Allan Buitendag
Nov 1991

Challenges to

Challenges to Empiricism

Edited by
Harold Morick

Rudolf Carnap
W. V. Quine
Wilfrid Sellars
Hilary Putnam
Karl R. Popper
Paul K. Feyerabend
Thomas S. Kuhn
Mary Hesse
Noam Chomsky
Nelson Goodman
R. Edgley
Jerry A. Fodor

HACKETT PUBLISHING COMPANY, INC.
Indianapolis • Cambridge

Copublished in the United Kingdom by
 Methuen and Company Ltd

Printed in the United States of America

Cover design by Laszlo J. Balogh

For further information, please address
Hackett Publishing Company, Inc.
Box 55573, Indianapolis, Indiana 46205

Library of Congress Cataloging in Publishing Data

Morick, Harold, comp.
  Challenges to empiricism.

  Reprint of the 1972 ed. published by Wadsworth Pub.
Co., Belmont, Calif.
  Bibliography: p.
  1. Empiricism—Addresses, essays, lectures.
I. Carnap, Rudolf, 1891–1970. II. Title
B816.M58 1980   146'.4   80–10731
ISBN 0–915144–89–1
ISBN 0–915144–90–5 (pbk.)

Contents

Many issues are decided by many people
on a basis of party spirit,
not of detailed examination of the problem
involved. In particular, whatever
presents itself as empiricism is sure
of widespread acceptance,
not on its merits, but because empiricism
is the fashion.

Bertrand Russell
The Philosophy of Bertrand Russell

Preface

Challenges to Empiricism is a concise introduction to the most important single development in philosophy and theory of science since World War II: the emergence of a full-blown criticism of the foundations of empiricism by scientists, historians of science, and science-oriented philosophers. This book provides, in their own words, their reasons for believing that the principles of empiricism in fact conflict with scientific methodology and with substantive results in linguistics and the psychology of perception.

The selections in this book are preceded by an introduction to the selections and to the basic ideas of empiricism, and are followed by an annotated bibliography and biographical notes on the contributors.

HAROLD MORICK
Albany, New York

Introduction

The Critique of Contemporary Empiricism

One of the main themes of philosophy and theory of science in the last twenty years is the critical assessment of the foundations of contemporary empiricism. Critics have questioned especially the empiricist conception of the role observation plays in our knowledge of matters of fact. The umbrella *contemporary empiricism* covers not only instrumentalism and operationalism in the physical and social sciences and "unliberalized" logical empiricism in philosophy but also the linguistic philosophy of Ludwig Wittgenstein and the Oxford school of Ordinary Language Analysis. In philosophy and theory of science, *empiricism* means the doctrine that experience rather than reason is the source of our knowledge of the world. This technical use of *empiricism* has obvious affinities with its ordinary use, in which it means the employment of methods based on practical experience rather than on theories or assumed principles.

Because the fundamental doctrines of contemporary empiricism are essentially refinements and modifications of David Hume's basic tenets in the theory of knowledge, the best entrance to an understanding of the foundations of contemporary empiricism is an understanding of the epistemological tenets of this great eighteenth century thinker. Although many of these basic ideas are not original to Hume, it is generally thought that he gave them their clearest, most coherent, and most uncompromising formulation. Let us turn to the groundwork that Hume laid for contemporary empiricism.

I am grateful to Kenneth Stern and Robert Meyers for their helpful criticisms of an early version of this introduction.

In Hume's view, the true nature and scope of ordinary and scientific knowledge can be revealed only by a "science of man," a study of the nature of man's ideas and of the principles of his reasoning processes. He thought that, as with all other sciences, the "science of man" must be founded on experience and observation.

Observation and experience teaches us that all thoughts are derived from past experience. For instance, unlike the blind, we can think about colors because we have seen them. In order to be precise, Hume expresses these points in semi-technical terminology: the nature of man's *ideas* are to be understood by contrast with the rest of his "perceptions" or mental contents—namely, by contrast with his *impressions*. It is from man's impressions that all his ideas are ultimately derived. Roughly speaking, Hume's "impressions" are what we call sensations and feelings: seeing a spider, feeling the pain of excessive heat, feeling anger. To remember or to imagine any of them is, in Hume's terminology, to have an idea; ideas, then, are what we call thoughts. Impressions are our forceful and lively perceptions, whereas our ideas are nothing but their faint copies; a remembered pain, for example, is obviously less vivid a perception than a felt pain.

An empiricist criterion of meaningfulness or significance follows from Hume's doctrine that every idea (i.e., thought) is a copy of a previous impression or set of impressions. According to Hume, we can think of a dragon without ever having seen one only because the idea of a dragon is a complex idea, a combination of simple ideas, each of which is a copy of some preceding impression. The idea of a golden mountain provides another example of a complex idea: "When we think of a golden mountain we only join two consistent ideas, *gold* and *mountain,* with which we were formerly acquainted."[1] That no one can have a particular simple idea unless he has experienced the impression of which it is the copy can be illustrated by the fact that blind men have no "idea" of colors, nor do deaf men have an "idea" of sounds. Thus, for Hume ideas divide up into the simple and the complex; all complex ideas are constructions out of simple ideas, and simple ideas are copies of impressions. This doctrine provides a criterion, or test of meaningfulness, a way of cleansing science and philosophy of empty verbiage. If we have "any suspicion that a philosophical term is employed without any meaning or idea (as is but too frequent), we need but inquire, *from what impression is that supposed idea derived?* And if it be impossible to assign any, this will serve to confirm our suspicion."[2]

In the following passage, Hume gives his conclusions as to what the science of man reveals about the principles of man's reasoning process.

All the objects of human reason or inquiry may naturally be divided into two kinds, to wit, relations of ideas *and* matters of fact. *Of the first kind are the sciences of geometry, algebra, and arithmetic, and, in short, every affirmation which is either intuitively or demonstratively certain.* That the square of the hypotenuse is equal to the square of the two sides *is a proposition which expresses a relation between these figures.* That three times five is equal to the half of thirty *expresses a relation between these numbers. Propositions of this kind are discoverable by the mere operation of thought, without dependence on what is anywhere existent in the universe. . . . Matters of fact, which are the second objects of human reason, are not ascertained in the same manner, nor is our evidence of their truth, however great, of a like nature with the foregoing. The contrary of every matter of fact is still possible, because it can never imply a contradiction and is conceived by the mind with the same facility and distinctness as if ever so comfortable to reality.* That the sun will not rise tomorrow *is no less intelligible a proposition and implies no more contradiction than the affirmation* that it will rise. *We should in vain, therefore, attempt to demonstrate its falsehood. Were it demonstratively false, it would imply a contradiction, and could never be distinctly conceived by the mind. . . . All reasonings concerning matter of fact seem to be founded on the relation of* cause and effect. *By means of that relation alone we can go beyond the evidence of our memory and senses. . . . A man finding a watch or any other machine in a desert island would conclude that there had once been men in that island. All our reasonings concerning fact are of the same nature.*[3]

In the technical language of contemporary philosophy, Hume is here maintaining that all knowledge about the world is a posteriori. An a posteriori statement is one which can be confirmed or disconfirmed only by experience and observation; for example, we cannot confirm or disconfirm "The sun will rise tomorrow" without looking to see what happens. On the other hand, "Three times five is equal to half of thirty" is a priori—that is, its truth is "discoverable by the mere operation of thought."[4] But in Hume's view, any truth discoverable by thought alone is never about the world but only about internal relations between our ideas; in the language of contemporary philosophy, a truth of this sort is *analytic*. Roughly, an analytic truth is a statement true by definition. Precisely, an analytic truth, as opposed to a *synthetic* truth, is a truth the denial of which is self-contradictory. For instance, "Three times five is equal to half of thirty" and "All spinsters are unmarried" are analytic because their denials—"Three times five is unequal to half of thirty" and "Some spinsters are married"—are presumably self-contradictory. Such truths tell us nothing about the world; they inform us only about the internal relations among our ideas, e.g., that the complex idea of a spinster contains the idea of someone unmarried.

With this terminology for Hume's distinctions, we can state succinctly what Hume thought the "science of man" tells us about the principles of our reasoning processes. All reasoning about relations of ideas—e.g., logic, arithmetic, geometry, algebra—is analytic and based on the principle of noncontradiction; all reasoning about matters of fact—e.g., physics, chemistry, everyday factual knowledge—is a posteriori, and whenever it goes beyond present direct observation and remembered past observation, it consists in generalizing from experience on the basis of the principle of cause and effect. So scientific reasoning consists in empirical generalization, or, more precisely, in induction by simple enumeration: the process of estimating what can truly be ascribed to a whole class of things or events on the basis of what has been observed to be true of part of that class. The following is an example of induction by simple enumeration: Because many cases of smallpox have undergone careful inspection, and because it has been found that all of these cases have been accompanied by a certain virus, we are entitled to infer that the uninspected cases of smallpox are also accompanied by that virus. Hume's own term for this is *experimental inference*.

According to Hume, these are the principles of human knowledge. They set our knowledge on a firm foundation, and their application enables us to purge science and philosophy of empty metaphysical speculation.

When we run over libraries, persuaded of these principles, what havoc must we make? If we take in our hand any volume of divinity or school metaphysics, for instance, let us ask, Does it contain any abstract reasoning concerning quantity or number? *No.* Does it contain any experimental reasoning concerning matter of fact and existence? *No. Commit it then to the flames, for it can contain nothing but sophistry and illusion.*[5]

Unfortunately, Hume's principles threaten to throw out the baby with the bath water. When his principles are applied consistently, they seem to narrow the scope of genuine knowledge almost to a vanishing point. It turns out that on Hume's principles most of what we take to be common knowledge, as well as what we take to be scientific knowledge, will not really be knowledge at all. When Hume applied what he took to be Newton's methods in natural science to the "science of man," he was led, paradoxically, to the conclusion that induction, or scientific method, cannot be rationally justified. Hume was led to this conclusion when he noted that empirical generalization is founded on the principle of cause and effect and that the principle of cause and effect cannot itself be justified rationally. Before we can attend to this claim of Hume's we need to understand his analysis of the nature of the cause-effect relation.

We say that the virus causes the symptoms of smallpox. But what do we mean by this? Roughly, that the presence of the symptoms is invariably preceded by the presence of the virus. Certainly not that there is an a priori relation between the virus and the symptoms; the proposition that the cause of the symptoms is something else, though of course false, is perfectly intelligible and self-consistent. We learn through experience alone that the symptoms are caused by the virus. "And experience only teaches us how one event constantly follows another, without instructing us in the secret connection which binds them together and renders them inseparable."[6] To see what Hume means by "without instructing us in the secret connection which binds [the cause and the effect] together," ask yourself how we discover that we can at will wiggle our thumbs but cannot wiggle our ears. The answer is that we learn only by making repeated tries which are followed by successes in the former case and by making repeated tries which are followed by failures in the latter case. After, say, a dozen tries at each, we know our will has an influence over our thumbs which it does not have over our ears. Yet there is nothing additional we observed in the twelfth try that we had not already observed in the very first try; we observe no subtle connection of "power" or "influence." Were we to observe the presence of such an influence, an otherwise normal man under paralysis ought to be able to know without trying to move a particular limb that he had lost his power to move that limb, for he should be able simply to observe the loss of the power directly. But the fact is that "a man suddenly struck with palsy in the leg or arm, or who had newly lost these members, frequently endeavors, at first, to move them and employ them in their usual offices."[7] With respect to moving one's thumb, there is something in fact absent at the very first try but present at the twelfth try: an irresistible expectation produced by habit or conditioning, the presence of which gives the illusion that there is more to the cause-effect relation than the invariant sequence of two contiguous events. In summary, to claim that a certain virus is the cause of smallpox is to claim an invariant sequence of symptoms-preceded-by-virus.

Turning from the meaning of a causal attribution, Hume considers its justification. Past instances of invariant conjunction of virus and symptoms lead us to infer that virus and symptoms are related as cause and effect and thus that they *will always be conjoined.* But what, Hume asks, actually entitles us to make this inference? There are only two types of legitimate inference: a priori demonstration (deduction) and a posteriori experimental inference. The inference from observed past instances to unobserved future instances clearly is not demonstrable. And to say that this inference is experimental is to beg the question, "for all inferences from experience suppose, as their foundation, that the future will resemble the past."[8] That is, because scientific method *presupposes* that the course of nature will not change, it can hardly be invoked to *prove* it. So Hume concludes that experimental inference, which is scientific method, is not rationally justifiable.

But Hume's empiricist principles also lead to skepticism beyond that about the legitimacy of experimental inference. "It is in vain," he said, "to ask whether there be body."[9] He meant that you cannot know whether there are any physical things—whether there are houses and trees and mountains, much less whether there are submicroscopic things like atoms and genes. Nor can you know whether there is any *you* who experiences your impressions and ideas, much less whether there are other people who experience their own impressions and ideas. All you can know is that there are and that there have been particular impressions and ideas. (Even this inventory of Hume's seems overblown, because his principles would seem to imply that you cannot even know whether there ever were any impressions or ideas in the past.) Indeed, if Hume's principles are correct, it is actually *meaningless* to ask whether there are people and physical objects external to your sensations. This is entailed by the empiricist criterion of meaning: because each and every idea you have is composed of simple ideas, and because every simple idea is a copy of a sensation or impression, the very suggestion of the existence of *anything* beyond your perceptions is unintelligible. Hume explicitly invokes his meaning-criterion to show that you cannot have any idea of a self who experiences your impressions and ideas. "From what impression could this idea be derived? This question it is impossible to answer without a manifest contradiction and absurdity; and yet it is a question which must necessarily be answered, if we would have the idea of self pass for clear and intelligible."[10] Now we can see that Hume's principles lead ultimately to solipsism: all you can conceivably know is that there are sensations here and now and *maybe* that there were sensations in the past as well.

Surprisingly perhaps, Hume does not proscribe belief in induction by simple enumeration, belief in the existence of a self, or belief in the existence of an external world for—on his view—it is silly to proscribe beliefs that are held on instinct. Fortunately for us, skeptical reason is but a feeble critic when faced with instinct and custom. Were it the other way around, "All discourse, all action would immediately cease, and men would remain in a total lethargy until the necessities of nature, unsatisfied, would put an end to their miserable existence."[11]

2. Phenomenalism

Recent empiricists have not agreed with Hume's conclusion that the belief in an external world is *rationally* unjustifiable. Until very recently—up to around 1950—most of Hume's followers thought that his own basic principles in fact implicitly contained the rational justification for this belief; this argument for belief in the external world is known as phenomenalism. According to this theory, anticipated by Hume and before him by George Berkeley, a physical thing is a kind of construction out of our experiences. Macbeth knew that the dagger he saw was hallucinatory and not real not because he knew that there was no external cause for his visual experience but rather because he knew that if he reached for the dagger he would see and feel his hand breeze right through the space where the dagger seemed to be. So, according to the phenomenalist, to have a visual experience of a real physical thing is to have an experience which belongs to a certain kind of group of experiences. This kind of set of experiences has a constancy and a rich and complex coherence that is lacking in the set of experiences of which hallucinations are a part. As John Stuart Mill, the main figure in nineteenth century empiricism, put it, matter is a permanent possibility of sensation.

I believe that Calcutta exists, though I do not perceive it, and that it would still exist if every percipient inhabitant were suddenly to leave the place, or be struck dead. But when I analyse the belief, all I find in it is, that were these events to take place, the Permanent Possibility of Sensation which I call Calcutta would still remain; that if I were suddenly transported to the banks of the Hoogly, I should still have the sensations which, if now present, would lead me to affirm that Calcutta exists here and now. We may infer, therefore, that both philosophers and the world at large, when they think of matter, conceive it really as a Permanent Possibility of Sensation.[12]

One's instinctive belief that there is an external world of other selves is explained and justified in a similar fashion. The phenomenalist believes that Hume's principles show us that each one of us is nothing but a bundle of experiences having a certain constancy and coherence. This gives rise to the illusion of a simple abiding thing which is over and above the experiences and which "has" them.

It is important to note that the phenomenalist claims not merely that all we can possibly *know* about daggers, Calcutta, and ourselves is confined to facts about our experiences; he affirms also that all we can possibly *mean* in speaking of these things is confined to our experiences. To say that there is a jackknife in your drawer at home *means* that were you or someone else to go home and open the drawer, that person would have such and such experiences were he to do such and such things (were he to reach for it, he would have sensations of resistance, weight, smoothness, and coolness; were he to drop it, he would hear a thump; were he accidentally to nick himself with it, he would feel pain, and so on). That this is what we mean by a real jackknife (as opposed to a hallucinatory jackknife, a dummy jackknife, or a real banana) follows directly from Hume's empiricist criterion of meaning. Hume's criterion, it will be recalled, states that every idea—and thus the idea of an "external" thing—is ultimately derived from sense impressions alone.

By the twentieth century, when empiricists had come to take statements or propositions rather than terms or ideas as the basic unit of meaning, the phenomenalist thesis that a physical object is a construction out of sensations was interpreted as the thesis that any statement about a physical object is translatable into a statement about sensations—that is, any statement about a physical object can be paraphrased into a statement about sensations. Thus, to make a categorical statement that there is along the banks of the Hoogly a particular drainage pipe is really to make a hypothetical statement about sense data. Such a hypothetical statement would be roughly that were a *normal* observer under *normal* observation conditions situated to view the banks of the Hoogly, and were he attentively to make such-and-such observations, he would then have such-and-such experiential data. (It is evident that a normality requirement is necessary, for obviously one thing *not* meant by "There is a new drainage pipe at the mouth of the Hoogly River" is: were a *blind* man to be suitably located he would have such-and-such visual sense data.) The phenomenalists believed that in these ways they could use Hume's own principles to analyze and justify the belief in the external world.

Although this general scheme was worked out to a remarkable degree of sophistication during the first part of this century (e.g., by Bertrand Russell and A. J. Ayer), the phenomenalist phase of post-Humean epiricism ended by the 1940s, for by that time it had become evident that statements about physical things could not be translated into propositions about actual and possible sense data. If a physical-object statement is to be translatable into a sense-data statement or into a set of sense-data statements, the former must at least be deducible from the latter. But it came to be realized that there is no finite set of statements about actual and possible sense data from which we can deduce even a single physical-object statement. Recall that the translating or paraphrasing statement must be couched in terms of normal observers in normal conditions of observation. There is, however, no *finite* set of statements that are couched in purely sensory terms and which can express the satisfaction of the condition of the presence of a normal observer. According to phenomenalism, to say in terms of actual and possible sense data that a normal observer is present is to make the hypothetical statement that were a doctor to inspect the observer, the observer would appear to the doctor to be normal. But, of course, not any old doctor will do but only one who himself is a normal observer. If we are to specify the doctor's normality in purely sensory terms, we must make reference to a second doctor who, when inspecting the sense organs of the first doctor, would himself have to have the sense data a normal observer has when inspecting the sense organs of a subject who is a normal observer. And if we are to specify in purely sensory terms that the second doctor is a normal observer, we must refer to yet a third doctor, and so on ad infinitum. In short, an objection fatal to phenomenalism is that its very formulation requires the use of a concept, that of a normal observer, which in principle cannot be defined phenomenalistically. Thus it is in principle impossible for anyone to provide a sense-data translation of even so banal a physical thing statement as "There is a new drainage pipe at the mouth of the Hoogly River."

3. Contemporary Empiricism

This brings us to the second and most recent major stage of post-Humean empiricism. Contemporary empiricism begins with the rejection of Hume's assumption that what we directly experience are always our own sensations. Physical things actually constitute the objects of perception, where "physical things" is taken in the wide sense that includes not only daggers and drainage pipes but also all the other sorts of objects common within the natural world—shadows, mirror images, and thunder claps. Hume and the phenomenalists were not unaware of this common-sense belief, of course, but what convinced them it was not sound is called the argument from illusion. Hume and the phenomenalists reasoned as follows. We sometimes undergo illusions—that is, we sometimes perceive physical things to have properties they do not really have. When approaching a table, what is in our visual field gets bigger, but of course the table does not grow. Thus what we see, which really is getting bigger, must be something else; but the only something else it could be is an experiential datum private to the perceiver—a mental image representing the table. Thus we perceive not the natural world but only mental images of it. We also sometimes fall prey to hallucinations: what we see may look like a table (or a dagger) when actually there is no table present. So what we perceive cannot be a table, because by hypothesis no physical thing is present where we are looking.

Thus the only alternative is that we are perceiving one of our own sense data. Moreover, because what we see when hallucinating a table is qualitatively indistinguishable from what we see when a table is actually present (or else we would not be fooled by the hallucination), what we directly see even when a table is present is not the table but rather our personal image of it. There are other variations of the argument from illusion, but the above cases bring out the essence of the argument. We may now turn to the contemporary empiricist objection to it.

As the contemporary empiricist sees it, neither the case of illusions nor the case of hallucinations requires us to introduce into the world special objects—impressions or mental images of tables, etc.—in addition to tables and the rest of the usual array of physical objects. In the illusion example above, we do not have to describe the state of affairs as one in which there is a queer something, a sense datum, which actually is growing larger. All we need say is what in fact in real life we actually do on such occasions say: *"It looks as if* the table is getting larger (although of course it isn't)."* And in the case of hallucination, we can say: "I thought I saw a table, but actually I didn't see anything since there is nothing there to see." And in general, if we take concrete cases of illusions, hallucinations, dreams, afterimages, etc. one by one, we can show that in each case there is no need to introduce sense data to account for any aspect of our experience.

Indeed, in the view of the typical contemporary empiricist, Hume's doctrine that the only objects of our experience are perceptions or sense data is not merely unnecessary to account for the facts of experience but it results in an incoherency as well. What brings the contemporary empiricist thus to the complete and utter rejection of one of Hume's basic principles is one or another version of what is called the private language argument, an argument based on or derived from some remarks of Ludwig Wittgenstein. The core of this argument is as follows. If all your experiences are only of your own impressions and ideas, as Hume believes, and if all words derive their meaning ultimately from impressions, another basic doctrine of Hume's, then the language you have acquired cannot possibly be understood by any other person. In order for another person to understand what you mean by *table* or *red* and in order for you to understand what he means by these words in his language, you and he would have to be able to experience one another's perceptions. But this is impossible on Hume's principle that the only objects of a person's experiences are *his own* impressions and ideas. According to Hume, because you use *red* to stand for a sense impression private to you and another speaker of English uses this word to stand for a sense impression private to him, it is possible that what he calls *red* is what, were you able to have his sense impressions, you would call *green*. Thus Hume's principles lead to the strange conclusion that English, say, is *not* a single language understood by millions of people but rather a kind of federation of languages, each of whose users may use words in a way different from every other language user. But the critic of Hume points out that any such doctrine which entails that we speak in private language must necessarily be false, because private languages turn out to be a logical impossibility.

Why are private languages impossible? Any language involves rules of use. A noise or a mark which is not used in accordance with rules of correct application is not a word. Thus, for example, were a child or a monkey to make the noise *red* in no consistent manner with respect to the presence or absence of red objects or with respect to the presence or absence of any other observable phenomenon, the noise *red* would not be used as a *word* of a language. So the words of a purportedly private language would have to be used consistently if they really are words. But in a private language, the notion of the consistent or inconsistent application of, say, *red* is without meaning. For there is no possible way you could tell that you now use *red* to stand for the same kind of sense impression for which you have used it in the past. You cannot ask other people whether you are consistent, for that is ruled out: your language is supposed to be intelligible to you alone. Nor can you bring back and pass under review the sense impression to which yesterday you attached the sound *red*. You have only your own memory impressions to rely on, which means that you have no independent justification whatsoever for your belief that today you use *red* to apply to the same kind of sense impression to which in the past you affixed *red*. The point of the critic of Hume is not that memory impressions per se cannot be used to justify or support claims we make; the point is rather that those memory impressions, the credibility of which can be vouched for only by yet more memory impressions, can provide only the illusion of justification. If you wonder if you are right about when the train leaves, you might call up a memory picture of the timetable in support. But the memory picture can thus serve as support of your recollection of the train's departure time only because the memory picture itself can be tested independently of your own personal memory impressions: you can phone the train station, ask a friend, or get the timetable and look at it. In contrast, the Humean private-language user, who has for support of any memory impression only other memory impressions, is like a man who gets extra copies of the *New York Times* to prove that what was said in the first copy is true.

To sum up, the structure of the argument against private language is that of reductio ad absurdum: assume as true for the sake of argument what you actually take to be false—in this case, that there is or can be a private language—and then show that this assumption leads to its denial, namely, that there cannot be such a language. This argument against private language was influential in bringing about the transition from Hume and phenomenalism to contemporary empiricism.

So the transition to contemporary emipiricism is made by replacing Hume's doctrine that private sense impressions are the objects of direct perception with the view that publicly observable physical things are the objects of perception. Observation claims about these, rather than about sense data, provide the foundations of empirical knowledge. That is, contemporary empiricism is Humean empiricism without sense data. Like Hume, the contemporary empiricist holds that a priori knowledge is analytic; he holds that observation—now of publicly observable things—together with memory is the only source of empirical or a posteriori knowledge; he holds that any reasoning taking us beyond this source, i.e., any nondemonstrative (nondeductive) reasoning is basically empirical generalization from observations; and he holds that all meaningful ideas must ultimately come from experience.

We can see how Hume's principles, cleansed of the doctrine of sense data, enable the contemporary empiricist to deal with the problem of the external world: once one sees that sense data are a myth born from conceptual confusion, the problem of the external world seems to vanish. There is then no question of whether we are rationally justified in believing that beyond the iron curtain of our sense data there is a world of tables, houses, mountains, and so on, because in every normal waking hour of our lives these items are precisely what we directly confront in perceiving. In this way contemporary empiricism justifies our instinctive belief in the existence of ordinary objects, the existence of which in no way depends upon our perceptions of them. But the nonphilosopher believes that there is more to the world beyond his own mind and conscious experiences than just the ordinary things like houses and mountains; he believes that there are other selves, with their own conscious experiences, and he believes that there are unobservable physical things which are not part of our day-to-day world, namely, the entities of theoretical science such as atoms, electrons, and genes. How does contemporary empiricism deal with this aspect of the problem of the external world?

The solution to the problem of justifying one's belief in the existence of other selves is implicit in contemporary empiricism's justification of our belief in the existence of everyday physical things. *Self* is simply a misleading label for persons, for flesh and blood creatures we confront every day in perception and in interaction. Like the account of our knowledge of ordinary physical things, this account of our knowledge of our *self* and of other *selves* accords with common sense: persons are a species of physical thing of which oneself is a member, and the others of which anyone but a hermit directly confronts every day.

However, a problem arises for the contemporary empiricist when he tries to explain one's knowledge of another person's experiences. Because the contemporary empiricist cannot observe or experience another person's experiences (he cannot feel his pains, for example), how on strict empiricist principles can he justify his day-to-day beliefs that, e.g., right now Jones is in pain? In order to see the contemporary empiricist's answer we must turn to his "linguistic" version of Hume's empiricist criterion of meaning: every genuine descriptive word must be either an ostensive word such as *red* or it must be a term definable in terms of ostensive words. An ostensive word cannot be defined verbally but only by pointing out examples of what it is to which the word applies. Thus one understands a descriptive word only if one knows the observable situations to which it can correctly apply.[13] Now Hume's criterion of meaning—when combined with the contemporary empiricist doctrine that the objects of perception are public and intersubjective—yields the requirement that if a word such as *pain* is to be counted as the genuinely descriptive word it obviously is, then it must in some way refer to publicly observable circumstances. One teaches a child what *pain* means by pointing out cases of crying with pain, grimacing with pain, etc.; and in the view of contemporary empiricism, this is no mere happenstance. If people did not behave in certain characteristic ways when having a pain, the very concept of pain could not become a part of our conceptual scheme. Thus we cannot separate pain-behavior from the very meaning of *pain*. Some contemporary empiricists believe that this entails that pain is nothing but a certain pattern of behavior. These are the operationalistic (or behavioristic) psychologists, linguists, and social scientists. However, most contemporary empiricists do not hold that *pain* means merely pain-behavior. In their view, the behavior is only an aspect of the meaning of *pain*—that aspect which guarantees its status as a genuinely descriptive word. Because the state of being in pain has both an inner and an outer aspect, we can rationally account for knowledge of a person's pains and other states of consciousness whether that person is oneself or some-one other than oneself. The pain Jones feels, so to say, from the inside is one and the same thing as what those of us in Jones' vicinity can observe from the outside. So it is roughly in this way that contemporary empiricism resolves the "other minds" aspect of the empiricist problem of the external world—the problem of accounting on strictly empiricist principles for all levels of our knowledge of the existence of anything outside of one's own states of consciousness.

With respect to justifying or analyzing the nonphilosopher's belief in the individually unobservable submicroscopic entities of theoretical science—atoms, electrons, genes, and such—strict empiricist standards oblige contemporary empiricists to conclude that theoretical talk is a kind of convenient shorthand fiction for talk about the behavior of such genuinely real and observable things as the movement of a meter-pointer or the path of a streak in a Wilson cloud chamber. We cannot see or touch an individual electron for precisely the same reason that we cannot see or shake hands with the average man.

4. The Critique of Contemporary Empiricism

I noted at the beginning of this essay that criticisms of the principles of contemporary empiricism focus mainly on the contemporary empiricist conception of the role observation plays in obtaining factual or empirical knowledge. I have been describing what this conception is in the context of the Hu-mean and phenomenalistic empiricism, which leads up to it. Although empiricism has never lacked critics, the present-day questioning of its foundations started to gain momentum only around 1950. These current criticisms issue in general from science-oriented philosophers, from historians of science, and from scientists who have argued that the principles of empiricism in fact conflict with actual scientific methodology and with certain substantive results in linguistics and in the psychology of perception. This group, which includes all the contributors to this volume, challenges and/or revises empiricism in light of the methodology and the results of scientific practice.

As we have seen, empiricist epistemology from Hume on is guided by the idea that observation provides a maximally certain and conceptually unrevisable foundation of empirical knowledge, a foundation that supplies the basic premises of all our reasoning and without which there would not even be any probable knowledge. This foundation picture of factual or a posteriori knowledge has come under severe attack on the grounds that it is not merely simplistic but that it is incorrect and consequently misleading. In the view of the critics, if one looks at actual scientific inquiry one sees that sense experience does not function as the foundation of knowledge at all. Instead, it serves as a stimulus, provoking us to make revisions in our system of beliefs—revisions from which our observation claims are not themselves immune.

Critics have raised three not entirely independent objections to this foundations picture. First, observation claims derive their credibility from background assumptions. It is simply false, the critics say, that what a scientific theory does is to explain established "facts" revealed by sense experience. The question of what the facts are is not one which can be answered except within a theory or network of background assumptions. Thus, for example, when we establish on the basis of eyewitnesses that it is a fact that Jones actually did go through a red light or that his dipped-in-acid litmus paper actually turned red, we presuppose that there actually exists at least one normal observer. This assumption, one which we all make, cannot be justified by either of the two empiricist-certified types of reasoning. Because this assumption is about what Hume calls "matters of fact and existence" and is thus not a truth about relations of ideas, it cannot be demonstrated. Nor can we support it by enumerative induction, for such extrapolation from observation claims presupposes the reliability of those claims and thus can hardly be invoked to support them. Thus there is no sharp distinction between observation claims, which were purported to report only what is directly observed, and theoretical claims, which assert more than what is directly experienced; every claim in one way or another transcends what is presently and directly experienced.

Second, according to the contemporary critics of empiricism, not only do observation claims derive their credibility from a network of background assumptions but they also derive their very meaning from this network. Thus observation terms, it is claimed, do not retain constant meanings through theory changes. For example, the scientific revolution of the sixteenth and seventeenth centuries replaced the Aristotelian conception of color as a continuous and perceiver-independent property of physical things with the conception of color as a certain power of physical things to stimulate an organism's sense organs. The critics hold that "being red" no longer means quite the same thing as it did to Aristotle, and thus that an observation claim like "The (litmus) paper turned red" has undergone a meaning-change.

Because this second objection applies to observation language, it applies to observation *words* as well as to observation *claims*. It will be recalled that the contemporary empiricists translated Hume's assumption that there are simple ideas into the claim that there are ostensive words—words which refer to and mean a simple experiential content and which imply nothing beyond that experiential content. But if there is no sharp distinction between observation claims and theoretical claims, then ostensive words are a myth. For when one points to a red thing and tells a child, "That is what *red* means," one has merely pointed out *one* aspect of the meaning of *red*. To be red is to be able to appear in a certain *multiplicity* of ways—under a multiplicity of conditions for observation for a multiplicity of kinds of observers (normal ones, color-blind ones, etc.)—and not just in a single way. Thus it is claimed that observation has no monopoly on meaning; instead, it is held that our theoretical claims and concepts give meaning to our observation claims and to experiential concepts such as color concepts.

Third, the critics of empiricism argue that not only are so-called observation claims and concepts theory-laden, but also our very *observations* are theory-infected. The principles of empiricism are proffered against the background presupposition that a person's perceptions are unaffected by the beliefs he has, by the assumptions he makes about the objects that he is observing. That is, empiricism rests on the background assumption that there is an absolutely stable and invariant correspondence between perceptions and the stimuli which produce them. The critics of contemporary empiricism believe that the results of empirical psychology disconfirm this empiricist presupposition. Observations are not "givens" or "data" but are always interpretations in the light of our background assumptions. The idea of unambiguous objects of perception is a myth. Take the familiar examples from gestalt psychology of the duck-rabbit figure and the figure which can be seen either as a black cross on a white background or as a white cross on a black background.* What someone sees in looking at such figures is not independent of his beliefs and expectations. For example, a person who is unacquainted with the ambiguity of such figures and who expects to see a rabbit-picture sees just that.

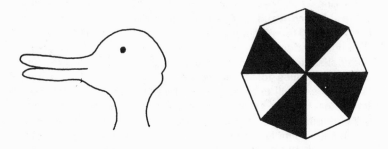

The result of these criticisms is that if they are correct, one must reject or severely alter the "foundations" picture of empirical knowledge, which lies at the heart of the empiricist vision. The empiricist picture is that all empirical knowledge is *founded* upon a set of independently intelligible and independently credible "observation claims." The critique suggested here, if sound, shows that it is a myth that there are such "basic" claims, and that the doctrine that all empirical knowledge could rest on such claims is incoherent.

5. The Critics and Their Criticisms

Any categorizing of the criticisms and revisions of contemporary empiricism can claim only a certain convenience, for these criticisms and revisions are largely interconnected. In particular, the issues of the first section of this collection spill over into those of the second section. In the first section the essays all deal with ontology, or the theory of reality, and its

* Figure from *Philosophical Investigations* by Ludwig Wittgenstein, 1953. Reprinted by permission of Basil Blackwell, Oxford.

relationship to empiricist epistemology. There is also much in these essays about the relationship between scientific inquiry and empiricist epistemology.

In "Empiricism, Semantics, and Ontology" Carnap distinguishes questions which are "internal" and those which are "external" to a conceptual scheme or language framework. He argues that while we can determine what things there are in the world by observation and by logical or mathematical demonstration *within a given conceptual scheme or language framework,* we can determine whether or not the conceptual scheme itself "exists," i.e., whether or not it provides a true map of reality, only on pragmatic or practical grounds. For example, given our actual conceptual scheme, "Are there brick houses on Elm Street?" is a factual question which is answerable by looking and seeing; whereas "Are there physical objects per se?" is not a factual question, for given our choice of a convenient language framework, its affirmative answer is merely analytically true, true "by definition." Carnap's position contrasts markedly with the empiricist view that it is an obvious factual truth about the world, revealed through the testimony of the senses, that there are physical things. Thus, whereas for the traditional empiricist only what is directly observable is real (everything else, it will be recalled, is a construction out of these foundational elements), for Carnap the empiricist's question as to which kinds of entities do and do not occur as immediate data is entirely irrelevant for ontology. So when seeking the best conceptual scheme, Carnap suggests we should ask not whether sense data, physical objects, numbers, etc. are observables but rather whether each of these categories serves as an efficient instrument of inquiry.

In "Two Dogmas of Empiricism" Quine argues that in "Empiricism, Semantics, and Ontology" and elsewhere Carnap fails to carry his pragmatism to its logical conclusion. The reason for this, Quine thinks, is that Carnap is unwilling to give up the empiricist synthetic-analytic dogma that some statements are about the world, whereas others are merely about language. Because the distinction between statements about the world and statements about language is illusory, says Quine, ontology is in fact a branch of science (although more abstract than most other branches, to be sure). Like *any* branch of science, its ultimate criterion of adequacy should be a pragmatic one. In Quine's view the analytic-synthetic dogma is ultimately one with the dogma of reductionism—the dogma that every descriptive statement is individually a report or summary of direct experience. He thinks that it is a mistake to think that scientists compare single individual statements with the world. We confront reality only with a totality or network of statements and beliefs, so that statements ought to be viewed as ingredients of a total system rather than as isolated reports or summaries of experience. And the ultimate purpose of the total enterprise of science is a pragmatic one: "Each man is given a scientific heritage plus a continuing barrage of sensory stimulation; and the considerations which guide him in warping his scientific heritage to fit his continuing sensory promptings are, where rational, pragmatic."

In the third selection Quine argues that there is no way we can tell for sure whether or not members of an alien culture divide the world into the kinds of objects that we do, or even whether or not they "cut up" the world into objects at all. Suppose they say "gavagai" whenever a rabbit passes by. Does this response to the rabbit-stimulation indicate that *gavagai* means rabbit for them? Apart from guesses about many other words of their language as well—what Quine calls "analytic hypotheses"—there can be no definite answer to this question. Within the context of one such system of analytic hypotheses *gavagai* may come out as "rabbit," but within other systems of hypotheses it may come out something like "rabbit-event," "rabbit-stage," "undetached rabbit-part," or something even stranger from the point of view of our ontology. Thus from the point of view of the question of the preconditions for translation, Quine challenges the empiricist doctrine that experience alone can reveal to us what kinds of things there are in the world. Quine also attacks empiricist ontology in a subtler way. The analytic-synthetic distinction holds that some propositions are true in virtue of their *meaning*. Bolstering the idea that there *are* meanings is the idea that translation consists of finding a sentence in, for instance, English that has the same meaning as a sentence in the alien language. If Quine is right, such a conception of the translator's project makes no sense, because it is a senseless idea that one could translate *gavagai* into English apart from *any* system of hypotheses at all.

Sellars, in "Empiricism and the Philosophy of Mind," argues that the scientific account of the world ought to take precedence over the common sense ontology of everyday life; for example, because colors have no place in the scientific framework, we ought to say that strictly speaking, i.e., scientifically speaking, they do not exist. He argues that those who find it preposterous to question the validity of our common-sense categories are victims of the empiricist myth that language hooks on to the world basically by means of ostensive definitions.

In "Brains and Behaviour" Putnam attacks the most plausible form of behaviorism in contemporary empiricism. This "soft" behaviorism, it will be recalled, holds that *part* of the meaning of any psychological term is its "outer" aspect—namely, behavior. Thus recall the example of pain: the "soft" behaviorist argues that we can teach children the meaning of *pain* only because people behave in certain characteristic ways when they feel pain; and from this the "soft" behaviorist infers that pain-behavior becomes part of the very meaning of *pain*. By various examples and arguments Putnam tries to show that a consideration of how scientific theories actually are constructed and supported leaves "soft" behaviorism as an enormously implausible theory. If we wish to theorize in accordance with the practices of the sciences, the plausible thing to conclude is that pain-behavior is in no way part of what we mean by *pain;* rather, it is merely the effect of a publicly *un*observable event—viz., a feeling of pain. More broadly, Putnam is here arguing against the contemporary empiricist doctrine that it is absurd or meaningless to say that there are publicly unobservable entities. In Putnam's view, there are cases in which the most plausible way to scientifically explain a "fact" is to posit the existence of entities which may be publicly unobservable.

In the second section of this collection the attention of the authors is focused directly upon the relationship between science and empiricist epistemology. According to Popper's "Science: Conjectures and Refutations," the traditional empiricist problem of justifying inductive inference is a pseudoproblem emanating from Hume's misconception of the nature of scientific method. Hume saw correctly that it is impossible to infer a theory from observation claims, but he failed to see that from this one should not conclude that a theory cannot be *refuted* by observations. Once we see that scientific method is essentially the method of trial and error, not essentially empirical generalization as the empiricist would have it, we see also that science is a perfectly rational activity. Rather than generalizing from observations, we jump to conclusions, make bold conjectures; we venture theories which we test not by trying to infer them from some imaginary foundation but by setting up experimental situations in which we try to refute or falsify them. Thus by the method of trial and error, or more aptly, conjectures and refutations, we use experience to weed out false theories.

In his compressed note, "Science without Experience," Feyerabend uses some discoveries and inventions of recent science and technology (computers, subliminal perception) to suggest the perhaps heretical possibility that science without experience is *conceivable*. This is a way, he suggests, to show the falsity of the empiricist doctrine that experience furnishes the foundations of knowledge. This note of Feyerabend's provides a good orientation for the perspective of his earlier and much fuller "How to Be a Good Empiricist." Feyerabend's recipe in this earlier essay is that a good empiricist is one who tries to proliferate theories rather than one who contents himself with merely sharpening the fashionable theories of the day. Because the good empiricist obviously cannot pull out of a hat a full-blown alternative to the going theories, he must start with the development of an alternative vision to the picture embedded in the going theory; he will try to formulate a general view not yet directly connected with observations. In a word, to be a good empiricist one must be a critical metaphysician. Traditional empiricism, in its attempt to rid science and philosophy of metaphysics, ignores the actual (and fruitful) way in which scientists carry on their enterprise in real life: "Elimination of metaphysics, far from increasing the empirical content of the remaining theories, is liable to turn those theories into dogmas." A one-theory system in science, says Feyerabend, would be as unproductive as a one-party system in the state.

In "Incommensurability and Paradigms" Kuhn defends the antiempiricist view that scientific frameworks are incommensurable with one another in roughly the same way that natural languages are incommensurable. Quine had argued that in translating, say, from Hopi to English, we cannot avoid gerrymandering Hopi to fit a mapping into English. Similarly, Kuhn argues, what Newton said must be "warped" to fit our Einsteinian space-time framework. Because there is no such thing as a theoretically neutral description of anything, "the choice of a new theory is a decision to adopt a different native language and to deploy it in a corresponding different world." Unlike English and Hopi, perhaps, it might appear that there are words in common—words at least spelled the same—between the languages of old and new scientific frameworks. Besides sharing certain scientific words like *mass,* Newton and the later Einstein used English and thus seem to share the observational vocabulary of English. But according to Kuhn and Feyerabend, terms like *mass* or *red* typically take on an altered meaning within a new theory, for words are implicitly defined by the theories which employ them.

In "Duhem, Quine and a New Empiricism" Mary Hesse argues

that this controversial thesis of meaning-variance between theories is a welcome antidote to the traditional empiricism in which statements, terms, and predicates are taken to have atomically independent and therefore stable meanings. She believes that by noting some of Quine's suggestions (which in key respects are refinements of Duhem's) holders of the meaning-variance thesis can avoid the paradoxes which would seem to make the thesis preposterous. Feyerabend and Kuhn are right to reject the traditional empiricist view that the meanings of terms are unaffected by the theories in which they are used: the meaning of a term in one theory is not the same as its meaning in another conflicting theory. Quine's doctrines support this view, she thinks, and they enable its defenders to avoid what would seem to be some absurd implications. Some of these implications are that no observation claim containing the term in one theory can contradict a statement containing the term in another theory and that there are no crucial experiments between theories. Hesse also questions to what extent Quine can reasonably be called an empiricist.

The third section of this book is devoted entirely to the Chomskian attack on the empiricist view of how language and knowledge are acquired. In the opening symposium Chomsky defends his claim that the empiricist account is inadequate; Putnam and Goodman attack this claim. Chomsky argues that the rules relating the underlying "deep" or logical structure to the surface structure of a sentence are so complicated and abstract as to challenge the adequacy of any empiricist stimulus-response or associationist account of how they are learned. We must suppose that the child has innate knowledge of the structure of his language—that is, that it has been programmed into his brain at birth. Only in this way can we account for the intellectual feat of his acquiring the rules of the grammar of a natural language.

In the critiques of Chomsky in this section, Putnam and Goodman hold that this innateness hypothesis of Chomsky's is probably unintelligible at bottom and is anyhow needless; an empiricist account of knowledge and language acquisition is perfectly capable of explaining the facts. In his discussion note, "Linguistics and Philosophy," Quine adds to this that Chomsky's criticism of empiricism is a red herring. He says that as a matter of fact empiricism cheerfully embraces innate mechanisms: "Externalized empiricism or behaviorism sees nothing uncongenial in the appeal to innate dispositions to overt behavior, innate readiness for language-learning." Thus when we blow away all the froth, Chomsky says nothing with which a behaviorist or externalized empiricist can disagree. "What would be interesting and valuable to find out, rather, is just what these endowments are in fact like in detail." And with respect to *that* question, Quine implies, Chomsky has nothing helpful to tell us. Finally, Edgley, in his essay "Innate Ideas," suggests that Chomsky illegitimately infers from certain empirical facts of language learning that we must have innate knowledge *that* certain things are true when all Chomsky could hope to infer is that we must have innate knowledge of *how* to apply certain abstract principles of grammar.

The last two selections in this collection show how Chomskians reply to these sorts of objections. If Fodor is right, then Quine is mistaken in suggesting that behaviorism can account for the empirical facts about language. "Behavioristic accounts of perception as involving the disposition to produce discriminative responses to physical differences are plausible only when isomorphism obtains between perceptual distinctions and specifiable stimulus differences." But when we hear, for example, a speaker say "The man hit the colorful ball," we perceive the longest pause on either side of *hit,* "although in acoustical fact, normal utterances of this sentence contain no energy drop at all." What we are in fact unconsciously doing is parsing this sentence in accordance with its conceptual or syntactic structure. This parsing cannot be explicated in terms of a "disposition" to provide a verbal report because normally we cannot say what we are doing; nor do our parsings correspond with any kind of characteristic nonverbal patterns of behavior.

"Perhaps the clearest and most explicit development of what appears to be a narrowly Humean theory of language acquisition in recent philosophy is that of Quine." With these words, Chomsky, in the concluding essay, launches a sustained and complex attack on the adequacy of Quine's attempt to use behavioristic stimulus-response psychology to "externalize" Hume's theory of language acquisition. Chomsky holds that Quine's definition of language as a "complex of dispositions to verbal behavior" is no more than an empty verbalism. In addition to his criticism of Quine, Chomsky ferrets out and criticizes Wittgenstein's empirical assumptions about language.

Notes

[1] David Hume, *An Enquiry Concerning Human Understanding,* in Hume, *Enquiries Concerning the Human Understanding and Concerning the Principles of Morals,* 2d ed., L. A. Selby-Bigge, ed. (Oxford: Clarendon Press,

1902), p. 19. The quotations from Hume's writings in this introductory essay follow that of the editions cited except that certain archaisms of spelling, punctuation, and the use of capital letters have been corrected.

2 Ibid., p. 22.

3 Ibid., pp. 25–26.

4 Ibid., p. 25.

5 Ibid., p. 165.

6 Ibid., p. 66.

7 Ibid.

8 Ibid., p. 37.

9 Hume, *A Treatise of Human Nature*, ed. L. A. Selby-Bigge (Oxford: Clarendon Press, 1888), p. 187.

10 Ibid., p. 251.

11 Hume, *Enquiries*, p. 160.

12 John Stuart Mill, *An Examination of Sir William Hamilton's Philosophy*, in *British Empirical Philosophers*, ed. A. J. Ayer and Raymond Winch (New York: Simon and Schuster, 1968), p. 552.

13 Some contemporary empiricists expand this meaning-criterion to statements: one understands a descriptive statement only if one knows the observable situations which would make it true. This move has not gained wide allegiance from contemporary empiricists, however.

The sketch given in the text is but a rough one of the empiricist doctrine of ostensive definition. Wittgenstein and others have made this position sophisticated. For example, Wittgenstein has argued persuasively that ostensive definitions can be used only with a pupil who already has a background of linguistic abilities.

For those already acquainted with the linguistic philosophy of Wittgenstein, I should mention that Wittgenstein's conception of *criterion* is nothing but the conception of ostensive definition qualified as noted above: where the falling of the barometer is a "symptom" of rain, its looking like *that* outside is the "criterion" of rain, the phenomenon to which we must point in order to explain the meaning of *rain* (see, e.g., Wittgenstein, *Philosophical Investigations* (Oxford: Blackwell, 1953), s. 354).

14 Bruce Aune has pointed this out in *Knowledge, Mind and Nature* (New York: Random House, 1967), pp. 266–67. This book of Aune's as well as his *Rationalism, Empiricism and Pragmatism: An Introduction* (New York: Random House, 1970) provides an excellent discussion of many of the issues treated in this collection.

I
Empiricism and Ontology

1. Rudolf Carnap

Empiricism, Semantics, and Ontology

1. The Problem of Abstract Entities

28 Empiricists are in general rather suspicious with respect to any kind of abstract entities like properties, classes, relations, numbers, propositions, etc. They usually feel much more in sympathy with nominalists than with realists (in the medieval sense). As far as possible they try to avoid any reference to abstract entities and to restrict themselves to what is sometimes called a nominalistic language, i.e., one not containing such references. However, within certain scientific contexts it seems hardly possible to avoid them. In the case of mathematics, some empiricists try to find a way out by treating the whole of mathematics as a mere calculus, a formal system for which no interpretation is given or can be given. Accordingly, the mathematician is said to speak not about numbers, functions, and infinite classes, but merely about meaningless symbols and formulas manipulated according to given formal rules. In physics it is more difficult to shun the suspected entities, because the language of physics serves for the communication of reports and predictions and hence cannot be taken as a mere calculus. A physicist who is suspicious of abstract entities may perhaps try to declare a certain part of the language of physics as uninterpreted and uninterpretable, that part which refers to real numbers as space-time coordinates or as values of physical magnitudes, to functions, limits, etc. More probably he will just speak about all these things like

From Rudolf Carnap, *Meaning and Necessity* (Chicago: University of Chicago Press). Copyright 1956 by The University of Chicago. Reprinted by permission.

The original version of this essay appeared in *Review Internationale de Philosophie*, IV, (1950). The present revised version was added to *Meaning and Necessity* in its second and enlarged (1956) edition.

anybody else but with an uneasy conscience, like a man who in his everyday life does with qualms many things which are not in accord with the high moral principles he professes on Sundays. Recently the problem of abstract entities has arisen again in connection with semantics, the theory of meaning and truth. Some semanticists say that certain expressions designate certain entities, and among these designated entities they include not only concrete material things but also abstract entities, e.g., properties as designated by predicates and propositions as designated by sentences.[1] Others object strongly to this procedure as violating the basic principles of empiricism and leading back to a metaphysical ontology of the Platonic kind.

It is the purpose of this article to clarify this controversial issue. The nature and implications of the acceptance of a language referring to abstract entities will first be discussed in general; it will be shown that using such a language does not imply embracing a Platonic ontology but is perfectly compatible with empiricism and strictly scientific thinking. Then the special question of the role of abstract entities in semantics will be discussed. It is hoped that the clarification of the issue will be useful to those who would like to accept abstract entities in their work in mathematics, physics, semantics, or any other field; it may help them to overcome nominalistic scruples.

2. Linguistic Frameworks

Are there properties, classes, numbers, propositions? In order to understand more clearly the nature of these and related problems, it is above all necessary to recognize a fundamental distinction between two kinds of questions concerning the existence or reality of entities. If someone wishes to speak in his language about a new kind of entities, he has to introduce a system of new ways of speaking, subject to new rules; we shall call this procedure the construction of a linguistic *framework* for the new entities in question. And now we must distinguish two kinds of questions of existence: first, questions of the existence of certain entities of the new kind *within the framework;* we call them *internal questions;* and second, questions concerning the existence or reality *of the system of entities as a whole,* called *external questions.* Internal questions and possible answers to them are formulated with the help of the new forms of expressions. The answers may be found either by purely logical methods or by empirical methods, depending upon whether the framework is a logical or a factual one. An external question is of a problematic character which is in need of closer examination.

The world of things.   Let us consider as an example the simplest kind of entities dealt with in the everyday language: the spatio-temporally ordered system of observable things and events. Once we have accepted the thing language with its framework for things, we can raise and answer internal questions, e.g., "Is there a white piece of paper on my desk?," "Did King Arthur actually live?," "Are unicorns and centaurs real or merely imaginary?," and the like. These questions are to be answered by empirical investigations. Results of observations are evaluated according to certain rules as confirming or disconfirming evidence for possible answers. (This evaluation is usually carried out, of course, as a matter of habit rather than a deliberate, rational procedure. But it is possible, in a rational reconstruction, to lay down explicit rules for the evaluation. This is one of the main tasks of a pure, as distinguished from a psychological epistemology.) The concept of reality occurring in these internal questions is an empirical, scientific, non-metaphysical concept. To recognize something as a real thing or event means to succeed in incorporating it into the system of things at a particular space-time position so that it fits together with the other things recognized as real, according to the rules of the framework.

From these questions we must distinguish the external question of the reality of the thing world itself. In contrast to the former questions, this question is raised neither by the man in the street nor by scientists, but only by philosophers. Realists give an affirmative answer, subjective idealists a negative one, and the controversy goes on for centuries without ever being solved. And it cannot be solved because it is framed in a wrong way. To be real in the scientific sense means to be an element of the system; hence this concept cannot be meaningfully applied to the system itself. Those who raise the question of the reality of the thing world itself have perhaps in mind not a theoretical question as their formulation seems to suggest, but rather a practical question, a matter of a practical decision concerning the structure of our language. We have to make the choice whether or not to accept and use the forms of expression in the framework in question.

In the case of this particular example, there is usually no deliberate choice because we all have accepted the thing language early in our lives as a matter of course. Nevertheless, we may regard it as a matter of decision in this sense: we are free to choose to continue using the thing language or not; in the latter case we could restrict ourselves to a language of sense-data and other "phenomenal" entities, or construct an alternative to the customary thing language with another structure, or, finally, we could refrain from speaking. If someone decides to accept the thing language, there is no objection against saying that he has accepted the world of things. But this must not be interpreted as if it meant his acceptance of a *belief* in the reality of the thing world; there is no such belief or assertion or assumption, because it is not a theoretical question. To accept the thing world means nothing more than to accept a certain form of language, in other words, to accept rules for forming statements and for testing, accepting, or rejecting them. The acceptance of the thing language leads, on the basis of observations made, also to the acceptance, belief, and assertion of certain statements. But the thesis of the reality of the thing world cannot be among these statements, because it cannot be formulated in the thing language or, it seems, in any other theoretical language.

The decision of accepting the thing language, although itself not of a cognitive nature, will nevertheless usually be influenced by theoretical knowledge, just like any other deliberate decision concerning the acceptance of linguistic or other rules. The purposes for which the language is intended to be used, for instance, the purpose of communicating factual knowledge, will determine which factors are relevant for the decision. The efficiency, fruitfulness, and simplicity of the use of the thing language may be among the decisive factors. And the questions concerning these qualities are indeed of a theoretical nature. But these questions cannot be identified with the question of realism. They are not yes-no questions but questions of degree. The thing language in the customary form works indeed with a high degree of efficiency for most purposes of everyday life. This is a matter of fact, based upon the content of our experiences. However, it would be wrong to describe this situation by saying: "The fact of the efficiency of the thing language is confirming evidence for the reality of the thing world"; we should rather say instead: "This fact makes it advisable to accept the thing language."

The system of numbers.   As an example of a system which is of a logical rather than a factual nature let us take the system of natural numbers. The framework for this system is constructed by introducing into the language new expressions with suitable rules: (1) numerals like "five" and sentence forms like "there are five books on the table"; (2) the general term "number" for new entities, and sentence forms like "five is a number"; (3) expressions for properties of numbers (e.g., "odd," "prime"), relations (e.g., "greater than"), and functions (e.g., "plus"), and sentence forms like "two plus three is five"; (4) numerical variables ("m," "n," etc.) and quantifiers for universal sentences ("for every $n, \ldots$") and existential sentences ("there is an n such that $\ldots$") with the customary deductive rules.

Here again there are internal questions, e.g., "Is there a prime number greater than a hundred?" Here, however, the answers are found, not by empirical investigation based on observations, but by logical analysis based on the rules for the new expressions. Therefore the answers are here analytic, i.e., logically true.

What is now the nature of the philosophical question concerning the existence or reality of numbers? To begin with, there is the internal question which, together with the affirmative answer, can be formulated in the new terms, say, by "There are numbers" or, more explicitly, "There is an n such that n is a number." This statement follows from the analytic statement "five is a number" and is therefore itself analytic. Moreover, it is rather trivial (in contradistinction to a statement like "There is a prime number greater than a million," which is likewise analytic but far from trivial), because it does not say more than that the new system is not empty; but this is immediately seen from the rule which states that words like "five" are substitutable for the new variables. Therefore nobody who meant the question "Are there numbers?" in the internal sense would either assert or even seriously consider a negative answer. This makes it plausible to assume that those philosophers who treat the question of the existence of numbers as a serious philosophical problem and offer lengthy arguments on either side, do not have in mind the internal question. And, indeed, if we were to ask them: "Do you mean the question as to whether the framework of numbers, *if* we were to accept it, would be found to be empty or not?" they would probably reply: "Not at all; we mean a question *prior* to the acceptance of the new framework." They might try to explain what they mean by saying that it is a question of the ontological status of numbers; the question whether or not numbers have a certain metaphysical characteristic called reality (but a kind of ideal reality, different from the material reality of the thing world) or subsistence or status of "independent entities." Unfortunately, these philosophers have so far not given a formulation of their question in terms of the common scientific language. Therefore our judgment must be that they have not succeeded in giving to the external question and to the possible answers any cognitive content. Unless and until they supply a clear cognitive interpretation, we are justified in our suspicion that their question is a pseudo-question, that is, one disguised in the form of a theoretical question while in fact it is non-theoretical; in the present case it is the practical problem whether or not to incorporate into the language the new linguistic forms which constitute the framework of numbers.

The system of propositions.   New variables, "p," "q," etc., are introduced with a rule to the effect that any (declarative) sentence may be substituted for a variable of this kind; this includes, in addition to the sentences of the original thing language, also all general sentences with variables of any kind which may have been introduced into the language. Further, the general term "proposition" is introduced. "p is a proposition" may be defined by "p or not p" (or by any other sentence form yielding only analytic sentences). Therefore, every sentence of the form "...is a proposition" (where any sentence may stand in the place of the dots) is analytic. This holds, for example, for the sentence:

(a) "Chicago is large is a proposition."

(We disregard here the fact that the rules of English grammar require not a sentence but a that-clause as the subject of another sentence; accordingly, instead of (a) we should have to say "That Chicago is large is a proposition.") Predicates may be admitted whose argument expressions are sentences; these predicates may be either extensional (e.g., the customary truth-functional connectives) or not (e.g., modal predicates like "possible," "necessary," etc.). With the help of the new variables, general sentences may be formed, e.g.,

(b) "For every p, either p or not-p."

(c) "There is a p such that p is not necessary and not-p is not necessary."

(d) "There is a p such that p is a proposition."

(c) and (d) are internal assertions of existence. The statement "There are propositions" may be meant in the sense of (d); in this case it is analytic (since it follows from (a)) and even trivial. If, however, the statement is meant in an external sense, then it is non-cognitive.

It is important to notice that the system of rules for the linguistic expressions of the propositional framework (of which only a few rules have here been briefly indicated) is sufficient for the introduction of the framework. Any further explanations as to the nature of the propositions (i.e., the elements of the system indicated, the values of the variables *"p," "q,"* etc.) are theoretically unnecessary because, if correct, they follow from the rules. For example, are propositions mental events (as in Russell's theory)? A look at the rules shows us that they are not, because otherwise existential statements would be of the form: "If the mental state of the person in question fulfils such and such conditions, then there is a *p* such that. . . ." The fact that no references to mental conditions occur in existential statements (like (*c*), (*d*), etc.) show that propositions are not mental entities. Further, a statement of the existence of linguistic entities (e.g., expressions, classes of expressions, etc.) must contain a reference to a language. The fact that no such reference occurs in the existential statements here shows that propositions are not linguistic entities. The fact that in these statements no reference to a subject (an observer or knower) occurs (nothing like: "There is a *p* which is necessary for Mr. *X*") shows that the propositions (and their properties, like necessity, etc.) are not subjective. Although characterizations of these or similar kinds are, strictly speaking, unnecessary, they may nevertheless be practically useful. If they are given, they should be understood, not as ingredient parts of the system, but merely as marginal notes with the purpose of supplying to the reader helpful hints or convenient pictorial associations which may make his learning of the use of the expressions easier than the bare system of the rules would do. Such a characterization is analogous to an extra-systematic explanation which a physicist sometimes gives to the beginner. He might, for example, tell him to imagine the atoms of a gas as small balls rushing around with great speed, or the electromagnetic field and its oscillations as quasi-elastic tensions and vibrations in an ether. In fact, however, all that can accurately be said about atoms or the field is implicitly contained in the physical laws of the theories in question.[2]

The system of thing properties.   The thing language contains words like "red," "hard," "stone," "house," etc., which are used for describing what things are like. Now we may introduce new variables, say *"f," "g,"* etc., for which those words are substitutable and furthermore the general term "property." New rules are laid down which admit sentences like "Red is a property," "Red is a color," "These two pieces of paper have at least one color in common" (i.e., "There is an *f* such that *f* is a color, and . . ."). The last sentence is an internal assertion. It is of an empirical, factual nature. However, the external statement, the philosophical statement of the reality of properties—a special case of the thesis of the reality of universals—is devoid of cognitive content.

The systems of integers and rational numbers.   Into a language containing the framework of natural numbers we may introduce first the (positive and negative) integers as relations among natural numbers and then the rational numbers as relations among integers. This involves introducing new types of variables, expressions substitutable for them, and the general terms "integer" and "rational number."

The system of real numbers.   On the basis of the rational numbers, the real numbers may be introduced as classes of a special kind (segments) of rational numbers (according to the method developed by Julius Dedekind and Gottlob Frege). Here again a new type of variables is introduced, expressions substitutable for them (e.g., "$\sqrt{2}$"), and the general term "real number."

The spatio-temporal coordinate system for physics.   The new entities are the space-time points. Each is an ordered quadruple of four real numbers, called its coordinates, consisting of three spatial and one temporal coordinate. The physical state of a spatio-temporal point or region is described either with the help of qualitative predicates (e.g., "hot") or by ascribing numbers as values of a physical magnitude (e.g., mass, temperature, and the like). The step from the system of things (which does not contain space-time points but only extended objects with spatial and temporal relations between them) to the physical coordinate system is again a matter of decision. Our choice of certain features, although itself not theoretical, is suggested by theoretical knowledge, either logical or factual. For example, the choice of real numbers rather than rational numbers or integers as coordinates is not much influenced by the facts of experience but mainly due to considerations of mathematical simplicity. The restriction to rational coordinates would not be in conflict with any experimental knowledge we have, because the result of any measurement is a rational number. However, it would prevent the use of ordinary geometry (which says, e.g., that the diagonal of a square with the side 1 has the irrational value $\sqrt{2}$) and thus lead to great complications. On the other hand, the decision to use three rather than two or four spatial coordinates is strongly suggested, but still not forced upon us, by the result of common observations. If certain events allegedly observed in spiritualistic séances, e.g., a ball moving out of a sealed box, were confirmed beyond any reasonable doubt, it might seem advisable to use four spatial coordinates. Internal questions are here, in general, empirical questions to be answered by empirical investigations. On the other hand, the external questions of the reality of physical space and physical time are pseudo-questions. A question like "Are there (really) space-time points?" is ambiguous. It may be meant as an internal question; then the affirmative answer is, of course, analytic and trivial. Or it may be meant in the external sense: "Shall we introduce such and such forms into our language?"; in this case it is not a theoretical but a practical question, a matter of decision rather than assertion, and hence the proposed formulation would be misleading. Or finally, it may be meant in the following sense: "Are our experiences such that the use of the lingistic forms in question will be expedient and fruitful?" This is a theoretical question of a factual, empirical nature. But it concerns a matter of degree; therefore a formulation in the form "real or not?" would be inadequate.

3. What Does Acceptance of a Kind of Entities Mean?

Let us now summarize the essential characteristics of situations involving the introduction of a new kind of entities, characteristics which are common to the various examples outlined above.

The acceptance of a new kind of entities is represented in the language by the introduction of a framework of new forms of expressions to be used according to a new set of rules. There may be new names for particular entities of the kind in question; but some such names may already occur in the language before the introduction of the new framework. (Thus, for example, the thing language contains certainly words of the type of "blue" and "house" before the framework of properties is introduced; and it may contain words like "ten" in sentences of the form "I have ten fingers" before the framework of numbers is introduced.) The latter fact shows that the occurrence of constants of the type in question—regarded as names of entities of the new kind after the new framework is introduced —is not a sure sign of the acceptance of the new kind of entities. Therefore the introduction of such constants is not to be regarded as an essential step in the introduction of the framework. The two essential steps are rather the following. First, the introduction of a general term, a predicate of higher level, for the new kind of entities, permitting us to say of any particular entity that it belongs to this kind (e.g., "Red is a *property*," "Five is a *number*"). Second, the introduction of variables of the new type. The new entities are values of these variables; the constants (and the closed compound expressions, if any) are substitutable for the variables.[3] With the help of the variables, general sentences concerning the new entities can be formulated.

After the new forms are introduced into the language, it is possible to formulate with their help internal questions and possible answers to them. A question of this kind may be either empirical or logical; accordingly a true answer is either factually true or analytic.

From the internal questions we must clearly distinguish external questions, i.e., philosophical questions concerning the existence or reality of the total system of the new entities. Many philosophers regard a question of this kind as an ontological question which must be raised and answered *before* the introduction of the new language forms. The latter introduction, they believe, is legitimate only if it can be justified by an ontological insight supplying an affirmative answer to the question of reality. In contrast to this view, we take the position that the introduction of the new ways of speaking does not need any theoretical justification because it does not imply any assertion of reality. We may still speak (and have done so) of "the acceptance of the new entities" since this form of speech is customary; but one must keep in mind that this phrase does not mean for us anything more than acceptance of the new framework, i.e., of the new linguistic forms. Above all, it must not be interpreted as referring to an assumption, belief, or assertion of "the reality of the entities." There is no such assertion. An alleged statement of the reality of the system of entities is a pseudo-statement without cognitive content. To be sure, we have to face at this point an important question; but it is a practical, not a theoretical question; it is the question of whether or not to accept the new linguistic forms. The acceptance cannot be judged as being either true or false because it is not an assertion. It can only be judged as being more or less expedient, fruitful, conducive to the aim for which the language is intended. Judgments of this kind supply the motivation for the decision of accepting or rejecting the kind of entities.[4]

Thus it is clear that the acceptance of a linguistic framework must not be regarded as implying a metaphysical doctrine concerning the reality of the entities in question. It seems to me due to a neglect of this important distinction that some contemporary nominalists label the admission of variables of abstract types as "Platonism."[5] This is, to say the least, an extremely misleading terminology. It leads to the absurd consequence, that the position of everybody who accepts the language of physics with its real number variables (as a language of communication, not merely as a calculus) would be called Platonistic, even if he is a strict empiricist who rejects Platonic metaphysics.

A brief historical remark may here be inserted. The non-cognitive character of the questions which we have called here external questions was recognized and emphasized already by the Vienna Circle under the leadership of Moritz Schlick, the group from which the movement of logical empiricism originated. Influenced by ideas of Ludwig Wittgenstein, the Circle rejected both the thesis of the reality of the external world and the thesis of its irreality as pseudo-statements;[6] the same was the case for both the thesis of the reality of universals (abstract entities, in our present terminology) and the nominalistic thesis that they are not real and that their alleged names are not names of anything but merely *flatus vocis*. (It is obvious that the apparent negation of a pseudo-statement must also be a pseudo-statement.) It is therefore not correct to classify the members of the Vienna Circle as nominalists, as is sometimes done. However, if we look at the basic anti-metaphysical and pro-scientific attitude of most nominalists (and the same holds for many materialists and realists in the modern sense), disregarding their occasional pseudo-theoretical formulations, then it is, of course, true to say that the Vienna Circle was much closer to those philosophers than to their opponents.

4. Abstract Entities in Semantics

The problem of the legitimacy and the status of abstract entities has recently again led to controversial discussions in connection with semantics. In a semantical meaning analysis certain expressions in a language are often said to designate (or name or denote or signify or refer to) certain extra-linguistic entities.[7] As long as physical things or events (e.g., Chicago or Caesar's death) are taken as designata (entities designated), no serious doubts arise. But strong objections have been raised, especially by some empiricists, against abstract entities as designata, e.g., against semantical statements of the following kind:

(1) "The word 'red' designates a property of things";

(2) "The word 'color' designates a property of properties of things";

(3) "The word 'five' designates a number";

(4) "The word 'odd' designates a property of numbers";

(5) "The sentence 'Chicago is large' designates a proposition."

Those who criticize these statements do not, of course, reject the use of the expressions in question, like "red" or "five"; nor would they deny that these expressions are meaningful. But to be meaningful, they would say, is not the same as having a meaning in the sense of an entity designated. They reject the belief, which they regard as implicitly presupposed by those semantical statements, that to each expression of the types in question (adjectives like "red," numerals like "five," etc.) there is a particular real entity to which the expression stands in the relation of designation. This belief is rejected as incompatible with the basic principles of empiricism or of scientific thinking. Derogatory labels like "Platonic realism," "hypostatization," or " 'Fido'-Fido principle" are attached to it. The latter is the name given by Gilbert Ryle (in his review of my *Meaning and Necessity* [*Philosophy*, XXIV (1949), 69–76]) to the criticized belief, which, in his view, arises by a naïve inference of analogy: just as there is an entity well known to me, viz. my dog Fido, which is designated by the name "Fido," thus there must be for every meaningful expression a particular entity to which it stands in the relation of designation or naming, i.e., the relation exemplified by "Fido"-Fido. The belief criticized is thus a case of hypostatization, i.e., of treating as names expressions which are not names. While "Fido" is a name, expressions like "red," "five," etc., are said not to be names, not to designate anything.

Our previous discussion concerning the acceptance of frameworks enables us now to clarify the situation with respect to abstract entities as designata. Let us take as an example the statement:

(a) " 'Five' designates a number."

The formulation of this statement presupposes that our language L contains the forms of expressions which we have called the framework of numbers, in particular, numerical variables and the general term "number." If L contains these forms, the following is an analytic statement in L:

(b) "Five is a number."

Further, to make the statement (a) possible, L must contain an expression like "designates" or "is a name of" for the semantical relation of designation. If suitable rules for this term are laid down, the following is likewise analytic:

(c) " 'Five' designates five."

(Generally speaking, any expression of the form " '. . .' designates . . ." is an analytic statement provided the term ". . ." is a constant in an accepted framework. If the latter condition is not fulfilled, the expression is not a statement.) Since (a) follows from (c) and (b), (a) is likewise analytic.

Thus it is clear that if someone accepts the framework of numbers, then he must acknowledge (c) and (b) and hence (a) as true statements. Generally speaking, if someone accepts a framework for a certain kind of entities, than he is bound to admit the entities as possible designata. Thus the question of the admissibility of entities of a certain type or of abstract entities in general as designata is reduced to the question of the acceptability of the linguistic framework for those entities. Both the nominalistic critics, who refuse the status of designators or names to expressions like "red," "five," etc., because they deny the existence of abstract entities, and the skeptics, who express doubts concerning the existence and demand evidence for it, treat the question of existence as a theoretical question. They do, of course, not mean the internal question; the affirmative answer to *this* question is analytic and trivial and too obvious for doubt or denial, as we have seen. Their doubts refer rather to the system of entities itself; hence they mean the external question. They believe that only after making sure that there really is a system of entities of the kind in question are we justified in accepting the framework by incorporating the linguistic forms into our language. However, we have seen that the external question is not a theoretical question but rather the practical question whether or not to accept those linguistic forms. This acceptance is not in need of a theoretical justification (except with respect to expediency and fruitfulness), because it does not imply a belief or assertion. Ryle says that the "Fido"-Fido principle is "a grotesque theory." Grotesque or not, Ryle is wrong in calling it a theory. It is rather the practical decision to accept certain frameworks. Maybe Ryle is historically right with respect to those whom he mentions as previous representatives of the principle, viz. John Stuart Mill, Frege, and Russell. If these philosophers regarded the acceptance of a system of entities as a theory, an assertion, they were victims of the same old, metaphysical confusion. But it is certainly wrong to regard *my* semantical method as involving a belief in the reality of abstract entities, since I reject a thesis of this kind as a metaphysical pseudo-statement.

The critics of the use of abstract entities in semantics overlook the fundamental difference between the acceptance of a system of entities and an internal assertion, e.g., an assertion that there are elephants or electrons or prime numbers greater than a million. Whoever makes an internal assertion is certainly obliged to justify it by providing evidence, empirical evidence in the case of electrons, logical proof in the case of the prime numbers. The demand for a theoretical justification, correct in the case of internal assertions, is sometimes wrongly applied to the acceptance of a system of entities. Thus, for example, Ernest Nagel (in his review of my *Meaning and Necessity* [*Journal of Philosophy,* XLV (1948), 467–72]) asks for "evidence relevant for affirming with warrant that there are such entities as infinitesimals or propositions." He characterizes the evidence required in these cases—in distinction to the empirical evidence in the case of electrons—as "in the broad sense logical and dialectical." Beyond this no hint is given as to what might be regarded as relevant evidence. Some nominalists regard the acceptance of abstract entities as a kind of superstition or myth, populating the world with fictitious or at least dubious entities, analogous to the belief in centaurs or demons. This shows again the confusion mentioned, because a superstition or myth is a false (or dubious) internal statement.

Let us take as example the natural numbers as cardinal numbers, i.e., in contexts like "Here are three books." The linguistic forms of the framework of numbers, including variables and the general term "number," are generally used in our common language of communication; and it is easy to formulate explicit rules for their use. Thus the logical characteristics of this framework are sufficiently clear (while many internal questions, i.e., arithmetical questions, are, of course, still open). In spite of this, the controversy concerning the external question of the ontological reality of the system of numbers continues. Suppose that one philosopher says: "I believe that there are numbers as real entities. This gives me the right to use the linguistic forms of the numerical framework and to make semantical statements about numbers as designata of numerals." His nominalistic opponent replies: "You are wrong; there are no numbers. The numerals may still be used as meaningful expressions. But they are not names, there are no entities designated by them. Therefore the word "number" and numerical variables must not be used (unless a way were found to introduce them as merely abbreviating devices, a way of translating them into the nominalistic thing language)." I cannot think of any possible evidence that would be regarded as relevant by both philosophers, and therefore, if actually found, would decide the controversy or at least make one of the opposite theses more probable than the other. (To construe the numbers as classes or properties of the second level, according to the Frege-Russell method, does, of course, not solve the controversy, because the first philosopher would affirm and the second deny the existence of the system of classes or properties of the second level.) Therefore I feel compelled to regard the external question as a pseudo-question, until both parties to the controversy offer a common interpretation of the question as a cognitive question; this would involve an indication of possible evidence regarded as relevant by both sides.

There is a particular kind of misinterpretation of the acceptance of abstract entities in various fields of science and in semantics, that needs to be cleared up. Certain early British empiricists (e.g., Berkeley and Hume) denied the existence of abstract entities on the ground that immediate experience presents us only with particulars, not with universals, e.g., with this red patch, but not with Redness or Color-in-General; with this scalene triangle, but not with Scalene Triangularity or Triangularity-in-General. Only entities belonging to a type of which examples were to be found within immediate experience could be accepted as ultimate constituents of reality. Thus, according to this way of thinking, the existence of abstract entities could be asserted only if one could show either that some abstract entities fall within the given, or that abstract entities can be defined in terms of the types of entity which are given. Since these empiricists found no abstract entities within the realm of sense-data, they either denied their existence, or else made a futile attempt to define universals in terms of particulars. Some contemporary philosophers, especially English philosophers following Bertrand Russell, think in basically similar terms. They emphasize a distinction between the data (that which is immediately given in consciousness, e.g., sense-data, immediately past experiences, etc.) and the constructs based on the data. Existence or reality is ascribed only to the data; the constructs are not real entities; the corresponding linguistic expressions are merely ways of speech not actually designating anything (reminiscent of the nominalists' *flatus vocis*). We shall not criticize here this general conception. (As far as it is a principle of accepting certain entities and not accepting others, leaving aside any ontological, phenomenalistic and nominalistic pseudo-statements, there cannot be any theoretical objection to it.) But if this conception leads to the view that other philosophers or scientists who accept abstract entities thereby assert or imply their occurrence as immediate data, then such a view must be rejected as a misinterpretation. References to space-time points, the electromagnetic field, or electrons in physics, to real or complex numbers and their functions in mathematics, to the excitatory potential or unconscious complexes in psychology, to an inflationary trend in economics, and the like, do not imply the assertion that entities of these kinds occur as immediate data. And the same holds for references to abstract entities as designata in semantics. Some of the criticisms by English philosophers against such references give the impression that, probably due to the misinterpretation just indicated, they accuse the semanticist not so much of bad metaphysics (as some nominalists would do) but of bad psychology. The fact that they regard a semantical method involving abstract entities not merely as doubtful and perhaps wrong, but as manifestly absurd, preposterous, and grotesque, and that they show a deep horror and indignation against this method, is perhaps to be explained by a misinterpretation of the kind described. In fact, of course, the semanticist does not in the least assert or imply that the abstract entities to which he refers can be experienced as immediately given either by sensation or by a kind of rational intuition. An assertion of this kind would indeed be very dubious psychology. The psychological question as to which kinds of entities do and which do not occur as immediate data is entirely irrelevant for semantics, just as it is for physics, mathematics, economics, etc., with respect to the examples mentioned above.[8]

For those who want to develop or use semantical methods, the decisive question is not the alleged ontological question of the existence of abstract entities but rather the question whether the use of abstract linguistic forms or, in technical terms, the use of variables beyond those for things (or phenomenal data), is expedient and fruitful for the purposes for which semantical analyses are made, viz., the analysis, interpretation, clarification, or construction of languages of communication, especially languages of science. This question is here neither decided nor even discussed. It is not a question simply of yes or no, but a matter of degree. Among those philosophers who have carried out semantical analyses and thought about suitable tools for this work, beginning with Plato and Aristotle and, in a more technical way on the basis of modern logic, with C. S. Peirce and Frege, a great majority accepted abstract entities. This does not, of course, prove the case. After all, semantics in the technical sense is still in the initial phases of its development, and we must be prepared for possible fundamental changes in methods. Let us therefore admit that the nominalistic critics may possibly be right. But if so, they will have to offer better arguments than they have so far. Appeal to ontological insight will not carry much weight. The critics will have to show that it is possible to construct a semantical method which avoids all references to abstract entities and achieves by simpler means essentially the same results as the other methods.

The acceptance or rejection of abstract linguistic forms, just as the acceptance or rejection of any other linguistic forms in any branch of science, will finally be decided by their efficiency as instruments, the ratio of the results achieved to the amount and complexity of the efforts required. To decree dogmatic prohibitions of certain linguistic forms instead of testing them by their success or failure in practical use, is worse than futile; it is positively harmful because it may obstruct scientific progress. The history of science shows examples of such prohibitions based on prejudices deriving from religious, mythological, metaphysical, or other irrational sources, which slowed up the developments for shorter or longer periods of time. Let us learn from the lessons of history. Let us grant to those who work in any special field of investigation the freedom to use any form of expression which seems useful to them; the work in the field will sooner or later lead to the elimination of those forms which have no useful function. *Let us be cautious in making assertions and critical in examining them, but tolerant in permitting linguistic forms.*

Notes

[1] The terms "sentence" and "statement" are here used synonymously for declarative (indicative, propositional) sentences.

[2] In my book *Meaning and Necessity* (Chicago, 1947) I have developed a semantical method which takes propositions as entities designated by sentences (more specifically, as intensions of sentences). In order to facilitate the understanding of the systematic development, I added some informal, extra-systematic explanations concerning the nature of propositions. I said that the term "proposition" "is used neither for a linguistic expression nor for a subjective, mental occurrence, but rather for something objective that may or may not be exemplified in nature. . . . We apply the term 'proposition' to any entities of a certain logical type, namely, those that may be expressed by (declarative) sentences in a language" (p. 27). After some more detailed discussions concerning the relation between propositions and facts, and the nature of false propositions, I added: "It has been the purpose of the preceding remarks to facilitate the understanding of our conception of propositions. If, however, a reader should find these explanations more puzzling than clarifying, or even unacceptable, he may disregard them" (p. 31) (that is, disregard these extra-systematic explanations, not the whole theory of the propositions as intensions of sentences, as one reviewer understood). In spite of this warning, it seems that some of those readers who were puzzled by the explanations, did not disregard them but thought that by raising objections against them they could refute the theory. This is analogous to the procedure of some laymen who by (correctly) criticizing the ether picture or other visualizations of physical theories, thought they had refuted those theories. Perhaps the discussions in the present paper will help in clarifying the role of the system of linguistic rules for the introduction of a framework for entities on the one hand, and that of extra-systematic explanations concerning the nature of the entities on the other.

[3] W. V. Quine was the first to recognize the importance of the introduction of variables as indicating the acceptance of entities. "The ontology to which one's use of language commits him comprises simply the objects that he treats as falling . . . within the range of values of his variables." "Notes on Existence and Necessity," *Journal of Philosophy,* XL (1943), 118. Compare Quine, "Designation and Existence," *Journal of Philosophy,* XXXVI (1939), 701–09, and "On Universals," *Journal of Symbolic Logic,* XII (1947), 74–84.

[4] For a closely related point of view on these questions see the detailed discussions in Herbert Feigl, "Existential Hypotheses," *Philosophy of Science,* 17 (1950), 35–62.

[5] Paul Bernays, "Sur le platonisme dans les mathématiques" (*L'Enseignement mathématique,* 34 (1935), 52–69). W. V. Quine, see previous footnote and "On What There Is," *Review of Metaphysics,* II (1948), 21–38. Quine does not acknowledge the distinction which I emphasize above, because according to his general conception there are no sharp boundary lines between logical and factual truth, between questions of meaning and questions of fact, between the acceptance of a language structure and the acceptance of an assertion formulated in the language. This conception, which seems to deviate considerably from customary ways of thinking, is explained in his "Semantics and Abstract Objects," *Proceedings of the American Academy*

of *Arts and Sciences*, LXXX (1951), 90–96. When Quine in "On What There Is" classifies my logicistic conception of mathematics (derived from Frege and Russell) as "platonic realism" [p. 33], this is meant (according to a personal communication from him) not as ascribing to me agreement with Plato's metaphysical doctrine of universals, but merely as referring to the fact that I accept a language of mathematics containing variables of higher levels. With respect to the basic attitude to take in choosing a language form (an "ontology" in Quine's terminology, which seems to me misleading), there appears now to be agreement between us: "the obvious counsel is tolerance and an experimental spirit" (*ibid.*, p. 38).

[6] See Carnap, *Scheinprobleme in der Philosophie; das Fremdpsychische und der Realismusstreit* (Berlin: 1928). Moritz Schlick, *Positivismus und Realismus,* reprinted in *Gesammelte Aufsätze* (Vienna, 1938).

[7] See *Meaning and Necessity* (Chicago, 1947). The distinction I have drawn in the latter book between the method of the name-relation and the method of intension and extension is not essential for our present discussion. The term "designation" is used in the present article in a neutral way; it may be understood as referring to the name-relation or to the intension-relation or to the extension-relation or to any similar relations used in other semantical methods.

[8] Wilfrid Sellars ("Acquaintance and Description Again," in *Journal of Philosophy*, XLVI (1949), 496–504; see pp. 502 f.) analyzes clearly the roots of the mistake "of taking the designation relation of semantic theory to be a reconstruction of *being present to an experience.*"

2. W. V. Quine

Two Dogmas of Empiricism

Modern empiricism has been conditioned in large part by two dogmas. One is a belief in some fundamental cleavage between truths which are *analytic,* or grounded in meanings independently of matters of fact, and truths which are *synthetic,* or grounded in fact. The other dogma is *reductionism:* the belief that each meaningful statement is equivalent to some logical construct upon terms which refer to immediate experience.

2 Dogma

From *From a Logical Point of View*, by W. V. Quine (Cambridge, Mass.: Harvard University Press). Copyright 1953, 1961 by the President and Fellows of Harvard College. First published in *The Philosophical Review*, 60 (1951). Reprinted by permission.

Both dogmas, I shall argue, are ill-founded. One effect of abandoning them is, as we shall see, a blurring of the supposed
boundary between speculative metaphysics and natural science.
Another effect is a shift toward pragmatism.

Effects.

1. Background for Analyticity

Kant's cleavage between analytic and synthetic truths was
foreshadowed in Hume's distinction between relations of ideas
and matters of fact, and in Leibniz's distinction between truths
of reason and truths of fact. Leibniz spoke of the truths of reason
as true in all possible worlds. Picturesqueness aside, this is
to say that the truths of reason are those which could not possibly be false. In the same vein we hear analytic statements
defined as statements whose denials are self-contradictory. But
this definition has small explanatory value; for the notion of
self-contradictoriness, in the quite broad sense needed for this
definition of analyticity, stands in exactly the same need of
clarification as does the notion of analyticity itself. The two
notions are the two sides of a single dubious coin.

Kant conceived of an analytic statement as one that attributes to its subject no more than is already conceptually contained in the subject. This formulation has two shortcomings:
① it limits itself to statements of subject-predicate form, and it
② appeals to a notion of containment which is left at a metaphorical level. But Kant's intent, evident more from the use he makes
of the notion of analyticity than from his definition of it, can be
restated thus: a statement is analytic when it is true by virtue
of meanings and independently of fact. Pursuing this line, let us
examine the concept of *meaning* which is presupposed.

Meaning, let us remember, is not to be identified with naming.[1] Frege's example of 'Evening Star' and 'Morning Star', and
Russell's of 'Scott' and 'the author of *Waverley*', illustrate that
terms can name the same thing but differ in meaning. The distinction between meaning and naming is no less important at
the level of abstract terms. The terms '9' and 'the number of
the planets' name one and the same abstract entity but presumably must be regarded as unlike in meaning; for astronomical observation was needed, and not mere reflection on
meanings, to determine the sameness of the entity in question.

The above examples consist of singular terms, concrete and
abstract. With general terms, or predicates, the situation is
somewhat different but parallel. Whereas a singular term pur-

ports to name an entity, abstract or concrete, a general term does not; but a general term is *true of* an entity, or of each of many, or of none.[2] The class of all entities of which a general term is true is called the *extension* of the term. Now paralleling the contrast between the meaning of a singular term and the entity named, we must distinguish equally between the meaning of a general term and its extension. The general terms 'creature with a heart' and 'creature with kidneys', for example, are perhaps alike in extension but unlike in meaning.

Confusion of meaning with extension, in the case of general terms, is less common than confusion of meaning with naming in the case of singular terms. It is indeed a commonplace in philosophy to oppose intension (or meaning) to extension, or, in a variant vocabulary, connotation to denotation.

The Aristotelian notion of essence was the forerunner, no doubt, of the modern notion of intension or meaning. For Aristotle it was essential in men to be rational, accidental to be two-legged. But there is an important difference between this attitude and the doctrine of meaning. From the latter point of view it may indeed be conceded (if only for the sake of argument) that rationality is involved in the meaning of the word 'man' while two-leggedness is not; but two-leggedness may at the same time be viewed as involved in the meaning of 'biped' while rationality is not. Thus from the point of view of the doctrine of meaning it makes no sense to say of the actual individual, who is at once a man and a biped, that his rationality is essential and his two-leggedness accidental or vice versa. Things had essences, for Aristotle, but only linguistic forms have meaning. Meaning is what essence becomes when it is divorced from the object of reference and wedded to the word.

For the theory of meaning a conspicuous question is the nature of its objects: what sort of things are meanings? A felt need for meant entities may derive from an earlier failure to appreciate that meaning and reference are distinct. Once the theory of meaning is sharply separated from the theory of reference, it is a short step to recognizing as the primary business of the theory of meaning simply the synonymy of linguistic forms and the analyticity of statements; meanings themselves, as obscure intermediary entities, may well be abandoned.[3]

The problem of analyticity then confronts us anew. Statements which are analytic by general philosophical acclaim are not, indeed, far to seek. They fall into two classes. Those of the first class, which may be called *logically true,* are typified by:

(1)   No unmarried man is married.

The relevant feature of this example is that it not merely is true as it stands, but remains true under any and all reinterpretations of 'man' and 'married'. If we suppose a prior inventory of *logical* particles, comprising 'no', 'un-', 'not', 'if', 'then', 'and', etc., then in general a logical truth is a statement which is true and remains true under all reinterpretations of its components other than the logical particles.

But there is also a second class of analytic statements, typified by:

(2)   No bachelor is married.

The characteristic of such a statement is that it can be turned into a logical truth by putting synonyms for synonyms; thus (2) can be turned into (1) by putting 'unmarried man' for its synonym 'bachelor'. We still lack a proper characterization of this second class of analytic statements, and therewith of analyticity generally, inasmuch as we have had in the above description to lean on a notion of "synonymy" which is no less in need of clarification than analyticity itself.

In recent years Carnap has tended to explain analyticity by appeal to what he calls state-descriptions.[4] A state-description is any exhaustive assignment of truth values to the atomic, or noncompound, statements of the language. All other statements of the language are, Carnap assumes, built up of their component clauses by means of the familiar logical devices, in such a way that the truth value of any complex statement is fixed for each state-description by specifiable logical laws. A statement is then explained as analytic when it comes out true under every state-description. This account is an adaptation of Leibniz's "true in all possible worlds." But note that this version of analyticity serves its purpose only if the atomic statements of the language are, unlike 'John is a bachelor' and 'John is married', mutually independent. Otherwise there would be a state-description which assigned truth to 'John is a bachelor' and to 'John is married', and consequently 'No bachelors are married' would turn out synthetic rather than analytic under the proposed criterion. Thus the criterion of analyticity in terms of state-descriptions serves only for languages devoid of extralogical synonym-pairs, such as 'bachelor' and 'unmarried man'

—synonym-pairs of the type which give rise to the "second class" of analytic statements. The criterion in terms of state-descriptions is a reconstruction at best of logical truth, not of analyticity.

I do not mean to suggest that Carnap is under any illusions on this point. His simplified model language with its state-descriptions is aimed primarily not at the general problem of analyticity but at another purpose, the clarification of probability and induction. Our problem, however, is analyticity; and here the major difficulty lies not in the first class of analytic statements, the logical truths, but rather in the second class, which depends on the notion of synonymy.

2. Definition

There are those who find it soothing to say that the analytic statements of the second class reduce to those of the first class, the logical truths, by *definition*; 'bachelor', for example, is *defined* as 'unmarried man'. But how do we find that 'bachelor' is defined as 'unmarried man'? Who defined it thus, and when? Are we to appeal to the nearest dictionary, and accept the lexicographer's formulation as law? Clearly this would be to put the cart before the horse. The lexicographer is an empirical scientist, whose business is the recording of antecedent facts; and if he glosses 'bachelor' as 'unmarried man' it is because of his belief that there is a relation of synonymy between those forms, implicit in general or preferred usage prior to his own work. The notion of synonymy presupposed here has still to be clarified, presumably in terms relating to linguistic behavior. Certainly the "definition" which is the lexicographer's report of an observed synonymy cannot be taken as the ground of the synonymy.

Definition is not, indeed, an activity exclusively of philologists. Philosophers and scientists frequently have occasion to "define" a recondite term by paraphrasing it into terms of a more familiar vocabulary. But ordinarily such a definition, like the philologist's, is pure lexicography, affirming a relation of synonymy antecedent to the exposition in hand.

Just what it means to affirm synonymy, just what the interconnections may be which are necessary and sufficient in order that two linguistic forms be properly describable as synonymous, is far from clear; but, whatever these interconnections may be, ordinarily they are grounded in usage. Definitions reporting selected instances of synonymy come then as reports upon usage.

There is also, however, a variant type of definitional activity which does not limit itself to the reporting of preëxisting synonymies. I have in mind what Carnap calls *explication*—an activity to which philosophers are given, and scientists also in their more philosophical moments. In explication the purpose is not merely to paraphrase the definiendum into an outright synonym, but actually to improve upon the definiendum by refining or supplementing its meaning. But even explication, though not merely reporting a preëxisting synonymy between definiendum and definiens, does rest nevertheless on *other* preexisting synonymies. The matter may be viewed as follows. Any word worth explicating has some contexts which, as wholes, are clear and precise enough to be useful; and the purpose of explication is to preserve the usage of these favored contexts while sharpening the usage of other contexts. In order that a given definition be suitable for purposes of explication, therefore, what is required is not that the definiendum in its antecedent usage be synonymous with the definiens, but just that each of these favored contexts of the definiendum, taken as a whole in its antecedent usage, be synonymous with the corresponding context of the definiens.

Two alternative definientia may be equally appropriate for the purposes of a given task of explication and yet not be synonymous with each other; for they may serve interchangeably within the favored contexts but diverge elsewhere. By cleaving to one of these definientia rather than the other, a definition of explicative kind generates, by fiat, a relation of synonymy between definiendum and definiens which did not hold before. But such a definition still owes its explicative function, as seen, to preexisting synonymies.

There does, however, remain still an extreme sort of definition which does not hark back to prior synonymies at all: namely, the explicitly conventional introduction of novel notations for purposes of sheer abbreviation. Here the definiendum becomes synonymous with the definiens simply because it has been created expressly for the purpose of being synonymous with the definiens. Here we have a really transparent case of synonymy created by definition; would that all species of synonymy were as intelligible. For the rest, definition rests on synonymy rather than explaining it.

The word 'definition' has come to have a dangerously reassuring sound, owing no doubt to its frequent occurrence in logical and mathematical writings. We shall do well to digress now into a brief appraisal of the role of definition in formal work.

In logical and mathematical systems either of two mutually antagonistic types of economy may be striven for, and each has its peculiar practical utility. On the one hand we may seek economy of practical expression—ease and brevity in the statement of multifarious relations. This sort of economy calls usually for distinctive concise notations for a wealth of concepts. Second, however, and oppositely, we may seek economy in grammar and vocabulary; we may try to find a minimum of basic concepts such that, once a distinctive notation has been appropriated to each of them, it becomes possible to express any desired further concept by mere combination and iteration of our basic notations. This second sort of economy is impractical in one way, since a poverty in basic idioms tends to a necessary lengthening of discourse. But it is practical in another way: it greatly simplifies theoretical discourse *about* the language, through minimizing the terms and the forms of construction wherein the language consists.

Both sorts of economy, though prima facie incompatible, are valuable in their separate ways. The custom has consequently arisen of combining both sorts of economy by forging in effect two languages, the one a part of the other. The inclusive language, though redundant in grammar and vocabulary, is economical in message lengths, while the part, called primitive notation, is economical in grammar and vocabulary. Whole and part are correlated by rules of translation whereby each idiom not in primitive notation is equated to some complex built up of primitive notation. These rules of translation are the so-called *definitions* which appear in formalized systems. They are best viewed not as adjuncts to one language but as correlations between two languages, the one a part of the other.

But these correlations are not arbitrary. They are supposed to show how the primitive notations can accomplish all purposes, save brevity and convenience, of the redundant language. Hence the definiendum and its definiens may be expected, in each case, to be related in one or another of the three ways lately noted. The definiens may be a faithful paraphrase of the definiendum into the narrower notation, preserving a direct synonymy[5] as of antecedent usage; or the definiens may, in the spirit of explication, improve upon the antecedent usage of the definiendum; or finally, the definiendum may be a newly created notation, newly endowed with meaning here and now.

In formal and informal work alike, thus we find that definition —except in the extreme case of the explicitly conventional introduction of new notations—hinges on prior relations of synonymy. Recognizing then that the notion of definition does not hold the key to synonymy and analyticity, let us look further into synonymy and say no more of definition.

3. Interchangeability

A natural suggestion, deserving close examination, is that the synonymy of two linguistic forms consists simply in their interchangeability in all contexts without change of truth value— interchangeability, in Leibniz's phrase, *salva veritate.*[6] Note that synonyms so conceived need not even be free from vagueness, as long as the vaguenesses match.

But it is not quite true that the synonyms 'bachelor' and 'unmarried man' are everywhere interchangeable *salva veritate.* Truths which become false under substitution of 'unmarried man' for 'bachelor' are easily constructed with the help of 'bachelor of arts' or 'bachelor's buttons'; also with the help of quotation, thus:

'Bachelor' has less than ten letters.

Such counterinstances can, however, perhaps be set aside by treating the phrases 'bachelor of arts' and 'bachelor's buttons' and the quotation ' 'bachelor' ' each as a single indivisible word and then stipulating that the interchangeability *salva veritate* which is to be the touchstone of synonymy is not supposed to apply to fragmentary occurrences inside of a word. This account of synonymy, supposing it acceptable on other counts, has indeed the drawback of appealing to a prior conception of "word" which can be counted on to present difficulties of formulation in its turn. Nevertheless some progress might be claimed in having reduced the problem of synonymy to a problem of wordhood. Let us pursue this line a bit, taking "word" for granted.

The question remains whether interchangeability *salva veritate* (apart from occurrences within words) is a strong enough condition for synonymy, or whether, on the contrary, some heteronymous expressions might be thus interchangeable. Now let us be clear that we are not concerned here with synonymy in the sense of complete identity in psychological associations or poetic quality; indeed no two expressions are synonymous in such a sense. We are concerned only with what may be called *cognitive* synonymy. Just what this is cannot be said without successfully finishing the present study; but we know something about it from the need which arose for it in connection with analyticity in §1. The sort of synonymy needed there was merely such that any analytic statement could be turned into a logical truth by putting synonyms for synonyms. Turning the tables and assuming analyticity, indeed, we could explain cognitive synonymy of terms as follows (keeping to the familiar example): to say that 'bachelor' and 'unmarried man' are cognitively synonymous is to say no more nor less than that the statement:

(3)   All and only bachelors are unmarried men

is analytic.[7]

What we need is an account of cognitive synonymy not presupposing analyticity—if we are to explain analyticity conversely with help of cognitive synonymy as undertaken in §1. And indeed such an independent account of cognitive synonymy is at present up for consideration, namely, interchangeability *salva veritate* everywhere except within words. The question before us, to resume the thread at last, is whether such interchangeability is a sufficient condition for cognitive synonymy. We can quickly assure ourselves that it is, by examples of the following sort. The statement:

(4)   Necessarily all and only bachelors are bachelors

is evidently true, even supposing 'necessarily' so narrowly construed as to be truly applicable only to analytic statements. Then, if 'bachelor' and 'unmarried man' are interchangeable *salva veritate*, the result:

(5)   Necessarily all and only bachelors are unmarried men

of putting 'unmarried man' for an occurrence of 'bachelor' in (4) must, like (4), be true. But to say that (5) is true is to say that (3) is analytic, and hence that 'bachelor' and 'unmarried man' are cognitively synonymous.

Let us see what there is about the above argument that gives it its air of hocus-pocus. The condition of interchangeability *salva veritate* varies in its force with variations in the richness of the language at hand. The above argument supposes we are working with a language rich enough to contain the adverb 'necessarily', this adverb being so construed as to yield truth when and only when applied to an analytic statement. But can we condone a language which contains such an adverb? Does the adverb really make sense? To suppose that it does is to suppose that we have already made satisfactory sense of 'analytic'. Then what are we so hard at work on right now?

Our argument is not flatly circular, but something like it. It has the form, figuratively speaking, of a closed curve in space.

Interchangeability *salva veritate* is meaningless until relativized to a language whose extent is specified in relevant respects. Suppose now we consider a language containing just the following materials. There is an indefinitely large stock of one-place predicates (for example, *'F'* where *'Fx'* means that *x* is a man) and many-place predicates (for example, *'G'* where *'Gxy'* means that *x* loves *y*), mostly having to do with extralogical subject matter. The rest of the language is logical. The atomic sentences consist each of a predicate followed by one or more variables *'x'*, *'y'*, etc.; and the complex sentences are built up of the atomic ones by truth functions ('not', 'and', 'or', etc.) and quantification.[8] In effect such a language enjoys the benefits also of descriptions and indeed singular terms generally, these being contextually definable in known ways.[9] Even abstract singular terms naming classes, classes of classes, etc., are contextually definable in case the assumed stock of predicates includes the two-place predicate of class membership.[10] Such a language can be adequate to classical mathematics and indeed to scientific discourse generally, except insofar as the latter involves debatable devices such as contrary-to-fact conditionals or modal adverbs like 'necessarily'.[11] Now a language of this type is extensional, in this sense: any two predicates which agree extensionally (that is, are true of the same objects) are interchangeable *salva veritate*.[12]

In an extensional language, therefore, interchangeability *salva veritate* is no assurance of cognitive synonymy of the desired type. That 'bachelor' and 'unmarried man' are interchangeable *salva veritate* in an extensional language assures us of no more than that (3) is true. There is no assurance here that the extensional agreement of 'bachelor' and 'unmarried man' rests on meaning rather than merely on accidental matters of fact, as does the extensional agreement of 'creature with a heart' and 'creature with kidneys'.

For most purposes extensional agreement is the nearest approximation to synonymy we need care about. But the fact remains that extensional agreement falls far short of cognitive synonymy of the type required for explaining analyticity in the manner of §1. The type of cognitive synonymy required there is such as to equate the synonymy of 'bachelor' and 'unmarried man' with the analyticity of (3), not merely with the truth of (3).

So we must recognize that interchangeability *salva veritate,* if construed in relation to an extensional language, is not a sufficient condition of cognitive synonymy in the sense needed for deriving analyticity in the manner of §1. If a language contains an intensional adverb 'necessarily' in the sense lately noted, or other particles to the same effect, then interchangeability *salva veritate* in such a language does afford a sufficient condition of cognitive synonymy; but such a language is intelligible only insofar as the notion of analyticity is already understood in advance.

The effort to explain cognitive synonymy first, for the sake of deriving analyticity from it afterward as in §1, is perhaps the wrong approach. Instead we might try explaining analyticity somehow without appeal to cognitive synonymy. Afterward we could doubtless derive cognitive synonymy from analyticity satisfactorily enough if desired. We have seen that cognitive synonymy of 'bachelor' and 'unmarried man' can be explained as analyticity of (3). The same explanation works for any pair of one-place predicates, of course, and it can be extended in obvious fashion to many-place predicates. Other syntactical categories can also be accommodated in fairly parallel fashion. Singular terms may be said to be cognitively synonymous when the statement of identity formed by putting '=' between them is analytic. Statements may be said simply to be cognitively synonymous when their biconditional (the result of joining them by 'if and only if') is analytic.[13] If we care to lump all categories into a single formulation, at the expense of assuming again the notion of "word" which was appealed to early in this section, we can describe any two linguistic forms as cognitively synonymous when the two forms are interchangeable (apart from occurrences within "words") *salva* (no longer *veritate* but) *analyticitate.* Certain technical questions arise, indeed, over cases of ambiguity or homonymy; let us not pause for them, however, for we are already digressing. Let us rather turn our backs on the problem of synonymy and address ourselves anew to that of analyticity.

Analyticity at first seemed most naturally definable by appeal to a realm of meanings. On refinement, the appeal to meanings gave way to an appeal to synonymy or definition. But definition turned out to be a will-o'-the-wisp, and synonymy turned out to be best understood only by dint of a prior appeal to analyticity itself. So we are back at the problem of analyticity.

I do not know whether the statement 'Everything green is extended' is analytic. Now does my indecision over this example really betray an incomplete understanding, an incomplete grasp of the "meanings" of 'green' and 'extended'? I think not. The trouble is not with 'green' or 'extended', but with 'analytic'.

It is often hinted that the difficulty in separating analytic statements from synthetic ones in ordinary language is due to the vagueness of ordinary language and that the distinction is clear when we have a precise artificial language with explicit "semantical rules." This, however, as I shall now attempt to show, is a confusion.

The notion of analyticity about which we are worrying is a purported relation between statements and languages: a statement S is said to be *analytic for* a language L, and the problem is to make sense of this relation generally, that is, for variable 'S' and 'L'. The gravity of this problem is not perceptibly less for artificial languages than for natural ones. The problem of making sense of the idiom 'S is analytic for L', with variable 'S' and 'L', retains its stubbornness even if we limit the range of the variable 'L' to artificial languages. Let me now try to make this point evident.

For artificial languages and semantical rules we look naturally to the writings of Carnap. His semantical rules take various forms, and to make my point I shall have to distinguish certain of the forms. Let us suppose, to begin with, an artificial language L_0 whose semantical rules have the form explicitly of a specification, by recursion or otherwise, of all the analytic statements of L_0. The rules tell us that such and such statements, and only those, are the analytic statements of L_0. Now here the difficulty is simply that the rules contain the word 'analytic', which we do not understand! We understand what expressions the rules attribute analyticity to, but we do not understand what the rules attribute to those expressions. In short, before we can understand a rule which begins 'A statement S is analytic for language L_0 if and only if . . .', we must understand the general relative term 'analytic for'; we must understand 'S is analytic for L' where 'S' and 'L' are variables.

Alternatively we may, indeed, view the so-called rule as a conventional definition of a new simple symbol 'analytic-for-L_0', which might better be written untendentiously as 'K' so as not to seem to throw light on the interesting word 'analytic'. Obviously any number of classes K, M, N, etc. of statements of L_0 can be specified for various purposes or for no purpose; what does it mean to say that K, as against M, N, etc., is the class of the "analytic" statements of L_0?

By saying what statements are analytic for L_0 we explain 'analytic-for-L_0' but not 'analytic', not 'analytic for'. We do not begin to explain the idiom 'S is analytic for L' with variable 'S' and 'L', even if we are content to limit the range of 'L' to the realm of artificial languages.

Actually we do know enough about the intended significance of 'analytic' to know that analytic statements are supposed to be true. Let us then turn to a second form of semantical rule, which says not that such and such statements are analytic but simply that such and such statements are included among the truths. Such a rule is not subject to the criticism of containing the un-understood word 'analytic'; and we may grant for the sake of argument that there is no difficulty over the broader term 'true'. A semantical rule of this second type, a rule of truth, is not supposed to specify all the truths of the language; it merely stipulates, recursively or otherwise, a certain multitude of statements which, along with others unspecified, are to count as true. Such a rule may be conceded to be quite clear. Derivatively, afterward, analyticity can be demarcated thus: a statement is analytic if it is (not merely true but) true according to the semantical rule.

Still there is really no progress. Instead of appealing to an unexplained word 'analytic', we are now appealing to an unexplained phrase 'semantical rule'. Not every true statement which says that the statements of some class are true can count as a semantical rule—otherwise *all* truths would be "analytic" in the sense of being true according to semantical rules. Semantical rules are distinguishable, apparently, only by the fact of appearing on a page under the heading 'Semantical Rules; and this heading is itself then meaningless.

We can say indeed that a statement is *analytic-for-L_0* if and only if it is true according to such and such specifically appended "semantical rules," but then we find ourselves back at essentially the same case which was originally discussed:

'S is analytic-for-L_0 if and only if. . . .' Once we seek to explain 'S is analytic for L' generally for variable 'L' (even allowing limitation of 'L' to artificial languages), the explanation 'true according to the semantical rules of L' is unavailing; for the relative term 'semantical rule of' is as much in need of clarification, at least, as 'analytic for'.

It may be instructive to compare the notion of semantical rule with that of postulate. Relative to a given set of postulates, it is easy to say what a postulate is: it is a member of the set. Relative to a given set of semantical rules, it is equally easy to say what a semantical rule is. But given simply a notation, mathematical or otherwise, and indeed as thoroughly understood a notation as you please in point of the translations or truth conditions of its statements, who can say which of its true statements rank as postulates? Obviously the question is meaningless—as meaningless as asking which points in Ohio are starting points. Any finite (or effectively specifiable infinite) selection of statements (preferably true ones, perhaps) is as much a set of postulates as any other. The word 'postulate' is significant only relative to an act of inquiry; we apply the word to a set of statements just insofar as we happen, for the year or the moment, to be thinking of those statements in relation to the statements which can be reached from them by some set of transformations to which we have seen fit to direct our attention. Now the notion of semantical rule is as sensible and meaningful as that of postulate, if conceived in a similarly relative spirit—relative, this time, to one or another particular enterprise of schooling unconversant persons in sufficient conditions for truth of statements of some natural or artificial language L. But from this point of view no one signalization of a subclass of the truths of L is intrinsically more a semantical rule than another; and, if 'analytic' means 'true by semantical rules', no one truth of L is analytic to the exclusion of another.[14]

It might conceivably be protested that an artificial language L (unlike a natural one) is a language in the ordinary sense *plus* a set of explicit semantical rules—the whole constituting, let us say, an ordered pair; and that the semantical rules of L then are specifiable simply as the second component of the pair L. But, by the same token and more simply, we might construe an artificial language L outright as an ordered pair whose second component is the class of its analytic statements; and then the analytic statements of L become specifiable simply as the statements in the second component of L. Or better still, we might just stop tugging at our bootstraps altogether.

Not all the explanations of analyticity known to Carnap and

his readers have been covered explicitly in the above considerations, but the extension to other forms is not hard to see.
Just one additional factor should be mentioned which sometimes enters: sometimes the semantical rules are in effect rules
of translation into ordinary language, in which case the analytic
statements of the artificial language are in effect recognized as
such from the analyticity of their specified translations in ordinary language. Here certainly there can be no thought of an
illumination of the problem of analyticity from the side of the
artificial language.

From the point of view of the problem of analyticity the
notion of an artificial language with semantical rules is a *feu
follet par excellence*. Semantical rules determining the analytic
statements of an artificial language are of interest only insofar
as we already understand the notion of analyticity; they are of
no help in gaining this understanding.

Appeal to hypothetical languages of an artificially simple
kind could conceivably be useful in clarifying analyticity, if the
mental or behavioral or cultural factors relevant to analyticity—
whatever they may be—were somehow sketched into the simplified model. But a model which takes analyticity merely as an
irreducible character is unlikely to throw light on the problem
of explicating analyticity.

It is obvious that truth in general depends on both language
and extralinguistic fact. The statement 'Brutus killed Caesar'
would be false if the world had been different in certain ways,
but it would also be false if the word 'killed' happened rather
to have the sense of 'begat'. Thus one is tempted to suppose
in general that the truth of a statement is somehow analyzable
into a linguistic component and a factual component. Given
this supposition, it next seems reasonable that in some statements the factual component should be null; and these are the
analytic statements. But, for all its a priori reasonableness, a
boundary between analytic and synthetic statements simply has
not been drawn. That there is such a distinction to be drawn
at all is an unempirical dogma of empiricists, a metaphysical
article of faith.

5. The Verification Theory and Reductionism

In the course of these somber reflections we have taken a dim
view first of the notion of meaning, then of the notion of cognitive synonymy, and finally of the notion of analyticity. But what,

it may be asked, of the verification theory of meaning? This phrase has established itself so firmly as a catchword of empiricism that we should be very unscientific indeed not to look beneath it for a possible key to the problem of meaning and the associated problems.

The verification theory of meaning, which has been conspicuous in the literature from Peirce onward, is that the meaning of a statement is the method of empirically confirming or infirming it. An analytic statement is that limiting case which is confirmed no matter what.

As urged in §1, we can as well pass over the question of meanings as entities and move straight to sameness of meaning, or synonymy. Then what the verification theory says is that statements are synonymous if and only if they are alike in point of method of empirical confirmation or infirmation.

This is an account of cognitive synonymy not of linguistic forms generally, but of statements.[15] However, from the concept of synonymy of statements we could derive the concept of synonymy for other linguistic forms, by considerations somewhat similar to those at the end of §3. Assuming the notion of "word," indeed, we could explain any two forms as synonymous when the putting of the one form for an occurrence of the other in any statement (apart from occurrences within "words") yields a synonymous statement. Finally, given the concept of synonymy thus for linguistic forms generally, we could define analyticity in terms of synonymy and logical truth as in §1. For that matter, we could define analyticity more simply in terms of just synonymy of statements together with logical truth; it is not necessary to appeal to synonymy of linguistic forms other than statements. For a statement may be described as analytic simply when it is synonymous with a logically true statement.

So, if the verification theory can be accepted as an adequate account of statement synonymy, the notion of analyticity is saved after all. However, let us reflect. Statement synonymy is said to be likeness of method of empirical confirmation or infirmation. Just what are these methods which are to be compared for likeness? What, in other words, is the nature of the relation between a statement and the experiences which contribute to or detract from its confirmation?

The most naïve view of the relation is that it is one of direct report. This is *radical reductionism*. Every meaningful statement is held to be translatable into a statement (true or false) about immediate experience. Radical reductionism, in one form or another, well antedates the verification theory of meaning explicitly so called. Thus Locke and Hume held that every idea must either originate directly in sense experience or else be compounded of ideas thus originating; and taking a hint from Tooke we might rephrase this doctrine in semantical jargon by saying that a term, to be significant at all, must be either a name of a sense datum or a compound of such names or an abbreviation of such a compound. So stated, the doctrine remains ambiguous as between sense data as sensory events and sense data as sensory qualities; and it remains vague as to the admissible ways of compounding. Moreover, the doctrine is unnecessarily and intolerably restrictive in the term-by-term critique which it imposes. More reasonably, and without yet exceeding the limits of what I have called radical reductionism, we may take full statements as our significant units—thus demanding that our statements as wholes be translatable into sense-datum language, but not that they be translatable term by term.

This emendation would unquestionably have been welcome to Locke and Hume and Tooke, but historically it had to await an important reorientation in semantics—the reorientation whereby the primary vehicle of meaning came to be seen no longer in the term but in the statement. This reorientation, seen in Bentham and Frege, underlies Russell's concept of incomplete symbols defined in use;[16] also it is implicit in the verification theory of meaning, since the objects of verification are statements.

Radical reductionism, conceived now with statements as units, set itself the task of specifying a sense-datum language and showing how to translate the rest of significant discourse, statement by statement, into it. Carnap embarked on this project in the *Aufbau*.

The language which Carnap adopted as his starting point was not a sense-datum language in the narrowest conceivable sense, for it included also the notations of logic, up through higher set theory. In effect it included the whole language of pure mathematics. The ontology implicit in it (that is, the range of values of its variables) embraced not only sensory events but classes, classes of classes, and so on. Empiricists there are who would boggle at such prodigality. Carnap's starting point is very parsimonious, however, in its extralogical or sensory part. In a series of constructions in which he exploits the resources of modern logic with much ingenuity, Carnap succeeds in defining a wide array of important additional sensory concepts which, but for his constructions, one would not have dreamed were definable on so slender a basis. He was the first empiricist who, not content with asserting the reducibility of science to terms of immediate experience, took serious steps toward carrying out the reduction.

If Carnap's starting point is satisfactory, still his constructions were, as he himself stressed, only a fragment of the full program. The construction of even the simplest statements about the physical world was left in a sketchy state. Carnap's suggestions on this subject were, despite their sketchiness, very suggestive. He explained spatio-temporal point-instants as quadruples of real numbers and envisaged assignment of sense qualities to point-instants according to certain canons. Roughly summarized, the plan was that qualities should be assigned to point-instants in such a way as to achieve the laziest world compatible with our experience. The principle of least action was to be our guide in constructing a world from experience.

Carnap did not seem to recognize, however, that his treatment of physical objects fell short of reduction not merely through sketchiness, but in principle. Statements of the form 'Quality q is at point-instant $x;y;z;t$' were, according to his canons, to be apportioned truth values in such a way as to maximize and minimize certain over-all features, and with growth of experience the truth values were to be progressively revised in the same spirit. I think this is a good schematization (deliberately oversimplified, to be sure) of what science really does; but it provides no indication, not even the sketchiest, of how a statement of the form 'Quality q is at $x;y;z;t$' could ever be translated into Carnap's initial language of sense data and logic. The connective 'is at' remains an added undefined connective; the canons counsel us in its use but not in its elimination.

Carnap seems to have appreciated this point afterward; for in his later writings he abandoned all notion of the translatability of statements about the physical world into statements about immediate experience. Reductionism in its radical form has long since ceased to figure in Carnap's philosophy.

But the dogma of reductionism has, in a subtler and more tenuous form, continued to influence the thought of empiricists. The notion lingers that to each statement, or each synthetic statement, there is associated a unique range of possible sensory events such that the occurrence of any of them would add to the likelihood of truth of the statement, and that there is associated also another unique range of possible sensory events whose occurrence would detract from that likelihood.

This notion is of course implicit in the verification theory of meaning.

The dogma of reductionism survives in the supposition that each statement, taken in isolation from its fellows, can admit of confirmation or infirmation at all. My countersuggestion, issuing essentially from Carnap's doctrine of the physical world in the *Aufbau*, is that our statements about the external world face the tribunal of sense experience not individually but only as a corporate body.[17]

The dogma of reductionism, even in its attenuated form, is intimately connected with the other dogma—that there is a cleavage between the analytic and the synthetic. We have found ourselves led, indeed, from the latter problem to the former through the verification theory of meaning. More directly, the one dogma clearly supports the other in this way: as long as it is taken to be significant in general to speak of the confirmation and infirmation of a statement, it seems significant to speak also of a limiting kind of statement which is vacuously confirmed, *ipso facto*, come what may; and such a statement is analytic.

The two dogmas are, indeed, at root identical. We lately reflected that in general the truth of statements does obviously depend both upon language and upon extralinguistic fact; and we noted that this obvious circumstance carries in its train, not logically but all too naturally, a feeling that the truth of a statement is somehow analyzable into a linguistic component and a factual component. The factual component must, if we are empiricists, boil down to a range of confirmatory experiences. In the extreme case where the linguistic component is all that matters, a true statement is analytic. But I hope we are now impressed with how stubbornly the distinction between analytic and synthetic has resisted any straightforward drawing. I am impressed also, apart from prefabricated examples of black and white balls in an urn, with how baffling the problem has always been of arriving at any explicit theory of the empirical confirmation of a synthetic statement. My present suggestion is that it is nonsense, and the root of much nonsense, to speak of a linguistic component and a factual component in the truth of any individual statement. Taken collectively, science has its double dependence upon language and experience; but this duality is not significantly traceable into the statements of science taken one by one.

The idea of defining a symbol in use was, as remarked, an advance over the impossible term-by-term empiricism of Locke and Hume. The statement, rather than the term, came with Bentham to be recognized as the unit accountable to an empiricist critique. But what I am now urging is that even in taking the statement as unit we have drawn our grid too finely. The unit of empirical significance is the whole of science.

6. Empiricism without the Dogmas

The totality of our so-called knowledge or beliefs, from the most casual matters of geography and history to the profoundest laws of atomic physics or even of pure mathematics and logic, is a man-made fabric which impinges on experience only along the edges. Or, to change the figure, total science is like a field of force whose boundary conditions are experience. A conflict with experience at the periphery occasions readjustments in the interior of the field. Truth values have to be redistributed over some of our statements. Reëvaluation of some statements entails reëvaluation of others, because of their logical interconnections—the logical laws being in turn simply certain further statements of the system, certain further elements of the field. Having reëvaluated one statement we must reëvaluate some others, which may be statements logically connected with the first or may be the statements of logical connections themselves. But the total field is so underdetermined by its boundary conditions, experience, that there is much latitude of choice as to what statements to reëvaluate in the light of any single contrary experience. No particular experiences are linked with any particular statements in the interior of the field, except indirectly through considerations of equilibrium affecting the field as a whole.

If this view is right, it is misleading to speak of the empirical content of an individual statement—especially if it is a statement at all remote from the experiential periphery of the field. Furthermore it becomes folly to seek a boundary between synthetic statements, which hold contingently on experience, and analytic statements, which hold come what may. Any statement can be held true come what may, if we make drastic enough adjustments elsewhere in the system. Even a statement very close to the periphery can be held true in the face of recalcitrant experience by pleading hallucination or by amending certain statements of the kind called logical laws. Conversely, by the same token, no statement is immune to revision. Revision even of the logical law of the excluded middle has been proposed as a means of simplifying quantum mechanics; and what difference is there in principle between such a shift and the shift whereby Kepler superseded Ptolemy, or Einstein Newton, or Darwin Aristotle?

For vividness I have been speaking in terms of varying distances from a sensory periphery. Let me try now to clarify this notion without metaphor. Certain statements, though *about* physical objects and not sense experience, seem peculiarly germane to sense experience—and in a selective way: some statements to some experiences, others to others. Such statements, especially germane to particular experiences, I picture as near the periphery. But in this relation of "germaneness" I envisage nothing more than a loose association reflecting the relative likelihood, in practice, of our choosing one statement rather than another for revision in the event of recalcitrant experience. For example, we can imagine recalcitrant experiences to which we would surely be inclined to accommodate our system by reëvaluating just the statement that there are brick houses on Elm Street, together with related statements on the same topic. We can imagine other recalcitrant experiences to which we would be inclined to accommodate our system by reëvaluating just the statement that there are no centaurs, along with kindred statements. A recalcitrant experience can, I have urged, be accommodated by any of various alternative reëvaluations in various alternative quarters of the total system; but, in the cases which we are now imagining, our natural tendency to disturb the total system as little as possible would lead us to focus our revisions upon these specific statements concerning brick houses or centaurs. These statements are felt, therefore, to have a sharper empirical reference than highly theoretical statements of physics or logic or ontology. The latter statements may be thought of as relatively centrally located within the total network, meaning merely that little preferential connection with any particular sense data obtrudes itself.

As an empiricist I continue to think of the conceptual scheme of science as a tool, ultimately, for predicting future experience in the light of past experience. Physical objects are conceptually imported into the situation as convenient intermediaries—not by definition in terms of experience, but simply as irreducible posits[18] comparable, epistemologically, to the gods of Homer. For my part I do, qua lay physicist, believe in physical objects and not in Homer's gods; and I consider it a scientific

error to believe otherwise. But in point of epistemological footing the physical objects and the gods differ only in degree and
not in kind. Both sorts of entities enter our conception only as
cultural posits. The myth of physical objects is epistemologically superior to most in that it has proved more efficacious
than other myths as a device for working a manageable structure into the flux of experience.

Positing does not stop with macroscopic physical objects.
Objects at the atomic level are posited to make the laws of
macroscopic objects, and ultimately the laws of experience,
simpler and more manageable; and we need not expect or
demand full definition of atomic and subatomic entities in terms
of macroscopic ones, any more than definition of macroscopic
things in terms of sense data. Science is a continuation of
common sense, and it continues the common-sense expedient
of swelling ontology to simplify theory.

Physical objects, small and large, are not the only posits.
Forces are another example; and indeed we are told nowadays
that the boundary between energy and matter is obsolete. Moreover, the abstract entities which are the substance of mathematics—ultimately classes and classes of classes and so on up
—are another posit in the same spirit. Epistemologically these
are myths on the same footing with physical objects and gods,
neither better nor worse except for differences in the degree
to which they expedite our dealings with sense experiences.

The over-all algebra of rational and irrational numbers is
underdetermined by the algebra of rational numbers, but is
smoother and more convenient; and it includes the algebra of
rational numbers as a jagged or gerrymandered part.[19] Total
science, mathematical and natural and human, is similarly but
more extremely underdetermined by experience. The edge of
the system must be kept squared with experience; the rest,
with all its elaborate myths or fictions, has as its objective the
simplicity of laws.

Ontological questions, under this view, are on a par with
questions of natural science.[20] Consider the question whether to
countenance classes as entities. This, as I have argued elsewhere,[21] is the question whether to quantify with respect to
variables which take classes as values. Now Carnap [1950a]
has maintained that is a question not of matters of fact but of
choosing a convenient language form, a convenient conceptual
scheme or framework for science. With this I agree, but only
on the proviso that the same be conceded regarding scientific
hypotheses generally. Carnap ([1950a], p. 32n) has recog-

nized that he is able to preserve a double standard for ontological questions and scientific hypotheses only by assuming
an absolute distinction between the analytic and the synthetic;
and I need not say again that this is a distinction which I
reject.[22]

The issue over there being classes seems more a question of
convenient conceptual scheme; the issue over there being centaurs, or brick houses on Elm Street, seems more a question of
fact. But I have been urging that this difference is only one of
degree, and that it turns upon our vaguely pragmatic inclination
to adjust one strand of the fabric of science rather than another in accommodating some particular recalcitrant experience. Conservatism figures in such choices, and so does the
quest for simplicity.

Carnap, Lewis, and others take a pragmatic stand on the question of choosing between language forms, scientific frameworks; but their pragmatism leaves off at the imagined
boundary between the analytic and the synthetic. In repudiating
such a boundary I espouse a more thorough pragmatism. Each
man is given a scientific heritage plus a continuing barrage
of sensory stimulation; and the considerations which guide him
in warping his scientific heritage to fit his continuing sensory
promptings are, where rational, pragmatic.

Notes

[1] See *From a Logical Point of View* (*FLPV*), p. 9.

[2] See *FLPV*, p. 10, and pp. 107–115.

[3] See *FLPV*, pp. 11f, and pp. 48f.

[4] Carnap [1947], pp. 9ff; [1950 b], pp. 70ff.

[5] According to an important variant sense of 'definition', the relation preserved may be the weaker relation of mere agreement in reference; see
FLPV, p. 132. But definition in this sense is better ignored in the present
connection, being irrelevant to the question of synonymy.

[6] Cf. Lewis [1918], p. 373.

[7] This is cognitive synonymy in a primary, broad sense. Carnap ([1947], pp.
56ff) and Lewis ([1946], pp. 83ff) have suggested how, once this notion is
at hand, a narrower sense of cognitive synonymy which is preferable for
some purposes can in turn be derived. But this special ramification of
concept-building lies aside from the present purposes and must not be
confused with the broad sort of cognitive synonymy here concerned.

[8] Pp. 81ff, *FLPV*, contain a description of just such a language except that
there happens there to be just one predicate, the two-place predicate 'e'.

[9] See *FLPV*, pp. 5–8; also pp. 85f, 166f.

[10] See *FLPV*, p. 87.

[11] On such devices see also Essay VIII, "Reference and Modality," in *FLPV*.

[12] This is the substance of Quine, *121.

[13] The 'if and only if' itself is intended in the truth functional sense. See
Carnap [1947], p. 14.

[14] The foregoing paragraph was not part of the present essay as originally published. It was prompted by Martin (see Bibliography), as was the end of Essay VII, "Notes on the Theory of Reference," in *FLPV*.

[15] The doctrine can indeed be formulated with terms rather than statements as the units. Thus Lewis describes the meaning of a term as *"a criterion in mind,* by reference to which one is able to apply or refuse to apply the expression in question in the case of presented, or imagined, things or situations" ([1946], p. 133).—For an instructive account of the vicissitudes of the verification theory of meaning, centered however on the question of meaning*fulness* rather than synonymy and analyticity, see Hempel.

[16] See *FLPV*, p. 6.

[17] This doctrine was well argued by Duhem, pp. 303–328. Or see Lowinger, pp. 132–140.

[18] Cf. *FLPV*, pp. 17f.

[19] Cf. p. 18, *FLPV*.

[20] "L'ontologie fait corps avec la science elle-même et ne peut en être separée." Meyerson, p. 439.

[21] *FLPV*, pp. 12f; pp. 102ff.

[22] For an effective expression of further misgivings over this distinction, see White.

References

Carnap, Rudolf, *Meaning and Necessity* (Chicago: University of Chicago Press, 1947).

———, "Empiricism, Semantics, and Ontology," *Revue Internationale de Philosophie* 4 (1950a), 20–40 [the first selection in this anthology].

———, *Logical Foundations of Probability* (Chicago: University of Chicago Press, 1950b).

Duhem, Pierre, *La Théorie physique: son objet et sa structure* (Paris, 1906).

Hempel, C. G., "Problems and changes in the empiricist criterion of meaning," *Revue internationale de philosophie* 4 (1950), 41–63.

———, "The concept of cognitive significance: a reconsideration," *Proceedings of American Academy of Arts and Sciences* 80 (1951), 61–77.

Lewis, C. I., *A Survey of Symbolic Logic* (Berkeley, 1918).

———, *An Analysis of Knowledge and Valuation* (Le Salle, III.: Open Court, 1946).

Lowinger, Armand, *The Methodology of Pierre Duhem* (New York: Columbia University Press, 1941).

Martin, R. M., "On 'analytic'," *Philosophical Studies* 3 (1952), 42–47.

Meyerson, Émile, *Identité et realité* (Paris, 1908; 4th ed., 1932).

Quine, W. V., *Mathematical Logic* (New York: Norton, 1940; Cambridge: Harvard University Press, 1947; rev. ed., Cambridge: Harvard University Press, 1951).

White, Morton, "The analytic and the synthetic: an untenable dualism," in Sidney Hook (ed.), *John Dewey: Philosopher of Science and Freedom* (New York: Dial Press, 1950), pp. 316–330.

3. W. V. Quine

Meaning and Translation

1. Stimulus Meaning

Empirical meaning is what remains when, given discourse together with all its stimulatory conditions, we peel away the verbiage. It is what the sentences of one language and their firm translations in a completely alien language have in common. So, if we would isolate empirical meaning, a likely position to project ourselves into is that of the linguist who is out to penetrate and translate a hitherto unknown language. Given are the native's unconstrued utterances and the observable circumstances of their occurrence. Wanted are the meanings; or wanted are English translations, for a good way to give a meaning is to say something in the home language that has it.

From *On Translation,* Reuben A. Brower, editor (Cambridge, Mass.: Harvard University Press). Copyright 1959 by the President and Fellows of Harvard College. Reprinted by permission.

This essay was an adaptation of part of a work then in progress, *Word and Object,* Cambridge, Mass.: M.I.T. Press, 1960. In the spring of 1957 I presented most of this essay as a lecture at the University of Pennsylvania, Columbia University, and Princeton University; and members of those audiences have helped me with their discussion. I used parts also at the fourth Colloque Philosophique de Royaumont, April 1958, in an address that since appeared as "Le myth de la signification" in the proceedings of the colloquium, *La Philosophie Analytique,* Paris: Editions de Minuit, 1962.

Translation between languages as close as Frisian and English is aided by resemblance of cognate word forms. Translation between unrelated languages, e.g., Hungarian and English, may be aided by traditional equations that have evolved in step with a shared culture. For light on the nature of meaning we must think rather of *radical* translation, i.e., translation of the language of a hitherto untouched people. Here it is, if anywhere, that austerely empirical meaning detaches itself from the words that have it.

The utterances first and most surely translated in such a case are perforce reports of observations conspicuously shared by the linguist and his informant. A rabbit scurries by, the native says "Gavagai," and our jungle linguist notes down the sentence "Rabbit" (or "Lo, a rabbit") as tentative translation. He will thus at first refrain from putting words into his informant's mouth, if only for lack of words to put. When he can, though, the linguist is going to have to supply native sentences for his informant's approval, despite some risk of slanting the data by suggestion. Otherwise he can do little with native terms that have references in common. For, suppose the native language includes sentences S_1, S_2, S_3, really translatable respectively as "Animal," "White," and "Rabbit." Stimulus situations always differ, whether relevantly or not; and, just because volunteered responses come singly, the classes of situations under which the native happens to have volunteered S_1, S_2, and S_3, are of course mutually exclusive, despite the hidden actual meanings of the words. How then is the linguist to perceive that the native would have been willing to assent to S_1 in all the situations where he happened to volunteer S_3, and in some but perhaps not all of the situations where he happened to volunteer S_2? Only by taking the initiative and querying combinations of native sentences and stimulus situations so as to narrow down his guesses to his eventual satisfaction.

Therefore picture the linguist asking "Gavagai?" in each of various stimulatory situations, and noting each time whether the native is prompted to assent or dissent or neither. Several assumptions are implicit here as to a linguist's power of intuition. For one thing, he must be able to recognize an informant's assent and dissent independently of any particular language. Moreover, he must be able ordinarily to guess what stimulation his subject is heeding—not nerve by nerve, but in terms at least of rough and ready reference to the environment. Moreover, he must be able to guess whether that stimulation actually prompts the native's assent to or dissent from the accompanying questions; he must be able to rule out the chance that the native assents to or dissents from the questioned sentence irrelevantly as a truth or falsehood on its own merits, without regard to the scurrying rabbit which happens to be the conspicuous circumstance of the moment.

The linguist does certainly succeed in these basic tasks of recognition in sufficiently numerous cases, and so can we all, however unconscious we be of our cues and method. The Turks' gestures of assent and dissent are nearly the reverse of ours, but facial expression shows through and sets us right pretty soon. As for what a man is noticing, this of course is commonly discernible from his orientation together with our familiarity with human interests. The third and last point of recognition is harder, but one easily imagines accomplishing it in typical cases: judging, without ulterior knowledge of the language, whether the subject's assent to or dissent from one's sudden question was prompted by the thing that had been under scrutiny at the time. One clue is got by pointing while asking; then, if the object is irrelevant, the answer may be accompanied by a look of puzzlement. Another clue to irrelevance can be that the question, asked without pointing, causes the native abruptly to shift his attention and look abstracted. But enough of conjectural mechanisms; the patent fact is that one does, by whatever unanalyzed intuitions, tend to pick up these minimum attitudinal data without special linguistic aid.

The imagined routine of proposing sentences in situations is suited only to sentences of a special sort: those which, like "Gavagai," "Red," "That hurts," "This one's face is dirty," etc., command assent only afresh in the light of currently observable circumstances. It is a question of *occasion sentences* as against *standing sentences.* Such are the sentences with which our jungle linguist must begin, and the ones for which we may appropriately try to develop a first crude concept of meaning.

The distinction between occasion sentences and standing sentences is itself definable in terms of the notion of prompted assent and dissent which we are supposing available. A sentence is an occasion sentence for a man if he can sometimes be got to assent to or dissent from it, but can never be got to unless the asking is accompanied by a prompting stimulation.

Not that there is no such prompted assent and dissent for standing sentences. A readily imaginable visual stimulation will prompt a geographically instructed subject, once, to assent to the standing sentence "There are brick houses on Elm Street." Stimulation implemented by an interferometer once prompted Michelson and Morley to dissent from the standing sentence "There is ether drift." But these standing sentences contrast with occasion sentences in that the subject may repeat his old assent or dissent unprompted by current stimulation, when we ask him again on later occasions; whereas an occasion sentence commands assent or dissent only as prompted all over again by current stimulation.

Let us define the *affirmative stimulus meaning* of an occasion sentence *S,* for a given speaker, as the class of all the stimulations that would prompt him to assent to *S*. We may define the *negative* stimulus meaning of *S* similarly in terms of dissent. Finally we may define the *stimulus meaning* of *S,* simply so-called, as the ordered pair of the affirmative and negative stimulus meanings of *S*. We could distinguish degrees of doubtfulness of assent and dissent, say, by reaction time, and elaborate our definition of stimulus meaning in easily imagined ways to include this information; but for the sake of fluent exposition let us forbear.

The several stimulations, which we assemble in classes to form stimulus meanings, must themselves be taken for present purposes not as dated particular events but as repeatable event forms. We are to say not that two stimulations have occurred that were just alike, but that the same stimulation has *recurred*. To see the necessity of this attitude consider again the positive stimulus meaning of an occasion sentence *S*. It is the class Σ of all those stimulations that *would* prompt assent to *S*. If the stimulations were taken as events rather than event forms, then Σ would have to be a class of events which largely did not and will not happen, but which would prompt assent to *S* if they were to happen. Whenever Σ contained one realized or unrealized particular event σ, it would have to contain all other unrealized duplicates of σ; and how many are there of *these?* Certainly it is hopeless nonsense to talk thus of unrealized particulars and try to assemble them into classes. Unrealized entities have to be construed as universals, simply because there are no places and dates by which to distinguish between those that are in other respects alike.

It is not necessary for present purposes to decide exactly when to count two events of surface irritation as recurrences of the same stimulation, and when to count them as occurrences of different stimulations. In practice certainly the linguist needs never care about nerve-for-nerve duplications of stimulating events. It remains, as always, sufficient merely to know, e.g., that the subject got a good glimpse of a rabbit. This is sufficient because of one's reasonable expectation of invariance of behavior under any such circumstances.

The affirmative and negative stimulus meanings of a sentence are mutually exclusive. We have supposed the linguist capable of recognizing assent and dissent, and we mean these to be so construed that no one can be said to assent to and dissent from the same occasion sentence on the same occasion. Granted, our subject might be prompted once by a given stimulation σ to assent to S, and later, by a recurrence of σ, to dissent from S; but then we would simply conclude that his meaning for S had changed. We would then reckon σ to his affirmative stimulus meaning of S as of the one date and to his negative stimulus meaning of S as of the other date. At any one given time his positive stimulus meaning of S comprises just the stimulations that *would* prompt him then to assent to S, and correspondingly for the negative stimulus meaning; and we may be sure that these two classes of stimulations are mutually exclusive.

Yet the affirmative and negative stimulus meaning do not determine each other; for the negative stimulus meaning of S does not ordinarily comprise all the stimulations that would not prompt assent to S. In general, therefore, the matching of whole stimulus meanings can be a better basis for translation than the matching merely of affirmative stimulus meanings.

What now of that strong conditional, the "would prompt" in our definition of stimulus meaning? The device is used so unquestioningly in solid old branches of science that to object to its use in a study as shaky as the present one would be a glaring case of misplaced aspiration, a compliment no more deserved than intended. What the strong conditional defines is a disposition, in this case a disposition to assent to or dissent from S when variously prompted. The disposition may be presumed to be some subtle structural condition, like an allergy and like solubility; like an allergy, more particularly, in not being understood. Whatever the ontological status of dispositions, or the philosophical status of talk of dispositions, we are familiar enough in a general way with how one sets about guessing, from judicious tests and samples and observed uniformities, whether there is a disposition of a specified sort.

2. The Inscrutability of Terms

Impressed with the interdependence of sentences, one may well wonder whether meanings even of whole sentences (let alone shorter expressions) can reasonably be talked of at all, except relative to the other sentences of an inclusive theory.

Such relativity would be awkward, since, conversely, the individual component sentences offer the only way into the theory. Now the notion of stimulus meaning partially resolves the predicament. It isolates a sort of net empirical import of each of various single sentences without regard to the containing theory, even though without loss of what the sentence owes to that containing theory. It is a device, as far as it goes, for exploring the fabric of interlocking sentences a sentence at a time. Some such device is indispensable in broaching an alien culture, and relevant also to an analysis of our own knowledge of the world.

We have started our consideration of meaning with sentences, even if sentences of a special sort and meaning in a strained sense. For words, when not learned as sentences, are learned only derivatively by abstraction from their roles in learned sentences. Still there are, prior to any such abstraction, the one-word sentences; and, as luck would have it, they are (in English) sentences of precisely the special sort already under investigation—occasion sentences like "White" and "Rabbit." Insofar then as the concept of stimulus meaning may be said to constitute in some strained sense a meaning concept for occasion sentences, it would in particular constitute a meaning concept for general terms like "White" and "Rabbit." Let us examine the concept of stimulus meaning for a while in this latter, conveniently limited, domain of application.

To affirm sameness of stimulus meaning on the part of a term for two speakers, or on the part of two terms for one or two speakers, is to affirm a certain sameness of applicability: the stimulations that prompt assent coincide, and likewise those that prompt dissent. Now is this merely to say that the term or terms have the same *extension*, i.e., are true of the same objects, for the speaker or speakers in question? In the case of "Rabbit" and "Gavagai" it may seem so. Actually, in the general case, more is involved. Thus, to adapt an example of Carnap's, imagine a general heathen term for horses and unicorns. Since there are no unicorns, the extension of that inclusive heathen term is that simply of "horses." Yet we would like somehow to say that the term, unlike "horse," *would* be true also of unicorns if there were any. Now our concept of stimulus meaning actually helps to make sense of that wanted further determination with respect to nonexistents. For stimulus meaning is in theory a question of direct surface irritations, not horses and unicorns. Each stimulation that would be occasioned by observing a unicorn is an assortment of nerve-hits, no less real and in principle no less specifiable than those occasioned by observing a horse. Such a stimulation can even be actualized, by papier-mâché trickery. In practice also we can do without deception, using descriptions and hypothetical questions, if we know enough of the language; such devices are indirect ways of guessing at stimulus meaning, even though external to the definition.

For terms like "Horse," "Unicorn," "White," and "Rabbit"—general terms for observable external objects—our concept of stimulus meaning thus seems to provide a moderately strong translation relation that goes beyond mere sameness of extension. But this is not so; the relation falls far short of sameness of extension on other counts. For, consider "Gavagai" again. Who knows but what the objects to which this term applies are not rabbits after all, but mere stages, or brief temporal segments, of rabbits? For in either event the stimulus situations that prompt assent to "Gavagai" would be the same as for "Rabbit." Or perhaps the objects to which "Gavagai" applies are all and sundry undetached parts of rabbits; again the stimulus meaning would register no difference. When from the sameness of stimulus meanings of "Gavagai" and "Rabbit" the linguist leaps to the conclusion that a gavagai is a whole enduring rabbit, he is just taking for granted that the native is enough like us to have a brief general term for rabbits and no brief general term for rabbit stages or parts.

Commonly we can translate something (e.g., "for the sake of") into a given language though nothing in that language corresponds to certain of the component syllables (e.g., to "the" and to "sake"). Just so the occasion sentence "Gavagai" is translatable as saying that a rabbit is there, though no part of "Gavagai" nor anything at all in the native language quite corresponds to the term "rabbit." Synonymy of "Gavagai" and "Rabbit" as sentences turns on considerations of prompted assent, which transcend all cultural boundaries; not so synonymy of them as terms. We are right to write "Rabbit," instead of "rabbit," as a signal that we are considering it in relation to what is synonymous with it as a sentence and not in relation to what is synonymous with it as a term.

Does it seem that the imagined indecision between rabbits, stages of rabbits, and integral parts of rabbits should be resoluble by a little supplementary pointing and questioning? Consider, then, how. Point to a rabbit and you have pointed to a stage of a rabbit and to an integral part of a rabbit. Point to an integral part of a rabbit and you have pointed to a rabbit and to a stage of a rabbit. Correspondingly for the third alternative.

Nothing not distinguished in stimulus meaning itself will be distinguished by pointing, unless the pointing is accompanied by questions of identity and diversity: "Is this the same gavagai as that? Do we have here one gavagai or two?" Such questioning requires of the linguist a command of the native language far beyond anything that we have as yet seen how to account for. More, it presupposes that the native conceptual scheme is, like ours, one that breaks reality down somehow into a multiplicity of identifiable and discriminable physical things, be they rabbits or stages or parts. For the native attitude might, after all, be very unlike ours. The term "gavagai" might be the proper name of a recurring universal rabbithood; and *still* the occasion sentence "Gavagai" would have the same stimulus meaning as under the other alternatives above suggested. For that matter, the native point of view might be so alien that from it there would be just no semblance of sense in speaking of objects at all, not even of abstract ones like rabbithood. Native channels might be wholly unlike Western talk of this and that, same and different, one and two. Failing some such familiar apparatus, surely the native cannot significantly be said to posit objects. Stuff conceivably, but not things, concrete *or* abstract. And yet, even in the face of this alien ontological attitude, the occasion sentence "Gavagai" could still have the same stimulus meaning as "(Lo, a) rabbit." Occasion sentences and stimulus meanings are general coin, whereas terms, conceived as variously applying to objects in some sense, are a provincial appurtenance of our object-positing kind of culture.

Can we even imagine any basic alternative to our object-positing pattern? Perhaps not; for we would have to imagine it in translation, and translation imposes our pattern. Perhaps the very notion of such radical contrast of cultures is meaningless, except in this purely privative sense: persistent failure to find smooth and convincing native analogues of our own familiar accessories of objective reference, such as the articles, the identity predicate, the plural ending. Only by such failure can we be said to perceive that the native language represents matters in ways not open to our own.

3. Observation Sentences

In §§ 1–2 we came to appreciate sameness of stimulus meaning as an in some ways serviceable synonymy relation when limited to occasion sentences. But even when thus limited, stimulus meaning falls short of the requirement implicit in ordinary uncritical talk of meaning. The trouble is that an informant's prompted assent to or dissent from an occasion sentence may depend only partly on the present prompting stimulation and all too largely on his hidden collateral information. In distinguishing between occasion sentences and standing sentences (§ 1), and deferring the latter, we have excluded all cases where the informant's assent or dissent might depend wholly on collateral information, but we have not excluded cases where his assent or dissent depends mainly on collateral information and ever so little on the present prompting stimulation. Thus, the native's assent to "Gavagai" on the occasion of nothing better than an ill-glimpsed movement in the grass can have been due mainly to earlier observation, in the linguist's absence, of rabbit enterprises near the spot. And there are occasion sentences the prompted assent to which will *always* depend so largely on collateral information that their stimulus meanings cannot be treated as their "meanings" by any stretch of the imagination. An example is "Bachelor"; one's assent to it is prompted genuinely enough by the sight of a face, yet it draws mainly on stored information and not at all on the prompting stimulation except as needed for recognizing the bachelor friend concerned. The trouble with "Bachelor" is that its meaning transcends the looks of the prompting faces and concerns matters that can be known only through other channels. Evidently then we must try to single out a subclass of the occasion sentences which will qualify as *observation sentences,* recognizing that what I have called stimulus meaning constitutes a reasonable notion of meaning for such sentences at most. Occasion sentences have been defined (§ 1) as sentences to which there is assent or dissent but only subject to prompting; and what we now ask of observation sentences, more particularly, is that the assent or dissent be prompted always without help of information beyond the prompting stimulation itself.

It is remarkable how sure we are that each assent to "Bachelor," or a native equivalent, would draw on data from the two sources—present stimulation and collateral information. We are not lacking in elaborate if unsystematic insights into the ways of using "Bachelor" or other specific words of our own language. Yet it does not behoove us to be smug about this easy sort of talk of meanings and reasons, for all its productivity; for, with the slightest encouragement, it can involve us in the most hopelessly confused beliefs and meaningless controversies.

Suppose it said that a particular class Σ comprises just those stimulations each of which suffices to prompt assent to an occasion sentence S outright, without benefit of collateral information. Suppose it said that the stimulations comprised in a further class Σ′, likewise sufficient to prompt assent to S, owe their efficacy rather to certain widely disseminated collateral information, C. Now couldn't we just as well have said, instead, that on acquiring C men have found it convenient implicitly to change the very *meaning* of S, so that the members of Σ′ now suffice outright like members of Σ? I suggest that we may say either; even historical clairvoyance would reveal no distinction, though it reveal all stages in the acquisition of C, since meaning can evolve *pari passu*. The distinction is illusory. What we objectively have is just an evolving adjustment to nature, reflected in an evolving set of dispositions to be prompted by stimulations to assent to or dissent from occasion sentences. These dispositions may be conceded to be impure in the sense of including worldly knowledge, but they contain it in a solution which there is no precipitating.

Observation sentences were to be occasion sentences the assent or dissent to which is prompted always without help of collateral information. The notion of help of collateral information is now seen to be shaky. Actually the notion of observation sentence is less so, because of a stabilizing statistical effect which I can suggest if for a moment I go on speaking uncritically in terms of the shaky notion of collateral information. Now some of the collateral information relevant to an occasion sentence S may be widely disseminated, some not. Even that which is widely disseminated may in part be shared by one large group of persons and in part by another, so that few if any persons know it all. Meaning, on the other hand, is social. Even the man who is oddest about a word is likely to have a few companions in deviation.

At any rate the effect is strikingly seen by comparing "Rabbit" with "Bachelor." The stimulus meaning of "Bachelor" will be the same for no two speakers short of Siamese twins. The stimulus meaning of "Rabbit" will be much alike for most speakers; exceptions like the movement in the grass are rare. A working concept that would seem to serve pretty much the purpose of the notion of observation sentence is then simply this: *occasion sentence possessing intersubjective stimulus meaning.*

In order then that an occasion sentence be an observation sentence, is it sufficient that there be *two* people for whom it has the same stimulus meaning? No, as witness those Siamese twins. Must it have the same stimulus meaning for all persons in the linguistic community (however *that* might be defined)? Surely not. Must it have *exactly* the same stimulus meaning for even two? Perhaps not, considering again that movement in the grass. But these questions aim at refinements that would simply be misleading if undertaken. We are concerned here with rough trends of behavior. What matters for the notion of observation sentence here intended is that for significantly many speakers the stimulus meanings deviate significantly little.

In one respect actually the intersubjective variability of the stimulus meaning of sentences like "Bachelor" has been understated. Not only will the stimulus meaning of "Bachelor" for one person differ from that of "Bachelor" for the next person; it will differ from that of any other likely sentence for the next person, in the same language or any other.

The linguist is not free to survey a native stimulus meaning *in extenso* and then to devise *ad hoc* a great complex English sentence whose stimulus meaning, for him, matches the native one by sheer exhaustion of cases. He has rather to extrapolate any native stimulus meaning from samples, guessing at the informant's mentality. If the sentence is as nonobservational as "Bachelor," he simply will not find likely lines of extrapolation. Translation by stimulus meaning will then deliver no wrong result, but simply nothing. This is interesting because what led us to try to define observation sentences was our reflection that they were the subclass of occasion sentences that seemed reasonably translatable by identity of stimulus meaning. Now we see that the limitation of this method of translation to this class of sentences is self-enforcing. When an occasion sentence is of the wrong kind, the informant's stimulus meaning for it will simply not be one that the linguist will feel he can plausibly equate with his own stimulus meaning for any English sentence.

The notion of stimulus meaning was one that required no multiplicity of informants. There is in principle the stimulus meaning of the sentence for the given speaker at the given time of his life (though in guessing at it the linguist may be helped by varying both the time and the speaker). The definition of observation sentence took wider points of reference: it expressly required comparison of various speakers of the same language. Finally the reflection in the foregoing paragraph reassures us that such widening of horizons can actually be done without. Translation of occasion sentences by stimulus meaning will limit itself to observation sentences without our ever having actually to bring the criterion of observation sentence to bear.

The phrase "observation sentence" suggests, for epistemologists or methodologists of science, datum sentences of science. On this score our version is by no means amiss. For our observation sentences as defined are just the occasion sentences on which there is pretty sure to be firm agreement on the part of well-placed observers. Thus they are just the sentences to which a scientist will finally recur when called upon to marshal his data and repeat his observations and experiments for doubting colleagues.

4. Intrasubjective Synonymy of Occasion Sentences

Stimulus meaning remains defined all this while for occasion sentences generally, without regard to observationality. But it bears less resemblance to what might reasonably be called meaning when applied to nonobservation sentences like "Bachelor." Translation of "Soltero" as "Bachelor" manifestly cannot be predicated on identity of stimulus meanings between persons; nor can synonymy of "Bachelor" and "Unmarried man."

Curiously enough, though, the stimulus meanings of "Bachelor" and "Unmarried man" are, despite all this, identical for any one speaker. An individual will at any one time be prompted by the same stimulations to assent to "Bachelor" and to "Unmarried man"; and similarly for dissent. What we find is that, though the concept of stimulus meaning is so very remote from "true meaning" when applied to the inobservational occasion sentences "Bachelor" and "Unmarried man," still synonymy is definable as sameness of stimulus meaning just as faithfully for these sentences as for the choicest observation sentences —as long as we stick to one speaker. For each speaker "Bachelor" and "Unmarried man" are synonymous in a defined sense (viz., alike in stimulus meaning) without having the same meaning in any acceptably defined sense of "meaning" (for stimulus meaning is, in the case of "Bachelor," nothing of the kind). Very well; let us welcome the synonymy and let the meaning go.

The one-speaker restriction presents no obstacle to saying that "Bachelor" and "Unmarried man" are synonymous for the whole community, in the sense of being synonymous for each member. A practical extension even to the two-language case is not far to seek if a bilingual speaker is at hand. "Bachelor" and "Soltero" will be synonymous for him by the intra-individual criterion, viz., sameness of stimulus meaning. Taking him as a sample, we may treat "Bachelor" and "Soltero" as synonymous for the translation purposes of the two whole linguistic communities that he represents. Whether he is a good enough sample would be checked by observing the fluency of his communication in both communities, by comparing other bilinguals, or by observing how well the translations work.

But such use of bilinguals is unavailable to the jungle linguist broaching an untouched culture. For radical translation the only concept thus far at our disposal is sameness of stimulus meaning, and this only for observation sentences.

The kinship and difference between intrasubjective synonymy and radical translation require careful notice. Intrasubjective synonymy, like translation, is quite capable of holding good for a whole community. It is intrasubjective in that the synonyms are joined for each subject by sameness of stimulus meaning for him; but it may still be community-wide in that the synonyms in question are joined by sameness of stimulus meaning for every single subject in the whole community. Obviously intrasubjective synonymy is in principle just as objective, just as discoverable by the outside linguist, as is translation. Our linguist may even find native sentences intrasubjectively synonymous without finding English translations—without, in short, understanding them; for he can find that they have the same stimulus meaning, for the subject, even though there may be no English sentence whose stimulus meaning for himself promises to be the same. Thus, to turn the tables: a Martian could find that "Bachelor" and "Unmarried man" were synonyms without discovering when to assent to either one.

"Bachelor" and "Yes" are two occasion sentences which we may instructively compare. Neither of them is an observation sentence, nor, therefore, translatable by identity of stimulus meaning. The heathen equivalent ("Tak," say) of "Yes" would fare poorly indeed under translation by stimulus meaning. The stimulations which—accompanying the linguist's question "Tak?"—would prompt assent to this queer sentence, even on the part of all natives without exception, are ones which (because exclusively verbal in turn, and couched in the heathen tongue) would never have prompted an unspoiled Anglo-Saxon to assent to "Yes" or anything like it. "Tak" is just what the linguist is fishing for by way of assent to whatever heathen occasion sentence he may be investigating, but it is a poor one, under these methods, to investigate. Indeed we may expect "Tak," or "Yes," like "Bachelor," to have the same stimulus meaning for no two speakers even of the same language; for "Yes" can have the same stimulus meaning only for speakers who agree on every single thing that can be blurted in a specious present. At the same time, sameness of stimulus meaning does define intrasubjective synonymy, not only between "Bachelor" and "Unmarried man" but equally between "Yes" and "Uh huh" or "Quite."

Note that the reservations of §2 regarding coextensiveness of terms still hold. Though the Martian find that "Bachelor" and "Unmarried man" are synonymous occasion sentences, still in so doing he will not establish that "bachelor" and "unmarried man" are coextensive general terms. Either term to the exclusion of the other might, so far as he knows, apply not to men but to their stages or parts or even to an abstract attribute; cf. §2.

Talking of occasion sentences as sentences and not as terms, however, we see that we can do more for synonymy within a language than for radical translation. It appears that sameness of stimulus meaning will serve as a standard of intrasubjective synonymy of occasion sentences without their having to be observation sentences.

Actually we do need this limitation: we should stick to short and simple sentences. Otherwise subjects' mere incapacity to digest long questions can, under our definitions, issue in difference of stimulus meanings between long and short sentences which we should prefer to find synonymous. A stimulation may prompt assent to the short sentence and not to the long one just because of the opacity of the long one; yet we should then like to say not that the subject has shown the meaning of the long sentence to be different, but merely that he has failed to penetrate it.

Certainly the sentences will not have to be kept so short but what some will contain others. One thinks of such containment as happening with help of conjunctions, in the grammarians' sense: "or," "and," "but," "if," "then," "that," etc., governing the contained sentence as clause of the containing sentence. But it can also happen farther down. Very simple sentences may contain substantives and adjectives ("red," "tile," "bachelor," etc.) which qualify also as occasion sentences in their own right, subject to our synonymy concept. So our synonymy concept already applies on an equal footing to sentences some of which recur as parts of others. Some extension of synonymy to longer occasion sentences, containing others as parts, is then possible by the following sort of construction.

Think of $R(S)$ first as an occasion sentence which, though moderately short, still contains an occasion sentence S as part. If now we leave the contained sentence blank, the partially empty result may graphically be referred to as $R(...)$ and called (following Peirce) a *rheme*. A rheme $R(...)$ will be called *regular* if it fulfills this condition: for each S and S', if S and S' are synonymous and $R(S)$ and $R(S')$ are idiomatically acceptable occasion sentences short enough for our synonymy concept, then $R(S)$ and $R(S')$ are synonymous. This concept of regularity makes reasonable sense thus far only for short rhemes, since $R(S)$ and $R(S')$ must, for suitably short S and S', be short enough to come under our existing synonymy concept. However, the concept of regularity now invites extension, in this very natural way: where the rhemes $R_1(...)$ and $R_2(...)$ are both regular, let us speak of the longer rheme $R_1(R_2(...))$ as regular too. In this way we may speak of regularity of longer and longer rhemes without end. Thereupon we can extend the synonymy concept to various long occasion sentences, as follows. Where $R(...)$ is any regular rheme and S and S' are short occasion sentences that are synonymous in the existing unextended sense and $R(S)$ and $R(S')$ are idiomatically acceptable combinations at all, we may by extension call $R(S)$ and $R(S')$ synonymous in turn—even though they be too long for synonymy as first defined. There is no limit now to length, since the regular rheme $R(...)$ may be as long as we please.

5. Truth Functions

In §§2–3 we accounted for radical translation only of observation sentences, by identification of stimulus meanings. Now there is also a decidedly different domain that lends itself directly to radical translation: that of *truth functions* such as negation, logical conjunction, and alternation. For, suppose as before that assent and dissent are generally recognizable. The sentences put to the native for assent or dissent may now be occasion sentences and standing sentences indifferently. Those that are occasion sentences will of course have to be accompanied by a prompting stimulation, if assent or dissent is to be elicited; the standing sentences, on the other hand, can be put without props. Now by reference to assent and dissent we can state *semantic criteria* for truth functions; i.e., criteria for determining whether a given native idiom is to be construed as expressing the truth function in question. The semantic criterion of negation is that it turns any short sentence to which one will assent into a sentence from which one will dissent, and vice versa. That of conjunction is that it produces compounds to which (so long as the component sentences are short) one is prepared to assent always and only when one is prepared to assent to each component. That of alternation is similar but with the verb "assent" changed twice to "dissent."

The point about short components is merely, as in §4, that when they are long the subject may get mixed up. Identification of a native idiom as negation, or conjunction, or alternation, is not to be ruled out in view of a subject's deviation from our semantic criteria when the deviation is due merely to confusion. Note well that no limit is imposed on the lengths of the component sentences to which negation, conjunction, or alternation may be applied; it is just that the test cases for first spotting such constructions in a strange language are cases with short components.

When we find a native construction to fulfill one or another of these three semantic criteria, we can ask no more toward an understanding of it. Incidentally we can then translate the idiom into English as "not," "and," or "or" as the case may be, but only subject to sundry humdrum provisos; for it is well known that these three English words do not represent negation, conjunction, and alternation exactly and unambiguously.

Any construction for compounding sentences from other sentences is counted in logic as expressing a truth function if it fulfills this condition: the compound has a unique "truth value" (truth or falsity) for each assignment of truth values to the components. Semantic criteria can obviously be stated for all truth functions along the lines already followed for negation, conjunction, and alternation.

One hears talk of prelogical peoples, said deliberately to accept certain simple self-contradictions as true. Doubtless overstating Levy-Bruhl's intentions, let us imagine someone to claim that these natives accept as true a certain sentence of the form "*p* ka bu *p*" where "ka" means "and" and "bu" means "not." Now this claim is absurd on the face of it, if translation of "ka" as "and" and "bu" as "not" follows our semantic criteria. And, not to be dogmatic, what criteria will you have? Conversely, to claim on the basis of a better dictionary that the natives *do* share our logic would be to impose our logic and beg the question, if there were really a meaningful question here to beg. But I do urge the better dictionary.

The same point can be illustrated within English, by the question of alternative logics. Is he who propounds heterodox logical laws really contradicting our logic, or is he just putting some familiar old vocables ("and," "or," "not," "all," etc.) to new and irrelevant uses? It makes no sense to say, unless from the point of view of some criteria or other for translating logical particles. Given the above criteria, the answer is clear.

We hear from time to time that the scientist in his famous freedom to resystematize science or fashion new calculi is bound at least to respect the law of contradiction. Now what are we to make of this? We do flee contradiction, for we are after truth. But what of a revision so fundamental as to count contradictions as true? Well, to begin with, it would have to be arranged carefully if all utility is not to be lost. Classical logical laws enable us from any one contradiction to deduce all statements indiscriminately; and such universal affirmation would leave science useless for lack of distinctions. So the revision which counts contradictions as true will have to be accompanied by a revision of other logical laws. Now all this can be done; but, once it is done, how can we say it is what it purported to be? This heroically novel logic falls under the considerations of the preceding paragraph, to be reconstrued perhaps simply as old logic in bad notation.

We *can* meaningfully contemplate changing a law of logic, be it the law of excluded middle or even the law of contradiction. But this is so only because while contemplating the change we continue to translate *identically:* "and" as "and," "or" as "or," etc. Afterward a more devious mode of translation will perhaps be hit upon which will annul the change of law; or perhaps, on the contrary, the change of law will be found to have produced an essentially stronger system, demonstrably not translatable into the old in any way at all. But even in the latter event any actual conflict between the old and the new logic proves illusory, for it comes only of translating identically.

At any rate we have settled a people's logical laws completely, so far as the truth-functional part of logic goes, once we have fixed our translations by the above semantic criteria. In particular the class of the *tautologies* is fixed: the truth-functional compounds that are true by truth-functional structure alone. There is a familiar tabular routine for determining, for sentences in which the truth functions are however immoderately iterated and superimposed, just what assignments of truth values to the ultimate component sentences will make the whole compound true; and the tautologies are the compounds that come out true under all assignments.

It is a commonplace of epistemology (and therefore occasionally contested) that just two very opposite spheres of knowledge enjoy irreducible certainty. One is the knowledge of what is directly present to sense experience, and the other is knowledge of logical truth. It is striking that these, roughly, are the two domains where we have made fairly direct behavioral sense of radical translation. One domain where radical translation seemed straightforward was that of the observation sentences. The other is that of the truth functions; hence also in a sense the tautologies, these being the truths to which only the truth functions matter.

But the truth functions and tautologies are only the simplest of the logical functions and logical truths. Can we perhaps do better? The logical functions that most naturally next suggest themselves are the *categoricals,* traditionally designated *A, E, I,* and *O,* and commonly construed in English by the construction "all are" ("All rabbits are timid"), "none are," "some are," "some are not." A semantic criterion for *A* perhaps suggests itself as follows: the compound commands assent (from a given speaker) if and only if the positive stimulus meaning (for him) of the first component is a subclass of the positive stimulus meaning of the second component. How to vary this for *E, I,* and *O* is obvious enough, except that the whole idea is wrong in view of §2. Thus take *A.* If "hippoid" is a general term intended to apply to all horses and unicorns, then all hippoids are horses (there being no unicorns), but still the positive stimulus meaning of "Hippoid" has stimulus patterns in it, of the sort suited to "Unicorn," that are not in the positive stimulus meaning of "Horse." On this score the suggested semantic criterion is at odds with "All *S* and *P*" in that it goes beyond extension. And it has a yet more serious failing of the opposite kind; for, whereas rabbit stages are not rabbits, we saw in §2 that in point of stimulus meaning there is no distinction.

The difficulty is fundamental. The categoricals depend for their truth on the objects, however external and however inferential, of which the component terms are true; and what those objects are is not uniquely determined by stimulus meanings. Indeed the categoricals, like plural endings and identity, make sense at all only relative to an object-positing kind of conceptual scheme; whereas, stressed in §2, stimulus meanings can be just the same for persons imbued with such a scheme and for persons as alien to it as you please. Of what we think of as logic, the truth-functional part is the only part the recognition of which, in a foreign language, we seem to be able to pin down to behavioral criteria.

6. Analytical Hypotheses

How then does our linguist push radical translation beyond the bounds of mere observation sentences and truth functions? In broad outline as follows. He segments heard utterances into conveniently short recurrent parts, and thus compiles a list of native "words." Various of these he hypothetically equates to English words and phrases, in such a way as to reproduce the already established translations of whole observation sentences. Such conjectural equatings of parts may be called *analytical hypotheses* of translation. He will need analytical hypotheses of translation not only for native words but also for native constructions, or ways of assembling words, since the native language would not be assumed to follow English word order. Taken together these analytical hypotheses of translation constitute a jungle-to-English grammar and dictionary, which the linguist then proceeds to apply even to sentences for the translation of which no independent evidence is available.

The analytical hypotheses of translation do not depend for their evidence exclusively upon those prior translations of observation sentences. They can also be tested partly by their conformity to intrasubjective synonymies of occasion sentences, as of §4. For example, if the analytical hypotheses direct us to translate native sentences S_1 and S_2 respectively as "Here is a bachelor" and "Here is an unmarried man," then we shall hope to find also that for each native the stimulus meaning of S_1 is the same as that of S_2.

The analytical hypotheses of translation can be partially tested in the light of the thence derived translations not only of occasion sentences but, sometimes, of standing sentences. Standing sentences differ from occasion sentences only in that assent to them and dissent from them may occur unprompted (cf. § 1), not in that they occur only unprompted. The concept of prompted assent is reasonably applicable to the standing sentence "Some rabbits are black" once, for a given speaker, if we manage to spring the specimen on him before he knows there are black ones. A given speaker's assent to some standing sentences can even be prompted repeatedly; thus his assent can genuinely be prompted anew each year to "The crocuses are out," and anew each day to "The *Times* has come." Standing sentences thus grade off toward occasion sentences, though there still remains a boundary, as defined midway in §1. So the linguist can further appraise his analytical hypotheses of translation by seeing how the thence derivable translations of standing sentences compare with the originals on the score of prompted assent and dissent.

Some slight further testing of the analytical hypotheses of translation is afforded by standing sentences even apart from prompted assent and dissent. If for instance the analytical hypotheses point to some rather platitudinous English standing sentence as translation of a native sentence S, then the linguist will feel reassured if he finds that S likewise commands general and unprompted assent.

The analytical hypotheses of translation would not in practice be held to equational form. There is no need to insist that the native word be equated outright to any one English word or phrase. One may specify certain contexts in which the word is to be translated one way and others in which the word is to be translated in another way. One may overlay the equational form with supplementary semantical instructions *ad libitum.* "Spoiled (*said of an egg*)" is as good a lexicographical definition as "addled," despite the intrusion of stage directions. Translation instructions having to do with grammatical inflections—to take an extreme case—may be depended on to present equation of words and equations of constructions in inextricable combination with much that is not equational. For the purpose is not translation of single words nor translation of single constructions, but translation of coherent discourse. The hypotheses the linguist arrives at, the instructions that he frames, are contributory hypotheses or instructions concerning translation of coherent discourse, and they may be presented in any form, equational or otherwise, that proves clear and convenient.

Nevertheless there is reason to draw particular attention to the simple form of analytical hypothesis which does directly equate a native word or construction to a hypothetical English equivalent. For hypotheses need thinking up, and the typical case of thinking up is the case where the English-bred linguist apprehends a parallelism of function between some component fragment of a translated whole native sentence S and some component word of the English translation of S. Only in some such way can we account for anyone's ever thinking to translate a native locution radically into English as a plural ending, or as the identity predicate "=," or as a categorical copula, or as any other part of our domestic apparatus of objective reference; for, as stressed in earlier pages, no scrutiny of stimulus meanings or other behavioral manifestations can even settle whether the native shares our object-positing sort of conceptual scheme at all. It is only by such outright projection of his own linguistic habits that the linguist can find general terms in the native language at all, or, having found them, match them with his own. Stimulus meanings never suffice to determine even what words are terms, if any, much less what terms are coextensive.

The linguist who is serious enough about the jungle language to undertake its definitive dictionary and grammar will not, indeed, proceed quite as we have imagined. He will steep himself in the language, disdainful of English parallels, to the point of speaking it like a native. His learning of it even from the beginning can have been as free of all thought of other languages as you please; it can have been virtually an accelerated counterpart of infantile learning. When at length he does turn his hand to translation, and to producing a jungle-to-English dictionary and grammar, he can do so as a bilingual. His own two personalities thereupon assume the roles which in previous pages were divided between the linguist and his informant. He equates "Gavagai" with "Rabbit" by appreciating a sameness of stimulus meaning of the two sentences for himself. Indeed he can even use sameness of stimulus meaning to translate nonobservational occasion sentences of the type of "Bachelor"; here the intrasubjective situation proves its advantage (cf. § 4). When he brings off other more recondite translations he surely does so by essentially the method of analytical hypotheses, but with the difference that he projects these hypotheses from his prior separate masteries of the two languages, rather than using them in mastering the jungle language. Now though it is such bilingual translation that does most justice to the jungle language, reflection upon it reveals least about the nature of meaning;

for the bilingual translator works by an intrasubjective com-
muning of a split personality, and we make operational sense
of his method only as we externalize it. So let us think still in
terms of our more primitive schematism of the jungle-to-English
project, which counts the native informant in as a live collabo-
rator rather than letting the linguist first ingest him.

7. A Handful of Meaning

The linguist's finished jungle-to-English manual is to be ap-
praised as a manual of sentence-to-sentence translation. Whatever be the details of its expository devices of word translation
and syntactical paradigm, its net accomplishment is an infinite
semantic correlation of sentences: the implicit specification of
an English sentence for every one of the infinitely many possible jungle sentences. The English sentence for a given jungle
one need not be unique, but it is to be unique to within any
acceptable standard of intrasubjective synonymy among English sentences; and conversely. Though the thinking up and
setting forth of such a semantic correlation of sentences depend on analyses into component words, the supporting evidence remains entirely at the level of sentences. It consists in
sundry conformities on the score of stimulus meaning, intrasubjective synonymies, and other points of prompted and unprompted assent and dissent, as noted in §6.

Whereas the semantic correlation exhausts the native sentences, its supporting evidence determines no such widespread
translation. Countless alternative over-all semantic correlations,
therefore, are equally compatible with that evidence. If the
linguist arrives at his one over-all correlation among many
without feeling that his choice was excessively arbitrary, this
is because he himself is limited in the correlations that he can
manage. For he is not, in his finitude, free to assign English
sentences to the infinitude of jungle ones in just any way whatever that will fit his supporting evidence; he has to assign them
in some way that is manageably systematic with respect to a
manageably limited set of repeatable speech segments. The
word-by-word approach is indispensable to the linguist in
specifying his semantic correlation and even in thinking it up.

Not only does the linguist's working segmentation limit the
possibilities of any eventual semantic correlation. It even contributes to defining, for him, the ends of translation. For he
will put a premium on structural parallels: on correspondence

between the parts of the native sentence, as he segments it, and the parts of the English translation. Other things being equal, the more literal translation is seen as more literally a translation.[1] Technically a tendency to literal translation is assured anyway, since the very purpose of segmentation is to make long translations constructible from short correspondences; but then one goes farther and makes of this tendency an objective—and an objective that even varies in detail with the practical segmentation adopted.

It is by his analytical hypotheses that our jungle linguist implicitly states (and indeed arrives at) the grand synthetic hypothesis which is his over-all semantic correlation of sentences. His supporting evidence, such as it is, for the semantic correlation is his supporting evidence also for his analytical hypotheses. Chronologically, the analytical hypotheses come before all that evidence is in; then such of the evidence as ensues is experienced as pragmatic corroboration of a working dictionary. But in any event the translation of a vast range of native sentences, though covered by the semantic correlation, can never be corroborated or supported at all except cantilever fashion: it is simply what comes out of the analytical hypotheses when they are applied beyond the zone that supports them. That those unverifiable translations proceed without mishap must not be taken as pragmatic evidence of good lexicography, for mishap is impossible.

We must then recognize that the analytical hypotheses of translation and the grand synthetic one that they add up to are only in an incomplete sense hypotheses. Contrast the case of translation of "Gavagai" as "Lo, a rabbit" by sameness of stimulus meaning. This is a genuine hypothesis from sample observations, though possibly wrong. "Gavagai" and "Lo, a rabbit" have stimulus meanings for the two speakers, and these are the same or different, whether we guess right or not. On the other hand no sense is made of sameness of meaning of the words that are equated in the typical analytical hypothesis. The point is not that we cannot be sure whether the analytical hypothesis is right, but that there is not even, as there was in the case of "Gavagai," an objective matter to be right or wrong about.

Complete radical translation does go on, and analytical hypotheses are indispensable. Nor are they capricious; on the contrary we have just been seeing, in outline, how they are supported. May we not then say that in those very ways of thinking up and supporting the analytical hypotheses a sense *is* after all given to sameness of meaning of the expressions which those hypotheses equate? No. We could claim this only if no two conflicting sets of analytical hypotheses were capable of being supported equally strongly by all theoretically accessible evidence (including simplicity considerations).

This indefinability of synonymy by reference to the methodology of analytical hypotheses is formally the same as the indefinability of truth by reference to scientific method. Also the consequences are parallel. Just as we may meaningfully speak of the truth of a sentence only within the terms of some theory or conceptual scheme, so on the whole we may meaningfully speak of interlinguistic synonymy of words and phrases only within the terms of some particular system of analytical hypotheses.

The method of analytical hypotheses is a way of catapulting oneself into the native language by the momentum of the home language. It is a way of grafting exotic shoots on to the old familiar bush until only the exotic meets the eye. Native sentences not neutrally meaningful are thereby tentatively translated into home sentences on the basis, in effect, of seeming analogy of roles within the languages. These relations of analogy cannot themselves be looked upon as the meanings, for they are not unique. And anyway the analogies weaken as we move out toward the theoretical sentences, farthest from observation. Thus who would undertake to translate "Neutrinos lack mass" into the jungle language? If anyone does, we may expect him to coin new native words or distort the usage of old ones. We may expect him to plead in extenuation that the natives lack the requisite concepts; also that they know too little physics. And he is right, but another way of describing the matter is as follows. Analytical hypotheses at best are devices whereby, indirectly, we bring out analogies between sentences that have yielded to translation and sentences that have not, and so extend the working limits of translation; and "Neutrinos lack mass" is way out where the effects of such analytical hypotheses as we manage to devise are too fuzzy to do much good.

Containment in the Low German continuum facilitated translation of Frisian into English (§1), and containment in a continuum of cultural evolution facilitated translation of Hungarian into English. These continuities, by facilitating translation, encourage an illusion of subject matter: an illusion that our so readily intertranslatable sentences are diverse verbal embodiments of some intercultural proposition or meaning, when they are better seen as the merest variants of one and the same intracultural verbalism. Only the discontinuity of radical translation tries our meanings: really sets them over against their verbal embodiments, or more typically, finds nothing there.

Observation sentences peel nicely; their meanings, stimulus meanings, emerge absolute and free of all residual verbal taint. Theoretical sentences such as "Neutrinos lack mass," or the law of entropy, or the constancy of the speed of light, are at the other extreme. For such sentences no hint of the stimulatory conditions of assent or dissent can be dreamed of that does not include verbal stimulation from within the language. Sentences of this extreme latter sort, and other sentences likewise that lie intermediate between the two extremes, lack linguistically neutral meaning.

It would be trivial to say that we cannot know the meaning of a foreign sentence except as we are prepared to offer a translation in our own language. I am saying more: that it is only relative to an in large part arbitrary manual of translation that most foreign sentences may be said to share the meaning of English sentences, and then only in a very parochial sense of meaning, viz., use-in-English. Stimulus meanings of observation sentences aside, most talk of meaning requires tacit reference to a home language in much the way that talk of truth involves tacit reference to one's own system of the world, the best that one can muster at the time.

There being (apart from stimulus meanings) so little in the way of neutral meanings relevant to radical translation, there is no telling how much of one's success with analytical hypotheses is due to real kinship of outlook on the part of the natives and ourselves, and how much of it is due to linguistic ingenuity or lucky coincidence. I am not sure that it even makes sense to ask. We may alternately wonder at the inscrutability of the native mind and wonder at how very much like us the native is, where in the one case we have merely muffed the best translation and in the other case we have done a more thorough job of reading our own provincial modes into the native's speech.

Usener, Cassirer, Sapir, and latterly B. L. Whorf have stressed that deep differences of language carry with them ultimate differences in the way one thinks, or looks upon the world. I should prefer not to put the matter in such a way as to suggest that certain philosophical propositions are affirmed in the one culture and denied in the other. What is really involved is difficulty or indeterminacy of correlation. It is just that there is less basis of comparison—less sense in saying what is good translation and what is bad—the farther we get away from sentences with visibly direct conditioning to nonverbal stimuli and the farther we get off home ground.

Note

[1] Hence also Carnap's concept of structural synonymy. See his *Meaning and Necessity* (Chicago, 1947), §§ 14–16.

4. Wilfrid Sellars

Empiricism and the Philosophy of Mind

**Does Empirical Knowledge
Have a Foundation?**

One of the forms taken by the Myth of the Given is the idea that there is, indeed *must be,* a structure of particular matter of fact such that (a) each fact can not only be noninferentially known to be the case, but presupposes no other knowledge either of particular matter of fact, or of general truths; and (b) such that the noninferential knowledge of facts belonging to this structure constitutes the ultimate court of appeals for all factual claims—particular and general—about the world. It is important to note that I characterized the knowledge of fact belonging to this stratum as not only noninferential, but as presupposing no knowledge of other matter of fact, whether particular or general. It might be thought that this is a redundancy, that knowledge (not belief or conviction, but knowledge) which logically presupposes knowledge of other facts *must* be

From Wilfrid Sellars, "Empiricism and the Philosophy of Mind," *Minnesota Studies in the Philosophy of Science,* Vol. 1, eds. Herbert Feigl and Michael Scriven (Minneapolis: University of Minnesota Press, 1956), pp. 293–305. Copyright © 1956 by the University of Minnesota. Reprinted by permission.

inferential. This, however, as I hope to show, is itself an episode in the Myth.

Now, the idea of such a privileged stratum of fact is a familiar
one, though not without its difficulties. Knowledge pertaining
to this level is *noninferential,* yet it is, after all, *knowledge.* It
is *ultimate,* yet it has *authority.* The attempt to make a consistent picture of these two requirements has traditionally taken
the following form:

Statements pertaining to this level, in order to 'express
knowledge' must not only be made, but, so to speak, must be
worthy of being made, *credible,* that is, in the sense of worthy
of credence. Furthermore, and this is a crucial point, they must
be made in a way which *involves* this credibility. For where
there is no connection between the making of a statement and
its authority, the assertion may express *conviction,* but it can
scarcely be said to express knowledge.

The authority—the credibility—of statements pertaining to
this level cannot exhaustively consist in the fact that they are
supported by *other* statements, for in that case all *knowledge*
pertaining to this level would have to be inferential, which not
only contradicts the hypothesis, but flies in the face of good
sense. The conclusion seems inevitable that if some statements
pertaining to this level are to express *noninferential* knowledge,
they must have a credibility which is not a matter of being supported by other statements. Now there does seem to be a class
of statements which fill at least part of this bill, namely, such
statements as would be said to *report observations,* thus: "This
is red." These statements, candidly made, have authority. Yet
they are not expressions of inference. How, then, is this authority to be understood?

Clearly, the argument continues, it springs from the fact that
they are made in just the circumstances in which they are
made, as is indicated by the fact that they characteristically,
though not necessarily or without exception, involve those so-
called token-reflexive expressions which, in addition to the
tenses of verbs, serve to connect the circumstances in which
a statement is made with its sense. (At this point it will be
helpful to begin putting the line of thought I am developing in
terms of the *fact-stating* and *observation-reporting* roles of certain sentences.) Roughly, two verbal performances which are
tokens of a non-token-reflexive sentence can occur in widely
different circumstances and yet make the same statement;
whereas two tokens of a token-reflexive sentence can make the
same statement only if they are uttered in the same circum-

stances (according to a relevant criterion of sameness). And two tokens of a sentence, whether it contains a token-reflexive expression—over and above a tensed verb—or not, can make the same *report* only if, made in all candor, they express the *presence*—in *some* sense of "presence"—of the state of affairs that is being reported; if, that is, they stand in that relation to the state of affairs, whatever the relation may be, by virtue of which they can be said to formulate observations of it.

It would appear, then, that there are two ways in which a sentence token can have credibility: (1) The authority may accrue to it, so to speak, from above, that is, as being a token of a sentence type *all* the tokens of which, in a certain use, have credibility, e.g., "2 + 2 = 4." In this case, let us say that token credibility is inherited from type authority. (2) The credibility may accrue to it from the fact that it came to exist in a certain way in a certain set of circumstances, e.g., "This is red." Here token credibility is not derived from type credibility.

Now, the credibility of *some* sentence types appears to be *intrinsic*— at least in the limited sense that it is *not* derived from other sentences, type or token. This is, or seems to be, the case with certain sentences used to make analytic statements. The credibility of *some* sentence types accrues to them by virtue of their logical relations to other sentence types, thus by virtue of the fact that they are logical consequences of more basic sentences. It would seem obvious, however, that the credibility of empirical sentence types cannot be traced without remainder to the credibility of other sentence types. And since no empirical sentence type appears to have *intrinsic* credibility, this means that credibility must accrue to *some* empirical sentence types by virtue of their logical relations to certain sentence tokens, and, indeed, to sentence tokens the authority of which is not derived, in its turn, from the authority of sentence types.

The picture we get is that of there being two *ultimate* modes of credibility: (1) The intrinsic credibility of analytic sentences, which accrues to tokens as being tokens of such a type; (2) the credibility of such tokens as "express observations," a credibility which flows from tokens to types.

Let us explore this picture, which is common to all traditional empiricisms, a bit further. How is the authority of such sentence tokens as "express observational knowledge" to be understood? It has been tempting to suppose that in spite of the obvious differences which exist between "observation reports" and "analytic statements," there is an essential similarity between the ways in which they come by their authority. Thus, it has been claimed, not without plausibility, that whereas *ordinary* empirical statements can be *correctly* made without being *true,* observation reports resemble analytic statements in that being correctly made is a sufficient as well as necessary condition of their truth. And it has been inferred from this—somewhat hastily, I believe—that "correctly making" the report "This is green" is a matter of "following the rules for the use of 'this,' 'is' and 'green.' "

Three comments are immediately necessary:

1. First a brief remark about the term "report." In ordinary usage a report is a report made *by* someone *to* someone. To make a report is to *do* something. In the literature of epistemology, however, the word "report" or *"Konstatierung"* has acquired a technical use in which a sentence token can play a reporting role (a) without being an *overt* verbal performance, and (b) without having the character of being "by someone to someone"—even oneself. There is, of course, such a thing as "talking to oneself"—*in foro interno*—but, as I shall be emphasizing in the closing stages of my argument, it is important not to suppose that all "covert" verbal episodes are of this kind.

2. My second comment is that while *we* shall not assume that because 'reports' *in the ordinary sense* are *actions,* 'reports' in the sense of *Konstatierungen* are also actions, the line of thought we are considering treats them as such. In other words, it interprets the correctness of *Konstatierungen* as analogous to the rightness of actions. Let me emphasize, however, that not all *ought* is *ought to do,* nor all correctness the correctness of *actions.*

3. My third comment is that if the expression "following a rule" is taken seriously, and is not weakened beyond all recognition into the bare notion of exhibiting a uniformity—in which case the lightning, thunder sequence would "follow a rule"— then it is the knowledge or belief that the circumstances are of a certain kind, and not the mere fact that they *are* of this kind, which contributes to bringing about the action.

In the light of these remarks it is clear that *if* observation reports are construed as *actions, if* their correctness is interpreted as the correctness of an *action, and if* the authority of an observation report is construed as the fact that making it is "following a rule" in the proper sense of this phrase, *then* we are face to face with givenness in its most straightforward form. For these stipulations commit one to the idea that the authority of *Konstatierungen* rests on nonverbal episodes of awareness

—awareness *that* something is the case, e.g., *that this is green* —which nonverbal episodes have an intrinsic authority (they are, so to speak 'self-authenticating') which the *verbal* performances (the *Konstatierungen*) properly performed "express." One is committed to a stratum of authoritative nonverbal episodes ("awareness") the authority of which accrues to a superstructure of *verbal actions,* provided that the expressions occurring in these actions are properly *used.* These self-authenticating episodes would constitute the tortoise on which stands the elephant on which rests the edifice of empirical knowledge. The essence of the view is the same whether these intrinsically authoritative episodes are such items as the awareness that a certain sense content is green or such items as the awareness that a certain physical object looks to someone to be green.

But what is the alternative? We might begin by trying something like the following: An overt or covert token of "This is green" in the presence of a green item is a *Konstatierung* and expresses observational knowledge if and only if it is a manifestation of a tendency to produce overt or covert tokens of "This is green"—given a certain set—if and only if a green object is being looked at in standard conditions. Clearly on this interpretation the occurrence of such tokens of "This is green" would be "following a rule" only in the sense that they are instances of a uniformity, a uniformity differing from the lightning-thunder case in that it is an acquired causal characteristic of the language user. Clearly the above suggestion, which corresponds to the "thermometer view" criticized by Professor Price, and which we have already rejected, won't do as it stands. Let us see, however, if it can't be revised to fit the criteria I have been using for "expressing observational knowledge."

The first hurdle to be jumped concerns the *authority* which, as I have emphasized, a sentence token must have in order that it may be said to express knowledge. Clearly, on this account the only thing that can remotely be supposed to constitute such authority is the fact that one can infer the presence of a green object from the fact that someone makes this report. As we have already noticed, the correctness of a report does not have to be construed as the rightness of an *action.* A report can be correct as being an instance of a general mode of behavior which, in a given linguistic community, it is reasonable to sanction and support.

The second hurdle is, however, the decisive one. For we have seen that to be the expression of knowledge, a report must not only *have* authority, this authority must *in some sense* be recognized by the person whose report it is. And this is a steep hurdle indeed. For if the authority of the report "This is green" lies in the fact that the existence of green items appropriately related to the perceiver can be inferred from the occurrence of such reports, it follows that only a person who is able to draw this inference, and therefore who has not only the concept *green,* but also the concept of uttering "This is green" —indeed, the concept of certain conditions of perception, those which would correctly be called 'standard conditions'—could be in a position to token "This is green" in recognition of its authority. In other words, for a *Konstatierung* "This is green" to "express observational knowledge," not only must it be a *symptom* or *sign* of the presence of a green object in standard conditions, but the perceiver must know that tokens of "This is green" are symptoms of the presence of green objects in conditions which are standard for visual perception.

Now it might be thought that there is something obviously absurd in the idea that before a token uttered by, say, Jones could be the expression of observational knowledge, Jones would have to know that overt verbal episodes of this kind are reliable indicators of the existence, suitably related to the speaker, of green objects. I do not think that it is. Indeed, I think that something very like it is true. The point I wish to make now, however, is that if it *is* true, then it follows, as a matter of simple logic, that one couldn't have observational knowledge of *any* fact unless one knew many *other* things as well. And let me emphasize that the point is not taken care of by distinguishing between *knowing how* and *knowing that,* and admitting that observational knowledge requires a lot of "know how." For the point is specifically that observational knowledge of any particular fact, e.g., that this is green, presupposes that one knows general facts of the form *X is a reliable symptom of Y.* And to admit this requires an abandonment of the traditional empiricist idea that observational knowledge "stands on its own feet." Indeed, the suggestion would be anathema to traditional empiricists for the obvious reason that by making observational knowledge *presuppose* knowledge of general facts of the form *X is a reliable symptom of Y,* it runs counter to the idea that we come to know general facts of this form only *after* we have come to know by observation a number of particular facts which support the hypothesis that X is a symptom of Y.

And it might be thought that there is an obvious regress in the view we are examining. Does it not tell us that observational knowledge at time t presupposes knowledge of the form *X is a reliable symptom of Y,* which presupposes *prior* observational knowledge, which presupposes *other* knowledge of the form *X is a reliable symptom of Y,* which presupposes still other, and *prior,* observational knowledge, and so on? This charge, however, rests on too simple, indeed a radically mistaken, conception of what one is saying of Jones when one says that he *knows* that p. It is not just that the objection supposes that knowing is an *episode;* for clearly there are episodes which we can correctly characterize as knowings, in particular, *observings.* The essential point is that in characterizing an episode or a state as that of *knowing,* we are not giving an empirical description of that episode or state; we are placing it in the logical space of reasons, of justifying and being able to justify what one says.

Thus, all that the view I am defending requires is that no tokening by S *now* of "This is green" is to count as "expressing observational knowledge" unless it is also correct to say of S that he *now* knows the appropriate fact of the form *X is a reliable symptom of Y,* namely that (and again I oversimplify) utterances of "This is green" are reliable indicators of the presence of green objects in standard conditions of perception. And while the correctness of this statement about Jones requires that Jones could *now* cite prior particular facts as evidence for the idea that these utterances *are* reliable indicators, it requires only that it is correct to say that Jones *now* knows, thus remembers, that these particular facts *did* obtain. It does not require that it be correct to say that at the time these facts did obtain he *then knew* them to obtain. And the regress disappears.

Thus, while Jones' ability to give inductive reasons *today* is built on a long history of acquiring and manifesting verbal habits in perceptual situations, and, in particular, the occurrence of verbal episodes, e.g., "This is green," which is superficially like those which are later properly said to express observational knowledge, it does not require that any episode in this prior time be characterizeable as expressing knowledge. . . .

The idea that observation "strictly and properly so-called" is constituted by certain self-authenticating nonverbal episodes, the authority of which is transmitted to verbal and quasi-verbal performances when these performances are made "in conformity with the semantical rules of the language," is, of course, the heart of the Myth of the Given. For the *given,* in epistemological tradition, is what is *taken* by these self-authenticating episodes. These 'takings' are, so to speak, the unmoved movers of empirical knowledge, the 'knowings in presence' which are presupposed by all other knowledge, both the knowledge of general truths and the knowledge 'in absence' of other particular matters of fact. Such is the framework in which traditional empiricism makes its characteristic claim that the perceptually given is the foundation of empirical knowledge.

Let me make it clear, however, that if I reject this framework, it is not because I should deny that observings are *inner* episodes, nor that *strictly speaking* they are *nonverbal* episodes. It will be my contention, however, that the sense in which they are nonverbal—which is also the sense in which thought episodes are nonverbal—is one which gives no aid or comfort to epistemological givenness. In the concluding sections of this paper, I shall attempt to explicate the logic of inner episodes, and show that we can distinguish between observations and thoughts, on the one hand, and their verbal expression on the other, without making the mistakes of traditional dualism. I shall also attempt to explicate the logical status of *impressions* or *immediate experiences,* and thus bring to a successful conclusion the quest with which my argument began.

One final remark before I begin this task. If I reject the framework of traditional empiricism, it is not because I want to say that empirical knowledge has *no* foundation. For to put it this way is to suggest that it is really "empirical knowledge so-called," and to put it in a box with rumors and hoaxes. There is clearly *some* point to the picture of human knowledge as resting on a level of propositions—observation reports—which do not rest on other propositions in the same way as other propositions rest on them. On the other hand, I do wish to insist that the metaphor of "foundation" is misleading in that it keeps us from seeing that if there is a logical dimension in which other empirical propositions rest on observation reports, there is another logical dimension in which the latter rest on the former.

Above all, the picture is misleading because of its static character. One seems forced to choose between the picture of an elephant which rests on a tortoise (What supports the tortoise?) and the picture of a great Hegelian serpent of knowledge with its tail in its mouth (Where does it begin?). Neither will do. For empirical knowledge, like its sophisticated extension, science, is rational, not because it has a *foundation* but because it is a self-correcting enterprise which can put *any* claim in jeopardy, though not *all* at once.

There are many strange and exotic specimens in the gardens of philosophy: Epistemology, Ontology, Cosmology, to name but a few. And clearly there is much good sense—not only rhyme but reason—to these labels. It is not my purpose, however, to animadvert on the botanizing of philosophies and things philosophical, other than to call attention to a recent addition to the list of philosophical flora and fauna, the Philosophy of Science. Nor shall I attempt to locate this new specialty in a classificatory system. The point I wish to make, however, can be introduced by calling to mind the fact that classificatory schemes, however theoretical their purpose, have practical consequences: nominal causes, so to speak, have real effects. As long as there was no such subject as 'philosophy of science,' all students of philosophy felt obligated to keep at least one eye part of the time on both the methodological and the substantive aspects of the scientific enterprise. And if the result was often a confusion of the task of philosophy with the task of science, and almost equally often a projection of the framework of the latest scientific speculations into the common-sense picture of the world (witness the almost unquestioned assumption, today, that the common-sense world of physical objects in Space and Time must be *analyzable* into spatially and temporally, or even spatiotemporally, related *events*), at least it had the merit of ensuring that reflection on the nature and implications of scientific discourse was an integral and vital part of philosophical thinking generally. But now that philosophy of science has nominal as well as real existence, there has arisen the temptation to leave it to the specialists, and to confuse the sound idea that philosophy is not science with the mistaken idea that philosophy is independent of science.

As long as discourse was viewed as a map, subdivided into a side-by-side of sub-maps, each representing a sub-region in a side-by-side of regions making up the total subject matter of discourse, and as long as the task of the philosopher was conceived to be the piecemeal one of analysis in the sense of *definition*—the task, so to speak, of "making little ones out of big ones"—one could view with equanimity the existence of philosophical specialists—specialists in formal and mathematical logic, in perception, in moral philosophy, etc. For if discourse were as represented above, where would be the harm of each man fencing himself off in his own garden? In spite, however, of the persistence of the slogan "philosophy is analysis," we now realize that the atomistic conception of philosophy is a snare and a delusion. For "analysis" no longer connotes the definition of terms, but rather the clarification of the logical structure—in the broadest sense—of discourse, and discourse no longer appears as one plane parallel to another, but as a tangle of intersecting dimensions whose relations with one another and with extra-linguistic fact conform to no single or simple pattern. No longer can the philosopher interested in perception say "let him who is interested in prescriptive discourse analyze its concepts and leave me in peace." Most if not all philosophically interesting concepts are caught up in more than one dimension of discourse, and while the atomism of early analysis has a healthy successor in the contemporary stress on journeyman tactics, the grand strategy of the philosophical enterprise is once again directed toward that articulated and integrated vision of man-in-the-universe—or, shall I say discourse-about-man-in-all-discourse—which has traditionally been its goal.

But the moral I wish specifically to draw is that no longer can one smugly say "Let the person who is interested in scientific discourse analyze scientific discourse and let the person who is interested in ordinary discourse analyze ordinary discourse." Let me not be misunderstood. I am not saying that in order to discern the logic—the polydimensional logic—of ordinary discourse, it is necessary to make use of the results or the methods of the sciences. Nor even that, within limits, such a division of labor is not a sound corollary of the journeyman's approach. My point is rather that what we call the scientific enterprise is the flowering of a dimension of discourse which already exists in what historians call the "prescientific stage," and that failure to understand this type of discourse "writ large"—in science—may lead, indeed, has often led to a failure to appreciate its role in "ordinary usage," and, as a result, to a failure to understand the full logic of even the most fundamental, the "simplest" empirical terms.

Another point of equal importance. The procedures of philosophical analysis as such may make no use of the methods or results of the sciences. But familiarity with the trend of scientific thought is essential to the *appraisal* of the framework categories of the common-sense picture of the world. For if the line of thought embodied in the preceding paragraphs is sound, if, that is to say, scientific discourse is but a continuation of a dimension of discourse which has been present in human discourse from the very beginning, then one would expect there to be a sense in which the scientific picture of the world *replaces* the common-sense picture; a sense in which the scientific account of "what there is" *supersedes* the descriptive ontology of everyday life.

Here one must be cautious. For there is a right way and a wrong way to make this point. Many years ago it used to be confidently said that science has shown, for example, that physical objects aren't really colored. Later it was pointed out that if this is interpreted as the claim that the sentence "Physical objects have colors" expresses an empirical proposition which, though widely believed by common sense, has been shown by science to be false, then, of course, this claim is absurd. The idea that physical objects aren't colored can make sense only as the (misleading) expression of one aspect of a philosophical critique of the very framework of physical objects located in Space and enduring through Time. In short, "Physical objects aren't really colored" makes sense only as a clumsy expression of the idea that there are no such things as the colored physical objects of the common-sense world, where this is interpreted, not as an empirical proposition—like "There are no nonhuman featherless bipeds"—*within* the common-sense frame, but as the expression of a rejection (in *some* sense) of this very framework itself, in favor of another built around different, if not unrelated, categories. This rejection need not, of course, be a *practical* rejection. It need not, that is, carry with it a proposal to brain-wash existing populations and train them to speak differently. And, of course, as long as the existing framework is used, it will be *incorrect* to say—otherwise than to make a philosophical point *about the framework*— that no object is really colored, or is located in Space, or endures through Time. But, *speaking as a philosopher,* I am quite prepared to say that the common-sense world of physical objects in Space and Time is unreal—that is, that there are no such things. Or, to put it less paradoxically, that in the dimension of describing and explaining the world, science is the measure of all things, of what is that it is, and of what is not that it is not.

There is a widespread impression that reflection on how we learn the language in which, in everyday life, we describe the world, leads to the conclusion that the categories of the common-sense picture of the world have, so to speak, an unchallengeable authenticity. There are, of course, different conceptions of just what this fundamental categorial framework is. For some it is sense contents and phenomenal relations between them; for others physical objects, persons, and processes in Space and Time. But whatever their points of difference, the philosophers I have in mind are united in the conviction that what is called the "ostensive tie" between our fundamental descriptive vocabulary and the world rules out of court as utterly absurd any notion that there are no such things as his framework talks about.

An integral part of this conviction is what I shall call (in an extended sense) the *positivistic conception of science,* the idea that the framework of theoretical objects (molecules, electromagnetic fields, etc.) and their relationships is, so to speak, an *auxiliary* framework. In its most explicit form, it is the idea that theoretical objects and propositions concerning them are "calculational devices," the value and status of which consist in their systematizing and heuristic role with respect to confirmable generalizations formulated in the framework of terms which enjoy a direct ostensive link with the world. One is tempted to put this by saying that according to these philosophers, the objects of ostensively linked discourse behave *as if* and *only as if* they were bound up with or consisted of scientific entities. But, of course, these philosophers would hasten to point out (and rightly so) that

X behaves as if it consisted of Y's

makes sense only by contrast with

X behaves as it does because it *does* consist of Y's

whereas their contention is exactly that where the Y's are *scientific* objects, no such contrast makes sense.

The point I am making is that as long as one thinks that there is a framework, whether of physical objects or of sense contents, the absolute authenticity of which is guaranteed by the fact that the learning of this framework involves an "ostensive step," so long one will be tempted to think of the authority of theoretical discourse as entirely derivative, that of a calculational auxiliary, an effective heuristic device. It is one of my prime purposes ... to convince the reader that this interpretation of the status of the scientific picture of the world rests on two mistakes: (1) a misunderstanding (which I have already exposed) of the ostensive element in the learning and use of a language—the Myth of the Given; (2) a reification of the *methodological* distinction between theoretical and non-theoretical discourse into a *substantive* distinction between theoretical and non-theoretical existence.

One way of summing up what I have been saying above is by saying that there is a widespread impression abroad, aided and abetted by a naive interpretation of concept formation, that philosophers of science deal with a mode of discourse which is, so to speak, a peninsular offshoot from the mainland of ordinary discourse. The study of scientific discourse is conceived to be a worthy employment for those who have the background and motivation to keep track of it, but an employment which is fundamentally a hobby divorced from the perplexities of the mainland. But, of course, this summing up won't quite do. For all philosophers would agree that no philosophy would be complete unless it resolved the perplexities which arise when one attempts to think through the relationship of the framework of modern science to ordinary discourse. My point, however, is not that any one would reject the idea that this is a proper task for philosophy, but that, by approaching the language in which the plain man describes and explains empirical fact with the presuppositions of *givenness,* they are led to a "resolution" of these perplexities along the lines of what I have called the positivistic or peninsular conception of scientific discourse—a "resolution" which, I believe, is not only superficial, but positively mistaken.

5. Hilary Putnam

Brains and Behaviour

Once upon a time there was a tough-minded philosopher who said, 'What is all this talk about "minds," "ideas," and "sensations"? Really—and I mean *really* in the real world—there is nothing to these so-called "mental" events and entities but certain processes in our all-too-material heads.'

And once upon a time there was a philosopher who retorted, 'What a masterpiece of confusion!' Even if, say, *pain* were perfectly correlated with any particular event in my brain (which I doubt) that event would obviously have certain properties—say, a certain numerical intensity measured in volts—which it would be *senseless* to ascribe to the feeling of pain. Thus, it is *two* things that are correlated, not *one*—and to call *two* things *one* thing is worse than being mistaken; it is utter contradiction.'

For a long time dualism and materialism appeared to exhaust the alternatives. Compromises were attempted ('double aspect' theories), but they never won many converts and practically no one found them intelligible. Then, in the mid-1930s, a seeming third possibility was discovered. This third possibility has been called *logical behaviourism*. To state the nature of this third possibility briefly, it is necessary to recall the treatment of the natural numbers (*i.e.,* zero, one, two, three . . .) in modern logic. Numbers are identified with *sets,* in various ways, depending on which authority one follows. For instance, Whitehead and Russell identified zero with the set of all empty sets, one with the set of all one-membered sets, two with the set of all two-membered sets, three with the set of all three-membered sets, and so on. (This has the appearance of circularity, but they

From *Analytical Philosophy,* Second Series, R. J. Butler, Editor (New York: Barnes & Noble, Inc.). Copyright 1965 by Basil Blackwell & Mott, Ltd. Reprinted by permission.

This paper was read as a part of the programme of The American Association for the Advancement of Science, Section L (History and Philosophy of Science), December 27th, 1961.

were able to dispel this appearance by defining 'one-membered set', 'two-membered set', 'three-membered set', &c., without using 'one', 'two', 'three', &c.) In short, numbers are treated as *logical constructions out of sets.* The number theorist is doing set theory without knowing it, according to this interpretation.

What was novel about this was the idea of getting rid of certain philosophically unwanted or embarrassing entities (numbers) without failing to do justice to the appropriate body of discourse (number theory) by treating the entities in question as logical constructions. Russell was quick to hold up this 'success' as a model to all future philosophers. And certain of those future philosophers—the Vienna positivists, in their 'physicalist' phase (about 1930)—took Russell's advice so seriously as to produce the doctrine that we are calling *logical behaviourism*—the doctrine that, just as numbers are (allegedly) logical constructions out of *sets,* so *mental events* are logical constructions out of actual and possible *behaviour events.*

In the set theoretic case, the 'reduction' of number theory to the appropriate part of set theory was carried out in detail and with indisputable technical success. One may dispute the philosophical significance of the reduction, but one knows exactly what one is talking about when one disputes it. In the mind-body case, the reduction was never carried out in even *one* possible way, so that it is not possible to be clear on just *how* mental entities or events are to be (identified with) logical constructions out of behaviour events. But, broadly speaking, it is clear what the view implies: it implies that all talk about mental events is translatable into talk about actual or potential overt behaviour.

It is easy to see in what way this view differs from both dualism and classical materialism. The logical behaviourist agrees with the dualist that what goes on in our brains has no connection whatsoever with what we *mean* when we say that someone is in pain. He can even take over the dualist's entire stock of arguments against the materialist position. Yet, at the same time, he can be as 'tough-minded' as the materialist in denying that ordinary talk of 'pains', 'thoughts', and 'feelings' involves reference to 'Mind' as a Cartesian substance.

Thus it is not surprising that logical behaviourism attracted enormous attention—both pro and con—during the next thirty years. Without doubt, this alternative proved to be a fruitful one to inject into the debate. Here, however, my intention is not to talk about the fruitfulness of the investigations to which logical behaviourism has led, but to see if there was any upshot to those investigations. Can we, after thirty years, say anything about the rightness or wrongness of logical behaviourism? Or must we say that a third alternative has been added to the old two; that we cannot decide between three any more easily than we could decide between two; and that our discussion is thus half as difficult again as it was before?

One conclusion emerged very quickly from the discussion pro and con logical behaviourism: that the extreme thesis of logical behaviourism, as we just stated it (that all talk about 'mental events' is translatable into talk about overt behaviour) is false. But, in a sense, this is not very interesting. An extreme thesis may be false, although there is 'something to' the way of thinking that it represents. And the more interesting question is this: what, if anything, can be 'saved' of the way of thinking that logical behaviourism represents?

In the last thirty years, the original extreme thesis of logical behaviourism has gradually been weakened to something like this:

(1) That there exist entailments between mind-statements and behaviour-statements; entailments that are not, perhaps, analytic in the way in which 'All bachelors are unmarried' is analytic, but that nevertheless follow (in some sense) from the meanings of mind words. I shall call these *analytic entailments.*

(2) That these entailments may not provide an actual *translation* of 'mind talk' into 'behaviour talk' (this 'talk' talk was introduced by Gilbert Ryle in his *Concept of Mind*), but that this is true for such superficial reasons as the greater ambiguity of mind talk, as compared with the relatively greater specificity of overt behaviour talk.

I believe that, although no philosopher would to-day subscribe to the older version of logical behaviourism, a great many philosophers[1] would accept these two points, while admitting the unsatisfactory imprecision of the present statement of both of them. If these philosophers are right, then there is much work to be done (*e.g.,* the notion of 'analyticity' has to be made clear), but the direction of work is laid out for us for some time to come.

I wish that I could share this happy point of view—if only for the comforting conclusion that first-rate philosophical research, continued for some time, will eventually lead to a solution to the mind-body problem which is independent of troublesome empirical facts about brains, central causation of behaviour, evidence for and against non-physical causation of at least some behaviour, and the soundness or unsoundness of psychical research and parapsychology. But the fact is that I come to bury logical behaviourism, not to praise it. I feel that the time has come for us to admit that logical behaviourism is a mistake, and that even the weakened forms of the logical behaviourist doctrine are incorrect. I cannot hope to establish this in so short a paper as this one[2]; but I hope to expose for your inspection at least the main lines of my thinking.

Logical Behaviourism

The logical behaviourist usually begins by pointing out what is perfectly true, that such words as 'pain' ('pain' will henceforth be our stock example of a mind word) are not taught by reference to standard examples in the way in which such words as 'red' are. One can point to a standard red thing, but one cannot point to a standard pain (that is, except by pointing to some piece of *behaviour*) and say: 'Compare the feeling you are having with this one (say, Jones's feeling at time t_1). If the two feelings have the identical *quality*, then your feeling is legitimately called a feeling of *pain*.' The difficulty, of course, is that I cannot have Jones's feeling at time t_1—unless I *am* Jones, and the time *is* t_1.

From this simple observation, certain things follow. For example, the account according to which the *intension* of the word 'pain' is a certain *quality* which 'I know from my own case' must be wrong. But this is not to refute dualism, since the dualist need not maintain that I know the intension of the English word 'pain' from my own case, but only that I experience the referent of the word.

What then is the intension of 'pain'? I am inclined to say that 'pain' is a cluster-concept. That is, the application of the word 'pain' is controlled by a whole cluster of criteria, *all of which can be regarded as synthetic*.[3] As a consequence, there is no satisfactory way of answering the question 'What does "pain" mean?' except by giving an exact synonym (*e.g.,* 'Schmerz'); but there are a million and one different ways of saying what pain *is*. One can, for example, say that pain is that feeling which is normally evinced by saying 'ouch', or by wincing, or in a variety of other ways (or often not evinced at all).

All this is compatible with logical behaviourism. The logical behaviourist would reply: 'Exactly. "Pain" is a cluster-concept —that is to say, it stands for a *cluster of phenomena.'* But that is not what I mean. Let us look at another kind of cluster-concept (cluster-concepts, of course, are not a homogeneous class): names of diseases.

We observe that, when a virus origin was discovered for polio, doctors said that certain cases in which all the symptoms of polio had been present, but in which the virus had been absent, had turned out not to be cases of polio at all. Similarly, if a virus should be discovered which normally (almost invariably) is the cause of what we presently call 'multiple sclerosis', the hypothesis that this virus is *the* cause of multiple sclerosis would not be falsified if, in some few exceptional circumstances, it was possible to have all the symptoms of multiple sclerosis for some other combination of reasons, or if this virus caused symptoms not presently recognized as symptoms of multiple sclerosis in some cases. These facts would certainly lead the lexicographer to *reject* the view that 'multiple sclerosis' means 'the simultaneous presence of such and such symptoms'. Rather he would say that 'multiple sclerosis' means 'that disease which is normally responsible for some or all of the following symptoms. . . .'

Of course, he does not have to say this. Some philosophers would prefer to say that 'polio' *used to mean* 'the simultaneous presence of such-and-such symptoms'. And they would say that the *decision* to accept the presence or absence of a virus as a criterion for the presence or absence of polio represented a *change of meaning.* But this runs strongly counter to our common sense. For example, doctors used to say 'I believe polio is caused by a virus'. On the 'change of meaning' account, those doctors were *wrong,* not *right. Polio, as the word was then used,* was not always caused by a virus; it is only what *we* call polio that is always caused by a virus. And if a doctor ever said (and many did) 'I believe this may not be a case of polio', knowing that all of the text-book symptoms were present, that doctor must have been contradicting himself (even if we, today, would say that he was right) or, perhaps, 'making a disguised linguistic proposal'. Also, this account runs counter to good linguistic methodology. The definition we proposed a paragraph back—'multiple sclerosis' means 'the disease that is normally *responsible* for the following symptoms. . . .'—has an exact analogue in the case of polio. This kind of definition leaves open the question whether there is a single cause or several. It is consonant with such a definition to speak of 'discovering a single origin for polio (or two or three or four)', to

speak of 'discovering X did not have polio' (although he exhibited all the symptoms of polio), and to speak of 'discovering
X did have polio' (although he exhibited *none* of the 'textbook
symptoms'). And, finally, such a definition does not require
us to say that any 'change of meaning' took place. Thus, this
is surely the definition that a good lexicographer would adopt.
But this entails *rejecting* the 'change of meaning' account as a
philosopher's invention.[4]

Accepting that this is the correct account of the names of
diseases, what follows? There *may* be analytic entailments connecting diseases and symptoms (although I shall argue against
this). For example, it looks plausible to say that:

'Normally people who have multiple sclerosis have some or
all of the following symptoms . . .'

is a necessary ('analytic') truth. But it does not follow that
'disease talk' is translatable into 'symptom talk'. Rather the
contrary follows (as is already indicated by the presence of the
word 'normally'): statements about multiple sclerosis are not
translatable into statements about the symptoms of multiple
sclerosis, not because disease talk is 'systematically ambiguous' and symptom talk is 'specific', but because *causes* are not
logical constructions out of their *effects.*

In analogy with the foregoing, both the dualist and the materialist would want to argue that, although the meaning of
'pain' may be *explained* by reference to overt behaviour, what
we mean by 'pain' is not the presence of a cluster of responses,
but rather the presence of an event or condition that normally
causes those responses. (Of course the pain is not the whole
cause of the pain behaviour, but only a suitably invariant part
of that cause[5]; but, similarly, the virus-caused tissue damage
is not the whole cause of the individual symptoms of polio in
some individual case, but a suitably invariant part of the cause.)
And they would want to argue further, that even if it *were* a
necessary truth that

'Normally, when one says "ouch" one has a pain'

or a necessary truth that

'Normally, when one has a pain one says "ouch" '

this would be an interesting observation about what 'pain'
means, but it would shed no metaphysical light on what pain *is*

(or *isn't*). And it certainly would not follow that 'pain talk' is translatable into 'response talk', or that the failure of translatability is only a matter of the 'systematic ambiguity' of pain talk as opposed to the 'specificity' of response talk: quite the contrary. Just as before, *causes* (pains) are *not* logical constructions out of their *effects* (behaviour).

The traditional dualist would, however, want to go farther, and deny the *necessity* of the two propositions just listed. Moreover, the traditional dualist is right: there is nothing self-contradictory, as we shall see below, in talking of hypothetical worlds in which there are pains but *no* pain behaviour.

The analogy with names of diseases is still preserved at this point. Suppose I identify multiple sclerosis as the disease that normally produces certain symptoms. If it later turns out that a certain virus is the cause of multiple sclerosis, using this newly discovered criterion I may then go on to find out that multiple sclerosis has quite different symptoms when, say, the average temperature is lower. I can then perfectly well talk of a hypothetical world (with lower temperature levels) in which multiple sclerosis does *not* normally produce the usual symptoms. It is true that if the *words* 'multiple sclerosis' are used in any world in such a way that the above lexical definition is a good one, *then* many victims of the disease must have had some or all of the following symptoms. . . . And in the same way it is true that *if* the explanation suggested of the word 'pain' is a good one (*i.e.,* 'pain is the feeling that is normally being evinced when someone says "ouch", or winces, or screams, &c.'), *then* persons in pain must have at some time winced or screamed or said 'ouch'—but this does *not* imply that 'if someone ever had a pain, then someone must at some time have winced or screamed or said "ouch".' To conclude this would be to confuse preconditions for *talking* about pain as *we* talk about pain with preconditions for the existence of pain.

The analogy we have been developing is not an identity: linguistically speaking, mind words and names of diseases are different in a great many respects. In particular, *first person uses* are very different: a man may have a severe case of polio and not know it, even if he knows the word 'polio', but one cannot have a severe pain and not know it. At first blush, this may look like a point in favour of logical behaviourism. The logical behaviourist may say: it is because the premisses 'John says he has a pain', 'John knows English', and 'John is speaking in all sincerity',[6] *entail* 'John has a pain', that pain reports have this sort of special status. But even if this is right, it does not follow that logical behaviorism is correct unless *sincerity* is a 'logical construction out of overt behaviour'! A far more reasonable account is this: one can have a 'pink elephant hallucination', but one cannot have a 'pain hallucination', or an 'absence of pain hallucination', simply because any situation that a person cannot discriminate from a situation in which he himself has a pain *counts* as a situation in which he has a pain, whereas a situation that a person cannot distinguish from one in which a pink elephant is present does not necessarily *count* as the presence of a pink elephant.

To sum up: I believe that pains are not clusters of responses, but that they are (normally, in our experience to date) the causes of certain clusters of responses. Moreover, although this is an empirical fact, it underlies the possibility of talking about pains in the particular way in which we do. However, it does not rule out in any way the possibility of worlds in which (owing to a difference in the environmental and hereditary conditions) pains are not responsible for the usual responses, or even are not responsible for any responses at all.

Let us now engage in a little science fiction. Let us try to describe some worlds in which pains are related to responses (and also to causes) in quite a different way than they are in our world.

If we confine our attention to non-verbal responses by full grown persons, for a start, then matters are easy. Imagine a community of 'super-spartans' or 'super-stoics'—a community in which the adults have the ability to successfully suppress *all* involuntary pain behaviour. They may, on occasion, admit that they feel pain, but always in pleasant well-modulated voices— even if they are undergoing the agonies of the damned. They do *not* wince, scream, flinch, sob, grit their teeth, clench their fists, exhibit beads of sweat, or otherwise act like people in pain or people suppressing the unconditioned responses associated with pain. However, they do feel pain, and they dislike it (just as we do). They even admit that it takes a great effort of will to behave as they do. It is only that they have what they regard as important ideological reasons for behaving as they do, and they have, through years of training, learned to live up to their own exacting standards.

It may be contended that children and not fully mature members of this community will exhibit, to varying degrees, normal unconditioned pain behaviour, and that this is all that is necessary for the ascription of pain. On this view, the *sine qua non* for the significant ascription of pain to a species is that its immature members should exhibit unconditioned pain responses.

One might well stop to ask whether this statement has even a clear meaning. Supposing that there are Martians: do we have any criterion for something being an 'unconditioned pain response' for a Martian? Other things being equal, one *avoids* things with which one has had painful experiences: this would suggest that *avoidance* behaviour might be looked for as a universal unconditioned pain response. However, even if this were true, it would hardly be specific enough, since avoidance can also be an unconditioned response to many things that we do not associate with pain—to things that disgust us, or frighten us, or even merely bore us.

Let us put these difficulties aside, and see if we can devise an imaginary world in which there are not, even by lenient standards, any unconditioned pain responses. Specifically, let us take our 'super-spartans', and let us suppose that after millions of years they begin to have children who are born fully acculturated. They are born speaking the adult language, knowing the multiplication table, having opinions on political issues, and *inter alia* sharing the dominant spartan beliefs about the importance of not evincing pain (except by way of a verbal report, and even that in a tone of voice that suggests indifference). Then there would not *be* any 'unconditioned pain responses' in this community (although there might be unconditioned *desires* to make certain responses—desires which were, however, always suppressed by an effort of will). Yet there is a clear absurdity to the position that one cannot ascribe to these people a capacity for feeling pain.

To make this absurdity evident, let us imagine that we succeed in converting an adult 'super-spartan' to *our* ideology. Let us suppose that he begins to evince pain in the normal way. Yet he reports that the pains he is feeling are not more *intense* than are the ones he experienced prior to conversion—indeed, he may say that giving expression to them makes them *less* intense. In this case, the logical behaviourist would have to say that, through the medium of this one member, we had demonstrated the existence of unconditioned pain responses in the whole species, and hence that ascription of pain to the species is 'logically proper'. But this is to say that had this one man never lived, and had it been possible to demonstrate only indirectly (via the use of *theories*) that these beings feel pain, then pain ascriptions *would* have been improper.

We have so far been constructing worlds in which the relation of pain to its non-verbal *effects* is altered. What about the relation of pain to *causes?* This is even more easy for the imagination to modify. Can one not imagine a species who feel pain only when a magnetic field is present (although the magnetic field causes no detectable damage to their bodies or nervous systems)? If we now let the members of such a species become converts *to* 'super-spartanism', we can depict to ourselves a world in which pains, in our sense, are clearly present, but in which they have neither the normal causes nor the normal effects (apart from verbal reports).

What about verbal reports? Some behaviourists have taken these as the characteristic form of pain behaviour. Of course, there is a difficulty here: If 'I am in pain' means 'I am disposed to utter this kind of verbal report' (to put matters crudely), then how do we tell that any particular report is 'this kind of verbal report'? The usual answer is in terms of the unconditioned pain responses and their assumed supplantation by the verbal reports in question. However, we have seen that there are no *logical* reasons for the existence of unconditioned pain responses in all species capable of feeling pain (there *may* be logical reasons for the existence of avoidance desires, but avoidance *desires* are not themselves behaviour any more than pains are).

Once again, let us be charitable to the extent of waiving the first difficulty that comes to mind, and let us undertake the task of trying to imagine a world in which there are not even pain *reports.* I will call this world the 'X-world'. In the X-world we have to deal with 'super-super-spartans'. These have been super-spartans for so long, that they have begun to suppress even *talk* of pain. Of course, each individual X-worlder may have his private way of thinking about pain. He may even have the *word* 'pain' (as before, I assume that these beings are born fully acculturated). He may *think* to himself: 'This pain is intolerable. If it goes on one minute longer I shall scream. Oh No! I mustn't do that! That would disgrace my whole family. . . .' But X-worlders do not even admit to *having* pains. They pretend not to know either the word or the phenomenon to which it refers. In short, if pains are 'logical constructs out of behaviour', then our X-worlders behave so as not to have pains!—Only, of course, they do have pains, and they know perfectly well that they have pains.

If this last fantasy is not, in some disguised way, self-contradictory, then logical behaviourism is simply a mistake. Not only is the second thesis of logical behaviourism—the existence of a near-translation of pain talk into behaviour talk—false, but so is even the first thesis—the existence of 'analytic entailments'. Pains *are* responsible for certain kinds of behaviour—but only in the context of our beliefs, desires, ideological attitudes, and so forth. From the statement 'X has a pain' by itself *no* behavioural statement follows—not even a behavioural statement with a 'normally' or a 'probably' in it.

In our concluding section we shall consider the logical behaviourist's stock of counter-moves to this sort of argument. If the logical behaviourist's positive views are inadequate owing to an oversimplified view of the nature of cluster words— amounting, in some instances, to an open denial that it is *possible* to have a word governed by a cluster of indicators, *all* of which are synthetic—his negative views are inadequate owing to an oversimplified view of empirical reasoning. It is unfortunately characteristic of modern philosophy that its problems should overlap three different areas—to speak roughly, the areas of linguistics, logic, and 'theory of theories' (scientific methodology)—and that many of its practitioners should try to get by with an inadequate knowledge of at least two out of the three.

Some Behaviourist Arguments

We have been talking of 'X-worlders' and 'super-spartans'. No one denies that, in *some* sense of the term, such fantasies are 'intelligible'. But 'intelligibility' can be a superficial thing. A fantasy may be 'intelligible', at least at the level of 'surface grammar', although we may come to see, on thinking about it for a while, that some absurdity is involved. Consider, for example, the supposition that last night, just on the stroke of midnight, all distances were instantaneously doubled. Of course, we did not notice the change, for *we* ourselves also doubled in size! This story may seem intelligible to us at first blush, at least as an amusing possibility. On reflection, however, we come to see that a logical contradiction is involved. For 'length' means nothing more nor less than a relation to a standard, and it is a contradiction to maintain that the length of everything doubled, while the relations to the standards remained unchanged.

What I have just said (speaking as a logical behaviourist might speak) is false, but not totally so. It is false (or at least the last part is false), because 'length' does *not* mean 'relation to a standard'. If it did (assuming a 'standard' has to be a macroscopic material object, or anyway a material object), it would make no sense to speak of distances in a world in which there were only gravitational and electromagnetic fields, but no material objects. Also, it would make no sense to speak of the *standard* (whatever it might be) as having changed its length. Consequences so counter-intuitive have led many physicists (and even a few philosophers of physics) to view 'length' not as something operationally defined, but as a theoretical magnitude (like electrical charge), which can be measured in a virtual infinity of ways, but which is not explicitly and exactly definable in terms of any of the ways of measuring it. Some of these physicists—the 'unified field' theorists—would even say that, far from it being the case that 'length' (and hence 'space') depends on the existence of suitably related material bodies, material bodies are best viewed as local variations in the curvature of space—that is to say, local variations in the intensity of a certain magnitude (the tensor g_{ik}), one aspect of which we experience as 'length'.

Again, it is far from true that the hypothesis 'last night, on the stroke of midnight, everything doubled in length' has no testable consequences. For example, if last night everything did double in length, and the velocity of light did not also double, then this morning we would have experienced an apparent halving of the speed of light. Moreover, if g (the gravitational constant) did not double, then we would have experienced an apparent halving in the intensity of the gravitational field. And if h (Planck's constant) did not change, then.... In short, our world would have been bewilderingly different. And if we could survive at all, under so drastically altered conditions, no doubt some clever physicist would figure out what had happened.

I have gone into such detail just to make the point that in philosophy things are rarely so simple as they seem. The 'doubling universe' is a favourite classroom example of a 'pseudo-hypothesis'—yet it is the worst possible example if a 'clear case' is desired. In the first place, what is desired is a hypothesis with no testable consequences—yet *this* hypothesis, as it is always stated, *does* have testable consequences (perhaps some more complex hypothesis does not; but then we have to see this more complex hypothesis stated before we can be expected to discuss it). In the second place, the usual argument for the absurdity of this hypothesis rests on a simplistic theory of the meaning of 'length'—and a full discussion of *that* situation is hardly possible without bringing in considerations from unified field theory and quantum mechanics (the latter comes in in connection with the notion of a 'material standard'). But, the example aside, one can hardly challenge the point that a superficially coherent story may contain a hidden absurdity.

Or can one? Of course, a superficially coherent story may contain a hidden logical contradiction, but the whole point of the logical behaviourist's sneering reference to 'surface grammar' is that *linguistic coherence, meaningfulness of the individual terms,* and *logical consistency,* do not by themselves guarantee freedom from another kind of absurdity—there are 'depth absurdities' which can only be detected by more powerful techniques. It is fair to say that to-day, after thirty years of this sort of talk, we lack both a single *convincing* example of such a depth absurdity, and a technique of detection (or alleged technique of detection) which does not reduce to 'untestable, *therefore* nonsense'.

To come to the case at hand: the logical behaviourist is likely to say that our hypothesis about 'X-worlders' is untestable in principle (if there *were* 'X-worlders', by hpothesis we couldn't distinguish them from people who really didn't know what pain is); and *therefore* meaningless (apart from a certain 'surface significance' which is of no real interest). If the logical behaviourist has learned a little from 'ordinary language philosophy', he is likely to shy away from saying 'untestable, therefore *meaningless',* but he is still likely to say or at least think: 'untestable, therefore in *some* sense absurd'. I shall try to meet this 'argument' *not* by challenging the premiss, be it overt or covert, that 'untestable synthetic statement' is some kind of contradiction in terms (although I believe that premiss to be mistaken), but simply by showing that, on any but the most naive view of testability, our hypothesis *is* testable.

Of course, I could not do this if it were true that 'by hypothesis, we couldn't distinguish X-worlders from people who *really* didn't know what pain is'. But that isn't true—at any rate, it isn't true 'by hypothesis'. What is true by hypothesis is that we couldn't distinguish X-worlders from people who really didn't know what pain is *on the basis of overt behaviour alone.* But that still leaves many other ways in which we might determine what is going on 'inside' the X-worlders—in both the figurative and literal sense of 'inside'. For example, we might examine their *brains.*

It is a fact that when pain impulses are 'received' in the brain, suitable electrical detecting instruments record a characteristic 'spike' pattern. Let us express this briefly (and too simply) by saying that 'brain spikes' are one-to-one correlated with experiences of pain. If our X-worlders belong to the human species, then we can verify that they do feel pains, notwithstanding their claim that they don't have any idea what pain is, by applying our electrical instruments and detecting the tell-tale 'brain spikes'.

This reply to the logical behaviourist is far too simple to be convincing. 'It is true,' the logical behaviourist will object, 'that experiences of pain are one-to-one correlated with "brain spikes" in the case of normal human beings. But you don't know that the X-worlders are normal human beings, in this sense—in fact, you have every reason to suppose that they are *not* normal human beings.' This reply shows that no *mere* correlation, however carefully verified in the case of normal human beings, can be used to verify ascriptions of pain to X-worlders. Fortunately, we do not have to suppose that our knowledge will always be restricted to mere correlations, like the pain-'brain spike' correlation. At a more advanced level, considerations of simplicity and coherence can begin to play a rôle in a way in which they cannot when only crude observational regularities are available.

Let us suppose that we begin to detect waves of a new kind, emanating from human brains—call them 'V-waves'. Let us suppose we develop a way of 'decoding' V-waves so as to reveal people's unspoken thoughts. And, finally, let us suppose that our 'decoding' technique also works in the case of the V-waves emanating from the brains of X-worlders. How does this correlation differ from the pain-'brain spike' correlation?

Simply in this way: it is reasonable to say that 'spikes'—momentary peaks in the electrical intensity in certain parts of the brain—could have almost any cause. But waves which go over into coherent English (or any other language), under a relatively simple decoding scheme, could not have just any cause. The 'null hypothesis'—that this is just the operation of 'chance'—can be dismissed at once. And if, in the case of human beings, we verify that the decoded waves correspond to what we are in fact thinking, then the hypothesis that this same correlation holds in the case of X-worlders will be assigned an immensely high probability, simply because no other likely explanation readily suggests itself. But 'no other likely explanation readily suggests itself' isn't verification, the logical behaviourist may say. On the contrary. How, for example, have we verified that cadmium lines in the spectrographic analysis of sunlight indicate the presence of cadmium in the sun? Mimicking the logical behaviourist, we might say: 'We have verified that under normal circumstances, cadmium lines only occur when heated cadmium is present. But we don't know that circumstances on the sun are normal in this sense.' If we took this seriously, we would have to *heat cadmium on the sun* before we could say that the regularity upon which we base our spectrographic analysis of sunlight had been verified. In fact, we have verified the regularity under 'normal' circumstances, and we can *show* (deductively) that *if* many other laws, that have also been verified under 'normal' circumstances and *only* under 'normal' circumstances (*i.e.*, never on the surface of the sun), hold on the sun, *then* this regularity holds also under 'abnormal' circumstances. And if someone says, 'But perhaps *none* of the usual laws of physics hold on the sun', we reply that this is like supposing that a random process always produces coherent English. The fact is that the 'signals' (sunlight, radio waves, &c.) which we receive from the sun cohere with a vast body of theory. Perhaps there is some other explanation than that the sun obeys the usual laws of physics; but *no other likely explanation suggests itself.* This sort of reasoning *is* scientific verification; and if it is not reducible to simple Baconian induction—well, then, philosophers must learn to widen their notions of verification to embrace it.

The logical behaviourist might try to account for the decodability of the X-worlders' 'V-waves' into coherent English (or the appropriate natural language) without invoking the absurd 'null hypothesis'. He might suggest, for example, that the 'X-worlders' are having fun at our expense—they are able, say, to produce misleading V-waves at will. If the X-worlders have brains quite unlike ours, this may even have some plausibility. But once again, in an advanced state of knowledge, considerations of coherence and simplicity may quite conceivably 'verify' that this is false. For example, the X-worlders may have brains quite like ours, rather than unlike ours. And we may have built up enough theory to say how the brain of a human being should 'look' if that human being were pretending not to be in pain when he was, in fact, in pain. Now consider what the 'misleading V-waves' story requires: it requires that the X-worlders produce V-waves in quite a different way than we do, without specifying what that different way is. Moreover, it requires that this be the case, although the reverse hypothesis— that X-worlders' brains function *exactly* as human brains do— in fact, that they *are* human brains—fits all the data. Clearly, this story is in serious methodological difficulties, and any other 'counter-explanation' that the logical behaviourist tries to invoke will be in similar difficulties. In short, the logical behaviourist's argument reduces to this: 'You cannot verify "psycho-physical" correlations in the case of X-worlders (or at least, you can't verify ones having to do, directly or indirectly, with *pain*), because, by hypothesis, X-worlders won't tell you (or indicate behaviourally) when they are in pain. 'Indirect verification'—verification using theories which have been 'tested' only in the case of human beings—is not verification at all, because X-worlders *may* obey different laws than human beings. And it is not incumbent upon *me* (the logical behavourist says) to suggest what those laws might be: it is incumbent upon *you* to rule out *all* other explanations.' And this is a silly argument. The scientist does not have to rule out all the ridiculous theories that someone *might* suggest; he only has to show that he has ruled out any reasonable alternative theories that one might put forward on the basis of present knowledge.

Granting, then, that we might discover a technique for 'reading' the unspoken thoughts of X-worlders: we would then be in the same position with respect to the X-worlders as we were with respect to the original 'super-spartans'. The super-spartans were quite willing to tell us (and each other) about their pains; and we could see that their pain talk was linguistically coherent and situationally appropriate (*e.g.,* a super-spartan will tell you that he feels intense pain when you touch him with a red hot poker). On this basis, we were quite willing to grant that the super-spartans did, indeed, feel pain—all the more readily, since the deviancy in their behaviour had a perfectly convincing ideological explanation. (Note again the rôle played here by considerations of coherence and simplicity). But the X-worlders also 'tell' us (and, perhaps, each other), exactly the same things, albeit *un*willingly (by the medium of the involuntarily produced 'V-waves'). Thus we have to say—at least, we have to say as long as the 'V-wave' theory has not broken down—that the X-worlders are what they, in fact, are—just 'super-super-spartans'.

Let us now consider a quite different argument that a logical behaviourist might use. 'You are assuming,' he might say, 'the following principle:

If someone's brain is in the same state as that of a human being in pain (not just at the moment of the pain, but before and after for a sufficient interval), then he is in pain.

'Moreover, this principle is one which it would never be reasonable to give up (on your conception of "methodology"). Thus, you have turned it into a tautology. But observe what turning this principle into a tautology involves: it involves changing the meaning of "pain". What "pain" means for *you* is: the presence of pain, in the colloquial sense of the term, *or* the presence of a brain state identical with the brain state of someone who feels pain. Of course, in that sense we can verify that your "X-worlders" experience "pain"—but that is not the sense of "pain" at issue.'

The reply to this argument is that the premiss is simply false. It is just not true that, on my conception of verification, it would *never* be reasonable to give up the principle stated. To show this, I have to beg your pardons for engaging in a little more science fiction. Let us suppose that scientists discover yet another kind of waves—call them 'W-waves'. Let us suppose that W-waves do not emanate from human brains, but that they are detected emanating from the brains of X-worlders. And let us suppose that, once again, there exists a simple scheme for decoding W-waves into coherent English (or whatever language X-worlders speak), and that the 'decoded' waves 'read' like this: 'Ho, ho! are we fooling those Earthians! They think that the V-waves they detect represent our thoughts! If they only knew that instead of pretending not to have pains when we really have pains, we are really pretending to pretend not to have pains when we really do have pains when we really don't have pains!' Under these circumstances, we would 'doubt' (to put it mildly) that the same psycho-physical correlations held for normal humans and for X-worlders. Further investigations might lead us to quite a number of different hypotheses. For example, we might decide that X-worlders don't think with their brains at all—that the 'organ' of thought is not just the brain, in the case of X-worlders, but some larger structure—perhaps even a structure which is not 'physical' in the sense of consisting of elementary particles. The point is that what is necessarily true is not the principle stated two paragraphs back, but rather the principle:

If someone (some organism) is in the same state as a human being in pain in all relevant respects, then he (that organism) is in pain.

—And *this* principle *is* a tautology by anybody's lights! The only *a priori* methodological restriction I am imposing here is this one:

If some organism is in the same state as a human being in pain in all respects *known* to be relevant, and there is no reason to suppose that there exist *unk*nown relevant respects, then don't postulate any.

—But this principle is not a 'tautology'; in fact, it is not a *statement* at all, but a methodological directive. And deciding to conform to this directive is not (as hardly needs to be said) changing the meaning of the word 'pain', or of *any* word.

There are two things that the logical behaviourist can do: he can claim that ascribing pains to X-worlders, or even super-spartans, involves a 'change of meaning',[7] or he can claim that ascribing pains to super-spartans, or at least to X-worlders, is 'untestable'. The first thing is a piece of unreasonable linguistics; the second, a piece of unreasonable scientific method. The two are, not surprisingly, mutually supporting: the unreasonable scientific method makes the unreasonable linguistics appear more reasonable. Similarly, the normal ways of thinking and talking are mutually supporting: reasonable linguistic field techniques are, needless to say, in agreement with reasonable conceptions of scientific method. Madmen sometimes have consistent delusional systems; so madness and sanity can both have a 'circular' aspect. I may not have succeeded, in this paper, in breaking the 'delusional system' of a committed logical behaviourist; but I hope to have convinced the uncommitted that that system need not be taken seriously. If we have to choose between 'circles', the circle of reason is to be preferred to any of the many circles of unreason.

Notes

[1] *E.g.,* these two points are fairly explicitly stated in Strawson's *Individuals.* Strawson has told me that he no longer subscribes to point (1), however.

[2] An attempted fourth alternative—*i.e.,* an alternative to dualism, materialism, *and* behaviourism—is sketched in 'The Mental Life of Some Machines', which appeared in the Proceedings of the Wayne Symposium on the Philosophy of Mind. This fourth alternative is materialistic in the wide sense of being compatible with the view that organisms, including human beings, are physical systems consisting of elementary particles and obeying the laws of physics, but does not require that such 'states' as *pain* and *preference* be defined in a way which makes reference to either overt behaviour or physical-chemical constitution. The idea, briefly, is that predicates which apply to a system by virtue of its *functional organization* have just this characteristic: a given functional organization (*e.g.,* a given inductive logic, a given rational preference function) may realize itself in almost any kind of overt behaviour, depending upon the circumstances, and is capable of being 'built into' structures of many different logically possible physical (or even metaphysical) constitutions. Thus the statement that a creature prefers A to B does not tell us whether the creature has a carbon chemistry, or a silicon chemistry, or is even a disembodied mind, nor does it tell us how the creature would behave under any circumstances specifiable without reference to the creature's other preferences and beliefs, but it does not thereby become something 'mysterious'.

³ I mean not only that *each* criterion can be regarded as synthetic, but also that the cluster is *collectively* synthetic, in the sense that we are free in certain cases to say (for reason of inductive simplicity and theoretical economy) that the term applies although the whole cluster is missing. This is completely compatible with saying that the cluster serves to fix the meaning of the word. The point is that when we specify something by a cluster of indicators we assume that people will *use their brains*. That criteria may be over-ridden when good sense demands is the sort of thing we may regard as a 'convention associated with discourse' (Grice) rather than as something to be stipulated in connection with the individual words.

⁴ Cf. 'Dreaming and "Depth Grammar",' *Analytical Philosophy*, First Series.

⁵ Of course, 'the cause' is a highly ambiguous phrase. Even if it is correct in certain contexts to say that certain events in the brain are 'the cause' of my pain behaviour, it does *not* follow (as has sometimes been suggested) that my pain must be 'identical' with these neural events.

⁶ This is suggested in Wittgenstein's *Philosophical Investigations*.

⁷ This popular philosophical move is discussed in 'Dreaming and "Depth Grammar",' *Analytical Philosophy*, First Series.

II
Empiricism and Science

6. Karl R. Popper
Science: Conjectures and Refutations

Mr. Turnbull had predicted evil consequences, ... and was now doing the best in his power to bring about the verification of his own prophecies.

Anthony Trollope

I

128 When I received the list of participants in this course and realized that I had been asked to speak to philosophical colleagues I thought, after some hesitation and consultation, that you would probably prefer me to speak about those problems which interest me most, and about those developments with which I am most intimately acquainted. I therefore decided to do what I have never done before: to give you a report on my own work in the philosophy of science, since the autumn of 1919 when I first began to grapple with the problem, *'When should a theory be ranked as scientific?'* or *'Is there a criterion for the scientific character or status of a theory?'*

The problem which troubled me at the time was neither, 'When is a theory true?' nor, 'When is a theory acceptable?' My problem was different. I *wished to distinguish between science and pseudo-science;* knowing very well that science often errs, and that pseudo-science may happen to stumble on the truth.

Chapter 1 (excluding Appendix) of *Conjectures and Refutations* by Karl R. Popper. Copyright © 1963, 1965, 1969 by Karl R. Popper. Published by Routledge and Kegan Paul, London, and Basic Books, Inc., New York. Reprinted by permission.

A lecture given at Peterhouse, Cambridge, in Summer 1953, as part of a course on developments and trends in contemporary British philosophy, organized by the British Council; originally published under the title 'Philosophy of Science: a Personal Report' in *British Philosophy in Mid-Century*, ed. C. A. Mace, 1957.

I knew, of course, the most widely accepted answer to my problem: that science is distinguished from pseudo-science—or from 'metaphysics'—by its *empirical method,* which is essentially *inductive,* proceeding from observation or experiment. But this did not satisfy me. On the contrary, I often formulated my problem as one of distinguishing between a genuinely empirical method and a non-empirical or even a pseudo-empirical method—that is to say, a method which, although it appeals to observation and experiment, nevertheless does not come up to scientific standards. The latter method may be exemplified by astrology, with its stupendous mass of empirical evidence based on observation—on horoscopes and on biographies.

But as it was not the example of astrology which led me to my problem I should perhaps briefly describe the atmosphere in which my problem arose and the examples by which it was stimulated. After the collapse of the Austrian Empire there had been a revolution in Austria: the air was full of revolutionary slogans and ideas, and new and often wild theories. Among the theories which interested me Einstein's theory of relativity was no doubt by far the most important. Three others were Marx's theory of history, Freud's psycho-analysis, and Alfred Adler's so-called 'individual psychology'.

There was a lot of popular nonsense talked about these theories, and especially about relativity (as still happens even today), but I was fortunate in those who introduced me to the study of this theory. We all—the small circle of students to which I belonged—were thrilled with the result of Eddington's eclipse observations which in 1919 brought the first important confirmation of Einstein's theory of gravitation. It was a great experience for us, and one which had a lasting influence on my intellectual development.

The three other theories I have mentioned were also widely discussed among students at that time. I myself happened to come into personal contact with Alfred Adler, and even to co-operate with him in his social work among the children and young people in the working-class districts of Vienna where he had established social guidance clinics.

It was during the summer of 1919 that I began to feel more and more dissatisfied with these three theories—the Marxist theory of history, psycho-analysis, and individual psychology; and I began to feel dubious about their claims to scientific status. My problem perhaps first took the simple form, 'What is wrong with Marxism, psycho-analysis, and individual psychology?

Why are they so different from physical theories, from Newton's theory, and especially from the theory of relativity?'

To make this contrast clear I should explain that few of us at the time would have said that we believed in the *truth* of Einstein's theory of gravitation. This shows that it was not my doubting the *truth* of those other three theories which bothered me, but something else. Yet neither was it that I merely felt mathematical physics to be more *exact* than the sociological or psychological type of theory. Thus what worried me was neither the problem of truth, at that stage at least, nor the problem of exactness or measurability. It was rather that I felt that these other three theories, though posing as sciences, had in fact more in common with primitive myths than with science; that they resembled astrology rather than astronomy.

I found that those of my friends who were admirers of Marx, Freud, and Adler, were impressed by a number of points common to these theories, and especially by their apparent *explanatory power*. These theories appeared to be able to explain practically everything that happened within the fields to which they referred. The study of any of them seemed to have the effect of an intellectual conversion or revelation, opening your eyes to a new truth hidden from those not yet initiated. Once your eyes were thus opened you saw confirming instances everywhere: the world was full of *verifications* of the theory. Whatever happened always confirmed it. Thus its truth appeared manifest; and unbelievers were clearly people who did not want to see the manifest truth; who refused to see it, either because it was against their class interest, or because of their repressions which were still 'un-analysed' and crying aloud for treatment.

The most characteristic element in this situation seemed to me the incessant stream of confirmations, of observations which 'verified' the theories in question; and this point was constantly emphasized by their adherents. A Marxist could not open a newspaper without finding on every page confirming evidence for his interpretation of history; not only in the news, but also in its presentation—which revealed the class bias of the paper—and especially of course in what the paper did *not* say. The Freudian analysts emphasized that their theories were constantly verified by their 'clinical observations'. As for Adler, I was much impressed by a personal experience. Once, in 1919, I reported to him a case which to me did not seem particularly Adlerian, but which he found no difficulty in analysing in terms of his theory of inferiority feelings, although he had not even seen the child. Slightly shocked, I asked him how he could be so sure. 'Because of my thousandfold experience,' he replied; whereupon I could not help saying: 'And with this new case, I suppose, your experience has become thousand-and-one-fold.'

What I had in mind was that his previous observations may not have been much sounder than this new one; that each in its turn had been interpreted in the light of 'previous experience', and at the same time counted as additional confirmation. What, I asked myself, did it confirm? No more than that a case could be interpreted in the light of the theory. But this meant very little, I reflected, since every conceivable case could be interpreted in the light of Adler's theory, or equally of Freud's. I may illustrate this by two very different examples of human behaviour: that of a man who pushes a child into the water with the intention of drowning it; and that of a man who sacrifices his life in an attempt to save the child. Each of these two cases can be explained with equal ease in Freudian and in Adlerian terms. According to Freud the first man suffered from repression (say, of some component of his Oedipus complex), while the second man had achieved sublimation. According to Adler the first man suffered from feelings of inferiority (producing perhaps the need to prove to himself that he dared to commit some crime), and so did the second man (whose need was to prove to himself that he dared to rescue the child). I could not think of any human behaviour which could not be interpreted in terms of either theory. It was precisely this fact—that they always fitted, that they were always confirmed—which in the eyes of their admirers constituted the strongest argument in favour of these theories. It began to dawn on me that this apparent strength was in fact their weakness.

With Einstein's theory the situation was strikingly different. Take one typical instance—Einstein's prediction, just then confirmed by the findings of Eddington's expedition. Einstein's gravitational theory had led to the result that light must be attracted by heavy bodies (such as the sun), precisely as material bodies were attracted. As a consequence it could be calculated that light from a distant fixed star whose apparent position was close to the sun would reach the earth from such a direction that the star would seem to be slightly shifted away from the sun; or, in other words, that stars close to the sun would look as if they had moved a little away from the sun, and from one another. This is a thing which cannot normally be observed since such stars are rendered invisible in daytime by the sun's overwhelming brightness; but during an eclipse it is possible to take photographs of them. If the same constellation is photographed at night one can measure the distances on the two photographs, and check the predicted effect.

Now the impressive thing about this case is the *risk* involved in a prediction of this kind. If observation shows that the predicted effect is definitely absent, then the theory is simply refuted. The theory is *incompatible with certain possible results of observation*—in fact with results which everybody before Einstein would have expected.[1] This is quite different from the situation I have previously described, when it turned out that the theories in question were compatible with the most divergent human behaviour, so that it was practically impossible to describe any human behaviour that might not be claimed to be a verification of these theories.

These considerations led me in the winter of 1919–20 to conclusions which I may now reformulate as follows.

(1) It is easy to obtain confirmations, or verifications, for nearly every theory—if we look for confirmations.

(2) Confirmations should count only if they are the result of *risky predictions;* that is to say, if, unenlightened by the theory in question, we should have expected an event which was incompatible with the theory—an event which would have refuted the theory.

(3) Every 'good' scientific theory is a prohibition: it forbids certain things to happen. The more a theory forbids, the better it is.

(4) A theory which is not refutable by any conceivable event is non-scientific. Irrefutability is not a virtue of a theory (as people often think) but a vice.

(5) Every genuine *test* of a theory is an attempt to falsify it, or to refute it. Testability is falsifiability; but there are degrees of testability: some theories are more testable, more exposed to refutation, than others; they take, as it were, greater risks.

(6) Confirming evidence should not count *except when it is the result of a genuine test of the theory;* and this means that it can be presented as a serious but unsuccessful attempt to falsify the theory. (I now speak in such cases of 'corroborating evidence'.)

(7) Some genuinely testable theories, when found to be false, are still upheld by their admirers—for example by introducing *ad hoc* some auxiliary assumption, or by re-interpreting the theory *ad hoc* in such a way that it escapes refutation. Such a procedure is always possible, but it rescues the theory from

refutation only at the price of destroying, or at least lowering, its scientific status. (I later described such a rescuing operation as a *'conventionalist* twist' or a *conventionalist stratagem'*.)

One can sum up all this by saying that *the criterion of the scientific status of a theory is its falsifiability, or refutability, or testability.*

II

I may perhaps examplify this with the help of the various theories so far mentioned. Einstein's theory of gravitation clearly satisfied the criterion of falsifiability. Even if our measuring instruments at the time did not allow us to pronounce on the results of the tests with complete assurance, there was clearly a possibility of refuting the theory.

Astrology did not pass the test. Astrologers were greatly impressed, and misled, by what they believed to be confirming evidence—so much so that they were quite unimpressed by any unfavourable evidence. Moreover, by making their interpretations and prophecies sufficiently vague they were able to explain away anything that might have been a refutation of the theory had the theory and the prophecies been more precise. In order to escape falsification they destroyed the testability of their theory. It is a typical soothsayer's trick to predict things so vaguely that the predictions can hardly fail: that they become irrefutable.

The Marxist theory of history, in spite of the serious efforts of some of its founders and followers, ultimately adopted this soothsaying practice. In some of its earlier formulations (for example in Marx's analysis of the character of the 'coming social revolution') their predictions were testable, and in fact falsified.[2] Yet instead of accepting the refutations the followers of Marx re-interpreted both the theory and the evidence in order to make them agree. In this way they rescued the theory from refutation; but they did so at the price of adopting a device which made it irrefutable. They thus gave a 'conventionalist twist' to the theory; and by this stratagem they destroyed its much advertised claim to scientific status.

The two psycho-analytic theories were in a different class. They were simply non-testable, irrefutable. There was no conceivable human behaviour which could contradict them. This does not mean that Freud and Adler were not seeing certain things correctly: I personally do not doubt that much of what they say is of considerable importance, and may well play its part one day in a psychological science which is testable. But it does mean that those 'clinical observations' which analysts naïvely believe confirm their theory cannot do this any more than the daily confirmations which astrologers find in their practice.[3] And as for Freud's epic of the Ego, the Super-ego, and the Id, no substantially stronger claim to scientific status can be made for it than for Homer's collected stories from Olympus. These theories describe some facts, but in the manner of myths. They contain most interesting psychological suggestions, but not in a testable form.

At the same time I realized that such myths may be developed, and become testable; that historically speaking all—or very nearly all—scientific theories originate from myths, and that a myth may contain important anticipations of scientific theories. Examples are Empedocles' theory of evolution by trial and error, or Parmenides' myth of the unchanging block universe in which nothing ever happens and which, if we add another dimension, becomes Einstein's block universe (in which, too, nothing ever happens, since everything is, four-dimensionally speaking, determined and laid down from the beginning). I thus felt that if a theory is found to be non-scientific, or 'metaphysical' (as we might say), it is not thereby found to be unimportant, or insignificant, or 'meaningless', or 'nonsensical'.[4] But it cannot claim to be backed by empirical evidence in the scientific sense—although it may easily be, in some genetic sense, the 'result of observation'.

(There were a great many other theories of this pre-scientific or pseudo-scientific character, some of them, unfortunately, as influential as the Marxist interpretation of history; for example, the racialist interpretation of history—another of those impressive and all-explanatory theories which act upon weak minds like revelations.)

Thus the problem which I tried to solve by proposing the criterion of falsifiability was neither a problem of meaningfulness or significance, nor a problem of truth or acceptability. It was the problem of drawing a line (as well as this can be done) between the statements, or systems of statements, of the empirical sciences, and all other statements—whether they are of a religious or of a metaphysical character, or simply pseudo-scientific. Years later—it must have been in 1928 or 1929—I called this first problem of mine the *'problem of demarcation'*. The criterion of falsifiability is a solution to this problem of demarcation, for it says that statements or systems of statements, in order to be ranked as scientific, must be capable of conflicting with possible, or conceivable, observations.

III

Today I know, of course, that this *criterion of demarcation*—the criterion of testability, or falsifiability, or refutability—is far from obvious; for even now its significance is seldom realized. At that time, in 1920, it seemed to me almost trivial, although it solved for me an intellectual problem which had worried me deeply, and one which also had obvious practical consequences (for example, political ones). But I did not yet realize its full implications, or its philosophical significance. When I explained it to a fellow student of the Mathematics Department (now a distinguished mathematician in Great Britain), he suggested that I should publish it. At the time I thought this absurd; for I was convinced that my problem, since it was so important for me, must have agitated many scientists and philosophers who would surely have reached my rather obvious solution. That this was not the case I learnt from Wittgenstein's work, and from its reception; and so I published my results thirteen years later in the form of a criticism of Wittgenstein's *criterion of meaningfulness.*

Wittgenstein, as you all know, tried to show in the *Tractatus* (see for example his propositions 6.53; 6.54; and 5) that all so-called philosophical or metaphysical propositions were actually non-propositions or pseudo-propositions: that they were senseless or meaningless. All genuine (or meaningful) propositions were truth functions of the elementary or atomic propositions which described 'atomic facts', i.e.—facts which can in principle be ascertained by observation. In other words, meaningful propositions were fully reducible to elementary or atomic propositions which were simple statements describing possible states of affairs, and which could in principle be established or rejected by observation. If we call a statement an 'observation statement' not only if it states an actual observation but also if it states anything that *may* be observed, we shall have to say (according to the *Tractatus,* 5 and 4.52) that every genuine proposition must be a truth-function of, and therefore deducible from, observation statements. All other apparent propositions will be meaningless pseudo-propositions; in fact they will be nothing but nonsensical gibberish.

This idea was used by Wittgenstein for a characterization of science, as opposed to philosophy. We read (for example in 4.11, where natural science is taken to stand in opposition to philosophy): 'The totality of true propositions is the total natural science (or the totality of the natural sciences).' This means that the propositions which belong to science are those deductible from *true* observation statements; they are those propositions which can be *verified* by true observation statements. Could we know all true observation statements, we should also know all that may be asserted by natural science.

This amounts to a crude verifiability criterion of demarcation. To make it slightly less crude, it could be amended thus: 'The statements which may possibly fall within the province of science are those which may possibly be verified by observation statements; and these statements, again, coincide with the class of *all* genuine or meaningful statements.' For this approach, then, *verifiability, meaningfulness, and scientific character all coincide.*

I personally was never interested in the so-called problem of meaning; on the contrary, it appeared to me a verbal problem, a typical pseudo-problem. I was interested only in the problem of demarcation, i.e., in finding a criterion of the scientific character of theories. It was just this interest which made me see at once that Wittgenstein's verifiability criterion of meaning was intended to play the part of a criterion of demarcation as well; and which made me see that, as such, it was totally inadequate, even if all misgivings about the dubious concept of meaning were set aside. For Wittgenstein's criterion of demarcation—to use my own terminology in this context—is verifiability, or deducibility from observation statements. But this criterion is too narrow (*and* too wide): it excludes from science practically everything that is, in fact, characteristic of it (while failing in effect to exclude astrology). No scientific theory can ever be deduced from observation statements, or be described as a truth-function of observation statements.

All this I pointed out on various occasions to Wittgensteinians and members of the Vienna Circle. In 1931–2 I summarized my ideas in a largish book (read by several members of the Circle but never published; although part of it was incorporated in my *Logic of Scientific Discovery*); and in 1933 I published a letter to the Editor of *Erkenntnis* in which I tried to compress into two pages my ideas on the problems of demarcation and induction.[5] In this letter and elsewhere I described the problem of meaning as a pseudo-problem, in contrast to the problem of demarcation. But my contribution was classified by members of the Circle as a proposal to replace the verifiability criterion of *meaning* by a falsifiability criterion of *meaning*—which effectively made nonsense of my views.[6] My protests that I was trying to solve, not their pseudo-problem of meaning, but the problem of demarcation, were of no avail.

My attacks upon verification had some effect, however. They soon led to complete confusion in the camp of the verificationist philosophers of sense and nonsense. The original proposal of verifiability as the criterion of meaning was at least clear, simple, and forceful. The modifications and shifts which were now introduced were the very opposite.[7] This, I should say, is now seen even by the participants. But since I am usually quoted as one of them I wish to repeat that although I created this confusion I never participated in it. Neither falsifiability nor testability were proposed by me as criteria of meaning; and although I may plead guilty to having introduced both terms into the discussion, it was not I who introduced them into the theory of meaning.

Criticism of my alleged views was widespread and highly successful. I have yet to meet a criticism of my views.[8] Meanwhile, testability is being widely accepted as a criterion of demarcation.

IV

I have discussed the problem of demarcation in some detail because I believe that its solution is the key to most of the fundamental problems of the philosophy of science. I am going to give you later a list of some of these other problems, but only one of them—the *problem of induction*—can be discussed here at any length.

I had become interested in the problem of induction in 1923. Although this problem is very closely connected with the problem of demarcation, I did not fully appreciate the connection for about five years.

I approached the problem of induction through Hume. Hume, I felt, was perfectly right in pointing out that induction cannot be logically justified. He held that there can be no valid logical[9] arguments allowing us to establish '*that those instances, of which we have had no experience, resemble those, of which we have had experience*'. Consequently '*even after the observation of the frequent or constant conjunction of objects, we have no reason to draw any inference concerning any object beyond*

those of which we have had experience'. For 'shou'd it be said
that we have experience'[10]—experience teaching us that objects constantly conjoined with certain other objects continue
to be so conjoined—then, Hume says, 'I wou'd renew my question, *why from this experience we form any conclusion beyond
those past instances, of which we have had experience'.* In
other words, an attempt to justify the practice of induction by
an appeal to experience must lead to an *infinite regress.* As a
result we can say that theories can never be inferred from observation statements, or rationally justified by them.

I found Hume's refutation of inductive inference clear and
conclusive. But I felt completely dissatisfied with his psychological explanation of induction in terms of custom or habit.

It has often been noticed that this explanation of Hume's is
philosophically not very satisfactory. It is, however, without
doubt intended as a *psychological* rather than a philosophical
theory; for it tries to give a causal explanation of a psychological fact—*the fact that we believe in laws,* in statements asserting regularities or constantly conjoined kinds of events—by
asserting that this fact is due to (i.e., constantly conjoined
with) custom or habit. But even this reformulation of Hume's
theory is still unsatisfactory; for what I have just called a
'psychological fact' may itself be described as a custom or
habit—the custom or habit of believing in laws or regularities;
and it is neither very surprising nor very enlightening to hear
that such a custom or habit must be explained as due to, or
conjoined with, a custom or habit (even though a different one).
Only when we remember that the words 'custom' and 'habit'
are used by Hume, as they are in ordinary language, not merely
to *describe* regular behaviour, but rather to *theorize about its
origin* (ascribed to frequent repetition), can we reformulate his
psychological theory in a more satisfactory way. We can then
say that, like other habits, *our habit of believing in laws is the
product of frequent repetition*—of the repeated observation
that things of a certain kind are constantly conjoined with
things of another kind.

This genetico-psychological theory is, as indicated, incorporated in ordinary language, and it is therefore hardly as
revolutionary as Hume thought. It is no doubt an extremely
popular psychological theory—part of 'common sense', one
might say. But in spite of my love of both common sense and
Hume, I felt convinced that this psychological theory was mistaken; and that it was in fact refutable on purely logical grounds.

Hume's psychology, which is the popular psychology, was

mistaken, I felt, about at least three different things: (a) the typical result of repetition; (b) the genesis of habits; and especially (c) the character of those experiences or modes of behaviour which may be described as 'believing in a law' or 'expecting a law-like succession of events'.

(a) The typical result of repetition—say, of repeating a difficult passage on the piano—is that movements which at first needed attention are in the end executed without attention. We might say that the process becomes radically abbreviated, and ceases to be conscious: it becomes 'physiological'. Such a process, far from creating a conscious expectation of law-like succession, or a belief in a law, may on the contrary begin with a conscious belief and destroy it by making it superfluous. In learning to ride a bicycle we may start with the belief that we can avoid falling if we steer in the direction in which we threaten to fall, and this belief may be useful for guiding our movements. After sufficient practice we may forget the rule; in any case, we do not need it any longer. On the other hand, even if it is true that repetition may create unconscious expectations, these become conscious only if something goes wrong (we may not have heard the clock tick, but we may hear that it has stopped).

(b) Habits or customs do not, as a rule, *originate* in repetition. Even the habit of walking, or of speaking, or of feeding at certain hours, *begins* before repetition can play any part whatever. We may say, if we like, that they deserve to be called 'habits' or 'customs' only after repetition.has played its typical part; but we must not say that the practices in question originated as the result of many repetitions.

(c) Belief in a law is not quite the same thing as behaviour which betrays an expectation of a law-like succession of events; but these two are sufficiently closely connected to be treated together. They may, perhaps, in exceptional cases, result from a mere repetition of sense impressions (as in the case of the stopping clock). I was prepared to concede this, but I contended that normally, and in most cases of any interest, they cannot be so explained. As Hume admits, even a single striking observation may be sufficient to create a belief or an expectation—a fact which he tries to explain as due to an inductive habit, formed as the result of a vast number of long repetitive sequences which had been experienced at an earlier period of life.[11] But this, I contended, was merely his attempt to explain away unfavourable facts which threatened his theory; an unsuccessful attempt, since these unfavourable facts could be observed in very young animals and babies—as early, indeed, as we like. 'A lighted cigarette was held near the noses of the young puppies', reports F. Bäge. 'They sniffed at it once, turned tail, and nothing would induce them to come back to the source of the smell and to sniff again. A few days later, they reacted to the mere sight of a cigarette or even of a rolled piece of white paper, by bounding away, and sneezing.'[12] If we try to explain cases like this by postulating a vast number of long repetitive sequences at a still earlier age we are not only romancing, but forgetting that in the clever puppies' short lives there must be room not only for repetition but also for a great deal of novelty, and consequently of non-repetition.

But it is not only that certain empirical facts do not support Hume; there are decisive arguments of a *purely logical* nature against his psychological theory.

The central idea of Hume's theory is that of *repetition, based upon similarity* (or 'resemblance'). This idea is used in a very uncritical way. We are led to think of the water-drop that hollows the stone: of sequences of unquestionably like events slowly forcing themselves upon us, as does the tick of the clock. But we ought to realize that in a psychological theory such as Hume's, only repetition-for-us, based upon similarity-for-us, can be allowed to have any effect upon us. We must respond to situations as if they were equivalent; *take* them as similar; *interpret* them as repetitions. The clever puppies, we may assume, showed by their response, their way of acting or of reacting, that they recognized or interpreted the second situation as a repetition of the first: that they expected its main element, the objectionable smell, to be present. The situation was a repetition-for-them because they responded to it by *anticipating* its similarity to the previous one.

This apparently psychological criticism has a purely logical basis which may be summed up in the following simple argument. (It happens to be the one from which I originally started my criticism.) The kind of repetition envisaged by Hume can never be perfect; the cases he has in mind cannot be cases of perfect sameness; they can only be cases of similarity. Thus *they are repetitions only from a certain point of view.* (What has the effect upon me of a repetition may not have this effect upon a spider.) But this means that, for logical reasons, there must always be a point of view—such as a system of expectations, anticipations, assumptions, or interests—*before* there can be any repetition; which point of view, consequently, cannot be merely the result of repetition. (See now also appendix *x, (1), to my L.Sc.D.)

We must thus replace, for the purposes of a psychological theory of the origin of our beliefs, the naïve idea of events which *are* similar by the idea of events to which we react by *interpreting* them as being similar. But if this is so (and I can see no escape from it) then Hume's psychological theory of induction leads to an infinite regress, precisely analogous to that other infinite regress which was discovered by Hume himself, and used by him to explode the logical theory of induction. For what do we wish to explain? In the example of the puppies we wish to explain behaviour which may be described as *recognizing or interpreting* a situation as a repetition of another. Clearly, we cannot hope to explain this by an appeal to earlier repetitions, once we realize that the earlier repetitions must also have been repetitions-for-them, so that precisely the same problem arises again: that of *recognizing or interpreting* a situation as a repetition of another.

To put it more concisely, similarity-for-us is the product of a response involving interpretations (which may be inadequate) and anticipations or expectations (which may never be fulfilled). It is therefore impossible to explain anticipations, or expectations, as resulting from many repetitions, as suggested by Hume. For even the first repetition-for-us must be based upon similarity-for-us, and therefore upon expectations—precisely the kind of thing we wished to explain.

This shows that there is an infinite regress involved in Hume's psychological theory.

Hume, I felt, had never accepted the full force of his own logical analysis. Having refuted the logical idea of induction he was faced with the following problem: how do we actually obtain our knowledge, as a matter of psychological fact, if induction is a procedure which is logically invalid and rationally unjustifiable? There are two possible answers: (1) We obtain our knowledge by a non-inductive procedure. This answer would have allowed Hume to retain a form of rationalism. (2) We obtain our knowledge by repetition and induction, and therefore by a logically invalid and rationally unjustifiable procedure, so that all apparent knowledge is merely a kind of belief—belief based on habit. This answer would imply that even scientific knowledge is irrational, so that rationalism is absurd, and must be given up. (I shall not discuss here the age-old attempts, now again fashionable, to get out of the difficulty by asserting that though induction is of course logically invalid if we mean by 'logic' the same as 'deductive logic', it is not irrational by its own standards, as may be seen from the fact that every reasonable man applies it *as a matter of fact:* it was Hume's great achievement to break this uncritical identification of the question of fact—*quid facti?*—and the question of justification or validity—*quid juris?*)

It seems that Hume never seriously considered the first alternative. Having cast out the logical theory of induction by repetition he struck a bargain with common sense, meekly allowing the re-entry of induction by repetition, in the guise of a psychological theory. I proposed to turn the tables upon this theory of Hume's. Instead of explaining our propensity to expect regularities as the result of repetition, I proposed to explain repetition-for-us as the result of our propensity to expect regularities and to search for them.

Thus I was led by purely logical considerations to replace the psychological theory of induction by the following view. Without waiting, passively, for repetitions to impress or impose regularities upon us, we actively try to impose regularities upon the world. We try to discover similarities in it, and to interpret it in terms of laws invented by us. Without waiting for premises we jump to conclusions. These may have to be discarded later, should observation show that they are wrong.

This was a theory of trial and error—of *conjectures and refutations*. It made it possible to understand why our attempts to force interpretations upon the world were logically prior to the observation of similarities. Since there were logical reasons behind this procedure, I thought that it would apply in the field of science also; that scientific theories were not the digest of observations, but that they were inventions—conjectures boldly put forward for trial, to be eliminated if they clashed with observations; with observations which were rarely accidental but as a rule undertaken with the definite intention of testing a theory by obtaining, if possible, a decisive refutation.

V

The belief that science proceeds from observation to theory is still so widely and so firmly held that my denial of it is often met with incredulity. I have even been suspected of being insincere—of denying what nobody in his senses can doubt.

But in fact the belief that we can start with pure observations alone, without anything in the nature of a theory, is absurd; as may be illustrated by the story of the man who dedicated his life to natural science, wrote down everything he could observe, and bequeathed his priceless collection of observations to the Royal Society to be used as inductive evidence. This story should show us that though beetles may profitably be collected, observations may not.

Twenty-five years ago I tried to bring home the same point to a group of physics students in Vienna by beginning a lecture with the following instructions: 'Take pencil and paper; carefully observe, and write down what you have observed!' They asked, of course, *what* I wanted them to observe. Clearly the instruction, 'Observe!' is absurd.[13] (It is not even idiomatic, unless the object of the transitive verb can be taken as understood.) Observation is always selective. It needs a chosen object, a definite task, an interest, a point of view, a problem. And its description presupposes a descriptive language, with property words; it presupposes similarity and classification, which in its turn presupposes interests, points of view, and problems. 'A hungry animal', writes Katz,[14] 'divides the environment into edible and inedible things. An animal in flight sees roads to escape and hiding places.... Generally speaking, objects change ... according to the needs of the animal.' We may add that objects can be classified, and can become similar or dissimilar, *only* in this way—by being related to needs and interests. This rule applies not only to animals but also to scientists. For the animal a point of view is provided by its needs, the task of the moment, and its expectations; for the scientist by his theoretical interests, the special problem under investigation, his conjectures and anticipations, and the theories which he accepts as a kind of background: his frame of reference, his 'horizon of expectations'.

The problem 'Which comes first, the hypothesis (*H*) or the observation (*O*),' is soluble; as is the problem, 'Which comes first, the hen (*H*) or the egg (*O*)'. The reply to the latter is, 'An earlier kind of egg'; to the former, 'An earlier kind of hypothesis'. It is quite true that any particular hypothesis we choose will have been preceded by observations—the observations, for example, which it is designed to explain. But these observations, in their turn, presupposed the adoption of a frame of reference: a frame of expectations: a frame of theories. If they were significant, if they created a need for explanation and thus gave rise to the invention of a hypothesis, it was because they could not be explained within the old theoretical framework, the old horizon of expectations. There is no danger here of an infinite regress. Going back to more and more primitive theories and myths we shall in the end find unconscious, *inborn* expectations.

The theory of inborn *ideas* is absurd, I think; but every organism has inborn *reactions* or *responses;* and among them, responses adapted to impending events. These responses we may describe as 'expectations' without implying that these 'expectations' are conscious. The new-born baby 'expects', in this sense, to be fed (and, one could even argue, to be protected and loved). In view of the close relation between expectation and knowledge we may even speak in quite a reasonable sense of 'inborn knowledge'. This 'knowledge' is not, however, *valid a priori;* an inborn expectation, no matter how strong and specific, may be mistaken. (The newborn child may be abandoned, and starve.)

Thus we are born with expectations; with 'knowledge' which, although not *valid a priori,* is *psychologically or genetically a priori,* i.e., prior to all observational experience. One of the most important of these expectations is the expectation of finding a regularity. It is connected with an inborn propensity to look out for regularities, or with a *need* to *find* regularities, as we may see from the pleasure of the child who satisfies this need.

This 'instinctive' expectation of finding regularities, which is psychologically *a priori,* corresponds very closely to the 'law of causality' which Kant believed to be part of our mental outfit and to be *a priori* valid. One might thus be inclined to say that Kant failed to distinguish between psychologically *a priori* ways of thinking or responding and *a priori* valid beliefs. But I do not think that his mistake was quite as crude as that. For the expectation of finding regularities is not only psychologically *a priori,* but also logically *a priori:* it is logically prior to all observational experience, for it is prior to any recognition of similarities, as we have seen; and all observation involves the recognition of similarities (or dissimilarities). But in spite of being logically *a priori* in this sense the expectation is not valid *a priori.* For it may fail: we can easily construct an environment (it would be a lethal one) which, compared with our ordinary environment, is so chaotic that we completely fail to find regularities. (All natural laws could remain valid: environments of this kind have been used in the animal experiments mentioned in the next section.)

Thus Kant's reply to Hume came near to being right; for the distinction between an *a priori* valid expectation and one which is both genetically *and* logically prior to observation, but not *a priori* valid, is really somewhat subtle. But Kant proved too much. In trying to show how knowledge is possible, he proposed a theory which had the unavoidable consequence that our quest for knowledge must necessarily succeed, which is clearly mistaken. When Kant said, 'Our intellect does not draw its laws from nature but imposes its laws upon nature', he was right. But in thinking that these laws are necessarily true, or that we necessarily succeed in imposing them upon nature, he was wrong.[15] Nature very often resists quite successfully, forcing us to discard our laws as refuted; but if we live we may try again.

To sum up this logical criticism of Hume's psychology of induction we may consider the idea of building an induction machine. Placed in a simplified 'world' (for example, one of sequences of coloured counters) such a machine may through repetition 'learn', or even 'formulate', laws of succession which hold in its 'world'. If such a machine can be constructed (and I have no doubt that it can) then, it might be argued, my theory must be wrong; for if a machine is capable of performing inductions on the basis of repetition, there can be no logical reasons preventing us from doing the same.

The argument sounds convincing, but it is mistaken. In constructing an induction machine we, the architects of the machine, must decide *a priori* what constitutes its 'world'; what things are to be taken as similar or equal; and what *kind* of 'laws' we wish the machine to be able to 'discover' in its 'world'. In other words we must build into the machine a framework determining what is relevant or interesting in its world: the machine will have its 'inborn' selection principles. The problems of similarity will have been solved for it by its makers who thus have interpreted the 'world' for the machine.

VI

Our propensity to look out for regularities, and to impose laws upon nature, leads to the psychological phenomenon of *dogmatic thinking* or, more generally, dogmatic behaviour: we expect regularities everywhere and attempt to find them even where there are none; events which do not yield to these attempts we are inclined to treat as a kind of 'background noise'; and we stick to our expectations even when they are inadequate and we ought to accept defeat. This dogmatism is to some extent necessary. It is demanded by a situation which can only be dealt with by forcing our conjectures upon the world. Moreover, this dogmatism allows us to approach a good theory in stages, by way of approximations: if we accept defeat too easily, we may prevent ourselves from finding that we were very nearly right.

It is clear that this *dogmatic attitude*, which makes us stick to our first impressions, is indicative of a strong belief; while a *critical attitude,* which is ready to modify its tenets, which admits doubt and demands tests, is indicative of a weaker belief. Now according to Hume's theory, and to the popular theory, the strength of a belief should be a product of repetition; thus it should always grow with experience, and always be greater in less primitive persons. But dogmatic thinking, an uncontrolled wish to impose regularities, a manifest pleasure in rites and in repetition as such, are characteristic of primitives and children; and increasing experience and maturity sometimes create an attitude of caution and criticism rather than of dogmatism.

I may perhaps mention here a point of agreement with psycho-analysis. Psycho-analysts assert that neurotics and others interpret the world in accordance with a personal set pattern which is not easily given up, and which can often be traced back to early childhood. A pattern or scheme which was adopted very early in life is maintained throughout, and every new experience is interpreted in terms of it; verifying it, as it were, and contributing to its rigidity. This is a description of what I have called the dogmatic attitude, as distinct from the critical attitude, which shares with the dogmatic attitude the quick adoption of a schema of expectations—a myth, perhaps, or a conjecture or hypothesis—but which is ready to modify it, to correct it, and even to give it up. I am inclined to suggest that most neuroses may be due to a partially arrested development of the critical attitude; to an arrested rather than a natural dogmatism; to resistance to demands for the modification and adjustment of certain schematic interpretations and responses. This resistance in its turn may perhaps be explained, in some cases, as due to an injury or shock, resulting in fear and in an increased need for assurance or certainty, analogous to the way in which an injury to a limb makes us afraid to move it, so that it becomes stiff. (It might even be argued that the case of the limb is not merely analogous to the dogmatic response, but an instance of it.) The explanation of any concrete case will have to take into account the weight of the difficulties involved in making the necessary adjustments—difficulties which may be considerable, especially in a complex and changing world: we know from experiments on animals that varying degrees of neurotic behaviour may be produced at will by correspondingly varying difficulties.

I found many other links between the psychology of knowledge and psychological fields which are often considered remote from it—for example the psychology of art and music; in fact, my ideas about induction originated in a conjecture about the evolution of Western polyphony. But you will be spared this story.

VII

My logical criticism of Hume's psychological theory, and the considerations connected with it (most of which I elaborated in 1926-7, in a thesis entitled 'On Habit and Belief in Laws'[16]) may seem a little removed from the field of the philosophy of science. But the distinction between dogmatic and critical thinking, or the dogmatic and the critical attitude, brings us right back to our central problem. For the dogmatic attitude is clearly related to the tendency to *verify* our laws and schemata by seeking to apply them and to confirm them, even to the point of neglecting refutations, whereas the critical attitude is one of readiness to change them—to test them; to refute them; to *falsify* them, if possible. This suggests that we may identify the critical attitude with the scientific attitude, and the dogmatic attitude with the one which we have described as pseudo-scientific.

It further suggests that genetically speaking the pseudo-scientific attitude is more primitive than, and prior to, the scientific attitude: that it is a pre-scientific attitude. And this primitivity or priority also has its logical aspect. For the critical attitude is not so much opposed to the dogmatic attitude as superimposed upon it: criticism must be directed against existing and influential beliefs in need of critical revision—in other words, dogmatic beliefs. A critical attitude needs for its raw material, as it were, theories or beliefs which are held more or less dogmatically.

Thus science must begin with myths, and with the criticism of myths; neither with the collection of observations, nor with the invention of experiments, but with the critical discussion of myths, and of magical techniques and practices. The scientific tradition is distinguished from the pre-scientific tradition in having two layers. Like the latter, it passes on its theories;

but it also passes on a critical attitude towards them. The theories are passed on, not as dogmas, but rather with the challenge to discuss them and improve upon them. This tradition is Hellenic: it may be traced back to Thales, founder of the first *school* (I do not mean 'of the first *philosophical* school', but simply 'of the first school') which was not mainly concerned with the preservation of a dogma.[17]

The critical attitude, the tradition of free discussion of theories with the aim of discovering their weak spots so that they may be improved upon, is the attitude of reasonableness, of rationality. It makes far-reaching use of both verbal argument and observation—of observation in the interest of argument, however. The Greeks' discovery of the critical method gave rise at first to the mistaken hope that it would lead to the solution of all the great old problems; that it would establish certainty; that it would help to *prove* our theories, to *justify* them. But this hope was a residue of the dogmatic way of thinking; in fact nothing can be justified or proved (outside of mathematics and logic). The demand for rational proofs in science indicates a failure to keep distinct the broad realm of rationality and the narrow realm of rational certainty: it is an untenable, an unreasonable demand.

Nevertheless, the role of logical argument, of deductive logical reasoning, remains all-important for the critical approach; not because it allows us to prove our theories, or to infer them from observation statements, but because only by purely deductive reasoning is it possible for us to discover what our theories imply, and thus to criticize them effectively. Criticism, I said, is an attempt to find the weak spots in a theory, and these, as a rule, can be found only in the more remote logical consequences which can be derived from it. It is here that purely logical reasoning plays an important part in science.

Hume was right in stressing that our theories cannot be validly inferred from what we can know to be true—neither from observations nor from anything else. He concluded from this that our belief in them was irrational. If 'belief' means here our inability to doubt our natural laws, and the constancy of natural regularities, then Hume is again right: this kind of dogmatic belief has, one might say, a physiological rather than a rational basis. If, however, the term 'belief' is taken to cover our critical acceptance of scientific theories—a *tentative* acceptance combined with an eagerness to revise the theory if we succeed in designing a test which it cannot pass—then

Hume was wrong. In such an acceptance of theories there is nothing irrational. There is not even anything irrational in relying for practical purposes upon well-tested theories, for no more rational course of action is open to us.

Assume that we have deliberately made it our task to live in this unknown world of ours; to adjust ourselves to it as well as we can; to take advantage of the opportunities we can find in it; and to explain it, *if* possible (we need not assume that it is), and as far as possible, with the help of laws and explanatory theories. *If we have made this our task, then there is no more rational procedure than the method of trial and error—of conjecture and refutation:* of boldly proposing theories; of trying our best to show that these are erroneous; and of accepting them tentatively if our critical efforts are unsuccessful.

From the point of view here developed all laws, all theories, remain essentially tentative, or conjectural, or hypothetical, even when we feel unable to doubt them any longer. Before a theory has been refuted we can never know in what way it may have to be modified. That the sun will always rise and set within twenty-four hours is still proverbial as a law 'established by induction beyond reasonable doubt'. It is odd that this example is still in use, though it may have served well enough in the days of Aristotle and Pytheas of Massalia—the great traveller who for centuries was called a liar because of his tales of Thule, the land of the frozen sea and the *midnight sun.*

The method of trial and error is not, of course, simply identical with the scientific or critical approach—with the method of conjecture and refutation. The method of trial and error is applied not only by Einstein but, in a more dogmatic fashion, by the amoeba also. The difference lies not so much in the trials as in a critical and constructive attitude towards errors; errors which the scientist consciously and cautiously tries to uncover in order to refute his theories with searching arguments, including appeals to the most severe experimental tests which his theories and his ingenuity permit him to design.

The critical attitude may be described as the conscious attempt to make our theories, or conjectures, suffer in our stead in the struggle for the survival of the fittest. It gives us a chance to survive the elimination of an inadequate hypothesis—when a more dogmatic attitude would eliminate it by eliminating us. (There is a touching story of an Indian community which disappeared because of its belief in the holiness of life, including that of tigers.) We thus obtain the fittest theory within our reach by the elimination of those which are less fit. (By 'fitness' I do not mean merely 'usefulness' but truth; see chapters 3 and 10, *Conjectures and Refutations*.) I do not think that this procedure is irrational or in need of any further rational justification.

VIII

Let us now turn from our logical criticism of the *psychology of experience* to our real problem—the problem of *the logic of science.* Although some of the things I have said may help us here, in so far as they may have eliminated certain psychological prejudices in favour of induction, my treatment of the *logical problem of induction* is completely independent of this criticism, and of all psychological considerations. Provided you do not dogmatically believe in the alleged psychological fact that we make inductions, you may now forget my whole story with the exception of two logical points: my logical remarks on testability or falsifiability as the criterion of demarcation; and Hume's logical criticism of induction.

From what I have said it is obvious that there was a close link between the two problems which interested me at that time: demarcation, and induction or scientific method. It was easy to see that the method of science is criticism, i.e., attempted falsifications. Yet it took me a few years to notice that the two problems—of demarcation and of induction—were in a sense one.

Why, I asked, do so many scientists believe in induction? I found they did so because they believed natural science to be characterized by the inductive method—by a method starting from, and relying upon, long sequences of observations and experiments. They believed that the difference between genuine science and metaphysical or pseudo-scientific speculation depended solely upon whether or not the inductive method was employed. They believed (to put it in my own terminology) that only the inductive method could provide a satisfactory *criterion of demarcation.*

I recently came across an interesting formulation of this belief in a remarkable philosophical book by a great physicist— Max Born's *Natural Philosophy of Cause and Chance.*[18] He writes: 'Induction allows us to generalize a number of observations into a general rule: that night follows day and day follows night. . . . But while everyday life has no definite criterion for the validity of an induction, . . . science has worked out a code, or rule of craft, for its application.' Born nowhere reveals the contents of this inductive code (which, as his wording shows, contains a 'definite criterion for the validity of an induction'); but he stresses that 'there is no logical argument' for its acceptance: 'it is a question of faith'; and he is therefore 'willing to call induction a metaphysical principle'. But why does he believe that such a code of valid inductive rules must exist? This becomes clear when he speaks of the 'vast communities of people ignorant of, or rejecting, the rule of science, among them the members of anti-vaccination societies and believers in astrology. It is useless to argue with them; I cannot compel them to accept the same criteria of valid induction in which I believe: the code of scientific rules.' This makes it quite clear that *'valid induction' was here meant to serve as a criterion of demarcation between science and pseudo-science.*

But it is obvious that this rule or craft of 'valid induction' is not even metaphysical: it simply does not exist. No rule can ever guarantee that a generalization inferred from true observations, however often repeated, is true. (Born himself does not believe in the truth of Newtonian physics, in spite of its success, although he believes that it is based on induction.) And the success of science is not based upon rules of induction, but depends upon luck, ingenuity, and the purely deductive rules of critical argument.

I may summarize some of my conclusions as follows:

(1) Induction, i.e., inference based on many observations, is a myth. It is neither a psychological fact, nor a fact of ordinary life, nor one of scientific procedure.

(2) The actual procedure of science is to operate with conjectures: to jump to conclusions—often after one single observation (as noticed for example by Hume and Born).

(3) Repeated observations and experiments function in science as *tests* of our conjectures or hypotheses, i.e., as attempted refutations.

(4) The mistaken belief in induction is fortified by the need for a criterion of demarcation which, it is traditionally but wrongly believed, only the inductive method can provide.

(5) The conception of such an inductive method, like the criterion of verifiability, implies a faulty demarcation.

(6) None of this is altered in the least if we say that induction makes theories only probable rather than certain. (See especially chapter 10, *Conjectures and Refutations.*)

IX

If, as I have suggested, the problem of induction is only an instance or facet of the problem of demarcation, then the solution to the problem of demarcation must provide us with a solution to the problem of induction. This is indeed the case, I believe, although it is perhaps not immediately obvious.

For a brief formulation of the problem of induction we can turn again to Born, who writes: '... no observation or experiment, however extended, can give more than a finite number of repetitions'; therefore, 'the statement of a law—B depends on A—always transcends experience. Yet this kind of statement is made everywhere and all the time, and sometimes from scanty material.'[19]

In other words, the logical problem of induction arises from (a) Hume's discovery (so well expressed by Born) that it is impossible to justify a law by observation or experiment, since it 'transcends experience'; (b) the fact that science proposes and uses laws 'everywhere and all the time'. (Like Hume, Born is struck by the 'scanty material', i.e., the few observed instances upon which the law may be based.) To this we have to add (c) *the principle of empiricism* which asserts that in science, only observation and experiment may decide upon the *acceptance or rejection* of scientific statements, including laws and theories.

These three principles, (a), (b), and (c), appear at first sight to clash; and this apparent clash constitutes the *logical problem of induction*.

Faced with this clash, Born gives up *(c)*, the principle of empiricism (as Kant and many others, including Bertrand Russell, have done before him), in favour of what he calls a 'metaphysical principle'; a metaphysical principle which he does not even attempt to formulate; which he vaguely describes as a 'code or rule of craft'; and of which I have never seen any formulation which even looked promising and was not clearly untenable.

But in fact the principles (a) to (c) do not clash. We can see this the moment we realize that the acceptance by science of a law or of a theory is *tentative only;* which is to say that all laws and theories are conjectures, or tentative *hypotheses* (a position which I have sometimes called 'hypotheticism'); and that we may reject a law or theory on the basis of new evidence, without necessarily discarding the old evidence which originally led us to accept it.[20]

The principle of empiricism (c) can be fully preserved, since the fate of a theory, its acceptance or rejection, is decided by observation and experiment—by the result of tests. So long as a theory stands up to the severest tests we can design, it is accepted; if it does not, it is rejected. But it is never inferred, in any sense, from the empirical evidence. There is neither a psychological nor a logical induction. *Only the falsity of the theory can be inferred from empirical evidence, and this inference is a purely deductive one.*

Hume showed that it is not possible to infer a theory from observation statements; but this does not affect the possibility of refuting a theory by observation statements. The full appreciation of this possibility makes the relation between theories and observations perfectly clear.

This solves the problem of the alleged clash between the principles (a), (b), and (c), and with it Hume's problem of induction.

X

Thus the problem of induction is solved. But nothing seems less wanted than a simple solution to an age-old philosophical problem. Wittgenstein and his school hold that genuine philosophical problems do not exist;[21] from which it clearly follows that they cannot be solved. Others among my contemporaries do believe that there are philosophical problems, and respect them; but they seem to respect them too much; they seem to believe that they are insoluble, if not taboo; and they are shocked and horrified by the claim that there is a simple, neat, and lucid, solution to any of them. If there is a solution it must be deep, they feel, or at least complicated.

However this may be, I am still waiting for a simple, neat and lucid criticism of the solution which I published first in 1933 in my letter to the Editor of *Erkenntnis*,[22] and later in *The Logic of Scientific Discovery*.

Of course, one can invent new problems of induction, different from the one I have formulated and solved. (Its formulation was half its solution.) But I have yet to see any reformulation of the problem whose solution cannot be easily obtained from my old solution. I am now going to discuss some of these re-formulations.

One question which may be asked is this: how do we really jump from an observation statement to a theory?

Although this question appears to be psychological rather than philosophical, one can say something positive about it without invoking psychology. One can say first that the jump is not from an observation statement, but from a problem-situation, and that the theory must allow us *to explain* the observations which created the problem (that is, *to deduce* them from the theory strengthened by other accepted theories and by other observation statements, the so-called initial conditions). This leaves, of course, an immense number of possible theories, good and bad; and it thus appears that our question has not been answered.

But this makes it fairly clear that when we asked our question we had more in mind than, 'How do we jump from an observation statement to a theory?' The question we had in mind was, it now appears, 'How do we jump from an observation statement to a *good* theory?' But to this the answer is: by jumping first to *any* theory and then testing it, to find whether it is good or not; i.e., by repeatedly applying the critical method, eliminating many bad theories, and inventing many new ones. Not everybody is able to do this; but there is no other way.

Other questions have sometimes been asked. The original problem of induction, it was said, is the problem of *justifying* induction, i.e., of justifying inductive inference. If you answer this problem by saying that what is called an 'inductive inference' is always invalid and therefore clearly not justifiable, the following new problem must arise: how do you justify your method of trial and error? Reply: the method of trial and error is a *method of eliminating false theories* by observation statements; and the justification for this is the purely logical relationship of deducibility which allows us to assert the falsity of universal statements if we accept the truth of singular ones.

Another question sometimes asked is this: why is it reasonable to prefer non-falsified statements to falsified ones? To this question some involved answers have been produced, for example pragmatic answers. But from a pragmatic point of view the question does not arise, since false theories often serve well enough: most formulae used in engineering or navigation are known to be false, although they may be excellent approximations and easy to handle; and they are used with confidence by people who know them to be false.

The only correct answer is the straightforward one: because we search for truth (even though we can never be sure we have found it), and because the falsified theories are known or believed to be false, while the non-falsified theories may still be true. Besides, we do not prefer *every* non-falsified theory—only one which, in the light of criticism, appears to be better than its competitors: which solves our problems, which is well tested, and of which we think, or rather conjecture or hope (considering other provisionally accepted theories), that it will stand up to further tests.

It has also been said that the problem of induction is, 'Why is it *reasonable* to believe that the future will be like the past?', and that a satisfactory answer to this question should make it plain that such a belief is, in fact, reasonable. My reply is that it is reasonable to believe that the future will be very different from the past in many vitally important respects. Admittedly it is perfectly reasonable to *act* on the assumption that it will, in many respects, be like the past, and that well-tested laws will continue to hold (since we can have no better assumption to act upon); but it is also reasonable to believe that such a course of action will lead us at times into severe trouble, since some of the laws upon which we now heavily rely may easily prove unreliable. (Remember the midnight sun!) One might even say that to judge from past experience, and from our general scientific knowledge, the future will *not* be like the past, in perhaps most of the ways which those have in mind who say that it will. Water will sometimes not quench thirst, and air will choke those who breathe it. An apparent way out is to say that the future will be like the past *in the sense that the laws of nature will not change,* but this is begging the question. We speak of a 'law of nature' only if we think that we have before us a regularity which does not change; and if we find that it changes then we shall not continue to call it a 'law of nature'. Of course our search for natural laws indicates that we hope to find them, and that we believe that there are natural laws; but our belief in any particular natural law cannot have a safer basis than our unsuccessful critical attempts to refute it.

I think that those who put the problem of induction in terms of the *reasonableness* of our beliefs are perfectly right if they are dissatisfied with a Humean, or post-Humean, sceptical despair of reason. We must indeed reject the view that a belief in science is as irrational as a belief in primitive magical practices—that both are a matter of accepting a 'total ideology', a convention or a tradition based on faith. But we must be cautious if we formulate our problem, with Hume, as one of the reasonableness of our *beliefs*. We should split this problem into three—our old problem of demarcation, or of how to *distinguish* between science and primitive magic; the problem of the rationality of the scientific or critical *procedure,* and of the role of observation within it; and lastly the problem of the rationality of our *acceptance* of theories for scientific and for practical purposes. To all these three problems solutions have been offered here.

One should also be careful not to confuse the problem of the reasonableness of the scientific procedure and the (tentative) acceptance of the results of this procedure—i.e., the scientific theories—with the problem of the rationality or otherwise *of the belief that this procedure will succeed.* In practice, in practical scientific research, this belief is no doubt unavoidable and reasonable, there being no better alternative. But the belief is certainly unjustifiable in a theoretical sense, as I have argued (in section v). Moreover, if we could show, on general logical grounds, that the scientific quest is likely to succeed, one could not understand why anything like success has been so rare in the long history of human endeavours to know more about our world.

Yet another way of putting the problem of induction is in terms of probability. Let *t* be the theory and *e* the evidence: we can ask for $P(t,e)$, that is to say, the probability of *t,* given *e.* The problem of induction, it is often believed, can then be put thus: construct a *calculus of probability* which allows us to work out for any theory *t* what its probability is, relative to any given empirical evidence *e;* and show that $P(t,e)$ increases with the accumulation of supporting evidence, and reaches high values—at any rate values greater than ½.

In *The Logic of Scientific Discovery* I explained why I think that this approach to the problem is fundamentally mistaken.[23] To make this clear, I introduced there the distinction between *probability* and *degree of corroboration or confirmation.* (The term 'confirmation' has lately been so much used and misused that I have decided to surrender it to the verificationists and to use for my own purposes 'corroboration' only. The term 'probability' is best used in some of the many senses which satisfy the well-known calculus of probability, axiomatized, for example, by Keynes, Jeffreys, and myself; but nothing of course depends on the choice of words, as long as we do not *assume,* uncritically, that degree of corroboration must also be a probability—that is to say, that it must satisfy the calculus of probability.)

I explained in my book why we are interested in theories

with a *high degree of corroboration.* And I explained why it is a mistake to conclude from this that we are interested in *highly probable* theories. I pointed out that the probability of a statement (or set of statements) is always the greater the less the statement says: it is inverse to the content or the deductive power of the statement, and thus to its explanatory power. Accordingly every interesting and powerful statement must have a low probability; and *vice versa:* a statement with a high probability will be scientifically uninteresting, because it says little and has no explanatory power. Although we seek theories with a high degree of corroboration, *as scientists we do not seek highly probable theories but explanations; that is to say, powerful and improbable theories.*[24] The opposite view—that science aims at high probability—is a characteristic development of verificationism: if you find that you cannot verify a theory, or make it certain by induction, you may turn to probability as a kind of *'Ersatz'* for certainty, in the hope that induction may yield at least that much.

Notes

[1] This is a slight oversimplification, for about half of the Einstein effect may be derived from the classical theory, provided we assume a ballistic theory of light.

[2] See, for example, my *Open Society and Its Enemies,* ch. 15, section iii, and notes 13–14.

[3] 'Clinical observations', like all other observations, are *interpretations in the light of theories* (see below, sections iv ff.); and for this reason alone they are apt to seem to support those theories in the light of which they were interpreted. But real support can be obtained only from observations undertaken as tests (by 'attempted refutations'); and for this purpose *criteria of refutation* have to be laid down beforehand: it must be agreed which observable situations, if actually observed, mean that the theory is refuted. But what kind of clinical responses would refute to the satisfaction of the analyst not merely a particular analytic diagnosis but psychoanalysis itself? And have such criteria ever been discussed or agreed upon by analysts? Is there not, on the contrary, a whole family of analytic concepts, such as 'ambivalence' (I do not suggest that there is no such thing as ambivalence), which would make it difficult, if not impossible, to agree upon such criteria? Moreover, how much headway has been made in investigating the question of the extent to which the (conscious or unconscious) expectations and theories held by the analyst influence the 'clinical responses' of the patient? (To say nothing about the conscious attempts to influence the patient by proposing interpretations to him, etc.) Years ago I introduced the term *'Oedipus effect'* to describe the influence of a theory or expectation or prediction *upon the event which it predicts* or describes: it will be remembered that the causal chain leading to Oedipus' parricide was started by the oracle's prediction of this event. This is a characteristic and recurrent theme of such myths, but one which seems to have failed to attract the interest of the analysts, perhaps not accidentally. (The problem of confirmatory dreams suggested by the analyst is discussed by Freud, for example in *Gesammelte Schriften,* in, 1925, where he says on p. 314: 'If anybody asserts that most of the dreams which

can be utilized in an analysis . . . owe their origin to [the analyst's] suggestion, then no objection can be made from the point of view of analytic
theory. Yet there is nothing in this fact', he surprisingly adds, 'which
would detract from the reliability of our results.')

4 The case of astrology, nowadays a typical pseudo-science, may illustrate
this point. It was attacked, by Aristotelians and other rationalists, down to
Newton's day, for the wrong reason—for its now accepted assertion that
the planets had an 'influence' upon terrestrial ('sublunar') events. In fact
Newton's theory of gravity, and especially the lunar theory of the tides,
was historically speaking an offspring of astrological lore. Newton, it
seems, was most reluctant to adopt a theory which came from the same
stable as for example the theory that 'influenza' epidemics are due to an
astral 'influence'. And Galileo, no doubt for the same reason, actually rejected the lunar theory of the tides; and his misgivings about Kepler may
easily be explained by his misgivings about astrology.

5 My *Logic of Scientific Discovery* (1959, 1960, 1961), here usually referred
to as *L.Sc.D.*, is the translation of *Logik der Forschung* (1934), with a
number of additional notes and appendices, including (on pp. 312–14) the
letter to the Editor of *Erkenntnis* mentioned here in the text which was
first published in *Erkenntnis*, 3, 1933, pp. 426 f.

Concerning my never published book mentioned here in the text, see
R. Carnap's paper *'Ueber Protokollsätze'* (On Protocol-Sentences), *Erkenntnis*, 3, 1932, pp. 215–28 where he gives an outline of my theory on pp.
223–8, and accepts it. He calls my theory 'procedure B', and says (p. 224,
top): 'Starting from a point of view different from Neurath's' (who developed
what Carnap calls on p. 223 'procedure A'), 'Popper developed procedure
B as part of his system.' And after describing in detail my theory of tests,
Carnap sums up his views as follows (p. 228): 'After weighing the various
arguments here discussed, it appears to me that the second language
form with procedure B—that is in the form here described—is the most
adequate among the forms of scientific language at present advocated
. . . in the . . . theory of knowledge.' This paper of Carnap's contained the
first published report of my theory of critical testing. (See also my critical
remarks in *L.Sc.D.*, note 1 to section 29, p. 104, where the date '1933'
should read '1932'; and ch. 11, below, text to note 39.)

6 Wittgenstein's example of a nonsensical pseudo-proposition is: 'Socrates
is identical'. Obviously, 'Socrates is not identical' must also be nonsense.
Thus the negation of any nonsense will be nonsense, and that of a meaningful statement will be meaningful. *But the negation of a testable (or falsifiable) statement need not be testable,* as was pointed out, first in my
L.Sc.D., (e.g. pp. 38 f.) and later by my critics. The confusion caused by
taking testability as a criterion of *meaning* rather than of *demarcation* can
easily be imagined.

7 The most recent example of the way in which the history of this problem
is misunderstood is A. R. White's 'Note on Meaning and Verification', *Mind*,
63, 1954, pp. 66 ff. J. L. Evans's article, *Mind*, 62, 1953, pp. 1 ff., which Mr.
White criticizes, is excellent in my opinion, and unusually perceptive. Un-
derstandably enough, neither of the authors can quite reconstruct the
story. (Some hints may be found in my *Open Society*, notes 46, 51, and 52
to ch. 11; and a fuller analysis in ch. 11 of the present volume.)

8 In *L.Sc.D.* I discussed, and replied to, some likely objections which afterwards were indeed raised, without reference to my replies. One of them
is the contention that the falsification of a natural law is just as impossible as its verification. The answer is that this objection mixes two entirely
different levels of analysis (like the objection that mathematical demon-
strations are impossible since checking, no matter how often repeated,
can never make it quite certain that we have not overlooked a mistake).
On the first level, there is a logical asymmetry: one singular statement—say
about the perihelion of Mercury—can formally falsify Kepler's laws; but
these cannot be formally verified by any number of singular statements.
The attempt to minimize this asymmetry can only lead to confusion. On
another level, we may hesitate to accept any statement, even the simplest
observation statement; and we may point out that every statement involves

interpretation in the light of theories, and that it is therefore uncertain. This does not affect the fundamental asymmetry, but it is important: most dissectors of the heart before Harvey observed the wrong things—those, which they expected to see. There can never be anything like a completely safe observation, free from the dangers of misinterpretation. (This is one of the reasons why the theory of induction does not work.) The 'empirical basis' consists largely of a mixture of *theories* of lower degree of universality (of 'reproducible effects'). But the fact remains that, relative to whatever basis the investigator may accept (at his peril), he can test his theory only by trying to refute it.

9 Hume does not say 'logical' but 'demonstrative', a terminology which, I think, is a little misleading. The following two quotations are from the *Treatise of Human Nature,* Book 1, Part III, sections vi and xii. (The italics are all Hume's.)

10 This and the next quotation are from *loc. cit.,* section vi. See also Hume's *Enquiry Concerning Human Understanding,* section iv, Part II, and his *Abstract,* edited 1938 by J. M. Keynes and P. Sraffa, p. 15, and quoted in *L.Sc.D.,* new appendix *VII, text to note 6.

11 *Treatise,* section xiii; section xv, rule 4.

12 F. Bäge, 'Zur Entwicklung, etc.', *Zeitschrift f. Hundeforschung,* 1933; cp. D. Katz, *Animals and Men,* ch. vi, footnote.

13 See section 30 of *L.Sc.D.*

14 Katz, *loc. cit.*

15 Kant believed that Newton's dynamics was *a priori* valid. (See his *Metaphysical Foundations of Natural Science,* published between the first and the second editions of the *Critique of Pure Reason.*) But if, as he thought, we can explain the validity of Newton's theory by the fact that our intellect imposes its laws upon nature, it follows, I think, that our intellect *must succeed* in this; which makes it hard to understand why *a priori* knowledge such as Newton's should be so hard to come by. A somewhat fuller statement of this criticism can be found in ch. 2, especially section ix, and chs. 7 and 8 of *Conjectures and Refutations.*

16 A thesis submitted under the title *'Gewohnheit und Gesetzerlebnis'* to the Institute of Education of the City of Vienna in 1927. (Unpublished.)

17 Further comments on these developments may be found in chs. 4 and 5 of *Conjectures and Refutations.*

18 Max Born, *Natural Philosophy of Cause and Chance,* Oxford, 1949, p. 7.

19 *Natural Philosophy of Cause and Chance,* p. 6.

20 I do not doubt that Born and many others would agree that theories are accepted only tentatively. But the widespread belief in induction shows that the far-reaching implications of this view are rarely seen.

21 Wittgenstein still held this belief in 1946; see note 8 to ch. 2 of *Conjectures and Refutations.*

22 See note 5 above.

23 *L.Sc.D.* (see note 5 above), ch. x, especially sections 80 to 83, also section 34ff. See also my note 'A Set of Independent Axioms for Probability', *Mind,* N.S. 47, 1938, p. 275. (This note has since been reprinted, with corrections, in the new appendix *ii of *L.Sc.D.*)

24 A definition, in terms of probabilities, of $C(t,e)$, i.e., of the degree of corroboration (of a theory t relative to the evidence e) satisfying the demands indicated in my *L.Sc.D.,* sections 82 to 83, is the following:

$$C(t, e) = E(t,e) (1 + P(t)P(t,e)),$$

where $E(t,e) = (P(e,t) - P(e))/(P(e,t) + P(e))$ is a (non-additive) measure of the explanatory power of t with respect to e. Note that $C(t,e)$ is not a probability: it may have values between -1 (refutation of t by e) and $C(t,t) \leqslant +1$. Statements t which are lawlike and thus non-verifiable cannot even reach $C(t,e) = C(t,t)$ upon empirical evidence e. $C(t,t)$ is the *degree of corroborability* of t, and is equal to the *degree of testability* of t, or to the *content* of t. Because of the demands implied in point (6) at the end of section I above, I do not think, however, that it is possible to give a complete formalization of the idea of corrobration (or, as I previously used to say, of confirmation).

(Added 1955 to the first proofs of this paper:)

See also my note 'Degree of Confirmation', *British Journal for the Philosophy of Science*, 5, 1954, pp. 143 ff. (See also 5, pp. 334.) I have since simplified this definition as follows (*B.J.P.S.*, 5, 1955, p. 359:)

$$C(t,e) = (P(e,t) - P(e))/(P(e,t) - P(e,t) + P(e))$$

For a further improvement, see *B.J.P.S.*, 6, 1955, p. 56.

7. Paul K. Feyerabend

Science without Experience

One of the most important properties of modern science, at least according to some of its admirers, is its *universality: any* question can be attacked in a scientific way, leading either to an unambiguous answer or else to an explanation of why an answer cannot be had. In the present note I shall ask whether the *empirical hypothesis* is correct, i.e., whether experience can be regarded as a true source and foundation (testing ground) of knowledge.

Asking this question and expecting a scientific answer assumes that a science *without* experience is a *possibility;* that is, it assumes that the idea is neither absurd nor self-contradictory. It must be possible to imagine a natural science without sensory elements, and it should perhaps also be possible to indicate how such a science is going to work.

Now experience is said to enter science at three points: testing; assimilation of the results of test; understanding of theories.

A test may involve complex machinery and highly abstract auxiliary assumptions. But its final outcome has to be recognized by a human observer who *looks* at some piece of apparatus and *notices* some observable change. Communicating the

From *The Journal of Philosophy*, LXVI (1969). Reprinted by permission.

results of a test also involves the senses: we *hear* what somebody says to us; we *read* what somebody has written down.
Finally, the abstract principles of a theory are just strings of
signs, without relation to the external world, unless we know
how to connect them with experiment, and that means, according to the first item on the list, with experience, involving
simple and readily identifiable sensations.

It is easily seen that experience is needed at none of the
three points just mentioned.

To start with, it does not need to enter the process of *test:*
we can put a theory into a computer, provide the computer
with suitable instruments directed by him (her, it) so that relevant measurements are made which return to the computer,
leading there to an evaluation of the theory. The computer can
give a simple yes-no response from which a scientist may *learn*
whether or not a theory has been confirmed without having in
any way *participated* in the test (i.e., without having been sub-
jected to some relevant *experience*).

Learning what a computer says means being informed about
some simple occurrence in the macroscopic world. *Usually*
such information travels via the senses, giving rise to distinct
sensations. But this is not always the case. Subliminal perception leads to reactions directly, and without sensory data.
Latent learning leads to memory traces directly, and without
sensory data. Posthypnotic suggestion leads to (belated) reactions directly, and without sensory data. In addition there is
the whole unexplored field of telepathic phenomena. I am not
asserting that the natural sciences as we know them today
could be built on these phenomena alone and could be freed
from sensations entirely. Considering the peripheral nature of
the phenomena and considering also how little attention is
given to them in our education (we are not trained to use effectively our ability for latent learning) this would be both unwise
and impractical. But the point is made that sensations are not
necessary for the business of science and that they occur for
practical reasons only.

Considering now the objection that we *understand* our
theories, that we can *apply them,* only because we have been
told how they are connected with experience, one must point
out that experience arises *together with* theoretical assumptions, *not* before them, and that an experience without theories
is just as uncomprehended as is (allegedly) a theory without
experience: eliminate part of the theoretical knowledge of a
sensing subject and you have a person who is completely dis-

oriented, incapable of carrying out the simplest action. Eliminate further knowledge and his sensory world (his "observation language") will start disintegrating; even colors and other simple sensations will disappear until he is in a stage even more primitive than a small child. A small child, on the other hand, does not possess a stable perceptual world which he uses for making sense of the theories put before him. Quite the contrary. He passes through various perceptual stages which are only loosely connected with each other (earlier stages *disappear* when new stages take over) and which embody all the theoretical knowledge achieved at the time. Moreover, the whole process (including the very complex process of learning up to three or four languages) gets started only because the child reacts correctly toward signals, *interprets them correctly,* because he possesses means of interpretation even before he has experienced his first clear sensation. Again we can imagine that this interpretative apparatus acts without being accompanied by sensations (as do all reflexes and all well-learned movements such as typing). The theoretical knowledge it contains certainly can be *applied* correctly, though it is perhaps not *understood*. But what do sensations contribute to our understanding? Taken by themselves, i.e., taken as they would appear to a completely disoriented person, they are of no use, either for understanding, or for action. Nor is it sufficient to just *link them* to the existing theories. This would mean extending the theories by further elements so that we obtain longer expressions, not the understanding of the shorter expressions that we wanted. No—the sensations must be incorporated into our behavior in a manner that allows us to pass smoothly from them into action. But this returns us to the earlier situation where the theory was applied, but allegedly not yet understood. Understanding in the sense demanded here thus turns out to be ineffective and superfluous. Result: sensations can be eliminated from the process of understanding also (though they may of course continue to *accompany* it, just as a headache accompanies deep thought).

I conclude with a few remarks on the observational-theoretical dichotomy.

Most of the time the debates about this dichotomy concentrate on the question of its existence, *not* on the question of its purpose. We may readily admit the existence of statements that are examined by looking and of other statements that are examined with the help of complicated calculations, involving highly abstract theoretical assumptions. There are observational statements and theoretical statements in that sense. But there are also statements expressed by long sentences and statements expressed by short sentences, intuitively plausible statements and statments that either sound absurd or leave our intuitions unmoved, and so on and so forth. Why is it preferable to interpret theories on the basis of an *observation* language rather than on the basis of a language of intuitively evident statements (as was done only a few centuries ago and as must be done anyway, for observation does not help a disoriented person), or on the basis of a language containing short sentences (as is done in every elementary physics course)? Because observation is supposed to be a source (a testing ground) of knowledge. Is this supposition correct? And does it justify the use of observational languages for the explanation of theories?

It justifies such use only if observation can be shown to be the *only* or the only *trustworthy* source of knowledge. On pages 160–162 [this anthology] we have seen that the first part is far from true. Knowledge can *enter* our brain without touching our senses. And some knowledge *resides* in the individual brain without ever having entered it. Nor is observational knowledge the most reliable knowledge we possess. Science took a big step forward when the Aristotelian idea of the reliability of our everyday experience was given up and was replaced by an empiricism of a more subtle kind. Later on progress was often made by following theory, not observation, and by rearranging our observational world in conformance with theoretical assumptions. In the struggle for better knowledge theory and observation enter on an equal footing, just as do intuitive plausibility and intuitive absurdity: the absurd theory may win the day and the plausible theory may have to be given up just as the refuted theory may win the day, pushing aside, and making irrelevant, the refuting observations (this is what happened, for example, at the time of Galileo). Empiricism, insofar as it goes beyond the invitation not to forget considering observations, is therefore an unreasonable doctrine, not in agreement with scientific practice.

To sum up: a natural science without experience is *conceivable.* Conceiving a science without experience is an effective way of examining the empirical hypothesis that underlies much of science and is the *conditio sine qua non* of empiricism. Proceeding in this way, we may find methods that are more effective than plain and simple observation (just as Galileo found certain illusory phenomena to be more effective sources of

astronomical knowledge than plain, direct, undiluted observation). Proceeding in this way of course means leaving the con-
fines of empiricism and moving on to a more comprehensive and
more satisfactory kind of philosophy.

8. Paul K. Feyerabend

How to Be a Good Empiricist—A Plea for Tolerance in Matters Epistemological

*"Facts?" he repeated. "Take a drop more grog, Mr. Franklin,
and you'll get over the weakness of believing in facts! Foul play,
Sir!"*

Wilkie Collins
Moonstone

1. Contemporary Empiricism Liable to Lead to Establishment of a Dogmatic Metaphysics

Today empiricism is the professed philosophy of a good many
intellectual enterprises. It is the core of the sciences, or so at
least we are taught, for it is responsible both for the existence
and for the growth of scientific knowledge. It has been adopted
by influential schools in aesthetics, ethics, and theology. And

From *Philosophy of Science, The Delaware Seminar*, Vol. 2, Bernard
Baumrin, editor (New York: Interscience Publishers). Copyright 1963 by the
University of Delaware. Reprinted by permission.

Revised copy of paper originally appearing in *Inquiry*. For support of research the author is indebted to the National Science Foundation and the
Minnesota Center for the Philosophy of Science.

within philosophy proper the empirical point of view has been elaborated in great detail and with even greater precision. This predilection for empiricism is due to the assumption that only a thoroughly observational procedure can exclude fanciful speculation and empty metaphysics as well as to the hope that an empiristic attitude is most liable to prevent stagnation and to further the progress of knowledge. It is the purpose of the present paper to show that empiricism in the form in which it is practiced today cannot fulfill this hope.

Putting it very briefly, it seems to me that the contemporary doctrine of empiricism has encountered difficulties, and has created contradictions which are very similar to the difficulties and contradictions inherent in some versions of the doctrine of democracy. The latter are a well-known phenomenon. That is, it is well known that essentially totalitarian measures are often advertised as being a necessary consequence of democratic principles. Even worse—it not so rarely happens that the totalitarian character of the defended measures is not explicitly stated but covered up by calling them 'democratic,' the word 'democratic' now being used in a new, and somewhat mis-leading, manner. This method of (conscious or unconscious) verbal camouflage works so well that it has deceived some of the staunchest supporters of true democracy. What is not so well known is that modern empiricism is in precisely the same predicament. That is, some of the methods of modern em-piricism which are introduced in the spirit of anti-dogmatism and progress are bound to lead to the establishment of a dog-matic metaphysics and to the construction of defense mech-anisms which make this metaphysics safe from refutation by experimental inquiry. It is true that in the process of establish-ing such a metaphysics the words 'empirical' or 'experience' will frequently occur; but their sense will be as distorted as was the sense of 'democratic' when used by some concealed de-fenders of a new tyranny. (Popper, 1953). This, then, is my charge: Far from eliminating dogma and metaphysics and thereby encouraging progress, modern empiricism has found a new way of making dogma and metaphysics respectable, viz., the way of calling them 'well-confirmed theories,' and of de-veloping a method of confirmation in which experimental in-quiry plays a large though well controlled role. In this respect, modern empiricism is very different indeed from the empiricism of Galileo, Faraday, and Einstein, though it will of course try to represent these scientists as following its own paradigm of research, thereby further confusing the issue.[1]

From what has been said above it follows that the fight for tolerance in scientific matters and the fight for scientific progress must still be carried on. What has changed is the denomination of the enemies. They were priests, or 'school-philosophers,' a few decades ago. Today they call themselves 'philosophers of science,' or 'logical empiricists.'[2] There are also a good many scientists who work in the same direction. I maintain that all these groups work against scientific progress. But whereas the former did so openly and could be easily discerned, the latter proceed under the flag of progressivism and empiricism and thereby deceive a good many of their followers. Hence, although their presence is noticeable enough they may almost be compared to a fifth column, the aim of which must be exposed in order that its detrimental effect be fully appreciated. It is the purpose of this paper to contribute to such an exposure.

I shall also try to give a positive methodology for the empirical sciences which no longer encourages dogmatic petrification in the name of experience. Put in a nutshell, the answer which this method gives to the question in the title is: You can be a good empiricist only if you are prepared to work with many alternative theories rather than with a single point of view and 'experience.' This plurality of theories must not be regarded as a preliminary stage of knowledge which will at some time in the future be replaced by the One True Theory. Theoretical pluralism is assumed to be an *essential feature* of all knowledge that claims to be objective. Nor can one rest content with a plurality which is merely abstract and which is created by denying now this and now that component of the dominant point of view. Alternatives must rather be developed in such detail that problems already 'solved' by the accepted theory can again be treated in a new and perhaps also more detailed manner. Such development will of course take time, and it will not be possible, for example, at once to construct alternatives to the present quantum theory which are comparable to its richness and sophistication. Still, it would be very unwise to bring the process to a standstill in the very beginning by the remark that some suggested new ideas are undeveloped, general, metaphysical. *It takes time to build a good theory* [a triviality that seems to have been forgotten by some defenders of the Copenhagen point of view of the quantum theory]; and it also takes time to develop an alternative to a good theory. The *function* of such concrete alternatives is, however, this: They provide means of criticizing the accepted theory in a

manner which goes *beyond* the criticism provided by a comparison of that theory 'with the facts': however closely a theory
seems to reflect the facts, however universal its use, and however necessary its existence seems to be to those speaking the
corresponding idiom, its factual adequacy can be asserted only
after it has been confronted with alternatives *whose invention
and detailed development must therefore precede any final
assertion of practical success and factual adequacy.* This, then,
is the methodological justification of a plurality of *theories:*
Such a plurality allows for a much sharper criticism of accepted
ideas than does the comparison with a domain of 'facts' which
are supposed to sit there independently of theoretical considerations. The function of unusual *metaphysical* ideas which are
built up in a nondogmatic fashion and which are then developed in sufficient detail to give an (alternative) account even of
the most common experimental and observational situations is
defined accordingly: They play a decisive role in the criticism
and in the development of what is generally believed and 'highly
confirmed'; and they have therefore to be present at *any* stage
of the development of our knowledge.[3] A science that is free
from *metaphysics* is on the best way to become a *dogmatic*
metaphysical system. So far the summary of the method I shall
explain, and defend, in the present paper.

It is clear that this method still retains an essential element
of *empiricism:* The decision between alternative theories is
based upon *crucial experiments.* At the same time it must
restrict the range of such experiments. Crucial experiments
work well with theories of a low degree of generality whose
principles do not touch the principles on which the ontology
of the chosen observation language is based. They work well
if such theories are compared with respect to a much more
general background theory which provides a stable meaning
for the observation sentences. However, this background
theory, like any other theory, is itself in need of criticism.
Criticism must use alternatives. Alternatives will be the more
efficient the more radically they differ from the point of view
to be investigated. It is bound to happen, then, that the alternatives do not share a single statement with the theories they
criticize. Clearly, a crucial experiment is now impossible. It is
impossible, not because the experimental device is too complex, or because the calculations leading to the experimental
prediction are too difficult; it is impossible because there is
no statement capable of expressing what emerges from the
observation. This consequence, which severely restricts the

domain of empirical discussion, cannot be circumvented by any of the methods which are currently in use and which all try to work with relatively stable observation languages. It indicates that the attempt to make empiricism a universal basis of all our factual knowledge cannot be carried out. The discussion of this situation is beyond the scope of the present paper.

On the whole, the paper is a concise summary of results which I have explained in a more detailed fashion in the following essays: "Explanation, Reduction, and Empiricism"; "Problems of Microphysics"; "Problems of Empiricism"; "Linguistic Philosophy and the Mind–Body Problem."[4] All the relevant acknowledgements can be found there. Let me only repeat here that my general outlook derives from the work of K. R. Popper (London) and David Bohm (London) and from my discussions with both. It was severely tested in discussion with my colleague, T. S. Kuhn (Berkeley). It was the latter's skillful defense of a scientific conservatism which triggered two papers, including the present one. Criticism by A. Naess (Oslo), D. Rynin (Berkeley), Roy Edgley (Bristol), and J. W. N. Watkins (London) have been responsible for certain changes I made in the final version.

2. Two Conditions of Contemporary Empiricism

In this section I intend to give an outline of some assumptions of contemporary empiricism which have been widely accepted. It will be shown in the sections to follow that these apparently harmless assumptions which have been explicitly formulated by some logical empiricists, but which also seem to guide the work of a good many physicists, are bound to lead to exactly the results I have outlined above: dogmatic petrification and the establishment, on so-called 'empirical grounds,' of a rigid metaphysics.

One of the cornerstones of contemporary empiricism is its *theory of explanation*. This theory is an elaboration of some simple and very plausible ideas first proposed by Popper[5] and it may be introduced as follows: Let T and T' be two different scientific theories, T' the theory to be explained, or the explanandum, T the explaining theory, or the explanans. Explanation (of T') consists in the *derivation* of T' from T and initial conditions which specify the domain D' in which T' is applicable. Prima facie, this demand of derivability seems to be a very natural one to make for "otherwise the explanans would not constitute adequate grounds for the explanation" (Hempel). It implies two things: first, that the consequences of a satisfactory explanans, T, inside D' must be compatible with the explanandum, T'; and secondly, that the main descriptive terms of these consequences must either coincide, with respect to their meanings, with the main descriptive terms of T', or at least they must be related to them via an empirical hypothesis. The latter result can also be formulated by saying that the meaning of T' must be unaffected by the explanation. "It is of the utmost importance," writes Professor Nagel, emphasizing this point, "that the expressions peculiar to a science will possess meanings that are fixed by its *own* procedures, and are therefore intelligible in terms of its own rules of usage, whether or not the science has been, or will be [explained in terms of] the other discipline."

Now if we take it for granted that more general theories are always introduced with the purpose of explaining the existent successful theories, then every new theory will have to satisfy the two conditions just mentioned. Or, to state it in a more explicit manner,

(1) *only such theories are then admissible in a given domain which either* contain *the theories already used in this domain, or which are at least* consistent *with them inside the domain*[6]*; and*

(2) *meanings will have to be invariant with respect to scientific progress; that is, all future theories will have to be phrased in such a manner that their use in explanations does not affect what is said by the theories, or factual reports to be explained.*

These two conditions I shall call the *consistency condition* and the *condition of meaning invariance,* respectively.

Both conditions are *restrictive* conditions and therefore bound profoundly to influence the growth of knowledge. I shall soon show that the development of actual science very often violates them and that it violates them in exactly those places where one would be inclined to perceive a tremendous progress of knowledge. I shall also show that neither condition can be justified from the point of view of a tolerant empiricism. However, before doing so I would like to mention that both conditions have occasionally entered the domain of the sciences and have been used here in attacks against new developments and even in the process of theory construction itself.

Especially today, they play a very important role in the construction as well as in the defense of certain points of view
in microphysics.

Taking first an earlier example, we find that in his *Wärmelehre*, Ernst Mach (1897) makes the following remark:

> *Considering that there is, in a purely mechanical system of
> absolutely elastic atoms no real analogue for the* increase of
> entropy, *one can hardly suppress the idea that a violation of
> the second law ... should be possible if such a mechanical
> system were the* real *basis of thermodynamic processes.*

And referring to the fact that the second law is a highly confirmed physical law, he insinuates (in his *Zwei Aufsaetze,* 1912)
that for this reason the mechanical hypothesis must not be
taken too seriously. There were many similar objections against
the kinetic theory of heat.[7] More recently, Max Born has based
his arguments against the possibility of a return to determinism
upon the consistency condition and the assumption which we
shall here take for granted, that wave mechanics is incompatible with determinism.

> *If any future theory should be deterministic it cannot be a
> modification of the present one, but must be entirely different.
> How this should be possible without sacrificing a whole treas-
> ure of well established results [i.e., without contradicting highly
> confirmed physical laws and thereby violating the consistency
> condition] I leave the determinist to worry about.*

Most members of the so-called Copenhagen school of quantum
theory would argue in a similar manner. For them the idea of
complementarity and the formalism of quantization expressing
this idea do not contain any hypothetical element as they are
"uniquely determined by the facts" (Rosenfeld). Any theory
which contradicts this idea is factually inadequate and must
be removed. Conversely, an explanation of the idea of complementarity is acceptable only if it either contains this idea, or is
at least consistent with it. This is how the consistency condition
is used in arguments against theories such as those of Bohm,
de Broglie, and Vigier.[8]

The use of the consistency condition is not restricted to such
general remarks, however. A decisive part of the existing quantum theory *itself,* viz., the projection postulate,[9] is the result of
the attempt to give an account of the definiteness of macro objects and macro events that is in accordance with the consis-

tency condition. The influence of the condition of meaning invariance goes even further.

The Copenhagen-interpretation of the quantum theory [writes Heisenberg] starts from a paradox. Any experiment in physics, whether it refers to the phenomena of daily life or to atomic events is to be described in the terms of classical physics. . . . We cannot and should not replace these concepts by any others. *Still the application of these concepts is limited by the relation of uncertainty. We must keep in mind this limited range of applicability of the classical concepts while using them, but we cannot, and should not try to improve them.*

This means that the meaning of the classical terms must remain invariant with respect to any future explanation of microphenomena. Microtheories have to be formulated in such a manner that this invariance is guaranteed. The principle of correspondence and the formalism of quantization connected with it were explicitly devised for satisfying this demand. Altogether, the quantum theory seems to be the first theory after the downfall of the Aristotelian physics that has been quite explicitly constructed with an eye both on the consistency condition and the condition of (empirical) meaning invariance. In this respect it is very different indeed from, say, relativity which violates both consistency and meaning invariance with respect to earlier theories. Most of the arguments used for the defense of its customary interpretation also depend on the validity of these two conditions and they will collapse with their removal. An examination of these conditions is therefore very topical and bound deeply to affect present controversies in microphysics. I shall start this investigation by showing that some of the most interesting developments of physical theory in the past have violated both conditions.

3. These Conditions Not Invariably Accepted by Actual Science

The case of the consistency condition can be dealt with in a few words: it is well known (and has also been shown in great detail by Duhem) that Newton's theory is inconsistent with Galileo's law of the free fall and with Kepler's laws; that statistical thermodynamics is inconsistent with the second law of the phenomenological theory; that wave optics is inconsistent with geometrical optics; and so on. Note that what is being asserted here is *logical* inconsistency; it may well be that the differences of prediction are too small to be detectable by experiment. Note also that what is being asserted is not the inconsistency of, say, Newton's theory and Galileo's law, but rather the inconsistency of *some consequences* of Newton's theory in the domain of validity of Galileo's law, and Galileo's law. In this last case the situation is especially clear. Galileo's law asserts that the acceleration of the free fall is a constant, whereas application of Newton's theory to the surface of the earth gives an acceleration that is not a constant but *decreases* (although imperceptibly) with the distance from the center of the earth. Conclusion: If actual scientific procedure is to be the measure of method, then the consistency condition is inadequate.

The case of meaning invariance requires a little more argument, not because it is intrinsically more difficult, but because it seems to be much more closely connected with deep-rooted prejudices. Assume that an explanation is required, in terms of the special theory of relativity, of the classical conservation of mass in all reactions in a closed system S. If m', m'', m''', $\cdots$, $m^i \cdots$ are the masses of the parts P', P'', P''', $\cdots$, P^i, $\cdots$ of S, then what we want is an explanation of

$$\sum m^i = \text{const.} \tag{1}$$

for all reactions inside S. We see at once that the consistency condition cannot be fulfilled: According to special relativity Σm^i will vary with the velocities of the parts relative to the coordinate system in which the observations are carried out, and the total mass of S will also depend on the relative potential energies of the parts. However, if the velocities and the mutual forces are not too large, then the variation of Σm^i predicted by relativity will be so small as to be undetectable by experiment. Now let us turn to the *meanings* of the terms in the relativistic law and in the corresponding classical law. The first indication of a possible change of meaning may be seen in the fact that in the classical case the mass of an aggregate of parts equals the sum of the masses of the parts:

$$M(\sum P^i) = \sum M(P^i).$$

This is not valid in the case of relativity where the relative velocities and the relative potential energies contribute to the mass balance. That the relativistic concept and the classical concept of mass are very different indeed becomes clear if we also consider that the former is a *relation*, involving relative velocities, between an object and a coordinate system, whereas the latter is a *property* of the object itself and independent of its behavior in coordinate systems. True, there have been attempts to give a relational analysis even of the classical concept (Mach). None of these attempts, however, leads to the relativistic idea with its velocity dependence on the coordinate system, which idea must therefore be added even to a *relational* account of classical mass. The attempt to identify the classical mass with the relativistic rest mass is of no avail either. For although both may have the same numerical value, the one is still dependent on the coordinate system chosen (in which it is at rest and has that specific value), whereas the other is not so dependent. We have to conclude, then, that $(m)_c$ and $(m)_r$ mean very different things and that $(\Sigma m^i)_c = $ const. and $(\Sigma m^i)_r = $ const. are very different assertions. This being the case, the derivation from relativity of either equation (1) or of a law that makes slightly different quantitative predictions with Σm^i used in the classical manner, will be possible only if a further premise is added which establishes a relation between the $(m)_c$ and the $(m)_r$. Such a 'bridge law'—and this is a major point in Nagel's theory of reduction—is a hypothesis

according to which the occurrence of the properties designated by some expression in the premises of the [explanans] is a sufficient, or a necessary and sufficient condition for the occurrence of the properties designated by the expressions of the [explanandum].[10]

Applied to the present case this would mean the following: Under certain conditions the occurrence of relativistic mass of a given magnitude is accompanied by the occurrence of classical mass of a corresponding magnitude; this assertion is inconsistent with another part of the explanans, viz., the theory of relativity. After all, this theory asserts that there are no invariants which are directly connected with mass measurements and it thereby asserts that '$(m)_c$' does not express real features of physical systems. Thus we inevitably arrive at the conclusion that mass conservation cannot be explained in terms of relativity (or 'reduced' to relativity) without a violation of meaning invariance. And if one retorts, as has been done by some critics of the ideas expressed in the present paper,[11] that meaning invariance is an essential part of both reduction and explanation, then the answer will simply be that equation (1) can neither be explained by, nor reduced to relativity. Whatever the *words* used for describing the situation, the *fact* remains that actual science does not observe the requirement of meaning invariance.

This argument is quite general and is independent of whether the terms whose meaning is under investigation are observable or not. It is therefore stronger than may seem at first sight. There are some empiricists who would admit that the meaning of theoretical terms may be changed in the course of scientific progress. However, not many people are prepared to extend meaning *variance* to observational terms also. The idea motivating this attitude is, roughly, that the meaning of observational terms is uniquely determined by the procedures of observation such as looking, listening, and the like. These procedures remain unaffected by theoretical advance.[12] Hence, observational meanings, too, remain unaffected by theoretical advance. What is overlooked, here, is that the 'logic' of the observational terms is not exhausted by the procedures which are connected with their application 'on the basis of observation.' As will turn out later, it also depends on the more general ideas that determine the 'ontology' (in Quine's sense) of our discourse. These general ideas may change without any change of observational procedures being implied. For example, we may change our ideas about the nature, or the ontological status (property, relation, object, process, etc.) of the color of a self-luminescent object without changing the methods of ascertaining that color (looking, for example). Clearly, such a change is bound profoundly to influence the meanings of our observational terms.

All this has a decisive bearing upon some contemporary ideas concerning the interpretation of scientific theories. According to these ideas, theoretical terms receive their meanings via correspondence rules which connect them with an observational language *that has been fixed in advance* and independently of the structure of the theory to be interpreted. Now, our above analysis would seem to show that *if we interpret scientific theories in the manner accepted by the scientific community,* then most of these correspondence rules will be either false, or nonsensical. They will be *false* if they *assert* the existence of entities denied by the theory; they will be *nonsensical* if they *presuppose* this existence. Turning the argument around, we can also say that the attempt to interpret the calculus of some theory that has been voided of the meaning assigned to it by the scientific community with the help of the double language system, will lead to a very different theory. Let us again take the theory of relativity as an example: It can be safely assumed that the physical thing language of Carnap, and any similar language that has been suggested as an observation language, is not Lorentz-invariant. The attempt to interpret the *calculus* of relativity on *its* basis therefore cannot lead to the *theory* of relativity as it was understood by Einstein. What we shall obtain will be at the very most *Lorentz' interpretation* with its inherent asymmetries. This undesirable result cannot be evaded by the *demand* to use a different and more adequate observation language. The double language system assumes that theories which are not connected with some observation language do not possess an interpretation. The demand assumes that they do, and asks to choose the observation language most suited to it. It reverses the relation between theory and experience that is characteristic for the double language method of interpretation, which means, it gives up this method. Contemporary empiricism, therefore, has not led to any satisfactory account of the meanings of scientific theories.[13]

What we have shown so far is that the two conditions of Section 2 are frequently violated in the course of scientific practice and especially at periods of scientific revolution. This is not yet a very strong argument. True: There are empirically inclined philosophers who have derived some satisfaction from the assumption that they only make explicit what is implicitly contained in scientific practice. It is therefore quite important to show that scientific practice is not what it is supposed to be by them. Also, strict adherence to meaning invariance and consistency would have made impossible some very decisive advances in physical theory such as the advance from the physics of Aristotle to the physics of Galileo and Newton. However, how do we know (independently of the fact that they do exist, have a certain structure, and are very influential—a circumstance that will have great weight with opportunists only[14]) that the sciences are a desirable phenomenon, that they contribute to the advancement of knowledge, and that their analysis will therefore lead to reasonable methodological demands? And did it not emerge in the last section that meaning invariance and the consistency condition *are* adopted by some scientists? Actual scientific practice, therefore, cannot be our last authority. We have to find out whether consistency and meaning invariance are *desirable* conditions and this quite independently of who accepts and praises them and how many Nobel prizes have been won with their help.[15] Such an investigation will be carried out in the next sections.

4. Inherent Unreasonableness of Consistency Condition

Prima facie, the case of the consistency condition can be dealt with in very few words. Consider for that purpose a theory T' that successfully describes the situation in the domain D'. From this we can infer (a) that T' agrees with a *finite* number of observations (let their class be F); and (b) that it agrees with these observations inside a margin M of error only.[16] Any alternative that contradicts T' outside F and inside M is supported by exactly the same observations and therefore acceptable if T' was acceptable (we shall assume that F are the only observations available). The consistency condition is much less tolerant. It eliminates a theory not because it is in disagreement with the *facts;* it eliminates it because it is in disagreement with *another theory,* with a theory, moreover, whose confirming instances it shares. *It thereby makes the as yet untested part of that theory a measure of validity.* The only difference between such a measure and a more recent theory is age and familiarity. Had the younger theory been there first, then the consistency condition would have worked in its favor. In this respect the effect of the consistency condition is rather similar to the effect of the more traditional methods of transcendental deduction, analysis of essences, phenomenological analysis, linguistic analysis. It contributes to the preservation of the old and familiar not because of any inherent advantage in it—for example, not because it has a better foundation in observation than has the newly suggested alternative, or because it is more elegant—but just because it is old and familiar. This is not the only instance where on closer inspection a rather surprising similarity emerges between modern empiricism and some of the school philosophies it attacks.

Now it seems to me that these brief considerations, although leading to an interesting *tactical* criticism of the consistency condition, do not yet go to the heart of the matter. They show that an alternative of the accepted point of view which shares its confirming instances cannot be *eliminated* by factual reasoning. They do not show that such an alternative is *acceptable;* and even less do they show that it *should be used.* It is bad enough, so a defender of the consistency condition might point out, that the accepted point of view does not possess full empirical support. Adding new theories *of an equally unsatisfactory character* will not improve the situation; nor is there much sense in trying to *replace* the accepted theories by some of their possible alternatives. Such replacement will be no easy matter. A new formalism may have to be learned and familiar problems may have to be calculated in a new way. Textbooks must be rewritten, university curricula readjusted, experimental results reinterpreted. And what will be the result of all the effort? Another theory which, from an empirical point of view, has no advantage whatever over and above the theory it replaces. The only real improvement, so the defender of the consistency condition will continue, derives from the *addition of new facts.* Such new facts will either support the current theories, or they will force us to modify them by indicating precisely where they go wrong. In both cases they will precipitate real progress and not only arbitrary change. The proper procedure must therefore consist in the confrontation of the accepted point of view with as many relevant facts as possible. The exclusion of alternatives is then required for reasons of expediency: Their invention not only does not help, but it even hinders progress by absorbing time and manpower that could be devoted to better things. And the function of the consistency condition lies precisely in this. It eliminates such fruitless discussion and it forces the scientist to concentrate on the facts which, after all, are the only acceptable judges of a theory. This is how the practicing scientist will defend his concentration on a single theory to the exclusion of all empirically possible alternatives.[17]

It is worthwhile repeating the reasonable core of this argument: Theories should not be changed unless there are pressing reasons for doing so. The only pressing reason for changing a theory is disagreement with facts. Discussion of incompatible facts will therefore lead to progress. Discussion of incompatible alternatives will not. Hence, it is sound procedure to increase the number of relevant facts. It is not sound procedure to increase the number of factually adequate, but incompatible alternatives. One might wish to add that formal improvements such as increase of elegance, simplicity, generality, and coherence should not be excluded. But once these improvements have been carried out, the collection of facts for the purpose of test seems indeed to be the only thing left to the scientist.

And this it is—provided these facts *exist, and are available independently of whether or not one considers alternatives to the theory to be tested*. This assumption on which the validity of the argument in the last section depends in a most decisive manner I shall call the assumption of the relative autonomy of facts, or the autonomy principle. It is not asserted by this principle that the discovery and description of facts is independent of *all* theorizing. But it *is* asserted that the facts which belong to the empirical content of some theory are available whether or not one considers alternatives to *this* theory. I am not aware that this very important assumption has ever been explicitly formulated as a separate postulate of the empirical method. However, it is clearly implied in almost all investigations which deal with questions of confirmation and test. All these investigations use a model in which a *single* theory is compared with a class of facts (or observation statements) which are assumed to be 'given' somehow. I submit that this is much too simple a picture of the actual situation. Facts and theories are much more intimately connected than is admitted by the autonomy principle. Not only is the description of every single fact dependent on *some* theory (which may, of course, be very different from the theory to be tested). There exist also facts which cannot be unearthed except with the help of alternatives to the theory to be tested, and which become unavailable as soon as such alternatives are excluded. This suggests that the methodological unit to which we must refer when discussing questions of test and empirical content is constituted by a *whole set of partly overlapping, factually adequate, but mutually inconsistent theories*. In the present paper only the barest outlines will be given of such a test model. However, before doing this I want to discuss an example which shows very clearly the function of alternatives in the discovery of facts.

As is well known, the Brownian particle is a perpetual motion machine of the second kind and its existence refutes the phenomenological second law. It therefore belongs to the domain of relevant facts for this law. Now, could this relation between the law and the Brownian particle have been discovered in a *direct* manner, i.e., could it have been discovered by an investigation of the observational consequences of the phenomenological theory that did not make use of an alternative account of heat? This question is readily divided into two: (1) Could the *relevance* of the Brownian particle have been discovered in this manner? (2) Could it have been demonstrated that it actually *refutes* the second law? The answer to the first question is that we do not know. It is impossible to say what would have happened had the kinetic theory not been considered by some physicists. It is my guess, however, that in this case the Brownian particle would have been regarded as an oddity much in the same way in which some of the late Professor Ehrenhaft's astounding effects[18] are regarded as an oddity, and that it would not have been given the decisive position it assumes in contemporary theory. The answer to the second question is simply—No. Consider what the discovery of the inconsistency between the Brownian particle and the second law would have required! It would have required (a) measurement of the exact *motion* of the particle in order to ascertain the changes of its kinetic energy plus the energy spent on overcoming the resistance of the fluid; and (b) it would have required precise measurements of temperature and heat transfer in the surrounding medium in order to ascertain that any loss occurring here was indeed compensated by the increase of the energy of the moving particle and the work done against the fluid. Such measurements are beyond experimental possibilities (cf. Fürth). Neither is it possible to make precise measurements of the heat transfer; nor can the path of the particle be investigated with the desired precision. Hence a 'direct' refutation of the second law that considers only the phenomenological theory and the 'facts' of Brownian motion is impossible. And, as is well known, the actual refutation was brought about in a very different manner. It was brought about via the kinetic theory and Einstein's utilization of it in the calculation of the statistical properties of the Brownian motion.[19] In the course of this procedure the phenomenological theory (T') was incorporated into the wider context of statistical physics (T̄) *in such a manner that the consistency condition was violated;* and *then* a crucial experiment was staged (investigations of Svedberg and Perrin).

It seems to me that this example is typical for the relation between fairly general theories, or points of view, and 'the facts.' Both the relevance and the refuting character of many very decisive facts can be established only with the help of other theories which, although factually adequate, are yet not in agreement with the view to be tested. This being the case, the production of such refuting facts may have to be preceded by the invention and articulation of alternatives to that view. Empiricism demands that the empirical content of whatever knowledge we possess be increased as much as possible. Hence *the invention of alternatives in addition to the view that stands in the center of discussion constitutes an essential part of the empirical method.* Conversely, the fact that the consistency condition eliminates alternatives now shows it to be in disagreement with empiricism and not only with scientific practice. By excluding valuable tests it decreases the empirical content of the theories which are permitted to remain (and which, as we have indicated above, will usually be the theories which have been there first); and it especially decreases the number of those facts which could show their limitations. This last result of a determined application of the consistency condition is of very topical interest. It may well be that the refutation of the quantum-mechanical uncertainties presupposes just such an incorporation of the present theory into a wider context which is no longer in accordance with the idea of complementarity and which therefore suggests new and decisive experiments. And it may also be that the insistence, on the part of the majority of contemporary physicists, on the consistency condition will, if successful, forever protect these uncertainties from refutation. This is how modern empiricism may finally lead to a situation where a certain point of view petrifies into dogma by being, in the name of experience, completely removed from any conceivable criticism.

6. The Self-Deception Involved in All Uniformity

It is worthwhile to examine this apparently empirical defense of a dogmatic point of view in somewhat greater detail. Assume that physicists have adopted, either consciously or unconsciously, the idea of the uniqueness of complementarity and that they therefore elaborate the orthodox point of view and refuse to consider alternatives. In the beginning such a procedure may be quite harmless. After all, a man can do only so many things at a time and it is better when he pursues a theory in which he is interested rather than a theory he finds boring. Now assume that the pursuit of the theory he chose has led to successes and that the theory has explained in a satisfactory manner circumstances that had been unintelligible for quite some time. This gives empirical support to an idea which to start with seemed to possess only this advantage: It was interesting and intriguing. The concentration upon the theory will now be reinforced, the attitude towards alternatives will become less tolerant. Now if it is true, as has been argued in the last section, that many facts become available only with the help of such alternatives, then the refusal to consider them *will result in the elimination of potentially refuting facts.* More especially, it will eliminate facts whose discovery would show the complete and irreparable inadequacy of the theory.[20] Such facts having been made inaccessible, the theory will appear to be free from blemish and it will seem that "all evidence points with merciless definiteness in the ... direction ... [that] all the processes involving ... unknown interactions conform to the fundamental quantum law" (Rosenfeld, p. 44). This will further reinforce the belief in the uniqueness of the current theory and in the complete futility of any account that proceeds in a different manner. Being now very firmly convinced that there is only one good microphysics, the physicists will try to explain even adverse facts in its terms, and they will not mind when such explanations are sometimes a little clumsy. By now the success of the theory has become public news. Popular science books (and this includes a good many books on the philosophy of science) will spread the basic postulates of the theory; applications will be made in distant fields. More than ever the theory will appear to possess tremendous empirical support. The chances for the consideration of alternatives are now very slight indeed. The final success of the fundamental assumptions of the quantum theory and of the idea of complementarity will seem to be assured.

At the same time it is evident, on the basis of the considerations in the last section, that this appearance of success *cannot in the least be regarded as a sign of truth and correspondence with nature.* Quite the contrary, the suspicion arises that the absence of major difficulties is a result of the decrease of empirical content brought about by the elimination of alternatives, and of facts that can be discovered with the help of these alternatives only. In other words, *the suspicion arises that this alleged success is due to the fact that in the process of application to new domains the theory has been turned into a metaphysical system.* Such a system will of course be very 'successful' not, however, because it agrees so well with the facts, but because no facts have been specified that would constitute a test and because some such facts have even been removed. Its 'success' *is entirely manmade.* It was decided to stick to some ideas and the result was, quite naturally, the survival of these ideas. If now the initial decision is forgotten, or made only implicitly, then the survival will seem to constitute independent support, it will reinforce the decision, or turn it into an explicit one, and in this way close the circle. This is how empirical 'evidence' may be *created* by a procedure which quotes as its justification the very same evidence it has produced in the first place.

At this point an 'empirical' theory of the kind described (and let us always remember that the basic principles of the present quantum theory and especially the idea of complementarity are uncomfortably close to forming such a theory) becomes almost indistinguishable from a myth. In order to realize this, we need only consider that on account of its all-pervasive character a myth such as the myth of witchcraft and of demonic possession will possess a high degree of confirmation on the basis of observation. Such a myth has been taught for a long time; its content is enforced by fear, prejudice, and ignorance as well as by a jealous and cruel priesthood. It penetrates the most common idiom, infects all modes of thinking and many decisions which mean a great deal in human life. It provides models for the explanation of any conceivable event, conceivable, that is, for those who have accepted it.[21] This being the case, its key terms will be fixed in an unambiguous manner and the idea (which may have led to such a procedure in the first place) that they are copies of unchanging entities and that change of meaning, if it should happen, is due to human mistake—this idea will now be very plausible. Such plausibility reinforces all the maneuvers which are used for the preservation of the myth (elimination of opponents included). The conceptual apparatus of the theory and the emotions connected with its application having penetrated all means of communication, all actions, and indeed the whole life of the community, such methods as transcendental deduction, analysis of usage, phenomenological analysis which are means for further solidifying the myth will be extremely successful (which shows, by the way, that all these methods which have been the trademark of various philosophical schools old and new, have one thing in common: They tend to *preserve* the *status quo* of the intellectual life).[22] Observational results too, will speak in favor of the theory as they are formulated in its terms. It will seem that at last the truth has been arrived at. At the same time it is evident that all contact with the world has been lost and that the stability achieved, the semblance of absolute truth, *is nothing but the result of an absolute conformism.*[23] For how can we possibly test, or improve upon, the truth of a theory if it is built in such a manner that any conceivable event can be described, and explained, in terms of its principles? The *only* way of investigating such all-embracing principles is to compare them with a different set of *equally all-embracing* principles—but this way has been excluded from the very beginning. The myth is therefore of no objective relevance, it continues to exist solely as the result of the effort of the community of believers and of their leaders, be these now priests or Nobel prize winners. *Its 'success' is entirely manmade.* This, I think, is the most decisive argument against any method that encourages uniformity, be it now empirical or not. Any such method is in the last resort a method of deception. It enforces an unenlightened conformism, and speaks of truth; it leads to a deterioration of intellectual capabilities, of the power of imagination, and speaks of deep insight; it destroys the most precious gift of the young, their tremendous power of imagination, and speaks of education.

To sum up: *Unanimity of opinion may be fitting for a church, for the frightened victims of some (ancient, or modern) myth, or for the weak and willing followers of some tyrant; variety of opinion is a feature necessary for objective knowledge; and a method that encourages variety is also the only method that is compatible with a humanitarian outlook.* To the extent to which the consistency condition (and, as will emerge, the condition of meaning invariance) delimits variety, it contains a theological element (which lies, of course, in the worship of 'facts' so characteristic for nearly all empiricism).

7. Inherent Unreasonableness of Meaning Invariance

What we have achieved so far has immediate application to the question whether the meaning of certain key terms should be kept unchanged in the course of the development and improvement of our knowledge. After all, the meaning of every term we use depends upon the theoretical context in which it occurs. Hence, if we consider two contexts with basic principles which either contradict each other, or which lead to inconsistent consequences in certain domains, it is to be expected that some terms of the first context will not occur in the second context with exactly the same meaning. Moreover, if our methodology demands the use of mutually inconsistent, partly overlapping, and empirically adequate theories, then it thereby also demands the use of conceptual systems which are mutually *irreducible* (their primitives cannot be connected by bridge laws which are meaningful *and* factually correct) and it demands that meanings of terms be left elastic and that no binding commitment be made to a certain set of concepts.

It is very important to realize that such a tolerant attitude towards meanings, or such a change of meaning in cases where one of the competing conceptual systems has to be abandoned need not be the result of directly accessible observational difficulties. The law of inertia of the so-called *impetus theory* of the later Middle Ages[24] and Newton's own law of intertia are in perfect quantitative agreement: Both assert that an object that is not under the influence of any outer force will proceed along a straight line with constant speed. Yet despite this fact, the adoption of Newton's theory entails a conceptual revision that forces us to abandon the inertial law of the impetus theory, not because it is quantitatively incorrect but *because it achieves the correct predictions with the help of inadequate concepts.* The law asserts that the *impetus* of an object that is beyond the reach of outer forces remains constant.[25] The impetus is interpreted as an inner *force* which pushes the object along. Within the impetus theory such a force is quite conceivable as it is assumed here that forces determine *velocities* rather than accelerations. The concept of impetus is therefore formed in accordance with a law (forces determine velocities) and this law is inconsistent with the laws of Newton's theory and must be abandoned as soon as the latter is adopted. This is how the progress of our knowledge may lead to conceptual revisions for which no direct observational reasons are available. The occurrence of such changes quite obviously refutes the contention of some philosophers that the invariance of *usage* in the trivial and uninteresting contexts of the private lives of not too intelligent and inquisitive people indicates invariance of *meaning* and the superficiality of all scientific changes. It is also a very decisive objection against any crudely operationalistic account of both observable terms and theoretical terms.

What we have said applies even to singular statements of observation. Statements which are empirically adequate, and which are the result of observation (such as 'here is a table') may have to be reinterpreted, not because it has been found that they do not adequately express what is seen, heard, felt, but because of some changes in sometimes very remote parts of the conceptual scheme to which they belong. Witchcraft is again a very good example. Numerous eyewitnesses claim that they have actually *seen* the devil, or *experienced* demonic influence. There is no reason to suspect that they were lying. Nor is there any reason to assume that they were sloppy observers, for the phenomena leading to the belief in demonic influence are so obvious that a mistake is hardly possible (possession; split personality; loss of personality; hearing voices; etc.). These phenomena are well known today.[26] In the conceptual scheme that was the one generally accepted in the 15th and 16th centuries, the only way of describing them, or at least the way that seemed to express them most adequately, was by reference to demonic influences. Large parts of this conceptual scheme were changed for philosophical reasons and also under the influence of the evidence accumulated by the sciences. Descartes' materialism played a very decisive role in discrediting the belief in spatially localizable spirits. The language of demonic influences was no part of the new conceptual scheme that was created in this manner. It was for this reason that a reformulation was needed, and a reinterpretation of even the most common 'observational' statements. Combining this example with the remarks at the beginning of the present section, we now realize that according to the method of classes of alternative theories a lenient attitude must be taken with respect to the meanings of all the terms we use. We must not attach too great an importance to 'what we mean' by a phrase, and we must be prepared to change whatever little we have said concerning this meaning as soon as the need arises. Too great concern with meanings can only lead to dogmatism and sterility. Flexibility, and even sloppiness in semantical matters is a prerequisite of scientific progress.[27]

8. Some Consequences

Three consequences of the results so far obtained deserve a more detailed discussion. The first consequence is an evaluation of *metaphysics* which differs significantly from the standard empirical attitude. As is well known, there are empiricists who demand that science start from observable facts and proceed by generalization, and who refuse the admittance of metaphysical ideas at any point of this procedure. For them, only a system of thought that has been built up in a purely inductive fashion can claim to be genuine knowledge. Theories which are partly metaphysical, or 'hypothetical,' are suspect, and are best not used at all. This attitude has been formulated most clearly by Newton (see Cohen) in his reply to Pardies' second letter concerning the theory of colors:

if the possibility of hypotheses is to be the test of truth and reality of things, I see not how certainty can be obtained in any science; since numerous hypotheses may be devised, which shall seem to overcome new difficulties.

This radical position, which clearly depends on the demand for a theoretical monism, is no longer as popular as it used to be. It is now granted that metaphysical considerations may be of importance when the task is to *invent* a new physical theory; such invention, so it is admitted, is a more or less irrational act containing the most diverse components. Some of these components are, and perhaps must be, metaphysical ideas. However, it is also pointed out that as soon as the theory has been developed in a formally satisfactory fashion and has received sufficient confirmation to be regarded as empirically successful, it is pointed out that in the very same moment it can *and must* forget its metaphysical past; metaphysical speculation must *now* be replaced by empirical argument.

On the one side I would like to emphasize [writes Ernst Mach *on this point*[28]] *that* every and any *idea is admissible as a means for research, provided it is helpful; still, it must be pointed out, on the other side, that it is very necessary from time to time to free the presentation of the* results *of research from all inessential additions.*

This means that empirical considerations are still given the upper hand over metaphysical reasoning. Especially in the case of an inconsistency between metaphysics and some highly confirmed empirical theory it will be decided, *as a matter of course,* that the theory or the result of observation must stay, and that the metaphysical system must go. A very simple example is the way in which materialism is being judged by some of its opponents. For a materialist the world consists of material particles moving in space, of collections of such particles. Sensations, as introspected by human beings, do not look like collections of particles, and their observed existence is therefore assumed to refute and thereby to remove the metaphysical doctrine of materialism. Another example which I have analyzed in "Problems of Microphysics" is the attempt to eliminate certain very general ideas concerning the nature of microentities on the basis of the remark that they are inconsistent "with an immense body of experience" and that "to object to a lesson of experience by appealing to metaphysical preconceptions is unscientific" (Rosenfeld).

The methodology developed in the present paper leads to a very different evaluation of metaphysics. Metaphysical systems are scientific theories in their most primitive stage. If they *contradict* a well-confirmed point of view, then this indicates their usefulness as an alternative to this point of view. Alternatives are needed for the purpose of criticism. Hence, metaphysical systems which contradict observational results or well-confirmed theories *are most welcome* starting points of such criticism. Far from being misfired attempts at anticipating, or circumventing, empirical research which were deservedly exposed by a reference to experience, they are the only means at our disposal for examining those parts of our knowledge which have already become observational and which are therefore inaccessible to a criticism 'on the basis of observation.'

A second consequence is that a new attitude has to be adopted with respect to the *problem of induction*. This problem consists in the question of what justification there is for asserting the truth of a statement S given the truth of another statement, S', whose content is smaller than the content of S. It may be taken for granted that those who want to justify the truth of S also assume that after the justification the truth of S will be *known*. Knowledge to the effect that S implies the *stability* of S (we must not change, remove, criticize, what we know to be true). The method we are discussing at the present moment cannot allow such stability. It follows that the problem of induction at least in some of its formulations, is a problem whose solution leads to undesirable results. It may therefore be properly termed a pseudo problem.

The third consequence, which is more specific, is that *arguments from synonymy* (or from coextensionality), far from being that measure of adequacy as which they are usually introduced, are liable severely to impede the progress of knowledge. Arguments from synonymy judge a theory or a point of view not by its capability to mimic the world but rather by its capability to mimic the descriptive terms of another point of view which for some reason is received favorably. Thus for example, the attempt to give a materialistic, or else a purely physiological, account of human beings is criticized on the grounds that materialism, or physiology, cannot provide synonyms for 'mind,' 'pain,' 'seeing red,' 'thinking of Vienna,' in the sense in which these terms are used either in ordinary English (provided there is a well-established usage concerning these terms, a matter which I doubt) or in some more esoteric mentalistic idiom. Clearly, such criticism silently assumes the principle of meaning invariance, that is, it assumes that the meanings of at least some fundamental terms must remain unchanged in the course of the progress of our knowledge. It cannot therefore be accepted as valid.[29]

However, we can, and must go, still further. The ideas which we have developed above are strong enough not only to *reject* the demand for synonymy, wherever it is raised, but also to *support* the demand for irreducibility (in the sense in which this notion was used at the beginning of Section 7). The reason is that irreducibility is a presupposition of high critical ability on the part of the point of view shown to irreducible. An outer indication of such irreducibility which is quite striking in the case of an attack upon commonly accepted ideas is the feeling of *absurdity:* We deem absurd what goes counter to well-established linguistic habits. The absence, from a newly introduced set of ideas, of synonymy relations connecting it with parts of the accepted point of view; the feeling of absurdity therefore indicate that the new ideas are fit for the purpose of criticism, i.e., that they are fit for either leading to a strong *confirmation* of the earlier theories, or else to a very revolutionary *discovery:* absence of synonymy, clash of meanings, absurdity are desirable. Presence of synonymy, intuitive appeal, agreement with customary modes of speech, far from being *the* philosophical virtue, indicates that not much progress has been made and that the business of investigating what is commonly accepted *has not even started.*

9. How to Be a Good Empiricist

The final reply to the question put in the title is therefore as follows. A good empiricist will not rest content with the theory that is in the center of attention and with those tests of the theory which can be carried out in a direct manner. Knowing that the most fundamental and the most general criticism is the criticism produced with the help of alternatives, he will try to invent such alternatives.[30] It is, of course, impossible at once to produce a theory that is formally comparable to the main point of view and that leads to equally many predictions. His first step will therefore be the formulation of fairly general assumptions which are not yet directly connected with observations; this means that his first step will be the invention of a new *metaphysics*. This metaphysics must then be elaborated in sufficient detail in order to be able to compete with the theory to be investigated as regards generality, details of prediction, precision of formulation.[31] We may sum up both activities by saying that a good empiricist must be a critical metaphysician. Elimination of all metaphysics, far from increasing the empirical content of the remaining theories, is liable to turn these theories into dogmas. The consideration of alternatives together with the attempt to criticize each of them in the light of experience also leads to an attitude where meanings do not play a very important role and where arguments are based upon assumptions of fact rather than analysis of (archaic, although perhaps very precise) meanings. The effect of such an attitude upon the development of human capabilities should not be underestimated either. Where speculation and invention of alternatives is encouraged, bright ideas are liable to occur in great number and such ideas may then lead to a change of even the most 'fundamental' parts of our knowledge, i.e., they may lead to a change of assumptions which either are so close to observation that their truth seems to be dictated by 'the facts,' or which are so close to common prejudice that they seem to be 'obvious,' and their negation 'absurd.' In such a situation it will be realized that neither 'facts' nor abstract ideas can ever be used for defending certain principles come what may. Wherever facts play a role in such a dogmatic defense, we shall have to suspect foul play (see the opening quotation)— the foul play of those who try to turn good science into bad, because unchangeable, metaphysics. In the last resort, therefore, being a good empiricist means being critical, and basing one's criticism not just on an abstract principle of skepticism but upon *concrete suggestions* which indicate in every single case how the accepted point of view might be further tested and further investigated and which thereby prepare the next step in the development of our knowledge.

Notes

[1] It is very interesting to see how many so-called empiricists, when turning to the past completely fail to pay attention to some very obvious facts which are incompatible with their empiristic epistemology. Thus Galileo

has been represented as a thinker who turned away from the empty speculations of the Aristotelians and who based his own laws upon facts which
he had carefully collected beforehand. Nothing could be further from the
truth. *The Aristotelians could quote numerous observational results in
their favor.* The Copernican idea of the motion of the earth, on the other
hand, did not possess independent observational support, at least not in
the first 150 years of its existence. Moreover, it was inconsistent with facts
and highly confirmed physical theories. And *this* is how modern physics
started: not as an observational enterprise *but as an unsupported speculation that was inconsistent with highly confirmed laws.* For details and
further references see my "Realism and Instrumentalism," in *The Critical
Approach: Essays in Honor of Karl Popper.*

² One might be inclined to add those who base their pronouncements upon
an analysis of what they call 'ordinary language.' I do not think they deserve to be honored by a criticism. Paraphrasing Galileo, one might say
that they "deserve not even that name, for they do not talk plainly and
simply but are content to adore the shadows, philosophizing not with due
circumspection but merely from having memorized a few ill-understood
principles."

³ It is nowadays frequently assumed that "if one considers the history of a
special branch of science, one gets the impression that non-scientific elements . . . relatively frequently occur in the earlier stages of development,
but that they gradually retrogress in later stages and even tend to disappear
in such advanced stages which become ripe for more or less thorough
formalization." (H. J. Groenewold, *Synthese,* 1957, p. 305). Our considerations in the text would seem to show that such a development is very
undesirable and can only result in a well-formalized, precisely expressed,
and completely petrified metaphysics.

⁴ These essays were published in Volume III of the *Minnesota Studies in
the Philosophy of Science;* in Volumes I and II of the *Pittsburgh Studies
in the Philosophy of Science;* and in *Problems of Philosophy, Essays in
Honor of Herbert Feigl,* respectively.

⁵ See Popper, 1959. The decisive feature of Popper's theory, a feature which
was not at all made clear by earlier writers on the subject of explanation,
is the emphasis he puts on the initial conditions and the implied possibility of two kinds of laws, viz., (1) laws concerning the temporal sequence of events; and (2) laws concerning the space of initial conditions.
In the case of the quantum theory, the laws of the second kind provide
very important information about the nature of the elementary particles
and it is to *them* and *not* to the laws of motion that reference is made in
the discussions concerning the interpretation of the uncertainty relations.
In general relativity, the laws formulating the initial conditions concern the
structure of the universe at large and only by overlooking them could it be
believed that a purely relational account of space would be possible. For
the last point, cf. Hill.

⁶ It has been objected to this formulation that theories which are consistent
with a given explanandum may still contradict each other. This is quite
correct, but it does not invalidate my argument. For as soon as a single
theory is regarded as sufficient for explaining all that is known (and
represented by the other theories in question), it will have to be consistent
with all these other theories.

⁷ For a discussion of these objections, cf. ter Haar's review article in
Reviews of Modern Physics, 1957.

⁸ Cf. the discussions in *Observation and Interpretation* (see Rosenfeld).

⁹ For details and further literature, cf. Section 11 of my paper "Problems
of Microphysics."

¹⁰ E. Nagel, p. 302.

¹¹ Cf. Section 4.7 of M. Scriven's paper "Explanations, Predictions, and Laws,"
in Vol. III of the *Minnesota Studies in the Philosophy of Science.* Similar
objections have been raised by Kraft (Vienna) and Rynin (Berkeley).

¹² For an exposition and criticism of this idea cf. my 'Attempt at a Realistic
Interpretation of Experience,' *Proceedings of the Aristotelian Society,* New
Series, LVIII, 143–170 (1958).

[13] It must be admitted, however, that Einstein's original interpretation of the special theory of relativity is hardly ever used by contemporary physicists. For them the theory of relativity consists of two elements: (1) the Lorentz transformations; and (2) mass-energy equivalence. The Lorentz transformations are interpreted purely formally and are used to make a selection among possible equations. This interpretation does not allow to distinguish between Lorentz' original point of view and the entirely different point of view of Einstein. According to it Einstein achieved a very minor *formal* advance [this is the basis of Whittaker's attempt to 'debunk' Einstein]. It is also very similar to what application of the double language model would yield. Still, an undesirable philosophical procedure is not improved by the support it gets from an undesirable procedure in physics. [The above comment on the contemporary attitude towards relativity was made by E. L. Hill in discussions at the Minnesota Center for the Philosophy of Science.]

[14] In about 1925 philosophers of science were bold enough to stick to their theses even in those cases where they were inconsistent with actual science. They meant to be *reformers* of science, and not *imitators*. (This point was explicitly made by Mach in his controversy with Planck. Cf. again his *Zwei Aufsaetze*.) In the meantime they have become rather tame (or beat) and are much more prepared to change their ideas in accordance with the latest discoveries of the historians, or the latest fashion of the contemporary scientific enterprise. This is very regrettable, indeed, for it considerably decreases the number of the rational critics of the scientific enterprise. And it also seems to give unwanted support to the Hegelian thesis (which is now implicitly held by many historians and philosophers of science) that what exists has a 'logic' of its own and is for that very reason reasonable.

[15] Even the most dogmatic enterprise allows for discoveries (cf. the 'discovery' of so-called 'white Jews' among German physicists during the Nazi period). Hence, before hailing a so-called discovery, we must make sure that the system of thought which forms its background is not of a dogmatic kind.

[16] The indefinite character of all observations has been made very clear by Duhem, Chap. IX. For an alternative way of dealing with this indefiniteness, cf. S. Körner, *Conceptual Thinking*, New York, 1960.

[17] More detailed evidence for the existence of this attitude and for the way in which it influences the development of the sciences may be found in Kuhn's book *Structure of Scientific Revolutions*. The attitude is extremely common in the contemporary quantum theory. 'Let us enjoy the successful theories we possess and let us not waste our time with contemplating what *would* happen if *other* theories were used'—this seems to be the motto of almost all contemporary physicists (cf. Heisenberg, pp. 56, 144) and philosophers (cf. Hanson). It may be traced back to Newton's papers and letters (to Hooke and Pardies) on the theory of color. See also footnote 14 above.

[18] Having witnessed these effects under a great variety of conditions, I am much more reluctant to regard them as mere curiosities than is the scientific community of today. Cf. also my edition of Ehrenhaft's lectures, *Einzelne Magnetische Nord- und Südpole und deren Auswirkung in den Naturwissenschaften*, Vienna, 1947.

[19] For these investigations, cf. A. Einstein, *Investigations on the Theory of the Brownian Motion*, which contains all the relevant papers by Einstein and an exhaustive bibliography by R. Fürth. For the experimental work, cf. J. Perrin, *Die Atome*. For the relation between the phenomenological theory and the kinetic theory, cf. also Smoluchowski and Popper (1957). Despite Einstein's epoch-making discoveries and von Smoluchowski's splendid presentation of their effect (for the latter cf. also *oeuvres*), the present situation in thermodynamics is extremely unclear, especially in view of the continued presence of the ideas of reduction which we criticized in the text above. To be more specific, it is frequently attempted to determine the entropy balance of a complex *statistical* process by reference to the (refuted) *phenomenological* law after which procedure fluctua-

tions are superimposed in a most artificial fashion. For details cf. Popper, *loc. cit.*

[20] The quantum theory can be adapted to a great many difficulties. It is an open theory in the sense that apparent inadequacies can be accounted for in an *ad hoc* manner, by *adding* suitable operators, or elements in the Hamiltonian, rather than by recasting the whole structure. A refutation of its basic formalism (i.e., of the formalism of quantization, and of non-commuting operators in a Hilbert space or a reasonable extension of it) would therefore demand proof to the effect that *there is no conceivable adjustment of the Hamiltonian, or of the operators used* which makes the theory conform to a given fact. It is clear that such a general statement can only be provided by an *alternative theory* which of course must be detailed enough to allow for independent, and crucial tests.

[21] For a very detailed description of a once very influential myth, cf. C. H. Lea, *Materials for a History of Witchcraft*, 3 Vols., New York, 1957, as well as *Malleus Malleficarum,* translated by Montague Summers (who, by the way, counts it "among the most important, wisest [sic!], and weightiest books of the world") London, 1928.

[22] Quite clearly, analysis of usage, to take only one example, presupposes certain regularities concerning this usage. The more people differ in their fundamental ideas, the more difficult will it be to uncover such regularities. Hence, analysis of usage will work best in a closed society that is firmly held together by a powerful myth such as was the philosophy in the Oxford of about 10 years ago.

[23] Schizophrenics very often hold beliefs which are as rigid, all-pervasive, and unconnected with reality, as are the best dogmatic philosophies. Only such beliefs come to them naturally whereas a professor may sometimes spend his whole life in attempting to find arguments which create a similar state of mind.

[24] For details and further references, cf. Section 6 of my "Explanation, Reduction, and Empiricism," *loc. cit.*

[25] We assume here that a dynamical rather than a kinematic characterization of motion has been adopted. For a more detailed analysis cf. again the paper referred to in the previous footnote.

[26] For very vivid examples, cf. K. Jaspers, *Allgemeine Psychopathologie,* Berlin, 1959, pp. 75–123.

[27] Mae West is by far preferable to the precisionists: "I ain't afraid of pushin' grammar around so long as it sounds good" (*Goodness Had Nothing to Do with It,* New York, 1959, p. 19).

[28] 'Der Gegensatz zwischen der mechanischen und der phaenomenologischen Physik,' *Wärmelehre,* Leipzig, 1896, pp. 362 f.

[29] For details concerning the mind–body problem, cf. my "Materialism and the Mind–Body Problem," *Review of Metaphysics,* Sept. 1963.

[30] In my paper 'Realism and Instrumentalism,' I have tried to show that this is precisely the method which has brought about such spectacular advances of knowledge as the Copernican Revolution, the transition to relativity and to quantum theory.

[31] Cf. Section 13 of my "Realism and Instrumentalism."

References

M. Born, *Natural Philosophy of Cause and Chance,* Oxford University Press, New York, 1948, p. 109.

I. B. Cohen, Ed., *Isaac Newton's Papers & Letters on Natural Philosophy*, Harvard University Press, Cambridge, Massachusetts, 1958, p. 106.

P. Duhem, *La Théorie Physique: Son Objet, Sa Structure*, Paris, 1914, Chapters IX and X. See also K. R. Popper, "The Aim of Science," *Ratio*, Vol. I (1957).

A. Einstein, *Investigations on the Theory of the Brownian Motion*, New York, 1956.

P. K. Feyerabend, "Realism and Instrumentalism," in M. Bunge, Ed., *The Critical Approach: Essays in Honor of Karl Popper*, The Free Press, Glencoe, Illinois, 1964.

R. Fürth, *Zeitschrift für Physik*, 81, 143–162 (1933).

N. R. Hanson, "Five Cautions for the Copenhagen Critics," *Philosophy of Science*, XXVI, 325–337 (1959).

W. Heisenberg, *Physics and Philosophy*, New York, 1958, p. 44.

C. G. Hempel, "Studies in the Logic of Explanation," reprinted in H. Feigl and M. Brodbeck, Eds., *Readings in the Philosophy of Science*, New York, 1953, p. 321.

E. L. Hill, "Quantum Physics and the Relativity Theory," in H. Feigl and G. Maxwell, Eds., *Current Issues in the Philosophy of Science*, Holt, Rinehart and Winston, New York, 1961.

T. Kuhn, *Structure of Scientific Revolutions*, University of Chicago Press, Chicago, 1962.

E. Mach, *Wärmelehre*, Leipzig, 1897, p. 364.

E. Mach, *Zwei Aufsaetze*, Leipzig, 1912.

E. Nagel, "The Meaning of Reduction in the Natural Sciences," reprinted in A. C. Danto and S. Morgenbesser, Eds., *Philosophy of Science*, New York, 1960, p. 301.

Oeuvres de Marie Smoluchowski, Cracouvie, 1927, Vol. II, pp. 226 ff., 316 ff., 462 ff., and 530 ff.

J. Perrin, *Die Atome*, Leipzig, 1920.

K. R. Popper, *The Open Society and Its Enemies*, Princeton University Press, Princeton, New Jersey, 1953.

K. R. Popper, "Irreversibility, or, Entropy since 1905," *British Journal for the Philosophy of Science*, VIII, 151 (1957).

K. R. Popper, *Logic of Scientific Discovery*, New York, 1959, Section 12. This is a translation of his *Logik der Forschung* published in 1935.

L. Rosenfeld, "Misunderstandings about the Foundations of the Quantum Theory," in *Observation and Interpretation*, London, 1957, p. 42.

M. v. Smoluchowski, "Experimentell nachwiesbare, der üblichen Thermodynamik widersprechende Molekularphanomene," *Physikalische Zeitschrift*, XIII, 1069 (1912).

9. Thomas S. Kuhn

Incommensurability and Paradigms

194   At last we arrive at the central constellation of issues which
separate me from most of my critics. I regret the length of the
journey to this point but accept only partial responsibility for
the brush that has had to be cleared from the path. Unfortunately, the necessity of relegating these issues to my concluding section results in a relatively cursory and dogmatic treatment. I can hope only to isolate some aspects of my viewpoint
which my critics have generally missed or dismissed and to
provide motives for further reading and discussion.

The point-by-point comparison of two successive theories
demands a language into which at least the empirical consequences of both can be translated without loss or change.
That such a language lies ready to hand has been widely assumed since at least the seventeenth century when philosophers
took the neutrality of pure sensation-reports for granted and
sought a 'universal character' which would display all languages for expressing them as one. Ideally the primitive vocabulary of such a language would consist of pure sense-datum
terms plus syntactic connectives. Philosophers have now abandoned hope of achieving any such ideal, but many of them

From "Reflections on my Critics" by Thomas S. Kuhn in *Criticism and
the Growth of Knowledge,* Imre Lakatos and Alan Musgrave, editors (London: Cambridge University Press). Copyright 1970 by Cambridge University
Press. Reprinted by permission.

[In 1962 Kuhn published *The Structure of Scientific Revolutions* (Chicago:
University of Chicago Press). The book was widely discussed and in 1965
a symposium devoted to Kuhn's position was held in London. The papers
resulting from that meeting compose *Criticism and the Growth of Knowledge*
(in the footnotes here, abbreviated to *CGK*). The final paper of this book is
Kuhn's "Reflections on my Critics." "Incommensurability and Paradigms,"
here reprinted, is the last and culminating part of that paper. As Kuhn's opening lines indicate, in this passage he defends his most controversial theses.
These theses are also the center of his critique of empiricism. Other symposium contributors to whom Kuhn refers in the following selection are Sir
Karl Popper, Paul Feyerabend, Stephen Toulmin, Imre Lakatos, and Margaret
Masterman. Ed.]

continue to assume that theories can be compared by recourse to a basic vocabulary consisting entirely of words which are attached to nature in ways that are unproblematic and, to the extent necessary, independent of theory. That is the vocabulary in which Sir Karl's basic statements are framed. He requires it in order to compare the verisimilitude of alternate theories or to show that one is 'roomier' than (or includes) its predecessor. Feyerabend and I have argued at length that no such vocabulary is available. In the transition from one theory to the next words change their meanings or conditions of applicability in subtle ways.[1] Though most of the same signs are used before and after a revolution—e.g., force, mass, element, compound, cell—the ways in which some of them attach to nature has somehow changed. Successive theories are thus, we say, incommensurable.

Our choice of the term 'incommensurable' has bothered a number of readers. Though it does not mean 'incomparable' in the field from which it was borrowed, critics have regularly insisted that we cannot mean it literally since men who hold different theories do communicate and sometimes change each others' views.[2] More important, critics often slide from the observed existence of such communication, which I have underscored myself, to the conclusion that it can present no essential problems. Toulmin seems content to admit 'conceptual incongruities' and then go on as before.[3] Lakatos inserts parenthetically the phrase 'or from semantical reinterpretations' when telling us how to compare successive theories and thereafter treats the comparison as purely logical.[4] Sir Karl exorcises the difficulty in a way that has particular interest: 'It is just a dogma—a dangerous dogma—that the different frameworks are like mutually untranslatable languages. The fact is that even totally different languages (like English and Hopi, or Chinese) are not untranslatable, and that there are many Hopis or Chinese who have learnt to master English very well.'[5]

I accept the utility, indeed the importance, of the linguistic parallel, and shall therefore dwell for a bit upon it. Presumably Sir Karl accepts it too since he uses it. If he does, the dogma to which he objects is not that frameworks are like languages but that languages are untranslatable. But no one ever believed they were! What people have believed, and what makes the parallel important, is that the difficulties of learning a second language are different from and far less problematic than the difficulties of translation. Though one must know two languages in order to translate at all, and though translation can then always be managed up to a point, it can present grave difficulties to even the most adept bilingual. He must find the best available compromises between incompatible objectives. Nuances must be preserved but not at the price of sentences so long that communication breaks down. Literalness is desirable but not if it demands introducing too many foreign words which must be separately discussed in a glossary or appendix. People deeply committed both to accuracy and to felicity of expression find translation painful, and some cannot do it at all.

Translation, in short, always involves compromises which alter communication. The translator must decide what alterations are acceptable. To do that he needs to know what aspects of the original it is most important to preserve and also something about the prior education and experience of those who will read his work. Not surprisingly, therefore, it is today a deep and open question what a perfect translation would be and how nearly an actual translation can approach the ideal. Quine has recently concluded 'that rival systems of analytic hypotheses [for the preparation of translations] can conform to all speech dispositions within each of the languages concerned and yet dictate, in countless cases, utterly disparate translation. . . . Two such translations might even be patently contrary in truth value.[6] One need not go that far to recognize that reference to translation only isolates but does not resolve the problems which have led Feyerabend and me to talk of incommensurability. To me at least, what the existence of translations suggests is that recourse is available to scientists who hold incommensurable theories. That recourse need not, however, be to full restatement in a neutral language of even the theories' consequences. The problem of theory-comparison remains.

Why is translation, whether between theories or languages, so difficult? Because, as has often been remarked, languages cut up the world in different ways, and we have no access to a neutral sub-linguistic means of reporting. Quine points out that, though the linguist engaged in radical translation can readily discover that his native informant utters 'Gavagai' because he has seen a rabbit, it is more difficult to discover how 'Gavagai' should be translated. Should the linguist render it as 'rabbit', 'rabbit-kind', 'rabbit-part', 'rabbit-occurrence', or by some other phrase he may not even have thought to formulate? I extend the example by supposing that, in the community under examination, rabbits change colour, length of hair, characteristic gait, and so on during the rainy season, and that their appearance then elicits the term 'Bavagai'. Should 'Bavagai' be translated 'wet rabbit', 'shaggy rabbit', 'limping rabbit', all of these together, or should the linguist conclude that the native community has not recognized that 'Bavagai' and 'Gavagai' refer to the same animal? Evidence relevant to a choice among these alternatives will emerge from further investigation, and the result will be a reasonable analytic hypothesis with implication for the translation of other terms as well. But it will be only a hypothesis (none of the alternatives considered above need be right); the result of any error may be later difficulties in communication; when it occurs, it will be far from clear whether the problem is with translation and, if so, where the root difficulty lies.

These examples suggest that a translation manual inevitably embodies a theory, which offers the same sorts of reward, but also is prone to the same hazards, as other theories. To me they also suggest that the class of translators includes both the historian of science and the scientist trying to communicate with a colleague who embraces a different theory.[7] (Note, however, that the motives and correlated sensitivities of the scientists and historian are very different, which accounts for many systematic differences in their results.) They often have the inestimable advantage that the signs used in the two languages are identical or nearly so, that most of them function the same way in both languages, and that, where function has changed, there are nevertheless informative reasons for retaining the same sign. But those advantages bring with them penalties illustrated in both scientific discourse and history of science. They make it excessively easy to ignore functional changes that would be apparent if they had been accompanied by a change of sign.

The parallel between the task of the historian and the linguist highlights an aspect of translation with which Quine does not deal (he need not) and that has made trouble for linguists.[8] Teaching Aristotelian physics to students, I regularly point out that matter (in the *Physics,* not the *Metaphysics*), just because of its omnipresence and qualitative neutrality, is a physically dispensable concept. What populates the Aristotelian universe, accounting for both its diversity and regularity, is immaterial 'natures' or 'essences'; the appropriate parallel for the contemporary periodic table is not the four Aristotelian elements, but the quadrangle of four fundamental forms. Similarly, when teaching the development of Dalton's atomic theory, I point out that it implied a new view of chemical combination with the result that the line separating the referents of the terms 'mixture' and 'compound' shifted; alloys were compounds before Dalton, mixtures after.[9] Those remarks are part and parcel of my attempt to translate older theories into modern terms, and my students characteristically read source materials, though already rendered into English, differently after I have made them than they did before. By the same token, a good translation manual, particularly for the language of another region and culture, should include or be accompanied by discursive paragraphs explaining how native speakers view the world, what sorts of ontological categories they deploy. Part of learning to translate a language or a theory is learning to describe the world with which the language or theory functions.

Having introduced translation to illustrate the illumination that can be had by regarding scientific communities as language communities, I now leave it for a time in order to examine a particularly important aspect of the parallelism. In learning either a science or a language, vocabulary is generally acquired together with at least a minimal battery of generalizations which exhibit it applied to nature. In neither case, however, do the generalizations embody more than a fraction of the knowledge of nature which has been acquired in the learning process. Much of it is embodied instead in the mechanism, whatever it may be, which is used to attach terms to nature.[10] Both natural and scientific language are designed to describe the world as it is, not any conceivable world. The former, it is true, adapts to the unexpected occurrence more easily than the latter, but often at the price of long sentences and dubious syntax. Things which cannot *readily* be said in a language are things that its speakers do not expect to have occasion to say. If we forget this or underestimate its importance, that is probably because its converse does not hold. We can readily describe many things (unicorns, for example) which we do not expect to see.

How, then, do we acquire the knowledge of nature that is built into language? For the most part by the same techniques and at the same time as we acquire language itself, whether everyday or scientific. Parts of the process are well known. The definitions in a dictionary tell us something about what words mean and simultaneously inform us of the objects and situations about which we may need to read or speak. About some of these words we learn more, and about others everything we know, by encountering them in a variety of sentences.

Under those circumstances, as Carnap has shown, we acquire laws of nature together with a knowledge of meanings. Given a verbal definition of two tests, each definitive, for the presence of an electric charge, we learn both about the term 'charge' and also that a body which passes one test will also pass the other. These procedures for language-nature learning are, however, purely linguistic. They relate words to other words and thus can function only if we already possess some vocabulary acquired by a non-verbal or incompletely verbal process. Presumably that part of learning is by ostension or some elaboration of it, the direct matching of whole words or phrases to nature. If Sir Karl and I have a fundamental philosophic dispute, it is about the relevance of this last mode of language-nature learning to philosophy of science. Though he knows that many words needed by scientists, particularly for the formulation of basic sentences, are learned by a process not fully linguistic, he treats those terms and the knowledge acquired with them as unproblematic, at least in the context of theory-choice. I believe he misses a central point, the one which led me to introduce the notion of paradigms in my *Scientific Revolutions.*

When I speak of knowledge embedded in terms and phrases learned by some non-linguistic process like ostension, I am making the same point that my book aimed to make by repeated reference to the role of paradigms as concrete problem solutions, the exemplary objects of an ostension. When I speak of that knowledge as consequential for science and for theory-construction, I am identifying what Miss Masterman underscores about paradigms by saying that they 'can function when the theory is not there'.[11] These ties are not, however, likely to be apparent to anyone who has taken the notion of paradigm less seriously than Miss Masterman, for, as she quite properly emphasizes, I have used the term in a number of different ways. To discover what is presently the issue, I must briefly digress to unravel confusions, in this case ones that are entirely of my own making.

In Section 4 [of "Reflections on My Critics" in *CGK*] I remarked that a new version of my *Scientific Revolutions* would open with a discussion of community structure. Having isolated an individual specialists' group, I would next ask what its members shared that enabled them to solve puzzles and that accounted for their relative unanimity in problem-choice and in the evaluation of problem-solutions. One answer which my book licences to that question is 'a paradigm' or 'a set of paradigms'. (This is Miss Masterman's sociological sense of the term.) For it I should now like some other phrase, perhaps 'disciplinary matrix': 'disciplinary', because it is common to the practitioners of a specified discipline; 'matrix', because it consists of ordered elements which require individual specification. All of the objects of commitment described in my book as paradigms, parts of paradigms, or paradigmatic would find a place in the disciplinary matrix, but they would not be lumped together as paradigms, individually or collectively. Among them would be: shared symbolic generalizations, like '$f = ma$', or 'elements combine in constant proportion by weight'; shared models, whether metaphysical, like atomism, or heuristic, like the hydrodynamic model of the electric circuit; shared values, like the emphasis on accuracy of prediction, discussed above; and other elements of the sort. Among the latter I would particularly emphasize concrete problem solutions, the sorts of standard examples of solved problems which scientists encounter first in student laboratories, in the problems at the ends of chapters in science texts, and on examinations. If I could, I would call these problem-solutions paradigms, for they are what led me to the choice of the term in the first place. Having lost control of the word, however, I shall henceforth describe them as exemplars.[12]

Ordinarily problem-solutions of this sort are viewed as mere applications of theory that has already been learned. The student does them for practice, to gain facility in the use of what he already knows. Undoubtedly that description is correct after enough problems have been done, but never, I think, at the start. Rather, doing problems is learning the language of a theory and acquiring the knowledge of nature embedded in that language. In mechanics, for example, many problems involve applications of Newton's Second Law, usually stated as '$f = ma$.' That symbolic expression is, however, a law-sketch rather than a law. It must be rewritten in a different symbolic form for each physical problem before logical and mathematical deduction are applied to it. For free fall it becomes $mg = \dfrac{md^2s}{dt^2}$; for the pendulum it is $mg \operatorname{Sin} \theta = -ml\dfrac{d^2\theta}{dt^2}$; for coupled harmonic oscillators it becomes two equations, the first of which may be written $m_1\dfrac{d^2s_1}{dt^2}+k_1 s_1 = k_2(d+s_2-s_1)$; and so on.

Lacking space to develop an argument, I shall simply assert

that physicists share few rules, explicit or implicit, by which they make the transition from law-sketch to the specific symbolic forms demanded by individual problems. Instead, exposure to a series of exemplary problem-solutions teaches them to see different physical situations as like each other; they are, if you will, seen in a Newtonian gestalt. Once students have acquired the ability to see a number of problem-situations in that way, they can write down ad lib the symbolic forms demanded by other such situations as they arise. Before that acquisition, however, Newton's Second Law was to them little or no more than a string of uninterpreted symbols. Though they shared it, they did not know what it meant and it therefore told them little about nature. What they had yet to learn was not, however, embodied in additional symbolic formulations. Rather it was gained by a process like ostension, the direct exposure to a series of situations each of which, they were told, were Newtonian.

Seeing problem-situations as like each other, as subjects for the application of similar techniques, is also an important part of normal scientific work. One example may both illustrate the point and drive it home. Galileo found that a ball rolling down an incline acquires just enough velocity to return it to the same vertical height on a second incline of any slope, and he learned to see that experimental situation as like the pendulum with a point-mass for a bob. Huyghens then solved the problem of the centre of oscillation of a physical pendulum by imagining that the extended body of the latter was composed of Galilean point-pendula, the bonds between which could be released at any point in the swing. After the bonds were released, the individual point-pendula would swing freely, but their collective centre of gravity, when each was at its highest point, would be only at the height from which the centre of gravity of the extended pendulum had begun to fall. Finally, Daniel Bernoulli, still with no aid from Newton's Laws, discovered how to make the flow of water from an orifice in a storage tank resemble Huyghens's pendulum. Determine the descent of the centre of gravity of the water in tank and jet during an infinitesimal period of time. Next imagine that each particle of water afterwards moves separately upward to the maximum height obtainable with the velocity it possessed at the end of the interval of descent. The ascent of the centre of gravity of the separate particles must then equal the descent of the centre of gravity of the water in tank and jet. From that view of the problem the long sought speed of efflux followed at once. These examples display what Miss Masterman has in mind when she speaks of a paradigm as fundamentally an artefact which transforms problems to puzzles and enables them to be solved even in the absence of an adequate body of theory.

Is it clear that we are back to language and its attachment to nature? Only one law was used in all of the preceding examples. Known as the Principle of *vis viva,* it was generally stated as 'Actual descent equals potential ascent'. Contemplating the examples is an essential part (though only part) of learning what the words in that law mean individually and collectively, or in learning how they attach to nature. Equally, it is part of learning how the world behaves. The two cannot be separated. The same double role is played by the textbook problems from which students learn, for example, to discover forces, masses, accelerations in nature and in the process find out what *'f = ma'* means and how it attaches to and legislates for nature. In none of these cases do the examples function alone, of course. The student must know mathematics, some logic, and above all natural language and the world to which it applies. But the latter pair has to a considerable extent been learned in the same way, by a series of ostensions which have taught him to see mother as always like herself and different from father and sister, which have taught him to see dogs as similar to each other and unlike cats, and so on. These learned similarity-dissimilarity relationships are ones that we all deploy every day, unproblematically, yet without being able to name the characteristics by which we make the identifications and discriminations. They are prior, that is, to a list of criteria which, joined in a symbolic generalization, would enable us to define our terms. Rather they are parts of a language-conditioned or language-correlated way of seeing the world. Until we have acquired them, we do not see a world at all.

For a more leisurely and developed account of this aspect of the language-theory parallel, I shall have to refer readers to the previously cited paper from which much in the last few paragraphs is abstracted. Before returning to the problem of theory-choice, however, I must at least state the point which that paper primarily aims to defend. When I speak of learning language and nature together by ostension, and particularly when I speak of learning to cluster the objects of perception into similarity sets without answering questions like, 'similar with respect to what?', I am not calling upon some mystic process to be covered by the label 'intuition' and thereafter left alone. On the contrary, the sort of process I have in mind can perfectly well be modelled on a computer and thus compared with the more familiar mode of learning which resorts to criteria rather than to a learned similarity relationship. I am currently in the early stages of such a comparison, hoping, among other things, to discover something about the circumstances under which each of the two strategies works more effectively. In both programmes the computer will be given a series of stimuli (modelled as ordered sets of integers) together with the name of the class from which each stimulus was selected. In the criterion-learning programme the machine is instructed to abstract criteria which will permit the classification of additional stimuli, and it may thereafter discard the original set from which it learned to do the job. In the similarity-learning programme, the machine is instead instructed to retain all stimuli and to classify each new one by a global comparison with the clustered exemplars it has already encountered. Both programmes will work, but they do not give identical results. They differ in many of the same ways and for many of the same reasons as case law and codified law.

One of my claims is, then, that we have too long ignored the manner in which knowledge of nature can be tacitly embodied in whole experiences without intervening abstraction of criteria or generalizations. Those experiences are presented to us during education and professional initiation by a generation which already knows what they are exemplars of. By assimilating a sufficient number of exemplars, we learn to recognize and work with the world our teachers already know. My main past applications of that claim have, of course, been to normal science and the manner in which it is altered by revolutions, but an additional application is worth noting here. Recognizing the cognitive function of examples may also remove the taint of irrationality from my earlier remarks about the decisions I described as ideologically based. Given examples of what a scientific theory does and being bound by shared values to keep doing science, one need not also have criteria in order to discover that something has gone wrong or to make choices in case of conflict. On the contrary, though I have as yet no hard evidence, I believe that one of the differences between my similarity- and criteria-programmes will be the special effectiveness with which the former deals with situations of this sort.

Against that background return finally to the problem of theory-choice and the recourse offered by translation. One of the things upon which the practice of normal science depends is a learned ability to group objects and situations into similarity classes which are primitive in the sense that the grouping is done without an answer to the question, 'similar with respect to what?' One aspect of every revolution is, then, that some of the similarity relations change. Objects which were grouped in the same set before are grouped in different sets afterwards and *vice versa*. Think of the sun, moon, Mars, and earth before and after Copernicus; of free fall, pendular, and planetary motion before and after Galileo; or of salts, alloys, and a sulphur–iron filing mix before and after Dalton. Since most objects within even the altered sets continue to be grouped together, the names of the sets are generally preserved. Nevertheless, the transfer of a subset can crucially affect the network of interrelations among sets. Transferring the metals from the set of compounds to the set of elements was part of a new theory of combustion, of acidity, and of the difference between physical and chemical combination. In short order, those changes had spread through all of chemistry. When such a redistribution of objects among similarity sets occurs, two men whose discourse had proceeded for some time with apparently full understanding may suddenly find themselves responding to the same stimulus with incompatible descriptions or generalizations. Just because neither can then say, 'I use the word element (or mixture, or planet, or unconstrained motion) in ways governed by such and such criteria', the source of the breakdown in their communication may be extraordinarily difficult to isolate and by-pass.

I do not claim that there is no recourse in such situations, but before asking what it is, let me emphasize just how deep differences of this sort go. They are not simply about names or language but equally and inseparably about nature. We cannot say with any assurance that the two men even see the same thing, possess the same data, but identify or interpret it differently. What they are responding to differently is stimuli, and stimuli receive much neural processing before anything is seen or any data are given to the senses. Since we now know (as Descartes did not) that the stimulus-sensation correlation is neither one-to-one nor independent of education, we may reasonably suspect that it varies somewhat from community to community, the variation being correlated with the corresponding differences in the language-nature interaction. The sorts of communication breakdowns now being considered are likely evidence that the men involved are processing certain stimuli differently, receiving different data from them, seeing different things or the same things differently. I think it likely myself that much or all of the clustering of stimuli into similarity sets takes place in the stimulus-to-sensation portion of our neural processing apparatus; that the educational programming of that apparatus takes place when we are presented with stimuli that we are told emanate from members of the same similarity class; and that, after programming has been completed, we recognize, say, cats and dogs (or pick out forces, masses, and constraints) because they (or the situations in which they appear) then do, for the first time, look like the examples we have seen before.

Nevertheless, there must be recourse. Though they have no direct access to it, the stimuli to which the participants in a communication breakdown respond are, under pain of solipsism, the same. So is their general neural apparatus, however different the programming. Furthermore, except in a small, if all-important, area of experience, the programming must be the same, for the men involved share a history (except the immediate past), a language, an everyday world, and most of a scientific one. Given what they share, they can find out much about how they differ. At least they can do so if they have sufficient will, patience, and tolerance of threatening ambiguity, characteristics which in matters of this sort, cannot be taken for granted. Indeed, the sorts of therapeutic efforts to which I now turn are rarely carried far by scientists.

First and foremost, men experiencing communication breakdown can discover by experiment—sometimes by thought-experiment, armchair science—the area within which it occurs. Often the linguistic centre of the difficulty will involve a set of terms, like element and compound, which both men deploy unproblematically but which it can now be seen they attach to nature in different ways. For each, these are terms in a basic vocabulary, at least in the sense that their normal intra-group use elicits no discussion, request for explication, or disagreement. Having discovered, however, that for inter-group discussion, these words are the locus of special difficulties, our men may resort to their shared everyday vocbularies in a further attempt to elucidate their troubles. Each may, that is, try to discover what the other would see and say when presented with a stimulus to which his visual and verbal response would be different. With time and skill, they may become very good predictors of each other's behaviour, something that the historian regularly learns to do (or should) when dealing with older scientific theories.

What the participants in a communication breakdown have then found is, of course, a way to translate each other's theory into his own language and simultaneously to describe the world in which that theory or language applies. Without at least preliminary steps in that direction, there would be no process that one were even attempted to describe as theory-*choice*. Arbitrary conversion (except that I doubt the existence of such a thing in any aspect of life) would be all that was involved. Note, however, that the possibility of translation does not make the term 'conversion' inappropriate. In the absence of a neutral language, the choice of a new theory is a decision to adopt a different native language and to deploy it in a correspondingly different world. That sort of transition is, however, not one which the terms 'choice' and 'decision' quite fit, though the reasons for wanting to apply them after the event are clear. Exploring an alternative theory by techniques like those outlined above, one is likely to find that one is already using it (as one suddenly notes that one is thinking in, not translating out of, a foreign language). At no point was one aware of having reached a decision, made a choice. That sort of change is, however, conversion, and the techniques which induce it may well be described as therapeutic, if only because, when they succeed, one learns one had been sick before. No wonder the techniques are resisted and the nature of the change disguised in later reports.

Notes

[1] In his [1964], Shapere criticizes, in part quite properly, the way I discuss meaning-change in my book. In the process he challenges me to specify the 'cash difference' between a change in meaning and an alteration in the application of a term. Need I say that, in the present state of the theory of meaning, there is none. The identical point can be made using either term.

[2] See, for example, Stephen Toulmin, "Does the Distinction between Normal and Revolutionary Science Hold Water?" in *CGK*, pp. 43–4.

[3] Toulmin, *CGK*, p. 44.

[4] Imre Lakatos, "Falsification and the Methodology of Scientific Research Programmes," *CGK*, p. 118. Perhaps only because of its excessive brevity, Lakatos's other reference to this problem on p. 179, note 1, is equally little helpful.

[5] Karl Popper, "Normal Science and its Dangers," *CGK*, p. 56.

[6] Quine [1960], pp. 73 ff. [This reference is to part of chapter 2 of Quine's *Word and Object*. Selection 3 in this collection is an independently intelligible version of that chapter. Ed.]

[7] A number of these ideas about translation were developed in my Princeton seminar. I cannot now distinguish my contributions from those of the students and colleagues who attended. A paper by Tyler Burge was, however, particularly helpful.

[8] See particularly Nida [1964]. I am much indebted to Sarah Kuhn for calling this paper to my attention.

9 This example makes particularly clear the inadequacy of Scheffler's suggestion that the problems raised by Feyerabend and me vanish if one substitutes sameness-of-reference for sameness-of-meaning (Scheffler [1967], chapter 3). Whatever the reference of 'compound' may be, in this example it changes. But, as the following discussion will indicate, sameness-of-reference is no more free of difficulty than sameness-of-meaning in any of the applications that concern me and Feyerabend. Is the referent of 'rabbit' the same as that of 'rabbit-kind' or of 'rabbit-occurrence'? Consider the criteria of individuation and of self-identity which fit each of the terms.

10 For an extended example, see my [1964]. A more analytic discussion will be found in my [1970].

11 Margaret Masterman, "The Nature of a Paradigm," CGK, p. 66.

12 This modification and almost everything else in the remainder of this paper is discussed in far more detail and with more evidence in my [1970]. I refer readers to it even for bibliographical references. One additional remark is, however, in place here. The change just outlined in my text deprives me of recourse to the phrases 'pre-paradigm period' and 'post-paradigm period' when describing the maturation of a scientific specialty. In retrospect that seems to me all to the good, for, in both senses of the term, paradigms have throughout been possessed by any scientific community, including the schools of what I previously called the 'pre-paradigm period'. My failure to see that point earlier has certainly helped to make a paradigm seem a quasi-mystical entity or property that, like charisma, transforms those infected by it. Note, however, as Section 3 ("Reflections on My Critics" in CGK) indicates, that this alteration in terminology does not at all alter my description of the maturation process. The early stages in the development of most sciences are characterized by the presence of a number of competing schools. Later, usually in the aftermath of a notable scientific achievement, all or most of these schools vanish, a change which permits a far more powerful professional behaviour to the members of the remaining community. On this whole problem, Miss Masterman's remarks (Masterman, CGK, pp. 70–72) seem to me very telling.

References

Kuhn [1964]: 'A Function for Thought Experiments', in Cohen and Taton (eds.): Mélanges Alexandre Koyré, Vol, 2, L'aventure de l'esprit, pp. 307–34.

Kuhn [1970]: 'Second Thoughts on Paradigms', in Suppe (ed.): The Structure of Scientific Theory, 1970.

Nida [1964]: 'Linguistics and Ethnology in Translation-Problems', in Hymes (ed.): Language and Culture in Society, pp. 90–7.

Quine [1960]: Word and Object, 1960.

Scheffler [1967]: Science and Subjectivity, 1967.

Shapere [1964]: 'The Structure of Scientific Revolutions', Philosophical Review, 73, pp. 383–94.

10. Mary Hesse

Duhem, Quine and a New Empiricism

208   As in the case of great books in all branches of philosophy, Pierre Duhem's *Le Théorie Physique,* first published in 1906, can be looked to as the progenitor of many different and even conflicting currents in subsequent philosophy of science. On a superficial reading, it seems to be an expression of what later came to be called deductivist and instrumentalist analyses of scientific theory. Duhem's very definition of physical theory, put forward early in the book, is the quintessence of instrumentalism:

A physical theory is not an explanation. It is a system of mathematical propositions, deduced from a small number of principles, which aim to represent as simply, as completely, and as exactly as possible a set of experimental laws [p. 19].

The instrumentalist overtones of this become clear from the implications of the denial that theories are explanations. For Duhem an explanation is a metaphysical entity, and science should be independent of metaphysics. But this dictum is not intended, as with the positivists, to dispose of metaphysics as irrational or meaningless; it is rather an assertion of the autonomy and dignity of metaphysics as alone capable of expressing the truth of how things are in the world. Metaphysics according to Duhem is not independent of experience, but its methods are not those of science, and its conclusions stand independently of changing fashions in science. Thus it is for Duhem a grave error to interpret scientific theory as itself

From The Royal Institute of Philosophy Lectures, Vol. III, *Knowledge and Necessity* (London: Macmillan and Co., Ltd., New York: St. Martin's Press), pp. 191–209. Copyright 1970 by The Royal Institute of Philosophy. Reprinted by permission.

providing a metaphysics—a global theory drawn from science such as mechanism is not only false, because science outgrows it by its own methods, but also it is not the kind of theory that could ever be true, because it illegitimately uses the methods of mathematical representation of experimental facts to construct an ontology and to give answers to substantial questions about the nature of the world and of man. But only metaphysics, and in particular a religious metaphysics, can do that. The aim of science must be more modest. A non-interference pact must be established between the domains of science and metaphysics.

Duhem was not the first nor the last philosopher of religion to see the answer to teasing conflicts between science and religion in terms of a complete separation of their spheres of influence, but this is not the aspect of Duhem's thought that I want to discuss here. Indeed, if this were all there were to say about Duhem's philosophy of science it would deserve no more than a minor place in the history of positivism. But his extra-scientific preoccupations did not after all mislead him into so crude an analysis of science itself as his definition of scientific theory would entail. He is saved by a discussion of the observational basis of science that is far subtler than that presupposed by later deductivists and instrumentalists, and paradoxically it is a discussion which can be made to undermine the very foundations of the dichotomy of mathematical theory and explanation, science and metaphysics, that his theory of explanation presupposes.

Most empiricist accounts of science have been based, usually tacitly, on the notion of a comparatively unproblematic observation language. It matters little how this is construed—whether in terms of hard sense data, operational definitions, ordinary language, or what not—the essential point is that there are statements of some kind whose meaning as descriptions of states of affairs is supposed to be transparent, and whose truth-value is supposed to be directly and individually decidable by setting up the appropriate observation situations. It is a long time since anyone seriously claimed that the truth of such statements can be known *incorrigibly*, but most eyes have been averted from the consequences of the significant admission of fallibility of even observation statements, and attention has been concentrated on the way in which meaning and truth-value is conveyed to theories, regarded as in these respects parasitic upon observation statements and clearly distinguishable from them. The consequences for deductivism have been proliferation of a number of insoluble and unnecessary problems regarding the meaning of theoretical statements and the possibility of confirming them, and the result has been a slide into instrumentalism in which, in the end, only observation statements and not theories have empirical interpretation. What that interpretation and its significance is still remains unanalysed.

Duhem introduces two important modifications into this type of classical empiricism. They may be expressed as a new theory of *correspondence* and a new theory of *coherence.*

(i) In his theory of *correspondence*, attention is shifted away from the empirical basis of traditional empiricism to the theoretical *interpretation* of that basis. Duhem sees that what is primarily significant for science is not the precise nature of what we directly observe, which in the end is a *causal* process, itself susceptible of scientific analysis. What is significant is the interpretive expression we give to what is observed, what he calls the *theoretical facts,* as opposed to the 'raw data' represented by *practical facts.* This distinction may best be explained by means of his own example. Consider the theoretical fact 'The temperature is distributed in a certain manner over a certain body' (p. 133). This, says Duhem, is susceptible of precise mathematical formulation with regard to the geometry of the body and the numerical specification of the temperature distribution. Contrast the practical fact. Here geometrical description is at best an idealisation of a more or less rigid body with a more or less indefinite surface. The temperature at a given point cannot be exactly fixed, but is only given as an average value over vaguely defined small volumes. The theoretical fact is an imperfect translation, or interpretation, of the practical fact. Moreover, the relation between them is not one-one, but rather many-many, for an infinity of idealisations may be made to more or less fit the practical fact, and an infinity of practical facts may be expressed by means of one theoretical fact.

Duhem is not careful in his exposition to distinguish *facts* from *linguistic expressions of facts.* Sometimes both practical and theoretical facts seem to be intended as linguistic statements (for instance, where the metaphor of 'translation' is said to be appropriate). But even if this is his intention, it is clear that he does not wish to follow traditional empiricism into a search for forms of expression of practical facts which will constitute the basis of science. Practical facts are not the appropriate place to look for such a basis—they are imprecise,

ambiguous, corrigible, and on their own ultimately meaningless. Moreover, there is a sense in which they are literally inexpressible. The absence of distinction between fact and linguistic expression here is not accidental. As soon as we begin
to try to capture a practical fact in language, we are committed to some theoretical interpretation. Even to say of the
solid body that 'its points are more or less worn down and
blunt' is to commit ourselves to the categories of an ideal
geometry.

What, then, is the 'basis' of scientific knowledge for Duhem?
If we are to use this conception at all, we must say that the
basis of science is the set of theoretical facts in terms of which
experience is interpreted. But we have just seen that theoretical facts have only a more or less loose and ambiguous relation with experience. How can we be sure that they provide a
firm empirical foundation? The answer must be that we cannot be sure. There is no such foundation. It must be admitted
that Duhem himself is not consistent on this point, for he sometimes speaks of the persistence of the network of theoretical
facts as if this, once established, takes on the privileged character ascribed to observation statements in classical positivism.
But this is not the view that emerges from his more careful
discussion of examples. For he is quite clear, as in the case of
the correction of the 'observational' laws of Kepler by Newton's
theory (p. 193), that more comprehensive mathematical representations may show particular theoretical facts to be false.

However, we certainly seem to have a problem here, because
if it is admitted that subsets of the theoretical facts may be removed from the corpus of science, and if we yet want to retain
emipiricism, the decision to remove them can be made only by
reference to *other* theoretical facts, whose status is in principle
equally insecure. The correspondence with experience, though
loose and corrigible, must still be retained, and still remains
unanalysed.

(ii) Duhem's theory of *coherence* is indispensable to a satisfactory resolution of this problem. The theory has been much
discussed, but unfortunately not always in the context in which
Duhem set it, with the result that it has often been misunderstood and even trivialised.

Theoretical facts do not stand on their own, but are bound
together, in a network of laws which constitutes the total mathematical representation of experience. The putative theoretical
fact that was Kepler's third law of planetary motion, for example, does not fit the network of laws established by Newton's

theory. It is therefore modified, and this modification is possible without violating experience because of the many-one relation between the theoretical fact and that practical fact understood as the ultimately inexpressible situation which obtains in regard to the orbits of planets. It follows that neither the truth nor the falsity of a theoretical fact or a lawlike relation connecting such facts can be determined in isolation from the rest of the network. Systems of hypotheses have to come to the test of experience as wholes. Individual hypotheses are not individually falsifiable any more than they are individually verifiable.

Quine, as is well known, has taken up both aspects of Duhem's new empiricism. A bare remnant of empirical correspondence is implied by his dictum that 'our statements about the external world face the tribunal of sense experience not individually but only as a corporate body'—for Quine they do face it; how they face it has come in his recent writings to be a question for a stimulus-response psychology (Quine, 1960, 1968). The coherence of our knowledge is also implied, in the very strong sense (which is never explicitly claimed by Duhem) not only that generally speaking hypotheses cannot individually be shown to be false by experience, but that *no* statement can be; any statement can be maintained true in the face of any evidence: 'Any statement can be held true come what may, if we make drastic enough adjustments elsewhere in the system' (Quine, 1953, p. 43). Because it is doubtful whether we ever want to 'hold a hypothesis *true*' rather than highly confirmed or highly probable, and because I do not here want to beg or examine that question, I shall discuss Quine's claim in a slightly more weakened form than is implied by this quotation. The weaker form, which I shall call the Q-thesis, is that

No descriptive statement can be individually falsified by evidence, whatever the evidence may be, since adjustments in the rest of the system can always be devised to prevent its falsification.

It has seemed to many commentators that to replace the observational basis of science with this shifting network is to open the floodgates to conventionalism, and to a vicious circularity of truth-value and meaning which is in effect an abandonment of empiricism. Popper (1959, p. 78), for example, classes Duhem with Poincaré as a conventionalist. But if by conventionalism is meant, as Poincaré apparently intended in regard to the geometry of physical space, that any given total theoretical system can be imposed upon any logically possible experience, then surely to class Duhem as a conventionalist is a mistake. For neither Duhem nor Quine say anything to imply that a total system is not refutable by experience; indeed that it is so refutable is entailed by their contrast between refutability of individual hypotheses and refutability of the linked system of hypotheses. Once parts of the system have been fixed, perhaps conventionally, there are some extensions of it that are empirically excluded.

But elsewhere Popper (1963, p. 238 ff.) demands something more than this:

We can be reasonably successful in attributing our refutations to definite portions of the theoretical maze. (For we are reasonably successful in this—a fact which must remain inexplicable for one who adopts Duhem's or Quine's views on the matter) [*p. 243*].

The 'holistic argument goes much too far' if it denies that it is ever possible to find out which is the guilty hypothesis. There are, he suggests, three ways in which it may in fact be identified:

(i) We may provisionally take for granted the background knowledge common to two theories for which we design a crucial experiment, and regard the experiment as refuting one or other of the theories rather than the background knowledge. But neither Duhem nor Quine would ever deny this possibility, and it is of course not sufficient to refute Q, since it does not require acceptance of the background knowledge to be anything but *provisional*.

(ii) We may be able to axiomatise the whole theoretical system in such a way as to isolate the effect of a single axiom, which may then be refuted in isolation. But even if we disregard the extreme impracticability of such axiomatisation in the case of most interesting scientific theories, its ideal possibility still does not refute Q, because no axiomatisation can fully account for the empirical applicability of the system, and the correctness of the conditions of application (the so-called 'correspondence rules') might always be called into question to avoid abandonment of any of the axioms.

(iii) Theories need to make successful predictions (to be 'corroborated' in Popper's terminology) as well as being refuted if false. When successful predictions have occurred, Popper seems to suggest, we are more reluctant to abandon those parts of the theory responsible for them, and more willing to locate the responsibility for subsequent refutations in other, less well corroborated parts of the network. Popper's notion of corroboration here as elsewhere is far from clear, but it is difficult to interpret this suggestion in any sense other than in terms of relative inductive *confirmation* of some parts of the system in comparison with others. Some theory of confirmation of the system by experience does indeed seem to be a requirement of the network analysis, and I shall return to this requirement below; but as far as Popper's suggestion goes, he only regards this method of picking out a guilty hypothesis as indicative and not conclusive, and so the method in any case would not refute Q.

The Q-thesis has also recently come under attack from Adolf Grunbaum (1963, ch. 4; 1966). In a series of articles Grunbaum has sought to show that Q is true only in trivial cases in which 'drastic adjustments elsewhere in the system' are construed as allowing *ad hoc* changes in the rules of English usage. Clearly if a hypothesis predicts that roses are red, and they turn out to be black, Q is not satisfied except trivially by interchanging the uses of 'red' and 'black' in observation reports in English. 'Hence', Grunbaum continues, 'a *necessary* condition for the non-triviality of Duhem's thesis is that *the theoretical language be semantically stable* in the relevant respects' (1966, p. 278). He does not, however, claim to give general sufficient conditions for the non-triviality of auxiliary hypotheses or rules which would preserve the truth of a hypothesis H in the face of apparently contrary evidence, nor does he attempt to spell out in detail what it would be for the theoretical language to be 'semantically stable' or for H to remain the 'same hypothesis', arguing only that Quine's suggestion of resort to a non-standard logic must at least be regarded as trivial, as must *ad hoc* changes in the meanings of descriptive terms.[1]

This criticism suggests, therefore, a second requirement for the Q-thesis to be viable, namely some theory of change and retention of *meaning* within the network, in addition to the first requirement of some theory of confirmation.

To summarise these important and pervasive kinds of doubt about the viability of the Q-thesis, it is convenient to quote further from Grunbaum. Discussing Einstein's assertion that any metric geometry can be preserved in the face of any empirical evidence, he says:

Indeed, if the Duhemian is to maintain, as he does, that a total
theoretical system *is falsifiable by observations, then surely he
must assume that the relevant falsifying observations present
us with sufficient relatively stubborn fact to be falsifying. . . .
And if there were no relatively stubborn fact . . . how could
the Duhemian avoid the following conclusion: 'Observational
findings are always so unrestrictedly ambiguous as not to permit
even the refutation of any given total theoretical system'? But
such a result would be tantamount to the absurdity that any
total theoretical system can be espoused* a priori (1966, p. 288).

One could earn a quick point against this passage by remark-
ing a *non sequitur* between 'if there were no *relatively* stubborn
fact' and 'observational findings are always so *unrestrictedly*
ambiguous . . .'. Might there not, one wants to ask, be relatively *un*stubborn facts which were nevertheless not *so* unrestrictedly ambiguous as to warrant the conclusion that any
theory might be espoused as true *a priori?* Neither does it obviously follow that if there is no conclusive refutation, any
theory goes, for there may be available a theory of relative confirmation. More fundamentally, it should be noted that Grunbaum has almost unwittingly fallen into just the habit of distinguishing the theoretical system from the 'relatively stubborn
facts' that are called in question by the Q-thesis. That the facts
are only *relatively* stubborn does not save him, for the whole
thrust of Q is against the practice of looking in the system for
those statements which can, even relatively, form its basis, and
upon which the rest of the system is propped up. 'Relatively'
in this context is always taken in classical empiricist accounts
to imply 'relative to some *more* basic statements which we
could uncover if we had time or necessity'. But the only relativity of stubbornness that can be allowed in a Q-system is
relativity with respect to the *other theoretical* statements. The
structure is mutually supporting. Where the points of external support are applied is a subsidiary matter which cannot be decided independently of the character of the network itself. Grunbaum might well reply that this leaves the
theory completely up in the air, and removes it from empirical
control in just the way he fears. So we are left with the two
requirements of a network theory as constituting problems for
explication:
   (i) That some relative empirical confirmation should be provided, and that without being able to identify any statement of
the system which expresses the evidence incorrigibly.

(ii) That some means of analysing stability and change of meaning in the network should be provided.

2. Criteria of Confirmation

When faced with a philosophical tangle which seems to involve logical circularities or contradictions, it is often illuminating to try to conceive of a mechanism which simulates the conditions of the problem, and to see whether a self-consistent model of it is possible. What we need in this case is a machine capable of representing and theorising about its environment according to the conditions just described. We can distinguish in the usual way between the hardware and the software of the machine: the machine has a certain physical constitution, the hardware, which we will assume remains fIxed (the machine is not at present regarded as a structurally evolving organism), and its software includes a certain system of coding according to which some of its physical states can be represented in its own 'language', and the representation perhaps printed on an output tape, so that the machine is capable of 'reporting' on its environment. Suppose the machine goes through the following stages of operation:

(i) Physical input from the environment causally modifies part of the machine (its 'receptor').

(ii) The information thus conveyed to the receptor is represented in the machine language according to a code present in the machine. We may assume at this stage that the code is not, at least in practice, infinitely and exactly competent, so that (a) if the input is potentially infinitely various, some information present in the receptor is lost at the coding stage, and (b) the mechanism may make mistakes in a small proportion of translation of the input into code. The product of this stage will be called the *coded input* (C.I.), and corresponds to the set of observation statements produced by a human investigator as the representation in language resulting from experienced sensory input. Notice in particular that C.I. is not necessarily a complete or accurate representation of the input.

(iii) C.I. is examined for repetitions which yield inductive generalisations, and for more complex patterns which yield theories. If the machine is inductivist it may run through all possible systems of generalisations seeking that which is in some specified sense most probable or most simple. If it is deductivist it may have a small stock of patterns to try out on

C.I., rejecting those whose fit is too bad, and retaining those whose fit is 'best' or good enough. In either case it is not necessary that the theory arrived at by the machine should be consistent with *every* piece of C.I., only that *most* of it should be consistent. Moreover, *which* parts of C.I. are going to be consistent with the best theory cannot be determined in advance, but only by examining the theory in the light of the complete C.I., and adjusting it to make the best fit. In other words, no single statement of C.I. is incorrigible relative to a good theory, only most of it must be. There are no epistemologically privileged protocol statements, but the element of correspondence which implies an empiricist check on the theory is still present in the whole set of observation statements. Thus the first requirement of the network model of science regarding the possibility of confirmation can be met by providing (*a*) the empirical check or correspondence element present in the whole of C.I., and (*b*) some principles of probability or simplicity of theories which are used as the coherence element to choose the best theory and modify and perhaps discard some small part of C.I.

Does the Q-thesis hold for such a machine? No C.I. statement (say C_1) is logically immune from correction by the best theory or theories, and therefore if some given descriptive statement S is contradicted by C_1, S can in principle always be regarded as unfalsified by taking C_1 to be itself false. But what does 'false' mean here? It cannot mean that C_1 is false as a direct representation of the input, because all that can be known about this is that a certain small proportion of such C.I. statements are false, not which ones. It must mean false relative to a 'best' theory constructed in the light of the whole C.I. and the internal coherence criteria for construction of theories. If these criteria are sufficiently modified no doubt C_1 could be made consistent with some theory which satisfies them, but it does not follow that this could be done according to any criteria which would be accepted as reasonable for a good theory. However, this limitation on the applicability of Q only highlights the importance for judging 'truth' and 'falsity' of what are taken to be reasonable criteria, and indicates that these are not immediately determined by the input, but are in a sense *a priori* relative to that input. They may, of course, possibly be regarded as modifiable in a second order sense in the light of the type of theories which seem to be successful for large amounts of input, but then the principles of modification would presuppose yet higher-level criteria, and so on. I shall not pursue here the problem of specifying and justifying criteria for 'best' theories,

for in the light of current discussion of various kinds of confirmation theory the only thing that is clear is that the problem
is turning out to be unexpectedly deep and difficult, and as yet
hardly rewarding. But it does seem important to emphasise that
some statement of confirmation criteria for theories seems to
be a necessary condition of rebutting the charge that the
Q-thesis effectively abandons empiricism.

It may seem that this requirement contradicts the claim that
is also integral to the Quinean approach, namely that there is
no ultimate distinction between the *a priori* and the *a posteriori,*
the analytic and the synthetic. Quine himself (1968) has recently
willingly accepted that the possession of some 'innate ideas' is
a corollary of his network model of language. This is in reply
to objections by Chomsky (1968), who curiously reads Quine,
not as abandoning empiricism, but as sticking too closely to it in
his analysis of sensory conditioning as the foundation of language learning. There is no empirical evidence, Chomsky
claims, for the kind of language learning Quine seems to require, rather all the evidence we have (which incidentally is
from syntax rather than semantics, and therefore not clearly
relevant to the conditions of applicability of descriptive predicates—but let us take Chomsky for the moment at his own
valuation) points to the presence of innate, interlingual dispositions to certain standard linguistic principles. Quine's acceptance of this point seems motivated rather by desire to conform
to the present state of empirical linguistics and psychology of
perception than by general arguments such as have been put
forward here. Innate principles which are understood merely
as conditions causally operating on sensory data perhaps need
not count for Quine as *a priori* principles which refute his conflation of the prior and the posterior. However, we can hardly
be content with this understanding of the principles. To remain
so would be like accepting a physico-physiological account of
the processes which go on when we do sums, and regarding
this as excluding rational discussion of the logically systematic
principles involved in doing sums correctly. To adapt the
favourite metaphor which Quine takes from Neurath, modifying
parts of the network while relying on other parts may be like
rebuilding a boat plank by plank while it is afloat, but there are
right and wrong ways of doing the rebuilding. To provide a
normative inductive logic in which the innate principles are
systematically explicated does not *preclude* empirical investigations of the scientific and social facts about inductive reason-

ing, but it tells us more about them, by showing why and under what conditions they can be regarded as rational. There is a close parallel here with the programme of rational decision theory, which may be assisted, but is not determined, by empirical investigations of practical decision making. In the sense of a rational inductive logic, then, the innate principles would be *a priori* relative to the data which they process, but this sense need not be objectionable to Quine, since no claim is made about the eternal immutability of the principles—different external conditions may cause adaptive organisms to modify these principles too.

3. Meaning

The alternative possibility of saving S from falsification, which has been dismissed by Grunbaum as trivial, is to so 'change the meaning of S' that it no longer contradicts the evidence. How can we understand in terms of the machine model the demand that meanings shall be stable in order to exclude trivial satisfaction of Q? We cannot directly and immediately apply the usual empiricist interpretation of 'the meaning of S' as the empirical conditions necessary and sufficient for S to have the truth-value true, because the only criteria of truth we have are relative to the coherence of the system as well as to its empirical constraints. Indeed, the truth- or probability-value of S *relative to the current best theory* may change as additional evidence replaces best theory by another, and that without direct observation of the empirical conditions of satisfaction of S. So in this sense the meaning of S, like its truth-value, is not invariant to accumulating evidence. Is such instability of meaning an objection to the network model?

It can certainly be interpreted in such a way as to constitute a *reductio ad absurdum* of any model of science which attempts to retain an element of empiricism, including the network model. It has been so interpreted by several recent writers in the guise of what has come to be called the 'meaning variance thesis' (Hanson, 1958; Feyerabend, 1962; Kuhn, 1962), and since I want to distinguish the network model from this thesis in important respects, I shall start by stating and examining the thesis itself.

The original context of the meaning variance thesis was an attack upon the deductive model of theories with its accompanying assumption that there is a comparatively stable and transparent observation language, upon which theoretical language is parasitic. It is pointed out, first, that reliance on deducibility in the deductive account of explanation of observation by theory, and reduction of one theory to another, is vain, because there is always a measure of approximation in such inferences, and hence it is always possible for the same data to be 'explained' in mutually contradictory forms by mutually contradictory theories. For example, Galileo's law is not a logical consequence of Newton's theory; in fact it is contradicted by that theory, because the law asserts that the acceleration of bodies falling along the earth's radii is constant. It was possible to hold Galileo's law to be true only because this discrepancy was concealed by experimental error. And yet Newton's theory is held to *explain* the facts about falling bodies in spite of contradicting the experimental law which had been accepted up to then as a description of those facts. Again, Newtonian mechanics cannot simply be reduced by deduction to the more comprehensive relativity mechanics, because relativity mechanics entails, among other things, that space and time are mutually dependent and inseparable dimensions, and that the mass of a body is not an invariant property, but a function of the body's speed relative to whatever happens to be taken as the rest frame. Such consequences of relativity are strictly *inconsistent* with Newtonian mechanics. Similar objections may be made to the alleged deductive reduction of phenomenological thermodynamics to statistical mechanics, and of quantum to classical electrodynamics. Many of these examples involve something even more radical than mere numerical approximations. It is meaningless, for example, to speak of Newtonian mechanics 'approximating' to relativistic mechanics 'when the constant velocity of light c is taken as infinite', or of quantum theory 'approximating' to classical physics 'when the quantum of action h is taken as zero', because it is of the essence of relativity and quantum theory that the respective constants c and h are *finite constants,* having experimentally specifiable values. Moreover, in passing from one theory to another there are *conceptual* as well as numerical changes in the predicates involved: mass as invariant property becomes variable relation, temperature as property becomes a relational function of velocity, atom as indestructible homogeneous stuff becomes divisible and internally structured.

Such examples as these lead to the second, and more radical, part of the meaning variance thesis, namely that deducibility is impossible not only because numerical fit between theory and observation is at best approximate, but also because the concepts of different theories are governed by rules of syntax and use implicit in the respective theories, and since different theories in a given experimental domain in general conflict, these rules of usage are in general inconsistent. Hence explanation of observation by theory, or reduction of one theory to another, cannot take place by identification of the concepts of one theory with those of observation or of another theory, nor by empirically established relations between them. We cannot even know that different theories are 'about' the same observational subject matter, for if the meaning of the predicates of observation statements are determined by the theoretical beliefs held by their reporters, and if these meanings differ in different theories, then we seem to have an incommensurability between theories which allows no logical comparison between them, and in particular allows no relations of consistency, incompatibility or relative confirmation.

The thrust of the meaning variance thesis is therefore primarily against the notion of a neutral observation language which has meaning invariant to changes of theory. But the thesis becomes impaled on a dilemma. Either there is such an independent observation language, in which case according to the thesis its predicates cannot be related deductively or in any other logical fashion with any theoretical language, or there is no such observation language, in which case every theory provides its own 'theory-laden' observation predicates, and no theory can be logically compared with any other. The consequences of meaning variance can be put in paradoxical form as follows:

(1) The meaning of a term in one theory is not the same as its meaning in another prima facie conflicting theory.

(2) Therefore no statement, and in particular no observation statement, containing the predicate in one theory can contradict a statement containing the predicate in the other.

(3) Therefore no observation statement which belongs to one theory can be used as a test for another theory. There are no crucial experiments between theories.

A similar paradox can be derived from (1) with regard to both explanation and confirmation.

(1a) The meaning of a predicate in the pre-theoretical observation language is different from its meaning in a theory which is said to explain that domain of observation and to be confirmed by it.

(*2a*) Therefore if the theory entails some observation statement, that statement cannot be the same as any pre-theoretical observation statement, even if it is typographically similar to it.

(*3a*) Therefore no theory can explain or be confirmed by the statements of the pre-theoretical observation language.

That such paradoxes seem to follow from the meaning variance thesis has been taken to be a strong objection to the thesis, and hence strong support for the view, presupposed in the deductive account, that observation statements have meaning independent of theories. On the other hand there is certainly a prima facie case for item (1) of the meaning variance thesis, and the network model itself is committed to a similar abandonment of the theory-neutral observation language. Must the notion of a theory-laden observation language lead to paradox?

First, it may be wondered whether so radical a departure from deductivism as indicated by (2) is really warranted by the argument for (1). Suppose we grant for the moment (1) in some sense of 'the meaning of a predicate' which could be incorporated into deductivism, for example that the predicates of a theory are 'implicitly defined' by the postulates of that theory, which entails (1). Even so, for the paradoxes to go through, a further step is required. It must be shown either (i) that the sense of 'meaning' required to make (2) true is the same as that required for the truth of (1), or (ii) that another concept of 'meaning' is implicit in (2), that for this concept meaning is also theory-variant, hence that (2) is still true, and the paradoxes follow. (i) can be disposed of very quickly. In order to establish (i) it would be necessary to show that the difference of meaning of 'P' in different theories which is asserted in (1) is such as to preclude substitutivity of 'P' in one theory T for 'P' in the other theory T', so that no relations of consistency, entailment or contradiction could be set up between statements of T and T'. If this were true, however, it would also be impossible to speak of the difference of meaning *of* 'P' in T and T', for this formulation already presupposes some meaning-identity of 'P' which is not theory-variant. Hence (1) would be not just false, but inexpressible. What, then, is the relevant identity of 'P' presupposed by the possibility of asserting (1) which will also make (2) false and hence dissolve the paradoxes? Here typographic similarity will clearly not do. We must appeal somehow to the external empirical reference of T and T' to give the meaning-identity of 'P' that will allow substitutivity of 'P' between the theories.

The suggestion that naturally springs to mind within the deductive framework is to take the class of objects that satisfy P, that is, the extension of 'P', and identify the relevant meaning of 'P' with this extension. In pursuit of this suggestion Israel Scheffler (1967, ch. 3) proposes to construe 'meaning' in the classic Fregean manner as having two separable components: 'sense' and 'reference'. (1) may be regarded as the assertion that the sense, or definition, or synonymy relations of predicates differ in different theories, but in considering the logical relations of deducibility, consistency, contradiction, and so on, it is sameness of reference or extension that is solely involved. Difference of sense does not imply difference of reference, hence (2) and (3) do not follow from (1). Thus Scheffler claims to reconcile variance of meaning between theories, and between theory and observation, with invariance of reference and hence of logical relations.

Unfortunately this reconciliation does not work even within the deductive framework. Waiving difficulties about construing sense in terms of definitional synonymy relations, the most serious objection is that 'same reference' is neither necessary nor sufficient for the logical comparability that is required of different theories. It is not *sufficient* because the properties ascribed to objects in science are not extensional properties. Suppose two theories T_1 and T_2 are 'about' two quite distinct aspects of a domain of objects: say their colour relations, and their shapes. It may happen that T_1 and T_2 are such that there is an exact one-to-one correspondence between the sets of predicates of T_1 and T_2 respectively, and that as far as is known T_1 is true of any set of objects if and only if T_2 is also true of it. Then the corresponding predicates of the two theories have the same referential meaning. But this does not imply that the theories are the same. So long as no predicates are added to their respective predicate-sets, no development of T_1 can be either consistent with or contradictory to any development of T_2. In other words, because science is about *intensional* properties, sameness of extension does not suffice for logical comparability. Furthermore, sameness of reference is not *necessary* for logical comparability. Two different theories may make use of different categorisations or classifications of objects: thus Dalton's atoms have different extensions from Cannizzaro's atoms, yet we want to be able to say of some of Cannizzaro's statements that they entail or contradict some of Dalton's.

The network model gives promise of resolving the paradoxes by, first, giving a more subtle analysis of the observation language than that presupposed by deductivism, in terms of which what I have called 'intension' of predicates as well as their extension has a place, and second by allowing a distinction to be made between meanings which are internal to a theory, and meanings which are empirically related. Return for a moment to the observing machine described earlier. We have already noticed that the meaning of descriptive statements is internally related to the best theory and its criteria in something like the way the meaning variance theorists describe. It is also the case that no simple account of the meaning of descriptive predicates in terms of their extension is possible in this model, because all we can know about extension is also relative to the state of the evidence. It may be true or highly probable that P applies to a given object according to one best theory, but false or highly improbable according to another theory adopted on different evidence. There is, however, a relation between machine hardware and input that does remain constant during the process of data collection and theory building that has been described. This is the set of physical conditions under which input becomes coded input. These conditions do not demand infinite exactness nor complete freedom from error, but in what has been said so far they have been assumed sufficiently stable to permit the assertion that a high proportion of statements in the C.I. are true, though we don't know which. This stability is sufficient to ensure that trivial changes of meaning are not resorted to to save theories come what may. Translated into terms of human language-users, this stability does not require that they be aware of some transparent empirical relation between observed properties and linguistic predicates, nor even that they always entertain the same theories; it requires only that by learning to apply predicates in an intersubjectively acceptable manner, they have acquired physical dispositions which are invariant to change of evidence.

To express the matter thus is to invite the comment: does not this kind of stability entail undue inflexibility in the use of descriptive predicates? Do not the meanings of our predicates sometimes change even in this respect under pressure of evidence? In other words, does not evidence also educate our dispositions? It seems fairly clear from the history of science that it does. Consider the predicates 'heavy' and 'light' after Newton's theory had been accepted. It then became incorrect to use the word 'light' of air, and correct to use the word 'heavy', because in Newton's theory all material substances are heavy by definition, even if they can be made to cause a balloon to rise. In such cases there is indeed no substitutibility with retention of truth-value of 'heavy' before and after the change, and so the meaning paradoxes seem to arise. But consider the reason why such a change might occur. In machine terms, we might find that certain applications in observational situations of a given predicate to objects of a certain kind were always contradicted by the best theory for a wide variety of evidence. This would not of course *force* on us a change of disposition to apply that predicate to those objects under the appropriate input, because we expect a small proportion of such applications to be in error relative to the best theory. But if these errors seemed to be concentrated in an unexpected way around certain predicates, we might well decide to change the use of these predicates to fit better the best theories as determined by the large proportion of other observation statements which are assumed true. It might even be possible to state explicit rules for such changes of use and disposition, depending for example on the small probability values of the observation statements involved relative to the rest of the evidence. But all this of course depends on any particular occasion on the presence of many predicates which are not so subject to change of use. The solution of the meaning variance paradoxes requires that there are always many stable predicates when one theory gives way to another.

The possibility of some change of use according to empirically controlled rules shows, however, that Grunbaum's requirement of 'stability of meaning' to save the Q-thesis from triviality is too stringent. Allowing the sort of flexibility of meaning which has obviously often occurred in the development of science need not open the floodgates to apriorism.

4. Summary

In summary let me try to state explicitly the main principles of the new Duhem–Quine empiricism in distinction from the old.

(i) There is no need to make a fundamental epistemological distinction between the theoretical and observational aspects of science, either in regard to decidability of truth-value, or transparency of empirical meaning. The network of relatively observational statements can be imagined to be continuous with a network of theoretical relationships. Indeed much of the recent argument in the literature which has been designed to show that there is no sharp line between theory and observation has depended upon examples of quasi-direct recognition in some circumstances of the empirical applicability of what are normally called *theoretical* predicates (such as 'particle-pair annihilation', 'glaciation'). The corresponding theoretical properties cannot, of course, be directly observed independently of the surrounding network of theory and empirical laws, but neither can the so-called observable properties. The difference between them is pragmatic and dependent on causal conditions of sense-perception rather than epistemological.

(ii) The corollary is that empirical applications of observation predicates are not incorrigible, and the empirical laws accepted as holding between them are not infallible. A whole theoretical network may force corrections upon empirical laws in any part of it, but not all, or even most, of it can be corrected at once. Moreover, there is no way of telling *a priori* by separating the theoretical from the observational, *which* part may need correction in the light of subsequent evidence and theory.

(iii) Corrections may strongly suggest changes in the conditions of correct intersubjective application of some of the descriptive predicates, and these changes may be made explicitly according to rules which presuppose that other predicates are not subject to change on the same occasion. To save the notion of 'same theory' which is required to avoid the meaning variance paradoxes, there must be some such stability, indeed the majority of descriptive predicates must be stable in this sense, but just as we do not know *a priori* which observation statements will be retained as true in the next theory, neither do we know which observation predicates will retain stability of meaning. Had Aristotle been a Carnapian, 'heavy' would undoubtedly have appeared in his list of primary observation predicates, and he would have held it to be observable that air is not heavy.

(iv) To avoid total arbitrariness in adoption of the 'best' theory on given sensory input, some prior principles of selection of well-confirmed theories, and criteria for shifts of applicability of some observation predicates, must be assumed. This does not seem, however, to be an objectionable apriorism in the context of the new empiricism, since it is always possible that these principles themselves might change under pressure of the evidence in second or higher order network adjustments.

(v) Lurking within many of these elements of the new empiricism is a systematic conflation of certain aspects of the epistemological problem with causal mechanisms. This occurs at the point of what has been called 'coding' of the input into the coded input, and the identification of this process in human observers with the causal process by means of which descriptive language has been learned. Doubtless to the old empiricism this is a fatal circularity in the network model, because the question will immediately be asked: How do we know anything about the causal coding and the input it processes except in terms of the usual scientific method of observation and theorising? And if this in turn is subject to the conditions of the network model is not the regress irreducibly vicious? Similar objection, it will be recalled, was made to Russell's causal account of the reception of sense data. But there is a crucial difference between the aims of the new empiricism and those of Russell. Russell, in common with most old empiricists, was looking for 'hard data'; new empiricists accept that these are not to be had. This, incidentally, suggests that the approach suggested here to the relatively prior principles of data processing, via a search for a rational inductive logic, is a better reflection of new empiricism than is the purely scientific search for invariants of language which Chomsky favours, or for psychological and machine models of human learning with which some investigators replace the study of inductive logic. Such empirical approaches are always open to the regressive argument, and leave unanswered the question of what prior principles they themselves depend on. The approach via a rational inductive theory, on the other hand, has the merit of exploring possible rational strategies in possible worlds, independently at least of the details of actual learning processes. But it provides no assurance like that sought by old empiricists, that our knowledge of *this* world is firmly based, only that *if* we were given certain interconnected prior conditions, of whose actuality we can never in practice be certain (for example, that the world is not infinitely various), then we could give reasons for our conscious methods of developing science in a world where these conditions obtain. Duhem might hasten to applaud this conclusion as confirming his view that after all scientific knowledge is superficial and transient compared to the revealed truths of a theological metaphysics. We, who do not have this assurance either, must make do with what we have, a poor thing perhaps, but enough.

Note

---

[1] *Note added in proof:* Professor Grunbaum has now developed these arguments further in 'Can we ascertain the falsity of a scientific hypothesis?', a Thalheimer Lecture, 1969, to be published by the Johns Hopkins Press.

References

N. Chomsky, 'Quine's empirical assumptions', in *Synthese* (1968) 19, 53. [This essay is excerpted from "Some Empirical Assumptions in Modern Philosophy of Language," which is the fifteenth selection in the present collection. Ed.]

P. Duhem, *The Aim and Structure of Physical Theory* (Princeton, N.J., 1906; trans. Wiener, Oxford, 1954).

P. K. Feyerabend, 'Explanation, reduction and empiricism', in *Minnesota Studies,* III, ed. H. Feigl and G. Maxwell (Minneapolis, 1962), p. 28.

A. Grunbaum, *Philosophical Problem of Space and Time* (New York, 1963).

——— 'The falsifiability of a component of a theoretical system', in *Mind, Matter, and Method,* ed. P. K. Feyerabend and G. Maxwell (Minneapolis, 1966), p. 273.

N. R. Hanson, *Patterns of Discovery* (Cambridge, 1958).

T. S. Kuhn, *The Structure of Scientific Revolutions* (Chicago, 1962).

K. R. Popper, *The Logic of Scientific Discovery* (London, 1959).

——— *Conjectures and Refutations* (London, 1963).

W. v. O. Quine, *From a Logical Point of View* (Cambridge, Mass., 1953).

——— *Word and Object* (New York, 1960).

——— 'Replies', in *Synthese* (1968) 19, 264.

I. Scheffler, *Science and Subjectivity* (Indianapolis, 1967).

III

Empiricism and Linguistics

11. Symposium on Innate Ideas

A. Noam Chomsky

Recent Contributions to the Theory of Innate Ideas: Summary of Oral Presentation

230

I think that it will be useful to separate two issues in the discussion of our present topic—one is the issue of historical interpretation, namely, what in fact was the content of the classical doctrine of innate ideas, let us say, in Descartes and Leibniz; the second is the substantive issue, namely, in the light of the information presently available, what can we say about the prerequisites for the acquisition of knowledge—what can we postulate regarding the psychologically a priori principles that determine the character of learning and the nature of what is acquired.

These are independent issues; each is interesting in its own right, and I will have a few things to say about each. What I would like to suggest is that contemporary research supports a theory of psychological a priori principles that bears a striking resemblance to the classical doctrine of innate ideas. The separateness of these issues must, nevertheless, be kept clearly in mind.

The particular aspect of the substantive issue that I will be concerned with is the problem of acquisition of language. I think that a consideration of the nature of linguistic structure can shed some light on certain classical questions concerning the origin of ideas.

From *Boston Studies in the Philosophy of Science* Vol. III, Robert S. Cohen and Marx W. Wartofsky, editors (Dordrecht, Holland: D. Reidel, 1967). Reprinted by permission.

To provide a framework for the discussion, let us consider the problem of designing a model of language-acquisition, an abstract 'language-acquisition device' that duplicates certain aspects of the achievement of the human who succeeds in acquiring linguistic competence. We can take this device to be an input-output system

$$\text{data}\rightarrow \boxed{\text{LA}} \rightarrow\text{knowledge}$$

To study the substantive issue, we first attempt to determine the nature of the output in many cases, and then to determine the character of the function relating input to output. Notice that this is an entirely empirical matter; there is no place for any dogmatic or arbitrary assumptions about the intrinsic, innate structure of the device LA. The problem is quite analogous to the problem of studying the innate principles that make it possible for a bird to acquire the knowledge that expresses itself in nest-building or in song-production. On a priori grounds, there is no way to determine the extent to which an instinctual component enters into these acts. To study this question, we would try to determine from the behavior of the mature animal just what is the nature of its competence, and we would then try to construct a second-order hypothesis as to the innate principles that provide this competence on the basis of presented data. We might deepen the investigation by manipulating input conditions, thus extending the information bearing on this input-output relation. Similarly, in the case of language-acquisition, we can carry out the analogous study of language-acquisition under a variety of different input conditions, for example, with data drawn from a variety of languages.

In either case, once we have developed some insight into the nature of the resulting competence, we can turn to the investigation of the innate mental functions that provide for the acquisition of this competence. Notice that the conditions of the problem provide an upper bound and a lower bound on the structure that we may suppose to be innate to the acquisition device. The upper bound is provided by the diversity of resulting competence—in our case, the diversity of languages. We cannot impose so much structure on the device that acquisition of some attested language is ruled out. Thus we cannot suppose that the specific rules of English are innate to the device and these alone, since this would be inconsistent with the observation that Chinese can be learned as readily as

English. On the other hand, we must attribute to the device a sufficiently rich structure so that the output can be attained within the observed limits of time, data, and access.

To repeat, there is no reason for any dogmatic assumptions about the nature of LA. The only conditions we must meet in developing such a model of innate mental capacity are those provided by the diversity of language, and by the necessity to provide empirically attested competence within the observed empirical conditions.

When we face the problem of developing such a model in a serious way, it becomes immediately apparent that it is no easy matter to formulate a hypothesis about innate structure that is rich enough to meet the condition of empirical adequacy. The competence of an adult, or even a young child, is such that we must attribute to him a knowledge of language that extends far beyond anything that he has learned. Compared with the number of sentences that a child can produce or interpret with ease, the number of seconds in a lifetime is ridiculously small. Hence the data available as input is only a minute sample of the linguistic material that has been thoroughly mastered, as indicated by actual performance. Furthermore, great diversity of input conditions does not lead to a wide diversity in resulting competence, so far as we can detect. Furthermore, vast differences in intelligence have only a small effect on resulting competence. We observe further that the tremendous intellectual accomplishment of language acquisition is carried out at a period of life when the child is capable of little else, and that this task is entirely beyond the capacities of an otherwise intelligent ape. Such observations as these lead one to suspect, from the start, that we are dealing with a species-specific capacity with a largely innate component. It seems to me that this initial expectation is strongly supported by a deeper study of linguistic competence. There are several aspects of normal linguistic competence that are crucial to this discussion.

I. Creative Aspect of Language Use

By this phrase I refer to the ability to produce and interpret new sentences in independence from 'stimulus control'—i.e., external stimuli or independently identifiable internal states. The normal use of language is 'creative' in this sense, as was widely noted in traditional rationalist linguistic theory. The sentences used in everyday discourse are not 'familiar sentences' or 'generalizations of familiar sentences' in terms of any known process of generalization. In fact, even to speak of 'familiar sentences' is an absurdity. The idea that sentences or sentence-forms are learned by association or conditioning or 'training' as proposed in recent behaviorist speculations, is entirely at variance with obvious fact. More generally, it is important to realize that in no technical sense of these words can language use be regarded as a matter of 'habit' or can language be regarded as 'a complex of dispositions to respond'.

A person's competence can be represented by a *grammar,* which is a system of rules for pairing semantic and phonetic interpretations. Evidently, these rules operate over an infinite range. Once a person has mastered the rules (unconsciously, of course), he is capable, in principle, of using them to assign semantic interpretations to signals quite independently of whether he has been exposed to them or their parts, as long as they consist of elementary units that he knows are composed by the rules he has internalized. The central problem in designing a language-acquisition device is to show how such a system of rules can emerge, given the data to which the child is exposed. In order to gain some insight into this question, one naturally turns to a deeper investigation of the nature of grammars. I think real progress has been made in recent years in our understanding of the nature of grammatical rules and the manner in which they function to assign semantic interpretations to phonetically represented signals, and that it is precisely in this area that one can find results that have some bearing on the nature of a language-acquisition device.

II. Abstractness of Principles of Sentence Interpretation

A grammar consists of syntactic rules that generate certain underlying abstract objects, and rules of semantic and phonological interpretation that assign an intrinsic meaning and an ideal phonetic representation to these abstract objects.

Concretely, consider the sentence 'The doctor examined John'. The phonetic form of this sentence depends on the intrinsic phonological character of its minimal items ('The', 'doctor', 'examine', 'past tense', 'John'), the bracketing of the sentence (that is, as [[[the] [doctor]] [[examined] [John]]]), and the categories to which the bracketed elements belong (that is, the categories 'Sentence', 'Noun-Phrase', 'Verb-Phrase', 'Verb', 'Noun', 'Determiner', in this case). We can define the 'surface structure' of an utterance as its labeled bracketing, where the brackets are assigned appropriate categorial labels from a fixed, universal set. It is transparent that grammatical relations (e.g., 'Subject-of', 'Object-of', etc.) can be defined in terms of such a labeled bracketing. With terms defined in this way, we can assert that there is very strong evidence that the phonetic form of a sentence is determined by its labeled bracketing by phonological rules that operate in accordance with certain very abstract but quite universal principles of ordering and organization.

The meaning of the sentence 'the doctor examined John' is, evidently, determined from the meanings of its minimal items by certain general rules that make use of the grammatical relations expressed by the labeled bracketing. Let us define the 'deep structure' of a sentence to be that labeled bracketing that determines its intrinsic meaning, by application of these rules of semantic interpretation. In the example just given, we would not be far wrong if we took the deep structure to be identical with the surface structure. But it is obvious that these cannot in general be identified. Thus consider the slightly more complex sentences: 'John was examined by the doctor'; 'someone persuaded the doctor to examine John'; 'the doctor was persuaded to examine John'; 'John was persuaded to be examined by the doctor'. Evidently, the grammatical relations among *doctor, examine,* and *John,* as expressed by the deep structure, must be the same in all of these examples as the relations in 'the doctor examined John'. But the surface structures will differ greatly.

Furthermore, consider the two sentences:

someone expected the doctor to examine John
someone persuaded the doctor to examine John.

It is clear, in this case, that the similarity of surface structure masks a significant difference in deep structure, as we can see, immediately, by replacing 'the doctor to examine John' by 'John to be examined by the doctor' in the two cases.

So far, I have only made a negative point, namely, that deep structure is distinct from surface structure. Much more important is the fact that there is very strong evidence for a particular solution to the problem of how deep and surface structures are related, and how deep and surface structures are formed by the syntactic component of the grammar. The details of this theory need not concern us for the present. A crucial feature of it, and one which seems inescapable, is that it involves formal manipulations of structures that are highly abstract, in the sense that their relation to signals is defined by a long sequence of formal rules, and that, consequently, they have nothing remotely like a point by point correspondence to signals. Thus sentences may have very similar underlying structures despite great diversity of physical form, and diverse underlying structures despite similarity of surface form. A theory of language-acquisition must explain how this knowledge of abstract underlying forms and the principles that manipulate them comes to be acquired and freely used.

III. Universal Character of Linguistic Structure

So far as evidence is available, it seems that very heavy conditions on the form of grammar are universal. Deep structures seem to be very similar from language to language, and the rules that manipulate and interpret them also seem to be drawn from a very narrow class of conceivable formal operations. There is no a priori necessity for a language to be organized in this highly specific and most peculiar way. There is no sense of 'simplicity' in whch this design for language can be intelligibly described as 'most simple'. Nor is there any content to the claim that this design is somehow 'logical'. Furthermore, it would be quite impossible to argue that this structure is simply an accidental consequence of 'common descent'. Quite apart from questions of historical accuracy, it is enough to point out that this structure must be rediscovered by each child who learns the language. The problem is, precisely, to determine how the child determines that the structure of his language has the specific characteristics that empirical investigation of language leads us to postulate, given the meagre evidence available to him. Notice, incidentally, that the evidence is not only meagre in scope, but very degenerate in quality. Thus the child learns the principles of sentence formation and sentence interpretation on the basis of a corpus of data that consists, in large measure, of sentences that deviate in form from the idealized structures defined by the grammar that he develops.

Let us now return to the problem of designing a language-

LA Evidence ①

Incorporated in LA.

Process of Proposed LA.

acquisition device. The available evidence shows that the output of this device is a system of recursive rules that provide the basis for the creative aspect of language use and that manipulate highly abstract structures. Furthermore, the underlying abstract structures and the rules that apply to them have highly restricted properties that seem to be uniform over languages and over different individuals speaking the same language, and that seem to be largely invariant with respect to intelligence and specific experience. An engineer faced with the problem of designing a device meeting the given input-output conditions would naturally conclude that the basic properties of the output are a consequence of the design of the device. Nor is there any plausible alternative to this assumption, so far as I can see. More specifically, we are led by such evidence as I have mentioned to suppose that this device in some manner incorporates: a phonetic theory that defines the class of possible phonetic representations; a semantic theory that defines the class of possible semantic representations; a schema that defines the class of possible grammars; a general method for interpreting grammars that assigns a semantic and phonetic interpretation to each sentence, given a grammar; a method of evaluation that assigns some measure of 'complexity' to grammars.

Given such a specification, the device might proceed to acquire knowledge of a language in the following way: the given schema for grammar specifies the class of possible hypotheses; the method of interpretation permits each hypothesis to be tested against the input data; the evaluation measure selects the highest valued grammar compatible with the data. Once a hypothesis—a particular grammar—is selected, the learner knows the language defined by this grammar; in particular, he is capable of pairing semantic and phonetic interpretations over an indefinite range of sentences to which he has never been exposed. Thus his knowledge extends far beyond his experience and is not a 'generalization' from his experience in any significant sense of 'generalization' (except, trivially, the sense defined by the intrinsic structure of the language-acquisition device).

Proceeding in this way, one can seek a hypothesis concerning language-acquisition that falls between the upper and lower bounds, discussed above, that are set by the nature of the problem. Evidently, for language learning to take place the class of possible hypotheses—the schema for grammar—must be heavily restricted.

This account is schematic and idealized. We can give it content by specifying the language-acquisition system along the lines just outlined. I think that very plausible and concrete specifications can be given, along these lines, but this is not the place to pursue this matter, which has been elaborately discussed in many publications on transformational generative grammar.

I have so far been discussing only the substantive issue of the prerequisites for acquisition of knowledge of language, the a priori principles that determine how and in what form such knowledge is acquired. Let me now try to place this discussion in its historical context.

First, I mentioned three crucial aspects of linguistic competence: (1) creative aspect of language use; (2) abstract nature of deep structure; (3) apparent universality of the extremely special system of mechanisms formalized now as transformational grammar. It is interesting to observe that these three aspects of language are discussed in the rationalist philosophy of the 17th century and its aftermath, and that the linguistic theories that were developed within the framework of this discussion are, in essence, theories of transformational grammar.

Consequently, it would be historically accurate to describe the views regarding language structure just outlined as a rationalist conception of the nature of language. Furthermore, I employed it, again, in the classical fashion, to support what might fairly be called a rationalist conception of acquisition of knowledge, if we take the essence of this view to be that the general character of knowledge, the categories in which it is expressed or internally represented, and the basic principles that underlie it, are determined by the nature of the mind. In our case, the schematism assigned as an innate property to the language-acquisition device determines the form of knowledge (in one of the many traditional senses of 'form'). The role of experience is only to cause the innate schematism to be activated, and then to be differentiated and specified in a particular manner.

In sharp contrast to the rationalist view, we have the classical empiricist assumption that what is innate is (1) certain elementary mechanisms of peripheral processing (a receptor system), and (2) certain analytical mechanisms or inductive principles or mechanisms of association. What is assumed is that a preliminary analysis of experience is provided by the peripheral processing mechanisms and that one's concepts and knowledge, beyond this, are acquired by application of the innate inductive principles to this initially analyzed experience. Thus only the procedures and mechansms for acquisition of knowledge constitute an innate property. In the case of language-acquisition, there has been much empiricist speculation about what these mechanisms may be, but the only relatively clear attempt to work out some specific account of them is in modern structural linguistics, which has attempted to elaborate a system of inductive analytic procedures of segmentation and classification that can be applied to data to determine a grammar. It is conceivable that these methods might be somehow refined to the point where they can provide the surface structures of many utterances. It is quite inconceivable that they can be developed to the point where they can provide deep structures or the abstract principles that generate deep structures and relate them to surface structures. This is not a matter of further refinement, but of an entirely different approach to the question. Similarly, it is difficult to imagine how the vague suggestions about conditioning and associative nets that one finds in philosophical and psychological speculations of an empiricist cast might be refined or elaborated so as to provide for attested competence. A system of rules for generating deep structures and relating them to surface structures, in the manner characteristic of natural language, simply does not have the properties of an associative net or a habit family; hence no elaboration of principles for developing such structures can be appropriate to the problem of designing a language-acquisition device.

I have said nothing explicit so far about the doctrine that there are innate ideas and innate principles of various kinds that determine the character of what can be known in what may be a rather restricted and highly organized way. In the traditional view a condition for these innate mechanisms to become activated is that appropriate stimulation must be presented. This stimulation provides the occasion for the mind to apply certain innate interpretive principles, certain concepts that proceed from 'the power of understanding' itself, from the faculty of thinking rather than from external objects. To take a typical example from Descartes (Reply to Objections, V): "... When first in infancy we see a triangular figure depicted on paper, this figure cannot show us how a real triangle ought to be conceived, in the way in which geometricians consider it, because the true triangle is contained in this figure, just as the statue of Mercury is contained in a rough block of wood. But because we already possess within us the idea of a true triangle, and it can be more easily conceived by our mind than the more complex figure of the triangle drawn on paper, we, therefore, when we see the composite figure, apprehend not it itself, but rather the authentic triangle" (Haldane and Ross, vol. II, p. 227). In this sense, the idea of triangle is innate. For Leibniz what is innate is certain principles (in general, unconscious), that "enter into our thoughts, of which they form the soul and the connection". "Ideas and truths are for us innate as inclinations, dispositions, habits, or natural potentialities." Experience serves to elicit, not to form, these innate structures. Similar views are elaborated at length in rationalist speculative psychology.

It seems to me that the conclusions regarding the nature of language acquisition, discussed above, are fully in accord with the doctrine of innate ideas, so understood, and can be regarded as providing a kind of substantiation and further development of this doctrine. Of course, such a proposal raises nontrivial questions of historical interpretation.

What does seem to me fairly clear is that the present situation with regard to the study of language learning, and other aspects of human intellectual achievement of comparable intricacy, is essentially this. We have a certain amount of evidence about the grammars that must be the output of an acquisition model. This evidence shows clearly that knowledge of language cannot arise by application of step-by-step inductive operations (segmentation, classification, substitution procedures, 'analogy', association, conditioning, and so on) of any sort that have been developed or discussed within linguistics, psychology, or philosophy. Further empiricist speculations contribute nothing that even faintly suggests a way of overcoming the intrinsic limitations of the methods that have so far been proposed and elaborated. Furthermore, there are no other grounds for pursuing these empiricist speculations, and avoiding what would be the normal assumption, unprejudiced by doctrine, that one would formulate if confronted with empirical evidence of the sort sketched above. There is, in particular, nothing known in psychology or physiology that suggests that the empiricist approach is well-motivated, or that gives any grounds for skepticism concerning the rationalist alternative sketched above.

For further discussion of the question of historical interpretation, see Chomsky, *Aspects of the Theory of Syntax* (1965), ch. 1, and *Cartesian Linguistics* (1966). For further discussion of matters touched on here, see also Chomsky, 'Explanatory

Models in Linguistics', in *Logic, Methodology and Philosophy of Science,* ed. by E. Nagel, P. Suppes, and A. Tarski (1962); J. Katz, *The Philosophy of Language* (1966); P. M. Postal, Review of A. Martinet, *Elements of General Linguistics* (forthcoming); and the selections in section VI of *The Structure of Language, Readings in the Philosophy of Language,* ed. by J. Fodor and J. Katz (1964).

B. Hilary Putnam

The 'Innateness Hypothesis' and Explanatory Models in Linguistics

I. The Innateness Hypothesis

The 'innateness hypothesis' (henceforth, the 'I.H.') is a daring—or apparently daring; it may be meaningless, in which case it is not daring—hypothesis proposed by Noam Chomsky. I owe a debt of gratitude to Chomsky for having repeatedly exposed me to the I.H.; I have relied heavily in what follows on oral communications from him; and I beg his pardon in advance if I misstate the I.H. in any detail, or misrepresent any of the arguments for it. In addition to relying upon oral communications from Chomsky, I have also relied upon Chomsky's paper 'Explanatory Models in Linguistics', in which the I.H. plays a considerable rôle.

To begin, then, the I.H. is the hypothesis that the human brain is 'programmed' at birth in some quite *specific* and *structured* aspects of human natural language. The details of this programming are spelled out in some detail in 'Explanatory Models in Linguistics'. We should assume that the speaker has 'built in'[1] a function which assigns weights to the grammars G_1, G_2, G_3, ... in a certain class Σ of transformational grammars. Σ is not the class of all *possible* transformational grammars; rather all the members of Σ have some quite strong similarities. These similarities appear as 'linguistic universals'— i.e., as characteristics of *all* human natural languages. If intelligent non-terrestrial life—say, Martians—exists, and if the 'Martians' speak a language whose grammar does not belong to the subclass Σ of the class of all transformational grammars, then, I have heard Chomsky maintain, humans (except possibly for a few geniuses or linguistic experts) would be unable to learn Martian; a human child brought up by Martians would fail to acquire language; and Martians would, conversely, experience similar difficulties with human tongues. (Possible difficulties in *pronunciation* are not at issue here, and may be assumed *not* to exist for the purposes of this argument.) As examples of the similarities that all grammars of the subclass Σ are thought to possess (above the level of phonetics), we may mention the *active-passive* distinction, the existence of a *non-phrase-structure* portion of the grammar, the presence of such major categories as *concrete noun, verb taking an abstract subject,* etc. The project of delimiting the class Σ may also be described as the project of defining a *normal form for grammars.* Conversely, according to Chomsky, any non-trivial normal form for grammars, such that correct and perspicuous grammars of all human languages can and should be written in that normal form, "constitutes, in effect, a hypothesis concerning the innate intellectual equipment of the child".[2]

Given such a highly *restricted* class Σ of grammars (highly restricted in the sense that grammars not in the class are perfectly conceivable, not more 'complicated' in any absolute sense than grammars in the class, and may well be employed by non-human speakers, if such there be), the performance of the human child in learning his native language may be understood as follows, according to Chomsky. He may be thought of as operating on the following 'inputs'[3]: a list of utterances, containing both grammatical and ungrammatical sentences; a list of corrections, which enable him to classify the input utterances *as* grammatical or ungrammatical; and some information concerning which utterances count as *repetitions* of earlier utterances. Simplifying slightly, we may say that, on this model, the child is supplied with a list of grammatical sentence *types* and a list of ungrammatical sentence *types.* He then 'selects' the grammar in Σ compatible with this information to which his weighting function assigns the highest weight. On this scheme, the general *form* of grammar is not learned from experience, but is 'innate', and the 'plausibility ordering' of grammars compatible with given data of the kinds mentioned is likewise 'innate'.

So much for a statement of the I.H. If I have left the I.H. vague at many points, I believe that this is no accident—for the I.H. seems to me to be *essentially* and *irreparably* vague—but this much of a statement may serve to indicate *what* belief it is that I stigmatize as irreparably vague.

A couple of remarks may suffice to give some idea of the rôle that I.H. is supposed to play in linguistics. Linguistics relies heavily, according to Chomsky, upon 'intuitions' of grammaticality. But *what* is an intuition of 'grammaticality' an intuition *of?* According to Chomsky, the sort of theory-construction programmatically outlined above is what is needed to give this question the only answer it can have or deserves to have. Presumably, then, to 'intuit' (or assert, or conjecture, etc.) that a sentence is grammatical is to 'intuit' (or assert, or conjecture, etc.) that the sentence is generated by the highest-valued G_i in the class Σ which is such that it generates all the grammatical sentence types with which we have been supplied by the 'input' and none of the ungrammatical sentence types listed in the 'input'.[4]

Chomsky also says that the G_i which receives the highest value must do *more* than agree with 'intuitions' of grammaticality; it must account for certain ambiguities, for example.[5] At the same time, unfortunately, he lists no semantical information in the input, and he conjectures[6] that a child needs semantical information only to "provide motivation for language learning", and not to arrive at the *formal* grammar of its language. Apparently, then, the fact that a grammar which agrees with a sufficient amount of 'input' must be in the class Σ to be 'selected' by the child is what rules out grammars that generate all and only the grammatical sentences of a given natural language, but fail to correctly 'predict'[7] ambiguities (cf. E. M. in L., p. 533).

In addition to making clear what it *is* to be grammatical, Chomsky believes that the I.H. confronts the linguist with the following tasks: To *define* the normal form for grammars described above, and to *define* the weighing function. In *Syntactic Structures* Chomsky, indeed, gives this as an objective for linguistic theory: to give an *effective* procedure for choosing between rival grammars.

Lastly, the I.H. is supposed to justify the claim that what the linguist provides is "a hypothesis about the innate intellectual equipment that a child brings to bear in language learning".[8] Of course, even if language is *wholly* learned, it is still true that linguistics "characterizes the linguistic abilities of the mature speaker"[9], and that a grammar "could properly be called an explanatory model of the linguistic intuition of the native speaker".[10] However, one could with equal truth say that a driver's manual "characterizes the car-driving abilities of the mature driver" and that a calculus text provides "an explanatory model of the calculus-intuitions of the mathematician". Clearly, it is the idea that *these* abilities and *these* intuitions are close to the human *essence,* so to speak, that gives linguistics its 'sex appeal', for Chomsky at least.

II. The Supposed Evidence for the I.H.

A number of empirical facts and alleged empirical facts have been advanced to support the I.H. Since limitations of space make it impossible to describe all of them here, a few examples will have to suffice.

(a) The *ease* of the child's original language learning: "A young child is able to gain perfect mastery of a language with incomparably greater ease [*than an adult*—H.P.] and without any explicit instruction. Mere exposure to the language, and for a remarkably short period, seems to be all that the normal child requires to develop the competence of the native speaker".[11]

(b) The fact that reinforcement, "in any interesting sense", seems to be unnecessary for language learning. Some children have apparently even learned to speak without *talking*[12], and then displayed this ability at a relatively late age to startled adults who had given them up for mutes.

(c) The ability to "develop the competence of the native speaker" has been said not to depend on the intelligence level. Even quite low I.Q.'s 'internalize' the grammar of their native language.

(d) The 'linguistic universals' mentioned in the previous section are allegedly accounted for by the I.H.

(e) Lastly, of course, there is the 'argument' that runs *"what else* could account for language learning?" The task is so incredibly complex (analogous to learning, at least implicitly, a complicated physical theory, it is said), that it would be miraculous if even one tenth of the human race accomplished it without 'innate' assistance. (This is like Marx's 'proof' of the Labour Theory of Value in *Capital,* vol. III, which runs, in essence, "*What else* could account for the fact that commodities have different value *except* the fact that the labor-content is different?".)

III. Criticism of the Alleged Evidence

A. The irrelevance of linguistic universals.   *1. Not surprising on any theory.* Let us consider just how surprising the 'linguistic universals' cited above really are. Let us assume for the purpose a community of Martians whose 'innate intellectual equipment' may be supposed to be as different from the human as is compatible with their being able to speak a language at all. What could we expect to find in their language?

If the Martians' brains are not vastly richer than ours in complexity, then they, like us, will find it possible to employ a practically infinite set of expressions only if those expressions possess a 'grammar'—i.e., if they are built up by recursive rules from a limited stock of basic forms. Those basic forms need not be built up out of a *short* list of phonemes—the Martians might have vastly greater memory capacity than we do— but if Martians, like humans, find rote learning difficult, it will not be surprising if they too have *short* lists of phonemes in their languages.

Are the foregoing reflections arguments *for* or *against* the I.H.? I find it difficult to tell. If belief in 'innate intellectual equipment' is *just* that, then how *could* the I.H. be false? How could something with *no* innate intellectual equipment *learn* anything? *To be sure,* human 'innate intellectual equipment' is relevant to language learning; if this means that such parameters as memory span and memory capacity play a crucial role. But what rank Behaviorist is supposed to have ever denied *this?* On the other hand, that a particular mighty arbitrary set Σ of grammars is 'built in' to the brain of *both* Martians and Humans is *not* a hypothesis we would have to invoke to account for *these* basic similarities.

But for what similarities above the level of phonetics, where constitutional factors play a large role for obvious reasons, *would* the I.H. have to be invoked *save* in the trivial sense that memory capacity, intelligence, needs, interests, etc., are all relevant to language learning, and all depend, in part, on the biological makeup of the organism? If Martians are such strange creatures that they have no interest in physical objects, for example, their language will contain no concrete nouns; but would not this be *more,* not *less* surprising, on any *reasonable* view, than their having an interest in physical objects? (Would it be surprising if Martian contained devices for forming truth-functions and for quantification?)

Two more detailed points are relevant here. Chomsky has pointed out that no natural language has a phrase structure grammar. But this too is not surprising. The sentence 'John and Jim came home quickly' is not generated by a phrase-structure rule, in Chomsky's formalization of English grammar. But the sentence 'John came home quickly and Jim came home quickly' *is* generated by a phrase-structure rule in the grammar of mathematical logic, and Chomsky's famous 'and-transformation' is just an abbreviation rule. Again, the sentence 'That was the lady I saw you with last night' is not generated by a phrase-structure rule in English, or at least not in Chomsky's description of English. But the sentence 'That is $\iota x(x$ is a lady and I saw you with x last night)' is generated by a phrase-structure rule in the grammar of mathematical logic. And again the idiomatic English sentence *can* be obtained from its phrase-structure counterpart by a simple rule of abbreviation. Is it really surprising, does it really point to anything more interesting than *general intelligence,* that these operations which break the bounds of phrase-structure grammar appear in every natural language?[13]

Again, it may appear startling at first blush that such categories as noun, verb, adverb, etc. have 'universal' application. But, as Curry has pointed out, it is too easy to multiply 'facts' here. If a language contains nouns—that is, a phrase-structure category which contains the proper names—it contains noun phrases, that is, phrases which occupy the environments of nouns. If it contains noun phrases it contains verb phrases— phrases which when combined with a noun phrase by a suitable construction yield sentences. If it contains verb phrases, it contains adverb phrases—phrases which, when combined with a verb phrase yield a verb phrase. Similarly, adjective phrases, etc., can be defined in terms of the *two* basic categories 'noun' and 'sentence'. Thus the existence of nouns is all that has to be explained. And this reduces to explaining two facts: (1) The fact that all natural languages have a large phrase-structure portion in their grammar, in the sense just illustrated, in spite of the effect of what Chomsky calls 'transformations'. (2) The fact that all natural languages contain proper names. But (1) is not surprising in view of the fact that phrase-structure rules are extremely simple algorithms. Perhaps Chomsky would reply that 'simplicity' is subjective here, but this is just not so. The fact is that all the natural measures of complexity of an algorithm—size of the machine table, length of computations, time, and space required for the computation —lead to the same result here, quite independently of the detailed structure of the computing machine employed. Is it surprising that algorithms which are 'simplest' for virtually any computing system we can conceive of are also simplest for naturally evolved 'computing systems'? And (2)—the fact that all natural languages contain proper names—is not surprising in view of the utility of such names, and the difficulty of always finding a definite description which will suffice instead.

Once again, 'innate' factors are relevant *to be sure*—if choosing *simple* algorithms as the basis of the grammar is 'innate', and if the need for identifying persons rests on something innate—but what Behaviorist would or should be surprised? Human brains are computing systems and subject to some of the constraints that effect all computing systems; human beings have a natural interest in one another. If *that* is 'innateness', well and good!

2. Linguistic universals could be accounted for, even if surprising, without invoking the I.H.   Suppose that language-using human beings evolved *independently* in two or more places. Then, if Chomsky were *right,* there should be two or more *types* of human beings descended from the two or more original populations, and normal children of each type should fail to learn the languages spoken by the other types. Since we do not observe this, since there is only *one* class Σ built into *all* human brains, we have to conclude (if the I.H. is true) that language-using is an evolutionary 'leap' that occurred only *once.* But in that case, it is overwhelmingly likely that all human languages are descended from a single original language, and that the existence today of what are called 'unrelated' languages is accounted for by the great lapse of time and by countless historical changes. This is, indeed, likely even if the I.H. is false, since the human race itself is now generally believed to have resulted from a single evolutionary 'leap', and since the human population was extremely small and concentrated for millennia, and only gradually spread from Asia to other continents. Thus, even if language using was learned or invented rather than 'built in', or even if only some general dispositions in the direction of language using are 'built in'[14], it is likely that some one group of humans first developed language as we know it, and then spread this through conquest or imitation to the rest of the human population. Indeed, we do know that this is just how *alphabetic* writing spread. In any case, I repeat, this hypothesis —a single origin for human language—is certainly *required* by the I.H., but much weaker than the I.H.

But just this *consequence* of the I.H. is, in fact, enough to account for 'linguistic universals'! For, if all human languages are descended from a common parent, then just such highly useful features of the common parent as the presence of some kind of quantifiers, proper names, nouns, and verbs, etc., would be expected to survive. Random variation may, indeed, alter many things; but that it should fail to strip language of proper names, or common nouns, or quantifiers, is not *so* surprising as to require the I.H.

B. The 'ease' of language learning is not clear.   Let us consider somewhat closely the 'ease' with which children do learn their native language. A typical 'mature' college student seriously studying a foreign language spends three hours a week in lectures. In fourteen weeks of term he is thus exposed to forty-two hours of the language. In four years he may pick up over 300 hours of the language, very little of which is actual listening to native informants. By contrast, direct-method teachers estimate that 300 hours of direct-method teaching will enable one to converse fluently in a foreign language. Certainly 600 hours—say, 300 hours of direct-method teaching and 300 hours of reading—will enable any adult to speak and read a foreign language with ease, and to use an incomparably larger vocabulary than a young child.

It will be objected that the adult does not acquire a perfect accent. So what? The adult has been speaking one way all of his life, and has a huge set of habits to unlearn. What can equally well be accounted for by learning theory should not be cited as evidence for the I.H.

Now the child by the time it is four or five years old has been exposed to *vastly* more than 600 hours of direct-method instruction. Moreover, even if 'reinforcement' is not necessary, most children are consciously and repeatedly reinforced by adults in a host of ways—e.g., the constant repetition of simple one-word sentences ('cup', 'doggie') in the presence of babies. Indeed, any foreign adult living with the child for those years would have an incomparably better grasp of the language than the child does. The child indeed has a better accent. Also, the child's grammatical mistakes, which are numerous, arise not from carrying over previous language habits, but from not having fully acquired the first set. But it seems to me that this 'evidence' for the I.H. stands the facts on their head.

C. Reinforcement another issue.   As Chomsky is aware, the evidence is today slim that *any* learning requires reinforcement "in any interesting sense". Capablanca, for example, learned to play chess by simply watching adults play. This is comparable to Macaulay's achievement in learning language without speaking. Non-geniuses normally do require practice both to speak correctly and to play chess. Yet probably anyone *could* learn to speak *or* to play chess without practice if muffled, in the first case, or not allowed to play, in the second case, with sufficiently prolonged observation.

D. Independence of intelligence level an artifact.   *Every child learns to speak the native language*. What does this mean? If it means that children do not make serious grammatical blunders, even by the standards of descriptive as opposed to prescriptive grammar, this is just not true for the young child. By nine or ten years of age this has ceased to happen, perhaps (I speak as a parent), but nine or ten years is enough time to become pretty darn good at *anything*. What is more serious is what 'grammar' *means* here. It does not include mastery of vocabulary, in which even many adults are deficient, nor ability to understand *complex* constructions, in which many adults are *also* deficient. It means purely and simply the ability to learn what every normal adult learns. What this 'argument' reduces to is "Wow! How complicated a skill every normal adult learns. What else could it be but *innate*." Like the preceding argument, it reduces to the 'What Else' argument.

But what of the 'What Else?' argument? Just how impressed should we be by the failure of current learning theories to account for complex learning processes such as those involved in the learning of language? If Innateness were a *general* solution, perhaps we should be impressed. But the I.H. *cannot,* by its very nature, *be* generalized to handle all complex learning processes. Consider the following puzzle (called 'jump'):

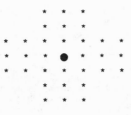

To begin with, all the holes but the center one are filled. The object of the game is to remove all the pegs but one by 'jumping' (as in checkers) and to end with the one remaining peg in the center. A clever person can get the solution in perhaps eight or ten hours of experimentation. A not so clever person can get a 'near-solution'—two pegs left—in the same time. No program exists, to my knowledge, that would enable a computer to solve even the 'near solution' problem without running out of both time and space, even though the machine can spend the equivalent of many human lifetimes in experimentation. When we come to the discovery of even the simplest mathematical theorem the situation is even more striking. The theorems of mathematics, the solutions to puzzles, etc., cannot on *any* theory be *individually* 'innate'; what must be 'innate' are heuristics, i.e., learning strategies. In the absence of any knowledge of what *general multipurpose learning strategies* might even look like, the assertion that such strategies (which absolutely must exist and be employed by all humans) cannot account for this or that learning process, that the answer or an answer schema must be 'innate', is utterly unfounded.

I will be told, of course, that *everyone* learns his native language (as well as everyone does), and that not everyone solves puzzles or proves theorems. But everyone does learn pattern recognition, automobile driving, etc., and everyone in fact can solve many problems that no computer can solve. In conversation Chomsky has repeatedly used precisely such skills as these to support the idea that humans have an "innate conceptual space". Well and good, if true. *But that is no help. Let a complete 17th-century Oxford University education be innate if you like;* still the solution to 'jump' was not innate; the Prime Number Theorem was not innate; and so on. *Invoking 'Innateness' only postpones the problem of learning; it does not solve it.* Until we understand the strategies which make general learning possible—and vague talk of 'classes of hypotheses'—and 'weighting functions' is utterly useless here—no discussion of the *limits* of learning can even begin.

[1] What 'built in' means is highly unclear in this context. The weighting function by itself determines only the relative ease with which various grammars can be learned by a human being. If a grammar G_1 can be learned more easily than a grammar G_2, then doubtless this is 'innate' in the sense of being a fact about human learning *potential*, as opposed to a fact about what has been learned. But this sort of fact is what learning theory tries to account for; *not* the explanation being sought. It should be noticed that Chomsky has never offered even a schematic account of the sort of device that is supposed to be present in the brain, and that is supposed to do the job of selecting the highest weighted grammar compatible with the data. But only a description, or at least a theory, of such a device could properly be called an innateness *hypothesis* at all.

[2] E. M. in L., p. 550.

[3] E. M. in L., pp. 530–531.

[4] I doubt that the child really is told which sentences it hears or utters are *ungrammatical*. At most it is told which are *deviant*—but it may not be told which are deviant for *syntactical* and which for *semantical* reasons.

[5] Many of these—e.g., the alleged 'ambiguity' in 'the shooting of the elephants was heard'—*require coaching to detect.* The claim that grammar "explains the ability to recognize ambiguities" thus lacks the impressiveness that Chomsky believes it to have. I am grateful to Paul Ziff and Stephen Leeds for calling this point to my attention.

[6] E. M. in L., p. 531, n. 5.

[7] A grammar 'predicts' an ambiguity, in Chomsky's formalism, whenever it assigns two or more structural descriptions to the same sentence.

[8] E. M. in L., p. 530.

[9] E. M. in L., p. 530.

[10] E. M. in L., p. 533.

[11] E. M. in L., p. 529.

[12] Macaulay's *first* words, it is said, were: "Thank you, Madam, the agony has somewhat abated" (to a lady who had spilled hot tea on him).

[13] Another example of a transformation is the 'active-passive' transformation (cf. *Syntactic Structures*). But (a) the presence of this, if it *is* a part of the grammar, is not surprising—why should not there be a systematic way of expressing the *converse* of a relation?—and (b) the argument for the existence of such a 'transformation' at all is extremely slim. It is contended that a grammar which 'defines' active and passive forms separately (this can be done by even a phrase-structure grammar) fails to represent something that every speaker knows, *viz.*, that active and passive forms are *related*. But why must every *relation* be mirrored by *syntax*? Every 'speaker' of the canonical languages of mathematical logic is aware that each sentence (x) $(Fx \supset Gx)$ is related to a sentence (x) $(\bar{G}x \supset \bar{F}x)$; yet the definition of 'well formed formula' fails to mirror 'what every speaker knows' in this respect, and is not inadequate on that account.

[14] It is very difficult to account for such phenomena as the spontaneous babbling of infants without *this* much 'innateness'. But this is not to say that a class Σ and a function f are 'built in', as required by the I.H.

C. Nelson Goodman

The Epistemological Argument

Anticus: Tell me about the resurrection.

Jason: After some centuries, the theory of Innate Ideas has been disinterred, and enthroned as the only adequate explanation for some striking facts concerning human linguistic proficiency.

A: What facts?

J: In the first place, that all natural languages, however diverse in origin and in superficials, have certain remarkable properties in common.

A: But is it remarkable that the elements of any collection have some remarkable properties in common? Surely we can find throughout the random deals of a pack of cards during an evening some very special uniformities; but we do not take them as posing a problem.

J: The claim is of course much stronger: that any language a human being can acquire has the properties in question.

A: I can imagine having a good deal of trouble mastering a language with an alphabet of a million letters and no word less than a million letters long. But does this call for elaborate explanation?

J: The properties in question are more interesting properties of grammatical form and of meaning.

A: Then the claim is indeed material and testable. I suppose these nomads have constructed languages lacking the properties in question, and found that earnest efforts to teach them

This recasting and expansion of the material in my symposium talk 'On Some Inimical Ideas' reflects no literary ambitions. The dialogue form offered advantages both in organization and in giving an appropriate tone to discussion of a theory that only my respect for its advocates enables me to take at all seriously.

Possible text → derive a language lacking the properti...
But No language lacking could be taken as an
initial language.

(4) to human beings fail. This seems to me not only remarkable
but incredible; for the human mind strikes me as agile enough
to learn, with appropriate instruction and explanation, almost
any transformation or distortion of an already familiar language.

J: I have done them an injustice. They hold only that no
language lacking the properties in question can be acquired
by a human being as an *initial* language. Once one language is
available and can be used for giving explanation and instruction, the limitations are transcended.

A: That answers my objection; but now I am puzzled as to
how they propose to examine the claim experimentally. Can
they really take an infant at birth, isolate it from all the influences of our language-bound culture, and attempt to inculcate
it with one of the 'bad' artificial languages?

(6) J: No. They readily admit this cannot be done. They regard
their claim as a hypothesis not subject to such direct experimental test, but supported by ancillary considerations and
evidence.

claim A: Very well; the claim is that certain statements about the
properties of languages that can be initially acquired are plausible, and a certain explanation illuminating. But so far we have
what are been speaking vaguely of 'certain properties' or 'the properties
the properties in question'. If we are to judge plausibility, we must surely have
a clearer formulation or illustrations of what these properties
are.

J: My informants are not always very explicit about this. They
cite some general grammatical properties now and then; but I
know you would say that each of these has been tailored to
fit the known natural languages and derives rather from the
conceptual apparatus we impose upon these languages than
from any remarkable affinities among them. One case that
might carry some weight with you, though, concerns a con-
cocted language called *Grubleen.* It differs from ordinary English only in that it contains the predicates 'grue' (for "examined
before *t* and green or not so examined and blue") and 'bleen'
(for "examined before *t* and blue or not so examined and
green") instead of the predicates 'green' and 'blue'. The claim
is that while a user of ordinary English might be taught to use
Grubleen, no human being could acquire Grubleen as an initial
language.

A: Though, as you say, experimental support for this can
hardly be expected. But I have another worry. Let us assume
that we now have before us an example of a language that can-

The claim cannot be tested experimentally but
supported by other means.

not be so acquired. Still, what in general is the difference between Grubleen-like and English-like languages? I see by your gesture that you are painfully aware of the difficulties of answering that question. So far we seem to have concluded first that the claim we are discussing cannot be experimentally tested even when we have an acknowledged example of a 'bad' language, and second that the claim has not even been formulated to the extent of citation of a single general property of 'bad' languages.

J: Nevertheless, important conjectures often cannot in the early stages be either precisely stated or actually tested. What you have said does not convince me that the claim ought to be rejected. If it is suggestive or promising enough, we ought rather to help examine and develop it.

A: You are right in principle; but I am not moved to try in this case, since the claim seems to me discredited by antecedent considerations.

J: Such as?

A: What we call a language is a fairly elaborate and sophisticated symbolic system. Don't you think, Jason, that before anyone acquires a language, he has had an abundance of practice in developing and using rudimentary prelinguistic symbolic systems in which gestures and sensory and perceptual occurrences of all sorts function as signs?

J: Yes; but *language*-acquisition is what is at issue.

A: You remember, though, that the real issue is over *initial* acquisition of languages, since once some language is available, acquisition of others is relatively easy.

J: True; but surely you do not call those rudimentary systems languages.

A: No; but I submit that our facility in going from one symbolic system to another is not much affected by whether each or either or neither is called a language; that acquisition of an initial language is acquisition of a secondary symbolic system; and that as we find no interesting limitations upon what we can acquire as a secondary language, we have no ground for believing that there are such limitations upon what we can acquire as a secondary symbolic system. In other words, when initial-language acquisition is seen as secondary-symbolic-system acquisition, the claim that there are rigid limitations upon initial-language acquisiton is deprived of plausibility by the fact that there are no such limitations upon secondary-language acquisition.

J: I am afraid that what you say undermines also a second claim: that initial-language acquisition is astonishingly fast.

A: Yes. If the language were the first symbolic system acquired, and the process of acquisition considered to begin with the first overt use of words, I suppose we might manage to work up some astonishment. But if acquisition of the first language is merely passage from a symbolic system already acquired to another that we are taught, that is a much easier step. On the other hand, if the process of acquiring the first language is thought of as beginning with the first use of symbols, then it must begin virtually at birth and takes a long time.

J: Does not all this just move the question back from the nature of languages that can be initially acquired to the nature of symbolic systems that can be so acquired? I suspect we would find remarkable uniformities and astonishing speed of acquisition here.

A: We'd certainly have an even harder time doing it. Little of the unimpressive evidence adduced with respect to languages would be pertinent here; and obviously we cannot argue back from uniformity of language to uniformity of prelinguistic system. We'd have to examine symbols that are not overt and articulate but rather inaccessible and ill-defined. And since the prelinguistic systems are likely to be fragmentary as well as rudimentary, we'd have trouble deciding when a system is acquired. And experimentation under all these difficulties would have to begin with symbol-using from the moment of birth. But I hardly have to refute your suspicions. Rather than facts crying for a theory, the theory is crying for the facts.

J: Your objections are more telling against my inadequate presentation than against the spirit and substance of what I am trying to present. All sophistry aside, is there nothing in human behavior you find striking enough to demand special explanation?

A: I can think of some remarkable behavioral facts that call for no such explanation as a theory of innate ideas.

J: For example?

A: Well, I learned instantly to fall when dropped, and moreover to fall, no matter where dropped, precisely toward the center of the earth.

J: And for this remarkable fact we do need a theory—the theory of gravitation.

A: A set of laws subsuming this behavior under a very general description; but I am not inclined to attribute knowledge of these laws to the falling objects.

J: But this is mechanical behavior, common to animate and inanimate objects alike. Living things obey more special laws framed in terms of other notions. And human beings, in their cognitive behavior, obey still more special laws that require reference to innate ideas.

A: Your speed there is remarkable enough. Let us take it more slowly. Are you saying that human cognition is explicable only by supposing that the mind is supplied at the start with the interpretation of certain symbols? If that means only that it responds in a fixed way to certain stimuli, this suggests a view of mind we would both reject. What seems to me notable is not the fixity but rather the flexibility of the mind; its ability to adapt, adjust, transform; its way of achieving unity in variety, constancy amid instability, of inventing rather than obeying. The mind does not merely kick when tapped; it gropes. The groping and grasping, the seeking and finding, seem to me more characteristic than any mere program-reading.

J: You Berkeleyans always overstress the groping.

A: And you Leibnizians overstress the predetermination.

J: We go from pettifogging analysis to loose metaphor, and now name-calling! But seriously, I think it is just those capacities of the mind that you praise that can be accounted for only by the instrumentation of innate ideas.

A: We have been paying much less attention to what the theory is than to what it is supposed to explain. Let us now assume that for certain remarkable facts I have no alternative explanation. Of course, that alone does not dictate acceptance of whatever theory may be offered; for that theory might be worse than none. Inability to explain a fact does not condemn me to accept an intrinsically repugnant and incomprehensible theory. Now I gather that the theory here proposed is that certain ideas are implanted in the mind as original equipment.

J: Roughly that.

A: And being ideas, they are in consciousness?

J: No, not necessarily; not even usually.

A: Then they are in the subconscious mind, operating upon cognitive processes, and capable of being brought into full consciousness?

J: Not even that, I may have no direct access to them at all. My only way of discovering them in my own mind may be by the same methods that someone else might use to infer that I have them, or I to infer that he does.

A: Then I am puzzled. You seem to be saying that these innate ideas are neither innate nor ideas.

J: What is innate are not concepts, images, formulae, or pictures, but rather 'inclinations, dispositions, habits, or natural potentialities'.

A: But I thought the ideas were posited to explain the capacities. If all that is claimed is that the mind has certain inclinations and capacities, how can you justify calling these ideas?

J: The justification is historical. Descartes and Leibniz used the term 'innate idea' in just this sense. But after all, it is the theory that counts, not the term 'innate idea'.

A: In that case, why all the effort at historical justification? And why, after admitting the term is controversial and claiming it is unnecessary, do these people go on using it? For a very compelling, but not very good, reason: that until the term 'innate idea' is applied, what is advocated is the rather trivial truth that the mind has certain capacities, tendencies, limitations. Once we apply the term, in anything like its normal use, the thesis becomes far from obvious; but unfortunately, it becomes false or meaningless. John Locke made all this acutely clear.

J: Again I am afraid I have not been careful enough. Rather than identify the innate ideas with capacities, etc., I probably should have said that these ideas exist as or are 'innate as' such capacities.

A: A few minutes ago you accused me of sophistry; but I bow before the subtlety of that last statement. Go again, Jason, and bring back to me all the mysteries of ideas being innate as capacities. Then, if you like, we can talk again about unsubstantiated conjectures that cry for explanation by implausible and untestable hypotheses that hypostatize ideas that are innate in the mind as non-ideas.

12. W. V. Quine

Linguistics and Philosophy

Chomsky has expressed general doubts as to how much philosophy stands to gain from linguistics or linguistics from philosophy. But he did express the belief that linguistics contributes
to philosophy in one quarter, by supporting rationalism as
against empiricism.

With the following claim of Chomsky's, at least, we are all
bound to agree:

*We must try to characterize innate structure in such a way as
to meet two kinds of empirical conditions. First we must attribute to the organism, as an innate property, a structure rich
enough to account for the fact that the postulated grammar is
acquired on the basis of the given conditions of access to data;
second, we must not attribute to the organism a structure so
rich as to be incompatible with the data.*

All this I find indisputable. If this is rationalism, and incompatible with Locke's empiricism, then so much the better for
rationalism and so much the worse for Locke. The connection
between this indisputable point about language, on the one
hand, and the disagreements of seventeenth-century philosophers on the other, is a scholarly matter on which I have no
interesting opinion. But what does require to be made clear is
that this indisputable point about language is in no conflict
with latter-day attitudes that are associated with the name of
empiricism, or behaviorism.

For, whatever we may make of Locke, the behaviorist is

From *Language and Philosophy,* a symposium edited by Sidney Hook
(New York: New York University Press). Copyright 1969 by New York University. Reprinted by permission.
[In this symposium Chomsky defends his innateness hypothesis and a
number of other philosophers comment on this thesis. Although Quine begins with a quotation from this defense of Chomsky's, it is clear his remarks apply to Chomsky's position in general. Ed.]

knowingly and cheerfully up to his neck in innate mechanisms of learning-readiness. The very reinforcement and extinction of responses, so central to behaviorism, depends on prior inequalities in the subject's qualitative spacing, so to speak, of stimulations. If the subject is rewarded for responding in a certain way to one stimulation, and punished for thus responding to another stimulation, then his responding in the same way to a third stimulation reflects an inequality in his qualitative spacing of the three stimulations; the third must resemble the first more than the second. Since each learned response presupposes some such prior inequalities, some such inequalities must be unlearned; hence innate. Innate biases and dispositions are the cornerstone of behaviorism, and have been studied by behaviorists. Chomsky mentioned some of that work himself, but still I feel I should stress the point.

This qualitative spacing of stimulations must therefore be recognized as an innate structure needed in accounting for any learning, and hence, in particular, language-learning. Unquestionably much additional innate structure is needed, too, to account for language-learning. The qualitative spacing of stimulations is as readily verifiable in other animals, after all, as in man; so the language-readiness of the human infant must depend on further endowments. It will be interesting to find out more and more, if we can, about what this additional innate structure is like and how it works. Such discoveries would illuminate not only language but learning processes generally.

It may well turn out that processes are involved that are very unlike the classical process of reinforcement and extinction of responses. This would be no refutation of behaviorism, in a philosophically significant sense of the term; for I see no interest in restricting the term "behaviorism" to a specific psychological schematism of conditioned response.

Conditioned response does retain a key role in language-learning. It is the entering wedge to any particular lexicon, for it is how we learn observation terms (or, better, simple observation sentences) by ostension. Learning by ostension is learning by simple induction, and the mechanism of such learning is conditioning. But this method is notoriously incapable of carrying us far in language. This is why, on the translational side, we are soon driven to what I have called analytical hypotheses. The as yet unknown innate structures, additional to mere quality space, that are needed in language-learning, are needed specifically to get the child over this great hump that lies beyond ostension, or induction. If Chomsky's antiempiricism or anti-behaviorism says merely that conditioning is insufficient to explain language-learining, then the doctrine is of a piece with my doctrine of the indeterminacy of translation.

When I dismiss a definition of behaviorism that limits it to conditioned response, am I simply extending the term to cover everyone? Well, I do think of it as covering all reasonable men. What matters, as I see it, is just the insistence upon couching all criteria in observation terms. By observation terms I mean terms that are or can be taught by ostension, and whose application in each particular case can therefore be checked intersubjectively. Not to cavil over the word "behaviorism," perhaps current usage would be best suited by referring to this orientation to observation simply as empiricism; but it is empiricism in a distinctly modern sense, for it rejects the naïve mentalism that typified the old empiricism. It does still condone the recourse to introspection that Chomsky has spoken in favor of, but it condones it as a means of arriving at conjectures or conclusions only insofar as these can eventually be made sense of in terms of external observation.

Empiricism of this modern sort, or behaviorism broadly so called, comes of the old empiricism by a drastic externalization. The old empiricist looked inward upon his ideas; the new empiricist looks outward upon the social institution of language. Ideas dwindle to meanings, seen as adjuncts of words. The old inner-directed empiricists—Hobbes, Gassendi, Locke, and their followers—had perforce to formulate their empiricist standard by reference to ideas; and they did so by exalting sense impressions and scouting innate ideas. When empiricism is externalized, on the other hand, the idea itself passes under a cloud; talk of ideas comes to count as unsatisfactory except insofar as it can be paraphrased into terms of dispositions to observable behavior. Externalized empiricism or behaviorism sees nothing uncongenial in the appeal to innate dispositions to overt behavior, innate readiness for language-learning. What would be interesting and valuable to find out, rather, is just what these endowments are in fact like in detail.

13. R. Edgley
Chomsky's Theory of Innate Ideas

260 Let us return to our earlier question: how close is the resemblance between Chomsky's theory and the classical doctrine
of innate ideas? One resemblance is clear: it shows some tendency to fluctuate between a dominant and a recessive version.
In identifying what is innate as ideas he moves sometimes
towards the dominant doctrine that these constitute information or knowledge, and sometimes towards the recessive doctrine that these are simply an aspect of mental structure. In
conformity with this latter recessive interpretation, Chomsky
usually represents empiricism, and even behaviourism, as
claiming not that we have no innate ideas but that we have
some, that is, some innate mental structure; though in Chomsky's view not enough to account for our knowledge. However,
in one combination of features Chomsky's theory is peculiar: in
general he clearly does not agree with the recessive doctrine
that all our ideas are innate; but on the other hand, the ideas
that he contends are innate are some of them highly contingent and thus very unlike the ideas of reason alleged to be
innate in the dominant doctrine. I shall argue that Chomsky
fails to show that what is innate is knowledge; but that given
this modification, it is its peculiar combination of the characteristics of the classical variations, a combination in which it
differs from and does not resemble the classical doctrine, that
constitutes one of the chief merits of Chomsky's theory and
saves it from both the incoherence of the dominant version and
the triviality of the recessive version.

In the Beckman Lectures,[1] Chomsky ascribes to one of his
critics, Hilary Putnam, an attitude that he finds typical of em-

From "Innate Ideas" by R. Edgley, in The Royal Institute of Philosophy
Lectures, Vol. III, *Knowledge and Necessity* (London: Macmillan and Co.,
Ltd., New York: St. Martin's Press), pp. 16–33. Copyright 1970 by The Royal
Institute of Philosophy. Reprinted by permission.
[This is the second half of Edgley's essay. In the earlier part Edgley as-
sesses various versions of the classical doctrine of innate ideas. Ed.]

piricism in general: namely, 'a curious distaste for the conclusion that the mind has intrinsic structure, as does every known
organism or physiological system'. Of course, this distaste
seems curious, not to say perverse, from that point of view
from which the mind is seen in profile, as a system causally
interacting with its environment: not only 'every known organism or physiological system' but everything whatsoever has
intrinsic structure in the sense that in its interaction with its
surroundings anything it does or that happens to it is attributable in part to its own characteristics. But, as my rational
reconstruction of the historical argument has shown, there is a
tension between this point of view and the requirement that if
those products of the mind's interaction with its surroundings
that the epistemologist is specially interested in, ideas,
thoughts, impressions, experience and so on, are to be acceptable or accurate, and thus if they are to constitute knowledge,
they must represent the mind's surroundings as they really are,
not simply as they appear to be. Any mental structure that
contributes something of itself to the shaping of these products
may be an obstacle to the satisfaction of that requirement;
and in this light the empiricist 'distaste' for mental structure
can be seen not as 'curious' or simply perverse but as a cautious economy. Creativity is no doubt a good thing. But a re-
porter who invents his story is not doing his job.

How then can we think of mental structure, which is essential, in such a way that it permits an undistorted view of things?
How can reality, its dumbness notwithstanding, be allowed to
speak for itself? For a start, accuracy of representation must
not be confused with total similarity between the representation and what it represents: simply as a representation, e.g., an
idea or an impression, it must have characteristics that the
thing or situation it represents perhaps does not and cannot
have; ideas are very different from physical objects, events,
states and situations, and that difference will be attributable to
the nature of the mind. These necessities of representation, as
we can call them, need not distort because with respect to the
question of accuracy of representation they are merely formal
characteristics: they do not affect the content of the representation and so do not make things appear otherwise than as they
are. In this way the mind, in its interaction with its environment,
will perform, by virtue of its structure, the causal function of
converting its input into something different, namely, ideas and
knowledge; but it will effect this conversion without introducing
into the content of these ideas and knowledge anything of its

own structure. What the mind contributes to our ideas of reality does not itself consist of ideas of reality.

This distinction between form and content is, of course, vague, but the mind's awareness of reality has been given some shapes, both literally and figuratively, that can be seen as attempts to avoid the implication that the mind itself contributes anything of the content of knowledge in the essential features of its representations. Thus a *tabula rasa* is not without structure; its structure is such that it receives information without adding to it. The mind should be transparent to reality; like good quality window glass its structure allows the view to be transmitted unaltered, as if it were not itself there. The mind is a mirror; not a distorting mirror, but one whose structure enables it to reflect things as they really are. Whatever their other shortcomings, one of the most conspicuous defects of these models is that in economising on the mind's contribution, they are too parsimonious. What the mind represents, according to these models, it represents as it really is, without distortion or addition. But it represents far too little of reality—generally, in fact, only its visual features. Underlying this limitation is another: knowing is depicted as a kind of seeing or perceiving. In general, traditional empiricism tends to claim not only that anything we know about reality must be perceptually testable, and perhaps reducible to perceptual judgments, but also that knowing and judging are themselves reducible to perceiving or having perceptual images. In the twentieth century this latter tendency has been counteracted in particular by recognition of the importance of language and its essential role in thinking, having ideas, and knowing things. Now language is certainly contributed by the mind, and to the extent that knowledge is expressible in language our knowledge may reflect that contribution. But again, empiricists have in effect argued that this is not a substantive contribution determining the content of our knowledge. The common claim that the rules of a language are conventional can be seen in this light. Part of this claim is that the differences between languages may reflect informative and interesting differences between the minds of one linguistic group and the minds of another; but to the extent that statements in one language are translatable into those of another, these different features do not enter into the content of anything that is said or thought. More generally, languages place no necessary restriction on what can be thought. The only essential features common to all languages are structural features of a logical kind, basic analytic principles allowing deductive inference from one assertion to another. These can be represented as truths, but in such a form they will not be truths about reality, since they give no information about reality.

Chomsky thinks that classical empiricism ascribes these deductive principles, and perhaps inductive principles, to the mind, as reflecting its innate structure, or as constituting 'analytical mechanisms or inductive principles or mechanisms of association';[2] and presumably he agrees with this ascription, his objection being that further principles or mechanisms must also be attributed to the mind as innate. What is the significance of this ascription? His general approach to his problem, and in particular that aspect of it most deeply committed to breaking down the barriers between philosophy and psychology, renders the answer ambiguous. The problem, he says, is the problem of designing an input-output device, the input being data and the output knowledge. To do this 'we first attempt to determine the nature of the output in many cases and then to determine the character of the function relating input to output; . . . this is an entirely empirical matter . . . quite analogous to the problem of studying the innate principles that make it possible for a bird to acquire the knowledge that expresses itself in nest-building or in song-production'.[3] His conclusion is that the device incorporates various theories;[4] but in the course of his linguistic investigations he also notes[5] 'that we are . . . using the term "theory" . . . with a systematic ambiguity, to refer both to the child's innate predisposition to learn a language . . . and to the linguist's account of this'. This ambiguity, of course, answers to the fluctuation between the dominant and recessive doctrines on the question of what exactly is innate, knowledge or a disposition of some sort. Let us for the moment consider its effect on the idea that analytical principles are attributable to the mind as reflecting its innate structure.

Suppose somebody argues: 'If the river burst its banks, the rainfall must have been unusually heavy; and the river did burst its banks. So the rainfall must have been unusually heavy.' This is an analytically valid argument, and the principle of the inference is *modus ponens:* 'If *p* and if *p* then *q,* then *q.*' The validity of the argument, and the truth of the principle, are not empirical matters. Let us now consider the person who argues in that way as an input-output device, with the premises of the argument, or data, as input, and his knowledge of the conclusion as output. What can we say about the character of the function relating input to output? Consider a question that sounds more familiar: if he knows the premises and knows the conclusion on the basis of those premises, i.e., because he drew it from those premises, can we say that he knows the analytic truth that is the principle of the argument? It seems to me that this too follows, and is again not an empirical matter. He may not be able to formulate what he knows on being asked, but he would at least know it implicitly in the sense already outlined. However, it is important to notice exactly what it is that is not an empirical matter in this latter case. What is analytic is that if he knows the premises and knows the conclusion because he drew it from those premises then he knows the analytic principle of *modus ponens*. But though this is analytic, and though the principle he implicitly knows is analytic, the fact that he knows that principle is not analytic. This is an empirical fact, and its empirical content is psychological, i.e., about his mind. That he knows it tells us something about his mind: not much, but a little, since he might have been an idiot, or a babe-in-arms, or a dog, so that having a mind does not entail having the knowledge; this is knowledge a sane person has, though perhaps only implicitly, when he comes to the age of reason.

Thus to say that somebody knows a certain analytic truth tells us something about his mind; and his knowledge, one might say, being knowledge, is in his mind. But these commonplaces cannot be all that is meant by arguing that to account for the fact that people get to know things by reasoning we must regard the structure of their minds as incorporating analytic principles; whatever anyone knows, whether something analytic or empirical, the fact that he knows it tells us something about his mind, and that knowledge is of course, being knowledge, in his mind. What more, then, is being claimed? Do we not have here, lurking in an obscurity that is understandable but hardly decent, an attempt to explain how it is that someone can have knowledge that is both non-empirical and not discovered by reasoning? Let us ask: what is it that is being said to be innate and to reflect the structure of the mind—knowledge of analytic principles or the analytic principles themselves? Given that an analytic principle can be regarded as a theory, in what sense is that theory *incorporated* in the device? Traditionally it was said sometimes that knowledge of truths, and sometimes that the truths themselves, are innate; and the commonest representation of this latter view is in the metaphor of truths inscribed on the soul, the information coming literally from inside, not outside, the mind. Nothing as unhelpful as this is possible today, of course. But Kant's refinement may still be with us, though in the cruder form of the suggestion that not only synthetic *a priori* but even analytic principles reflect mental structure: it is because the mind has the structure it does have that analytic principles are true and can be known to be true innately, neither from experience nor by reasoning. If this is the doctrine, it repeats, in cruder form, Kant's monumental error. It implies that as a logical possibility our minds could have had a different structure, not simply in our not knowing these analytic principles but in our having (and knowing) different ones, such that our present principles would have been false; and this is logically impossible.

The point can be made in another and perhaps clearer way. How on earth, it might be asked, could a principle such as *modus ponens* reflect or be a principle of mental structure? There are, for example, principles of atomic structure or of anatomic structure, and we could say that atoms and bodies are, or are modelled by, devices that incorporate these principles or theories: and this would presumably mean not that atoms or our bodies know these principles or theories, but that we know them and that these principles accurately describe, and perhaps explain and predict, the structure of atoms and bodies; so that (the structure of) atoms and bodies could be said to conform to these theories. Now the principle that if p and if p then q, then q clearly does not have that relation to minds and mental structure: if it describes, explains, or predicts anything at all, it is not upon minds in particular that it bears in these ways. However, this principle has a form that does relate it in a special fashion to minds, its form, namely, as a principle of derivability or deducibility: from the fact that p and if p then q, it is deducible (or inferable) that q. Deducing, inferring, drawing conclusions, arguing, and so on, are things that people do (in a broad sense of the word 'do'); and the fact that somebody draws a conclusion tells us in particular something about his mind, i.e., 'deduce', 'infer', 'conclude', etc., are psychological verbs. Thus, as atoms and bodies can conform to principles of atomic and anatomic structure, so also people's minds, in the inferences and deductions they make, in a word, in their reasoning, can conform to analytic principles; and just as atoms or bodies can conform to, without knowing, the principles that the physicists or anatomists know, so laymen in their reasoning can conform to, without knowing, at least explicitly, the principles that the logicians know. Analytic principles might then seem to reflect, or be principles of, mental structure in a way analogous to that in which atomic or anatomic principles or

theories reflect, or are principles of, atomic or anatomic structure; and minds could be said to incorporate analytic principles
as atoms and bodies could be said to incorporate atomic and
anatomic theories. If we design a model of an atom, a body, or
a mind, the sense in which the appropriate theories are incorporated will seem even stronger: the model is designed consciously to conform to those theories, so that the theories themselves are more or less literally built into the model, a situation
we might illustrate metaphorically by saying that the theories
are inscribed in that device.

I do not know whether this analogy is at work in Chomsky's
thinking on the subject, but it is almost certainly present in
some of the traditional versions of the doctrine of innate ideas.
It is in any case indefensible. In neither of its possible forms
does an analytic principle describe, explain, or predict the
structure of our minds or the course of our reasoning. In that
form in which it does relate specially to our minds its bearing
on them is not descriptive, explanatory or predictive, but
normative: *modus ponens*, for example, says that from the fact
that *p* and if *p* then *q*, it may legitimately or correctly be
deduced or inferred that *q*. Sometimes our reasoning con-
forms to principles of this kind, sometimes it does not, sometimes it contravenes such principles. Of course, our reasoning
cannot both contravene these principles and have knowledge
as its output; and our knowledge is sometimes the output of
such reasoning. Concentrating on this normative form of analytic
principles, we may suppose that as norms in general are simply
conventions we are as free to vary these rules of reasoning as
we are to vary the rules of tiddlywinks. The doctrine that these
are principles of deep psychological structure quite properly
rejects this conventionalism; but on the wrong grounds. For
though it implies that we are not free to vary the rules, it does
so for this reason, that it is psychologically impossible for us
to do so. But this in its turn implies that it is at least logically
possible, given a different psychological structure, that these
norms should have been different, and therefore that their non-
normative versions should have been false; and this is logically
impossible.

The general conclusion to be drawn from these considerations reveals a reversal of the normal roles of dominant and
recessive features in the doctrine of innate ideas. In the case
of simple analytic principles of inference, the dominant doctrine that what is innate is our *knowledge* of them, in the sense
outlined, is unobjectionable and unexciting; the doctrine that

the innateness of our knowledge is due to the innateness of the principles themselves, as reflecting or being principles of our psychological *structure,* is adventurous but incoherent. This incoherence is the effect of taking up the point of view from which the mind appears in profile, as an input-output system, and consequently treating the conceptual apparatus of the recessive doctrine as providing an explanatory framework for the phenomena of the dominant doctrine.

The version of empiricism I have outlined finds a place for deductive inference but not for induction. Radical empiricism rejects induction as a valid kind of argument, and if Chomsky is right this type of empiricism would be even less capable of accounting for our knowledge than a type admitting induction. Significantly, this does not prohibit radical empiricism from allowing either innate ideas, even an innate idea of induction, or ideas actively created by the mind. Hume argues that though induction cannot be justified as valid, we have a natural and perhaps innate tendency to think inductively. Popper sees the rejection of induction precisely as freeing the mind, and enabling us to conceive of it as free, for that creative activity in the invention of its own ideas that is supposed to be denied by classical empiricism and affirmed by rationalism. There is no paradox here, only the characteristic empiricist drive towards scepticism. For Hume, our belief in induction is simply a belief, not knowledge, and inductive arguments lead to belief, not knowledge. For Popper, the ideas the mind creates do not amount to knowledge but only hypotheses or conjectures; and even under stringent empirical tests, however firmly we may come to believe them, they still fall short of knowledge.

In view of this, can considerations of the sort Chomsky adduces be regarded as a refutation, and an empirical one, of empiricism itself? It may be true, as he claims, that these empiricist theories cannot account for our knowledge: the character of the function they assign to the input-output device, i.e., the intrinsic structure they attribute to the mind, is not sufficient to show that the knowledge we have would result as the output. Now that this is so seems to be a matter of logic rather than an empirical matter; though the topic is the 'psychological' topic of what characteristics we need to attribute to the person's mind if, given that he has some data as his input of knowledge, he is to derive other knowledge as output from it, the failure of empiricism in this respect seems to be its failure to meet a certain logical requirement, namely, that what he knows as output, the content of his consequential knowledge, should follow from what he knows as input, the content of the data, in accordance with whatever principles are ascribed to his mind; this seems to mean that the data we have do not entail what we consequentially know. The failure of empiricism even with induction would consist in the logical fact that this principle is still not logically sufficient to generate what we consequentially know from the data.

Objections of this logical type to empiricism are of course well known, to empiricists as well as to their critics. Do they amount to refutation? The typical empiricist reaction, as Hume and Popper illustrate, has been towards scepticism; it tends to deny that the output of 'knowledge' really is knowledge, and argues that our claims to such knowledge are not justified; the most that we can claim is probable belief, and perhaps no more than a degree of conviction without even benefit of probability. Now it may be and probably is the case that empiricism is wrong about this. Many contemporary philosophers would argue that empiricism is wrong about the data we have, and in particular that it cannot be as meagre and fragmentary as the sense-data or sense-impressions of classical empiricism, or as homogeneous as the purely physical data of behaviourism. Many would argue that empiricism is wrong about what knowledge is, and in particular that it sets impossibly high standards for its attainment. But whether right or wrong, sceptical empiricism rejects the very problem as Chomsky poses it, with output knowledge of this or that kind treated as a datum, and philosophers in general, whether empiricists or their critics, at least reserve the right, as these arguments show, to question the terms in which that problem is set up. We should perhaps, in a Kantian spirit, not protecting the specialism of our own trade union but simply distinguishing one topic from another, treat the philosophical discussion as transcendental and Chomsky's as empirical: as an empirical scientist he is fully entitled to employ concepts like that of knowledge in their ordinary and scientific ways, while the philosophical task is to analyse such concepts and show how, if at all, they are justified. To the extent that this Kantian approach assumes that concepts in ordinary and scientific employment cannot be repudiated by philosophical considerations, sceptical empiricism is already rejected. But the argument for rejection takes place on ground that Chomsky's problem presupposes: ground that the empiricist forces us onto, by accepting the substance of Chomsky's criticism, but as an objection to our claims to knowledge in general, not to empiricism itself.

If we allow knowledge of certain basic analytic principles to be innate in the sense already outlined, but reject the idea that this innateness is to be understood in terms of the way these principles reflect psychological structure, how, it might be asked, is such knowledge to be explained, when it is of truths that are neither empirical nor discovered by reasoning? A modern empiricist answer might be that this knowledge is implicitly acquired in the process of learning to think and reason, and that this is implicit in the process of learning a language. In learning the meanings of words we in effect learn certain simple analytic truths; for these truths are simple in this way, that knowing them to be true is a necessary condition of understanding their meaning. Empiricists have commonly regarded this account as a reduction and deflationary, i.e., as showing that the admission that some knowledge is innate commits us to nothing more extraordinary than admitting that we learn a language. Innate ideas, which seemed to be strange potentates ruling from the mind's mysterious hinterland, are revealed as intimate acquaintances of even the most ordinary chaps. Here Chomsky appears and reopens the debate at the very moment of the empiricist triumph. How extraordinary is learning a language? What exactly does it involve? What explanation can we give of how we learn a language? Far from getting rid of innate ideas, in the sense of unmasking their old familiar faces, learning a language, he claims, positively requires these powers, powers innate yet exotic, and certainly unsuspected. For what we know when we know a language has such a rich and complex structure that the data we are exposed to in learning a language would be logically inadequate to generate that knowledge without the aid of strong innate principles.

It is in being part of a theory of language learning that Chomsky's doctrine of innate ideas is most decisively distinguished from the rationalist doctrine he claims to inherit. The distinction has two connected aspects, and both are related to the fact that the classical doctrine, in its chief exponents, Plato, Descartes, and Leibniz, has no particular connection with linguistics. Descartes certainly says things about language that resemble parts of Chomsky's account, but as Chomsky himself reveals in *Cartesian Linguistics,* these occur in Descartes's arguments about the differences, and in particular the evidence of the differences, between mind and matter, and thus between human beings and machines (including animals); for Descartes at any rate, there is no step from Cartesian linguistics to the doctrine of innate ideas. The first difference, then, is that the classical doctrine represents innate ideas as ideas of or about not language but some reality independent of language or any other human artifact: things eternal and immutable, or God, mind and matter, or principles of inference. The second difference is that, as I have already pointed out, the classical theory, if it is to support the distinctive doctrine of rationalism, needs to attribute innate ideas not to the mind in general, or to the language faculty in particular, but to the reason. It is not enough to show simply that these ideas are not derived from experience. Thus the ideas identified as innate by the dominant doctrine, whether eternal and immutable ideas, or clear and distinct ones, or principles of inference, reveal their identity not simply by being not derived from experience but by being in some sense logically or rationally necessary: their denial may be self-contradictory, or unintelligible, or they may be necessary if any knowledge, or any rational knowledge, is to be logically possible at all. Chomsky's claim, however, is that our innate ideas at least include some that are contingent. As he has repeatedly emphasised, the universal grammar that reflects our innate language capacity is a rich and articulated structure, and the class of possible grammars that it defines is not the class of grammars that are merely logically possible in the sense of being self-consistent or intelligible. It is not even the class of grammars that are necessary from a utilitarian point of view for organisms of about our size and mobility, and with our interests and aims: the grammatical form that a language must have is not simply the form that it must have in order to function efficiently as a medium of human communication. The constraints are much more severe, and are imposed by necessities of a general biological or psychological kind.

This feature, constituting the second difference between Chomsky's theory and the dominant doctrine distinctive of rationalism, is regarded by Chomsky himself as one of the most interesting and important characteristics of his account; and it is easy to see why. It means that the universal grammar, and the psychological theory alleging that this grammar reflects our innate mental structure, have high information content and are far from degenerating into the vacuousness that traditionally threatens such claims.

The gap that this aspect opens up between Chomsky's theory and rationalism is evident from the fact that this is one important respect in which Chomsky's views link up with the theories of biologists about innate and instinctive tendencies and capacities in animals. I have quoted his reference to nest-building and song-production among birds, and he more than once places his views in this general context.[6] This seems unexalted company for the innate ideas of rationalism. But part of Chomsky's point is presumably that just as a bird has an innate tendency or capacity to sing a highly specific kind of song, so that a thrush hatched and reared in isolation from other thrushes will nevertheless sing the song characteristic of its species, so all natural languages exhibit specific uniformities that reflect the innate contribution of each child to the language-learning situation. It is perfectly possible to conceive of and construct a language lacking these features: the artificial language of Russellian logic, for instance, has a phrase-structure grammar that is uncharacteristic of natural languages. Such a language would be very difficult or even impossible for a child to learn as a first language, because its grammar would not answer to those innate species-specific mental capacities that enable the child to master any natural grammar with such ease and on the basis of such formally inadequate evidence. But in principle, at any rate, anything that could be said in a natural language could be said in an artificial language: the innate contribution is to our knowledge of the language and not to the content of our knowledge of any non-linguistic reality.

Put in this way, and in the context of biological theories about innate or instinctive tendencies and capacities in animals, Chomsky's theory is a plausible, illuminating, and informative hypothesis; but it is a hypothesis about innate tendencies, or capacities, or mental structure, or even, if you will, about innate information in some technical sense such as the word may have in, say, information theory. This is not sufficient to show that what is innate is knowledge. Chomsky talks of both innate knowledge and innate structure indifferently. But the difference is important if the theory is a theory of innate ideas that is to be essentially incompatible with empiricism. We can see this if we consider Hume's treatment of induction. Hume in effect agrees with Chomsky that in order to account for the output we must ascribe principles of induction to people; and there seems no reason why, as an empiricist, he should not allow other innate principles of 'human nature' to be similarly attributable. What his empiricism forbids him to allow is that such principles should be innately known to be true; they are at most beliefs, and the output also, therefore, is belief, not knowledge. To the extent that Chomsky treats his ascription of these principles as a matter of psychology, interpreting it in terms of some general psychological concept such as mental structure, his position on this matter differs from Hume's only in degree, that is, only on the question of how many and what principles are needed to account for the output. To distinguish his doctrine from empiricism, Chomsky must show that what is innate is not simply some disposition or capacity, nor, more specifically, mental structure, and not even, more specifically still, Hume's natural beliefs, but knowledge. We have here, from dispositions or capacities at one extreme, to knowledge at the other, an order of attribution of ascending logical strength: that is, these concepts are ordered by conditions of increasing stringency governing their application. Birds no doubt have a disposition to sing or build nests in a specic way, and this dispostion is perhaps innate: Chomsky's reference to this disposition as expressing knowledge seems venturesome, not to say reckless. Where the disposition or capacity involved is a mental one it may reach the level of being a belief but still, as Hume maintains, fall short of rational or justified belief, and shorter still of knowledge.

Empirical concepts in general are inexact or vague by comparison with the idealised concepts of pure logic or mathematics; and among empirical concepts those that are psychological or partly psychological tend to be vaguer than most. This means that though there are clear central cases that are paradigms for the application of the concepts, and clear central cases to which the concepts paradigmatically do not apply, between these two areas of clarity their application is more or less faltering and uncertain. Typically, correct application is determined by a range of criteria, and in the area of uncertainty some of these criteria are fulfilled and some are not. With psychological concepts this situation is radically complicated by the problem of other minds, i.e., by the asymmetry between first-person and second- and third-person uses of psychological words. These second- and third-person uses seem like second- and third-class uses, since they require as criteria behavioural, and in general observable, characteristics that seem logically less than adequate. When these second and third persons are, so to speak, not persons at all, but dogs, birds, or fish, whose behaviour may fulfil some of the criteria but does not include their use of these words, in the first or any other person, we have what we might call an essentially disputable area of application. When someone is able to use and understand words and so make statements, the concepts of belief and knowledge become clearly applicable, because what a person believes or knows can be identified as what he says. But for what he says to be something that he knows, more stringent conditions must be fulfilled than for it to be something that he believes.

What are these more stringent conditions? Let us consider a clear central case of knowledge that is not of some directly observed fact. If someone claims to know that it will snow tomorrow, what distinguishes this from a claim merely to believe that it will snow tomorrow? First, it must be true that it will snow tomorrow. Second, he must not only believe but believe with that degree of conviction that amounts to being sure or certain. Third, his certainty must be justified not simply by its being true that it will snow, nor even by there being good reasons for thinking that it will snow, but by his having good reasons for being certain—reasons good enough, that is, to exclude reasonable doubt that it will snow tomorrow. Fulfilment of these conditions would make this a paradigm case of knowledge.

If we had any innate knowledge it would necessarily fail this third condition, for this condition entails that the knowledge in this paradigm case is learned or discovered or inferred. The failure, moreover, would be total: the claim to knowledge would not just be inadequately supported, it would not be supported at all. But if what is alleged to be innately known were something so basic or rudimentary that it was from a logical point of view unnecessary for it to be justified, because, for example, it was involved in the very notion of justification, or because it could not be understood without its truth being accepted, this third condition would be inapplicable. The innate ideas of the dominant doctrine distinctive of rationalism are of this sort. Chomsky's universal grammar is not. The very contingency of its principles, which is one of its chief merits as grammar and which gives the associated psychological theory its informative content, is, in combination with their generality, an obstacle to its being both innate and knowledge; for since it leaves open as logically possible other forms of grammar, a claim that this was known to be the form of all natural grammars could hardly be justified in the absence of any considerations ruling out, as at least unlikely, some of the other logically possible candidates. The linguist may rule these out, by appealing to the evidence. The child learning the language cannot, and if he could, his knowledge would not be innate. For him, other logically possible grammars are ruled out not logically, by relevant considerations, but psychologically. He can't help thinking as he does. The conclusion he comes to happens to be right, but from a logical point of view he has jumped to it.

What is innate is from this point of view not knowledge but prejudice.

There is, of course, a good explanation in Chomsky's theory of how it comes about that the child happens to be right. It is not sheer luck or coincidence or a matter of God's grace or pre-established harmony. For the cunning of Chomsky's theory, by comparison with the classical doctrine, is that his innate ideas are ideas about language, which is a human product; and it is therefore plausible to suppose that the structure of this product will have features reflecting aspects of the human mind that are characteristic of the species, and that other human minds, having these characteristics, will in the learning situation automatically, from tenuous data, reconstruct the language according to the same model. Because the language that provides the input to Chomsky's language acquisition device is itself the output of language production devices there is a pre-established harmony, of an entirely natural and plausible kind, that explains how the learner's reconstruction inevitably tends to match the original. However, this explanation is not available to the child as a consideration justifying his confidence, and if it were that confidence would simply be a part of the child's evidence, not innate knowledge.

This objection faces us with the typical threat of scepticism. If the language-learning situation is this, that on the basis of inadequate data we jump to a conclusion in accordance with our innate prejudice, how can the conclusion be said to be known? Yet surely scepticism at this point is ludicrously academic? If we know anything, we know our language. It seems to me that so far as Chomsky has any argument for the strong claim that what is innate is not merely mental structure, and not merely Humean natural belief, but knowledge, it is this: that anything less would not account for the fact that the output of the language-learning situation is itself knowledge. In other words, Chomsky shares an important area of common ground with sceptical empiricism. Empiricism establishes sceptical conclusions by arguing in accordance with the following principle: if someone knows that something is the case on the basis of, or in consequence of, certain evidence or data, it follows that he must already know, explicitly or implicitly, whatever else (if anything) is necessary for what he consequentially knows to be logically derivable from what he already knows in conjunction with the data. Since the evidence is inadequate, he must know some suppressed major premise from which, in conjunction with the evidence, his consequential knowledge logically follows. Chomsky's input-output version of this is: if someone knows that something is the case on the basis of, or in consequence of, certain facts as input, we must, to explain that output of knowledge in terms of that input, ascribe to the person himself principles that are necessary to generate logically that output from that input. So far as there is any argument in Chomsky for the specific claim that what is innate is knowledge, rather than for the general claim that what is innate is psychological structure, it seems to depend on identifying his principle with the empiricist principle. Hume, doubting that we can have the innate knowledge required, uses the principle to throw doubt on our claims to consequential knowledge. Chomsky, taking our consequential knowledge as a datum, in effect seems to use the principle to show that we must have the required innate knowledge.

The weakness of this procedure is twofold: this condition on knowledge is too stringent even in normal cases; and the situation of the child learning his first language is anyway far from being a normal case of the acquisition of knowledge.

On this first matter, it is odd, on the face of it, that Chomsky should insist on such stringent conditions for consequential knowledge and allow such lax conditions for innate knowledge: to know a language a child needs not only the data but also knowledge of the general form of any human grammar; but he can apparently know the general form of any human grammar without so much as a scrap of evidence. Hume at least was consistent on this point. However, given his principle and a refusal to doubt commonplace claims to knowledge, the stringency and laxness of Chomsky's conditions on knowledge can be seen clearly as two sides of the same coin. If we try to account for knowledge by tightening up the standards to an almost impossible pitch in one place, we shall have to relax them beyond reason in another: as in other contexts, the price of a Puritanical exterior is an interior where anything goes.

It might be objected that my paradigm example of knowledge, though setting standards less stringent than Chomsky's for consequential knowledge, is still too rigorous to model the child's acquisition of knowledge of the language. The answer to this is that the example is, and was presented as, one central case of knowledge; there is no implication that its conditions are necessary for all cases. One good reason for not treating the child's acquisition of language as a central case of this sort is that until the process of acquisition has gone far enough to give the child a fair mastery of the language, he occupies, with the birds, bees and fishes, that area where the application of the concepts of belief and knowledge is essentially disputable. Even more disputable are the concepts of reasoning and inferring involved in my paradigm example. Positively inapplicable are the concepts in terms of which Chomsky models the child's acquisition of language—the concepts of forming hypotheses about linguistic structure and testing them against the evidence. Chomsky is, of course, fully aware that this picture of the child as a scientific genius is only a formal reconstruction of the language-learning situation. But it is only in the context of this picture that Chomsky's input-output principle can be plausibly identified with its counterpart in sceptical empiricism, the input represented as data or evidence, the process represented as the forming and testing of hypotheses against the evidence, and the consequential knowledge of the language represented as inferred from, or logically based on, the data, which then become the child's reasons justifying his claim to know the language. It is only in this context that the child's innate contribution can with any plausibility be identified as knowledge: the concept of knowledge here is part of the formal reconstruction, not literally applicable.

For the child to be correctly and literally described as knowing the language we do not need to interpret the picture literally. But as we relax the third condition in my paradigm, the condition requiring that the person to whom knowledge is ascribed should have reasons justifying his assurance, the application of the concept demands, in compensation, more stringent conditions of other kinds. The first condition, or some analogue, is tightened up, and we require not simply that the person concerned should believe what is true, or more generally get something right, on one occasion, but that he should continue to get things of that same sort right on other occasions: one and the same skill or competence is then attributed to him as being exercised on these different occasions, i.e., his getting these things right is an exercise of knowledge. The claim that this is knowledge is further strengthened precisely if the causal or quasi-causal explanation of how this competence was acquired appeals to facts that, if they were attributable to the person concerned as his reasons justifying the claim to knowledge, would logically support that claim. In this way, for example, a woman may be said to know intuitively or instinctively that her husband is worried or anxious. The force of these adverbs 'intuitively' and 'instinctively' is to imply on the one hand that the worry or anxiety were not directly observed in any publicly checkable sense, and on the other hand that she did not reason it out, come to the conclusion, or infer, that her husband was worried or anxious. We ascribe to her an intuition or instinct for things of this sort if she tends to be right about them on different occasions; and this 'faculty of knowledge' can be explained, and confirmed as knowledge, if on this occasion, for instance, she thought that her husband was worried or anxious because of the way he looked at her or because of the set of his shoulders as he walked or sat. The word 'because' here introduces a fact that is neither simply an explanatory cause of her thinking that he was worried or anxious, nor her reason for thinking that he was worried or anxious. But in being a fact that would have been her reason, and in her circumstances of close acquaintance a good one, if she had not only noticed it but had drawn her conclusion from it, the fact, in explaining her thought, also helps to justify it as knowledge. This is not a central case of knowledge, but it is sufficiently like a central case to make the application of the concept reasonable.

The same is true, it seems to me, of the child's knowledge of the language. The chief criterion for the application of the concept of knowledge in this case is the fact that the child is able to use words correctly, i.e., that he can get things right in a variety of situations. Support for this application of the concept is provided by the further fact that the child has been taught the use of words, i.e., that he has been exposed to the input data, and that these data constitute positive evidence that he could, if he were a scientist, cite in justification of his claim to knowledge. If this evidence is not only not evidence to him, in the sense in which he literally uses it to test hypotheses, but is moreover from the point of view of a formal reconstruction logically inadequate to generate what he consequentially knows, an explanation of the child's competence that links input to output through a mental structure that the child shares with all other language users will confirm rather than undermine the characterisation of the output as knowledge; for it will confirm the important practical implication of this characterisation, that the child's ability to use words correctly was not just a fluke but will survive in unforeseen circumstances in the future. This will not be a central case of knowledge; but in fulfilling these laxer conditions, which are, so to speak, natural analogues of the stricter logical conditions, it will be considerably closer to the centre than Chomsky's alternative of innate knowledge.

Notes

¹ [The Beckman Lectures were published as *Language and Mind* (New York, 1968). Ed.]
² "Recent Contributions to the Theory of Innate Ideas", in *Synthese,* XVII I (Mar. 1967), p. 9. [Reprinted in this volume, p. 237. Ed.]
³ Ibid., pp. 2–3. [Reprinted in this volume, p. 231. Ed.]
⁴ Ibid., pp. 7–8. [Reprinted in this volume, p. 236. Ed.]
⁵ *Aspects of the Theory of Syntax* (Cambridge, Mass., 1965), p. 25.
⁶ See also E. H. Lenneberg, 'The Capacity for Language Acquisition', in *The Structure of Language,* ed. Fodor and Katz (New York, 1964).

14. Jerry A. Fodor

Methodological Arguments for Behaviorism

It is universally acknowledged that a reasonable condition upon the acceptability of a scientific theory is that it be the simplest among those that are formally capable of accounting for the data. It must also be acknowledged that we do not at present possess a satisfactory, uniform measure of simplicity: that is, one that comes close to consistently giving intuitively plausible results in all the clear cases. The current situation is rather that the simplicity of a theory might reasonably be measured along any of a number of different dimensions, and it is by no means evident that all these measures produce the same ordering. One might, for example, maintain that the simplest theory is the one that recognizes the smallest number of "ultimate" laws (i.e., laws not deducible from covering laws of greater generality), or that the simplest theory is the one that can be specified with the smallest number of terms that denote unobservables, or with the smallest number of symbols in some designated vocabulary, and so on. Nor is it precluded that the most satisfactory definition of simplicity would require some weighted function of a number of such criteria.

Just as it seems plausible to argue that considerations of simplicity require us *ceteris paribus* to prefer a theory that postulates few unobservables to a theory that postulates many, so it may also be maintained that simplicity requires us to prefer a theory in which the terms that designate unobservables are logically connected to observation terms, as against a theory in which they are not. For it seems evident that theories of the latter sort are in some sense potentially more powerful than theories of the former sort, and clearly we must prefer the weaker of two theories when both are capable of accounting for the data.

We can imagine an array of increasingly powerful psychological theories, ordered in terms of increasing liberalization of the connections they permit between theoretical terms and observation terms. The least powerful such theory, and hence the one we would be committed most to prefer, all other things being equal, would presumably be the one in which all theoretical terms are eliminable in favor of observation terms—that is, a strict reductionism. The most powerful such theory, and hence the one we would be committed to prefer least, all other things being equal, would be one in which no theoretical terms are logically connected to any observation terms—that is, a strict realism in which all statements in the theory are independent, except as they are related by rules of formal logic (and, perhaps, by dictionary analyticities of the "Bachelors are unmarried" variety). Intermediate possibilities include theories in which theoretical terms are required to be mapped one-one (or one-many) to observables by correlating semantic rules—for example, theories that, though nonreductive, nevertheless require "criteria" for each of the theoretical terms.

We have been interpreting simplicity principles as rules that tell us which of a pair of competing theories it would be rational to choose, where two theories count as competitive only if they are formally incompatible and both capable of accounting for the known data. But it is also possible to adopt such principles as specifying a priori constraints on the notion of a putative explanation—for example, to decide that one will not regard as acceptable any theory that relaxes beyond a certain point the logical connection between theoretical and behavioral terms. To adopt such a principle in this way is tantamount to adopting what may prove a very strong assumption about the phenomena under investigation: that they are in fact no more complex than may be explained by theories constructed in accordance with the methodological rule in question. For example, to adopt the principle that one will not accept as a putative explanation of behavior any theory in which the theoretical terms are not definable in the observation language is tantamount to assuming that any intervening variable that is employed in the explanation of behavior is in principle elimi-nable—that is, that one will not in fact encounter behavior of such complexity that the simplest way of explaining it would require the uneliminable employment of an intervening variable.

Now, the important thing about such an assumption is that it is sometimes possible to provide rather convincing evidence of its falsehood. For it is sometimes possible to demonstrate the existence of phenomena the simplest available explanation of which requires the employment of theoretical entities in a way that violates the methodological rule at issue. Thus, in a famous psychological controversy, mediational learning theorists have argued that the phenomena of learning cannot be explained unless we abandon strictly reductive methodological principles in favor of principles that would permit some theoretical entities not eliminable in terms of observables.

It is worth considering one example of the sort of psycho-logical finding that may prove relevant to settling this sort of methodological question. It is well known that, under certain circumstances, conditioning (classical and operant) exhibits limited transitivity. Suppose, for example, that we condition a response B to a stimulus A and a response C to the event B. (Thus, A, B, and C might be paired-associate nonsense syl-lables, conditioned A-B, B-C.) Under such circumstances, it is relatively easy to demonstrate that presentations of A are sig-nificantly likely to produce C as a response, even though the pair A-C has not ever occurred during learning trials.

In such cases, one is very strongly tempted to assume the covert occurrence of B as an "unobserved," "mediating," or "intervening" response. That is, it is natural and plausible to suppose that the subject, upon being provided with A as stimulus, actually produces B as an unobserved response, and that it is this occurrence of B that serves in turn as the stimulus for the observed response C. This view would seem still more plausible if, for example, we could find data indicating that the latency for an overt response C to stimulus B is characteristically shorter than the latency for an overt response C to the stimulus A, for such data would suggest the presence of some intervening operation in the A-C situation that is absent in the B-C situation.

Since we can imagine data that would be directly relevant to the truth of the proposed explanation, it looks as though it is an empirical rather than a methodological question whether the explanation is correct. Yet, the explanation proposed is of a kind to which we are not entitled if we have adopted strict reductionism as a methodological principle. For such a principle requires that we introduce into psychological explanations no theoretical vocabulary that cannot be replaced by terms for observables. Thus there appears to be an impasse: either we give up this explanation (and all other explanations that are logically similar to it), or else we give up the methodological principle.

What we do in fact will, of course, be determined by a number of considerations: how sure we are of the relevant data; how much simplification the employment of explanations of this sort introduces into our general account of behavior (where "simplification" means "simplification as measured by indices other than the degree of logical connectedness between theoretical and observation terms"); what we take to be the precedents in other areas of science, and so on. The important point is that one can easily imagine situations in which it would be rational to abandon the methodological principle rather than the explanation—circumstances in which we would say that the arguments in favor of postulating the mediating response were overwhelming. It is in this rather devious way that our methodological commitments may themselves be required to face the data.

This point is extremely important for a discussion of the methodological arguments concerning behaviorism. It means that we may regard a commitment to behaviorism as involving a speculation about the complexity of those phenomena that psychological explanations will have to account for. This suggests in turn that it may be possible to conceive of circumstances in which the gross facts about the data, together with considerations of naturalness, general economy, and so on might require us to abandon the commitment to behaviorism. For example, if it is possible to demonstrate the occurrence of psychological phenomena for which the simplest available explanation requires us to hypothesize the occurrence of mental events that do not exhibit behavioral correlates, then, since even the weakest variety of behaviorism requires at least that such correlates exist for each type of mental event, we shall be in a situation of forced choice. In particular, we shall be required either to abandon the explanation or else to abandon the methodological principle that forbids explanations of that type.

It is, in fact, easy to find such cases in the psychological literature. The recent display of disenchantment with behaviorism on the part of a number of experimental psychologists is presumably the result of a growing awareness of the methodological significance of these cases.

We shall examine one such case in detail. It has to do with some recent experimentation involving the perception of speech. (The results that are informally discussed below are presented at length by Fodor and Bever [1965] and by Garrett, Bever, and Fodor [1966] where, however, a slightly different experimental paradigm is employed. Readers interested in the details should consult those two papers.)

It is a commonplace to describe speech in a language that one does not know as "torrential." Foreign languages are "spoken in a rush"; foreigners "talk too fast." If, however, one reflects upon the way speech in one's own language sounds, one notes that it appears to come in chunks, separated by pauses of greater or lesser duration. While foreign languages strike the ear as an almost continuous flow of sound, one's own language appears to be segmented in some quite definite way. Moreover, speakers exhibit considerable interjudge reliability when they are asked to describe the segmentation of particular sentences in their language. For example, they tend to agree on where the longest pauses in a sentence are, or which of two pauses in a sentence is the longer.

This situation is somewhat puzzling. If, as one might suppose, the perception of a pause in speech is simply the perception of a drop in the acoustical energy of the physical speech signal, it is hard to understand why the pausal characteristics of the languages one happens to know should appear to differ from those of languages one does not know. If, one the other hand, the perception of pause is in some way independent of the physical characteristics of the speech signal, it is difficult to understand why speakers agree when they are asked to indicate where the pauses are.

Since pause recognition appears to be in some way contingent upon linguistic competence, and since any clue to the nature of linguistic competence is ipso facto valuable, inquiries have been undertaken into the nature of the perception of pausal segmentation in speech. As a result of these inquiries, it is now possible to give a reasonably convincing account of this aspect of speech perception. That is, we can construct a theory that allows us to predict where the pauses are likely to be heard in speech and what relative length they are likely to be perceived as having. Moreover, this theory enables us to explain both why the perception of pausal structure should be contingent upon linguistic competence and why it should also exhibit the observed interjudge reliability.

The methodologically important point about the theory is this: to accept it is to abandon even the weakest variety of behaviorism since it requires postulating that very abstract and complex mental operations underlie the perception of pausation in speech. Although these operations are, of course, inferred from their behavioral effects (e.g., from the data about where pauses are perceived), there is no serious possibility of assigning individual behaviors as criteria, or even as correlates, to each such operation. Rather, on the view that is incorporated in this theory, the perceived sentence is understood as the product of some very complex integration of the speech signal with linguistic rules. Here, as elsewhere, we cannot associate each operation in the production of a complex artifact with some observable property of the finished product, if only because the traces of earlier operations are sometimes obliterated by the consequences of the later ones. To accept the theory we are about to present is therefore to abandon any methodological principles that require behavioral counterparts for mental events. Conversely, to adhere to methodological behaviorism is to reject this theory, along with whatever explanatory and predictive advantages it affords, and to do so without present hope of replacement.

It appears that the perception of pausation in speech is accounted for by the following generalization: the probability that a pause will be heard at a given point in a sentence is in large part a function of the constituent structure (i.e., of the "parsing") of the sentence at that point and is to that degree independent of the level of acoustic energy of the speech signal. For example, perceptual pauses are more likely to be heard at the syntactic boundaries between words than at those points at which acoustic pauses occur within words. Almost everyone who speaks English will locate a pause in the juncture of the phrase "Bob#Lees," though one can certify by spectrographic analysis (or, for many speakers, just by carefully attending to repetitions of the phrase) that the acoustic pattern is closer to "Bo#bLees"—that is, that the point of greatest acoustic energy drop is before the second "b," although the perceptual pause comes before the "L." In cases like this (and such cases are the norm), the *perceptual,* but not the *physical,* pause falls at the syntactic juncture. The syntactic structure is largely independent of the acoustic structure and it is by the former and not by the latter that the percept is determined.

Words are, of course, not the only sorts of syntactic constituents. It can be shown on purely linguistic grounds that the syntactic analysis of a sentence must involve a parsing (bracketing) of the sentence into nested units of various length. Thus, a simple sentence, such as "The man hit the colorful ball," has roughly the following constituent structure:

((The) (man)) ((hit) ((the) ((colorful) (ball))))

The generalization stated above (that pauses tend to be heard at constituent boundaries) may be sharpened to predict that the probability that a pause will be heard at a given point in a sentence varies with the number of constituents coterminous at that point. This turns out to be correct, at least for the major junctures. Thus, most speakers tend to locate the longest pause on one or the other side of "hit" in "The man hit the colorful ball"—although, in acoustic fact, normal utterances of this sentence contain no major energy drop at all.

It is at this point that the methodological problems arise. We have seen that the perception of a pause in a sentence is not typically a discriminative response to fluctuations in the acoustic energy of a speech signal. On the contrary, one apparently locates pauses largely by reference to the constituent structure of the sentences in which they are heard. When one perceives a pause in a sentence, what one is perceiving is determined by one's knowledge of the sentence's derived constituent structure.

Assuming then that recognition of the constituent structure is essential to the perception of segmental pause, and assuming too that the analysis of constituent structure is independent of the acoustics, the problem presents itself: How is the constituent structure of a sentence recognized by the persons who hear it?

The general outlines of the answer to this question are now fairly clear. The constituent structure of a sentence is automatically specified by the rules of certain sorts of grammars.

Such grammars also have a number of other properties that are clearly related to the capacities actually exhibited by speakers of natural languages: they afford a recursive characterization of the set of grammatical sequences of morphemes, they provide analyses of certain types of structural ambiguity that are exhibited by some sentences of all natural languages, they predict the obligatory stress patterns exhibited in spoken sentences, and so on.

The inference would appear to be that the data processing that is involved in the perception (or, for that matter, in the production) of a sentence in one's own language involves the application of the sort of rules that such grammars formulate. In particular, understanding a sentence in one's native language involves using such rules to assign the appropriate constituent analysis and it is that assignment, in turn, that dictates the perceived pausal segmentation the sentence bears. This hypothesis accounts for the fact that different speakers agree on the location of pauses in the sentences of their language, as well as for the fact that the ability to apprehend such pauses is confined to sentences uttered in a language one understands. For in the former case all speakers of a language presumably employ the same constituent structure rules and in the latter case learning the constituent structure rules for a language is part of learning the language.

But now, what of the operations that are involved in applying such rules? (Or, for that matter, in learning them; the following remarks apply, *mutatis mutandis,* to either performance.) In the first place, it is clear that they are *unconscious* operations, in the sense that they cannot be reported by subjects. Hence the justification for assuming that they occur is largely that they are required by such patterns of explanation as the one just rehearsed. More to the point, it is clear that there are no behavioral *correlates* for such operations and *a fortiori* no behavioral *criteria* for them. That is, just as it is patently false to assume that each assignment of brackets to some stretch of a sentence is associated with some disposition to provide a verbal report of that assignment, so it is also false to assume that such bracketings are associated with characteristic forms of nonverbal behavior. Behavior is produced when the sentence is understood, if it is produced at all; thus, individual mental operations are related to behavior only via the entire computational process of which they form a part. The justification for positing such operations in a psychological explanation can be, then, neither that subjects report their occurrence nor that some nonverbal behavioral index of their occurrence has been observed. Rather, we posit such operations simply because they are required for the construction of an adequate theory of speech perception.

To summarize: what happens when one hears a sentence in a language one knows is apparently that the acoustic signal is integrated by reference to some set of rules that the hearer has internalized during the course of learning the language. This integration is apparently the result of data-handling operations whose output is (*inter alia*) an analysis of the sentence into constituents. How many such operations must take place in the case of a particular sentence, and precisely what transformations are performed upon the acoustic input during the course of such analyses, are problems for psychological and linguistic theory. What is evident, however, is that these operations implicate behavior only in the very indirect sense that they are involved in understanding a sentence; and that, having understood a sentence, the hearer may (or may not) choose to act upon what he has understood.

It should be stressed that the example we have discussed, although perhaps relatively dramatic, is by no means atypical. The literature on the psychology of perception is filled with reports of phenomena whose most persuasive explanation would be precluded by adherence to any substantive form of behaviorism—that is, to any methodological canon about the relation of theoretical to observation terms that amounted to more than a warning against proliferating mental entities beyond necessity. Characteristically, such phenomena have to do with "constancies,"—that is, cases in which normal perception involves radical and uniform departure from the informational content of the physical input. It has been recognized since Helmholtz that such cases provide the best argument for unconscious mental operations, for there appears to be no alternative to invoking such operations if we are to explain the disparity between input and percept.

Behavioristic accounts of perception as involving the disposition to produce discriminative responses to physical differences among stimuli are plausible only when an isomorphism obtains between perceptual distinctions and specifiable stimulus differences. Where this isomorphism breaks down (as in the failure of perceptual pauses in sentences to correspond to anything that is acoustically marked) some unconscious data processing must be hypothesized. Philosophers who object to such explanations as a matter of principle, as well as philosophers who propose to defend behaviorism on simplicity grounds, would appear to owe a detailed account of these phenomena that avoided mentalistic postulations. The dignified silence that they have so far maintained on such matters does not really amount to an argument.

References

Fodor, J., and T. Bever (1965). "The Psychological Reality of Linguistic Segments," *Journal of Verbal Learning and Verbal Behavior,* IV (1965), 414–420.

Garrett, M., T. Bever, and J. Fodor (1966). "The Active Use of Grammar in Speech Perception," *Journal of Perception and Psychophysics,* I (1966), 30–32.

15. Noam Chomsky

Some Empirical Assumptions in Modern Philosophy of Language[1]

The classical empiricist theory of acquisition of knowledge is perhaps the clearest such theory that has received expression, and also, no doubt, the most influential. It is hardly necessary to document its influence—"dominance" might be a more accurate term—in linguistics and learning theory, for example. I would like to consider here some of the ways in which empiricist assumptions about acquisition of knowledge have ap-

From *Philosophy, Science and Method: Essays in Honor of Ernest Nagel* (New York: St. Martin's Press). Copyright 1969 by St. Martin's Press, Inc. Reprinted by permission.

peared in recent philosophy, specifically, in connection with the problem of language acquisition. The question seems to me worth pursuing because of the possibility of interpreting these assumptions as factual claims, claims which are, furthermore, highly debatable—in my opinion, quite erroneous—although no argument or evidence is given in support of them. Perhaps they are regarded as self-evident. My purpose here is not to demonstrate the falsity of these assumptions, but rather to try to determine how they enter into some recent and important thinking about the nature of language.

In its classical version, a narrow empiricist doctrine of acquisition of knowledge, as expressed most clearly by Hume, maintains that the mind, initially a blank tablet, receives impressions from the sense organs as a "passive mirror" (I omit, in this narrow theory, the matter of secondary impressions). Faded impressions—ideas—are associated with one another in accordance with certain fixed principles, which Hume enumerates as the principles of similarity, contiguity, and cause-effect relation, the latter being based on a certain "animal instinct." This proposal concerning the nature of mind becomes an empirical hypothesis of real substance when the various notions that appear in it are properly clarified. Thus properties of the sense organs will determine the nature of "impressions," and properties of the mind will determine just what counts as contiguity, similarity, and inductive evidence for establishment of causal relations. (Modern versions might add primitive S-R connections, certain assumptions about stimulus sampling, etc., but this is irrelevant here.) As an empirical hypothesis about the nature of mind, this empiricist view should be faced with evidence, as Hume, in his own way, insisted. Evidence can be brought to bear on this hypothesis at several levels. First, we might attempt to give a careful characterization of some system of human knowledge and then determine whether this system has the properties implied by the empiricist assumptions about how knowledge must be acquired. At this level, the question at issue is one of adequacy in principle of certain assumptions. Second, assuming the answer to the first question to be affirmative, or at least not obviously negative, we might go on to ask whether under empirically given conditions of access to data, this system could have been acquired by the mechanisms and in the manner postulated. This is a question of feasibility. Analogous questions can be asked about animals and their acquisition of knowledge and belief.

It is sometimes supposed that the empiricist assumptions

constitute a kind of null hypothesis, to be held until refuted, as the "simplest" or "most natural" thinkable. This is a curious point of view. The issue of relative "simplicity," even if this notion can be given some content relevant to choice among theories, can hardly be sensibly raised in connection with theories so meager in confirming evidence and explanatory force as those that have been proposed to account for learning and behavior. What is more, it is difficult to see on what rational grounds an empiricist theory can be shown to be "simpler" than, let us say, a pure reminiscence theory, which might also be characterized in a quite definite way, and held, irrelevantly, to be "simpler" in that it minimizes the role of learning. Surely, it cannot be maintained that there are some physical conditions of plausibility that support the empiricist view. It would, in fact, be quite remarkable if the physical conditions under which the brain develops and its detailed and intricate organization had no effect on the way associations can develop, as presupposed in the empiricist view, though it remains a logical possibility that this is so, just as it remains a logical possibility that all mental structures are developed through association. There would be no difficulty in designing a brain model that worked in quite a different way. Thus to adopt the empiricist position without argument or evidence would be mere dogmatism, *a priorism* of a sort that is no better founded in the study of mind than the study of any particular aspect of physiology, or in any other intellectual pursuit.

It might be supposed that the modern investigation of learning departs from the classical empirical approach in some fundamental way, avoiding its limitations and inadequacies. This question is irrelevant to the specific topic of this paper, but I think that anyone who explores the literature of learning theory will discover that despite much increase in knowledge and sharpening of technique, the theories that have been clearly formulated come no nearer to providing an account of normal learning—language learning, for example—than the classical approach. Either they remain within this framework in essential respects, or else they have shifted attention to such matters as control of behavior, establishment of behavioral repertoires or habit hierarchies, or the setting up of S-R connections through conditioning, and have thus largely abandoned the problem of accounting for acquisition of knowledge. To say this is to make no criticism of this work, which must be evaluated in terms of its own goals and interests, but simply to point out that there is, for the moment, no more reason to give it the

general designation "theory of learning" than to give this designation to molecular biology (which at least has the merit
of occupying itself with fundamental questions rather than with
phenomena and processes which may very well be quite marginal in normal learning or behavior).

Similarly, the commonly voiced argument that the basic
questions are begged in a nonempiricist account also seems
to me entirely without substance. How the mind reached its
present state of structure and organization is, of course, a fair
question, though it is one that can hardly be posed in any
sensible way until we have achieved some understanding of the
nature of that structure and organization. But the particular
assumptions of, let us say, a theory that attributes certain ideas
and principles to the mind as an innate property do not beg
that question any more or less than the conflicting assumptions
of the empiricist theory of mind. Of no greater substance is the
argument that whatever innate structure there may be developed through evolutionary mechanisms, so that the empiricist
approach is still basically correct, though on the phylogenetic
level.[2] For one thing, even if the notion of "development
through evolutionary mechanisms" can be made moderately
precise and the claims of "phylogenetic empiricism" verified
in terms of this now clear concept, the whole matter would have
nothing to do with the question of origin of knowledge or belief
in the case of a given organism. Furthermore, it is important to
bear in mind that this notion is, for the present, almost empty,
and with it, the claims of "phylogenetic empiricism"; it is, in
fact, perfectly posssble that the innate structure of mind is determined by principles of organization, by physical conditions,
even by physical laws that are now quite unknown, and that
such notions as "random mutation" and "natural selection"
are as much a cover for ignorance as the somewhat analogous
notions of "trial and error," "conditioning," "reinforcement,"
and "association." It is not that these notions do not have a
clear interpretation under certain restricted conditions; what
is in question is their significance when extended, in a purely
metaphorical way, well beyond the restricted conditions in
which they have been studied in many careful and important
investigations.

Finally, certain essentially terminological objections might
be raised against alternatives that have been proposed to an
empiricist hypothesis. For example, there is evidence that the
most primitive interpretation of visual phenomena by human
infants makes use of the basic perceptual constancies, but

one might ask whether the phrase "innate knowledge of the properties of objects in three-dimensional space" is one that should be used in describing the presumably innate schematism that underlies these abilities. In general, there is no refined or sufficiently elaborate terminology available for dealing with the "infinite amount of knowledge of which we are not always conscious," of which Liebniz spoke, or with the unconscious innate principles that determine the character of this knowledge. Therefore, one must extend, sharpen, or modify familiar usage when studying these problems. It is conceivable that this practice might lead to conceptual confusion of some sort, but unless this can be demonstrated, the terminological issues need not delay the attempt to study the innate structures and principles that serve as a precondition for experience and the basis for acquisition of knowledge. In the particular case of language, it is clear that at a certain state of maturation and development a child can properly be said to know his language (perfectly, by definition, language having no objective existence apart from its mental representation). We can then ask what role his experience played in determining the precise character of what he knows, for the most part unconsciously, at this stage. It is hard to see why we should withhold the term "innate knowledge of language" or "innate knowledge of the nature of language" from principles or systems of substantive elements that underlie and enter into the knowledge that is acquired, and that might be shown, through empirical investigation, to be independent of experience in their form and content. But the terminological question, in any event, hardly seems worth pursuing.

In short, it seems to me that the question of the basis for acquisition of knowledge is an open, empirical question, to be settled by empirical investigation rather than by *a priori* argument or by pure conceptual analysis. Specifically, the empiricist assumptions have no special status among the many theories that might be proposed to account for the acquisition of knowledge of language, or anything else.

Perhaps the clearest and most explicit development of what appears to be a narrowly Humean theory of language acquisition in recent philosophy is that of Quine, in the introductory chapters to his *Word and Object*.[3] If the Humean theory is roughly accurate, then a person's knowledge of language should be representable as a network of linguistic forms—let us say, to first approximation, sentences—associated with one another and, in part, associated to certain stimulus conditions. This formulation Quine presents as, I take it, a factual assertion. Thus he states that our "theories"—whether "deliberate," as chemistry, or "second nature," as "the immemorial doctrine of ordinary enduring middle-sized objects"—can each be characterized as "a fabric of sentences variously associated to one another and to nonverbal stimuli by the mechanism of conditioned response" (p. 11). Hence the whole of our knowledge (our total "theory," in this sense) can be characterized in these terms.

One difficulty that arises in interpreting such passages as these has to do with the relation between language and theory, where the latter term covers also general common-sense knowledge and belief. Quine's views about the interpenetration of theory and language are well-known, but, even accepting them fully, one could not doubt that a person's language and his "theory" are distinct systems. The point is too obvious to press, but it is, nevertheless, difficult to see how Quine distinguishes the two in his framework. In fact, throughout the discussion, he seems to use the terms interchangeably. For example, in Chapter 1, he discusses the learning of language in general terms, exemplifies it by an example from chemical theory leading up to the statement just quoted, then seemingly describes the "vast verbal structure" so constructed, the associative network that constitutes one's knowledge of sciences ("and indeed everything we ever say about the world"), as both the "body of theory" that one accepts and the language that one learns. Thus the discussion of how one constructs and uses a total theory of this sort concludes with the following statement:

Beneath the uniformity that unites us in communication there is a chaotic personal diversity of connections, and, for each of us, the connections continue to evolve. No two of us learn our language alike, nor, in a sense, does any finish learning it while he lives.

Since this comment merely summarizes the discussion of how the "single connected fabric" constituting our total theory is acquired (the latter discussion itself having been introduced to exemplify language-learning), it seems that Quine must be proposing that a language, too, is "a fabric of sentences variously associated to one another and to nonverbal stimuli by the mechanism of conditioned response." Other parts of this exposition reinforce the conclusion that this is what is intended, as we shall see in a moment. Nevertheless, interpretation of Quine's remarks is made difficult at points because of his tendency to use the terms "language" and "theory" interchangeably, though obviously he must be presupposing a fundamental difference between the two—he is, for example, surely not proposing that two monolingual speakers of the same language cannot disagree on questions of belief, that controversy over facts is necessarily as irrational as an argument between a monolingual speaker of English and a monolingual speaker of German.

Elsewhere, Quine states that he is considering a language as a "complex of present dispositions to verbal behavior, in which speakers of the same language have perforce come to resemble one another" (p. 27). Thus if a language is a network of sentences associated to one another and to external stimuli by the mechanism of conditioned response, then it follows that a person's disposition to verbal behavior can be characterized in terms of such a network. This factual assumption is far from obvious. I return to other aspects of this concept of "language" below.

How is knowledge of such a language acquired? As noted above, a Humean theory will acquire substance if such notions as "similarity" are characterized in some way. Quine therefore postulates a prelinguistic (and presumably innate) "quality space" with a built-in distance measure (pp. 83–84). Evidently, the structure of this space will determine the content of the theory of learning. For example, one could easily construct a theory of innate ideas of a rather classical sort in terms of a prelinguistic quality space with a built-in distance measure. Quine would, apparently, accept a very strong version of a theory of innate ideas as compatible with his framework. Thus he considers the possibility that "a red ball, a yellow ball, and a green ball are less distant from one another in . . . the child's . . . quality space than from a red kerchief." It is difficult to see how this differs from the assumption that "ball" is an innate idea, if we admit the same possibilities along other "dimensions" (particularly, if we allow these dimensions to be fairly abstract). In this respect, then, Quine seems to depart quite radically from the leading ideas that guided empiricist theory and to permit just about anything imaginable, so far as "learning" of concepts is concerned. In particular, consider the fact that a speaker of English has acquired the concept "sentence of English." Suppose that we were to postulate an innate quality space with a structure so abstract that any two sentences of

English are nearer to one another in terms of the postulated distance measure than a sentence of English and any sentence of another language. Then a learner could acquire the concept "sentence of English"—he could, in other words, know that the language to which he is exposed is English and "generalize" to any other sentence of English—from an exposure to one sentence. The same is true if we mean by "sentence of English" a pairing of a certain phonetic and semantic interpretation. We could, once again, construct a quality space sufficiently abstract so that the infinite set of English sentences could be "learned" from exposure to one sentence, by an organism equipped with this quality space.

The handful of examples and references that Quine gives suggests that he has something much narrower in mind, however; perhaps, a restriction to dimensions which have some simple physical correlate such as hue or brightness, with distance defined in terms of these physical correlates. If so, we have a very strong and quite specific version of a doctrine of innate ideas which now can be faced with empirical evidence.

It might be thought that Quine adds empirical content to his account by his insistence that "the child's early learning of a verbal response depends on society's reinforcement of the response in association with the stimulations that merit the response . . ." (p. 82) and his general insistence throughout that learning is based on reinforcement. But, unfortunately, Quine's concept of "reinforcement" is reduced to near vacuity. For example, he is willing to accept the possibility that "society's reinforcement consists in no more than corroborative usage, whose resemblance to the child's effort is the sole reward" (pp. 82–83). To say that learning requires reinforcement, then, comes very close to saying that learning cannot proceed without data. As Quine notes, his approach is "congenial . . . to Skinner's scheme, for . . . [Skinner] . . . does not enumerate the rewards." The remark is correct, but it should also be added that "Skinner's scheme" is almost totally empty, in fact, if anything even less substantive than Quine's version of it, since Skinner, as distinct from Quine, does not even require that reinforcing stimuli impinge on the organism—it is sufficient that they be imagined, hoped for, etc. In general, the invoking of "reinforcement" serves only a ritualistic function in such discussions as these, and one can safely disregard it in trying to determine the substantive content of what is being proposed.

However, Quine returns to a classical empiricist conception of a nonvacuous sort in his assumptions about how language is learned. Consistent with his view of language as a network of sentences,[4] he enumerates three possible mechanisms by which sentences can be learned—i.e., by which knowledge of language can be acquired (p. 9f.). First, sentences can be learned by "direct conditioning" to appropriate nonverbal stimulations, that is, by repeated pairing of a stimulation and a sentence under appropriate conditions; second, by association of sentences with sentences (let us put aside the objection that, in both cases, the associations should soon disappear, through extinction, under normal circumstances); third, new sentences can be produced by "analogical synthesis."[5] The third method at first seems to offer an escape to vacuity, once again. Thus if the first sentence of this paper is derivable by analogical synthesis from "the sky is blue" (both involve subject and predicate, are generated with their interpretations by the rules of English grammar, and share many other properties), then it is no doubt true that language can be learned by "analogical synthesis," by "generalization" along a dimension of the abstract sort suggested above (cf. pp. 293–294, this book). But it seems clear that Quine has nothing of this sort in mind. The one example that he gives is a case of substitution of one word for a similar one ("hand," "foot") in a fixed context. And he seems to imply that the process of analogical synthesis is theoretically dispensable, simply serving to speed matters up (see p. 9). Therefore, we can perhaps conform to his intentions by totally disregarding this process, and considering the knowledge attained by a long-lived adult using only the first two methods instead of the knowledge attained by a young child who has used all three (there being nothing that can be said about the latter case until the notion "analogical synthesis" is given some content). Noting further that a child of nine and a man of ninety share knowledge of language in fundamental respects—each can understand and use appropriately an astronomical number of sentences, for example—it would seem, further, that little is lost in omitting "analogical synthesis" from consideration entirely, even for the young child. Assuming that this interpretation of Quine's remarks is correct, we derive support for the conclusion that he regards a language as a finite network of associated sentences, some associated also to stimuli, since this is just the structure that would arise from the two postulated mechanisms of language learning. This interpretation of Quine's rather inexplicit comments on "analogic synthesis" is supported further by his practice of referring to acquisition of knowledge of language as a matter of "learning of sentences." It is unclear what sense there would be to the assertion that a person has "learned" a sentence that takes twice as long to say as his entire lifetime. Correspondingly, Quine's manner of formulating the process of language acquisition would permit no way of stating how this sentence might be encompassed in the person's knowledge of his language; thus Quine offers no way to describe the fact that the person has acquired rules or principles that determine the form and meaning of this sentence. If language-learning is based on the three mechanisms enumerated, it can yield a network of "associated" sentences, but not a generative system of rules and principles that determine the form and meaning of indefinitely many sentences. "Learning of sentences" is not "learning of language."

Against this interpretation of Quine's remarks on language we can bring the fact that it is inconsistent with a truism that he of course accepts, namely, that a language is an infinite set of sentences (with intrinsic meanings; cf., e.g., p. 71). A network derived by the postulated mechanisms must be finite; it can, in fact, contain only the sentences to which a person has been exposed (repeatedly, and under similar circumstances). If we return to the definition of "language" as a "complex of dispositions to verbal behavior," we reach a similar conclusion, at least if this notion is intended to have empirical content. Presumably, a complex of dispositions is a structure that can be represented as a set of probabilities for utterances in certain definable "circumstances" or "situations." But it must be recognized that the notion "probability of a sentence" is an entirely useless one, under any known interpretation of this term. On empirical grounds, the probability of my producing some given sentence of English—say, this sentence or the sentence "Birds fly" or "Tuesday follows Monday" or whatever—is indistinguishable from the probability of my producing a given sentence of Japanese. Introduction of the notion of "probability relative to a situation" changes nothing, at least if "situations" are characterized on any known objective grounds (we can, of course, raise the conditional probability of any sentence as high as we like, say to unity, relative to "situations" specified on ad hoc, invented grounds). Hence if a language is a totality of speech dispositions (in some empirically significant sense of this notion), then my language either does not include the sentences just cited as examples, or it includes all of Japanese. In fact if the "complex of dispositions" is determined on grounds of empirical observation, then only a few conventional greetings, clichés, and so on, have much chance of being associated to the complex defining the language, since few other sentences are likely to have a nonnull relative frequency, in the technical sense, in any reasonable corpus or set of observations—we would, for example, expect the attested frequency of any given sentence to decrease without limit as a corpus increases, under any but the most artificial conditions. One might imagine other ways of assigning probabilities to sentences on empirical grounds, but none, so far as I can see, that avoid these difficulties. Hence if a language is a complex of dispositions to respond under a normal set of circumstances, it would be not only finite (unless it included all languages) but also extremely small.

Adding to the confusion is the fact that Quine appears to vacillate somewhat in his use of the notion "speech dispositions." Thus he formulates the problem of "indeterminacy of translation" as resulting from the fact that "manuals for translating one language into another can be set up in divergent ways, all compatible with the totality of speech dispositions, yet incompatible with one another" (p. 27). As just noted, if we take the "totality of speech dispositions" of an individual to be characterized by probability distributions for utterances under detectable stimulus conditions, then the thesis quoted is true, near-vacuously, since except for a trivial set, all such probabilities will be empirically indistinguishable on empirical grounds, within or outside of the language. On the other hand, if we interpret the notion "disposition" and "situation" more loosely, it might be argued that the problem is really quite different, that there will be so few similarities among individuals in what they are inclined to say in given circumstances that no manual of translation can be set up at all, compatible with such inclinations. Actually, Quine avoids these problems in his exposition by shifting his ground from 'totality of speech dispostions" to "stimulus meanings," that is, dispositions to "assent or dissent" in a situation determined by one narrowly circumscribed experiment. He even goes so far as to say that this arbitrarily selected experiment provides all of the evidence that is available, in principle, to the linguist (equivalently, to the language learner—p. 39). Clearly, however, a person's total "disposition to verbal response" under arbitrary stimulus conditions is not the same as his "dispositions to be prompted to assent to or dissent from the sentence" under the particular conditions of the Gedankenexperiment that Quine outlines. One might argue that by arbitrarily limiting the "totality of evidence,"

Quine irrelevantly establishes the thesis that alternative theories (manuals of translation) exist compatible with all of the evidence (though the general thesis of indeterminacy of translation is nevertheless certainly true, in a sense to which we return in a moment). But my point here is only that this kind of vacillation makes it still more difficult to determine what Quine means by "disposition" or "language."

It is easy to imagine a way out of the difficulties posed by the implied finiteness of language and knowledge (or near emptiness, if the notion of "disposition" is taken very seriously). Thus one might assume that knowledge of a "universal grammar," in the widest sense, is an innate property of the mind, and that this given system of rules and principles determines the form and meaning of infinitely many sentences (and the infinite scope of our knowledge and belief) from the minute experiential base that is actually available to us. I do not doubt that this approach is quite reasonable, but it then raises the empirical question of the nature of this universal, *a priori* system; and, of course, any philosophical conclusions that may be drawn will depend on the answers proposed for this question.[6] Quine's attitude toward an approach of this sort is not easy to determine. It certainly seems inconsistent with his general point of view, specifically with his claim that even our knowledge of logical truths is derived by conditioning mechanisms that associate certain pairs of sentences (cf., e.g., p. 11f.), so that our knowledge of logical relations must be representable as a finite network of interconnected sentences. (How we can distinguish logical connections from causal ones or either type from sentences which happen to be paired by accident in our experience is unclear, just as it is unclear how either sort of knowledge can be applied, but it is pointless to pursue this issue in the light of the strangeness of the whole conception.) Elsewhere, however, Quine appears to take the view that truth-functional logic might provide a kind of "universal grammar." Thus he asserts (§ 13) that truth functions lend themselves to "radical translation" without "unverifiable analytical hypotheses," and hence can be learned directly from the available evidence. He gives no real argument for this beyond the statement, which appears quite irrelevant to the factual issue involved, that we can state truth conditions in terms of assent and dissent. The inference from what we can observe to a postulated underlying structure involving truth-functional connectives of course requires assumptions that go beyond evidence—mutually incompatible alternatives consistent with the evidence can easily be constructed. Hence Quine's willingness to place these matters within the framework of radical translation perhaps indicates that he is willing to regard the system of truth-functional logic as available, independently of experience, as a basis for language-learning. If so, it seems quite arbitrary to accept this framework as innate schematism and not to admit much else that can be imagined and described.[7] In view of the unclarity of this matter and the apparent inconsistency of the proposal just discussed with Quine's explicit characterization of "theory" and "language" and the mechanisms for acquiring them, I will put aside any further consideration of this topic.

We are left with the fact that Quine develops his explicit notion of "language" and "theory" within a narrowly conceived Humean framework (except for the possible intrusion of a rich system of innate ideas), and that he characterizes language-learning ("learning of sentences") in a way consistent with this narrow interpretation, although the conclusion that a language (or theory) is a finite fabric of sentences, constructed pairwise by training, or a set of sentences with empirically detectable probabilities of being produced (hence a nearly empty set) is incompatible with various truisms to which Quine would certainly agree.

Quine relies on his empirical assumptions about the acquisition of knowledge and learning of language to support some of his major philosophical conclusions. One critical example will serve to illustrate. Fundamental to knowledge are certain "analytical hypotheses" that go beyond the evidence. A crucial point, for Quine, is that the correctness of analytical hypotheses, in the case of ordinary language and "common sense knowledge," is not "an objective matter" that one can be "right or wrong about." These analytical hypotheses "exceed anything implicit in any native's disposition to speech behavior." Therefore, when we use these analytical hypotheses (as we must, beyond the most trivial cases) in translating, in learning a language in the first place, or in interpreting what is said to us under normal circumstances, we "impute our sense of linguistic analogy unverifiably to the native mind." The imputation is "unverifiable" in the sense that alternatives consistent with the data are conceivable; that is, it is "strong verifiability" that is in question. "There can be no doubt that rival systems of analytical hypotheses can fit the totality of speech behavior to perfection, and can fit the totality of dispositions to speech behavior as well, and still specify mutually incompatible translations of countless sentences insusceptible of independent control" (p. 72). These remarks Quine puts forth as the thesis of "indeterminacy of translation."

To understand the thesis clearly it is necessary to bear in mind that Quine distinguishes sharply between the construction of analytical hypotheses on the basis of data and the postulation of "stimulus meanings of observation sentences" on the basis of data. The latter, he states, involves only uncertainty of the "normal inductive" kind (p. 68). The same is true, apparently about the inductive inference involved in translation (similarly, "learning" and "understanding") of sentences containing truth-functional connectives. In these cases, induction leads us to "genuine hypotheses," which are to be sharply distinguished from the "analytical hypotheses" to which reference is made in the discussion of indeterminacy of translation. Hence Quine has in mind a distinction between "normal induction," which involves no serious epistemological problem, and "hypothesis formation" or "theory construction," which does involve such a problem. Such a distinction can no doubt be made; its point, however, is less than obvious. It is not clear what Quine is presupposing when he passes over the "normal uncertainty of induction" as within the range of radical translation. If clarified, this would add more content to his empirical theory of acquisition of knowledge, by specification of the *a priori* properties on which "normal induction" and the notions of relevant and sufficient evidence are based. It would then be necessary for him to justify the empirical assumption that the mind is natively endowed with the properties that permit "normal induction" to "genuine hypotheses" but not "theory construction" with some perhaps narrowly constrained class of "analytical hypotheses."

To return to the thesis of indeterminacy of translation, there can surely be no doubt that Quine's statement about analytical hypotheses is true, though the question arises why it is important. It is, to be sure, undeniable that if a system of "analytical hypotheses" goes beyond evidence, then it is possible to conceive alternatives compatible with the evidence, just as in the case of Quine's "genuine hypotheses" about stimulus meaning and truth-functional connectives. Thus the situation in the case of language, or "common sense knowledge," is, in this respect, no different from the case of physics. Accepting Quine's terms, for the purpose of discussion, we might say that "just as we may meaningfully speak of the truth of a sentence only within the terms of some theory or conceptual

scheme, so on the whole we may meaningfully speak of interlinguistic synonymy[8] only within the terms of some particular
system of analytical hypotheses" (p. 75). But, Quine answers:

*To be thus reassured is to misjudge the parallel. In being able to
speak of the truth of a sentence only within a more inclusive
theory, one is not much hampered; for one is always working
within some comfortably inclusive theory, however tentative.
. . . In short, the parameters of truth stay conveniently fixed
most of the time. Not so the analytical hypotheses that constitute the parameter of translation. We are always ready to wonder about the meaning of a foreigner's remark without reference
to any one set of analytical hypotheses, indeed even in the
absence of any; yet two sets of analytical hypotheses equally
compatible with all linguistic behavior can give contrary answers, unless the remark is of one of the limited sorts that can
be translated without recourse to analytical hypotheses* [pp.
75–76].

Thus what distinguishes the case of physics from the case
of language is that we are, for some reason, not permitted to
have a "tentative theory" in the case of language (except for
the "normal inductive cases" mentioned above). There can be
no fixed set of analytical hypotheses concerning language in
general. We need a new set for each language (to be more
precise, for each speaker of each language), there being nothing universal about the form of language. This problem, then,
is one that faces the linguist, the child learning a language (or
acquiring "common sense knowledge," given the intercon-
nection between these processes), and the person who hears
or reads something in his own language.

To summarize, Quine supposes an innate quality space with
a built-in distance measure that is, apparently, correlated to
certain "obvious" physical properties. Furthermore, certain
kinds of inductive operations (involving, perhaps, generalization in this quality space) are based on innate properties of the
mind, as are also, perhaps, certain elements of truth-functional
logic. Utilizing these properties, the child (or the linguist doing
radical translation) can form certain genuine hypotheses,
which might be wrong but are at least right-or-wrong, about
stimulus meanings and truth-functional connectives. Beyond
this, language-learning (acquisition of knowledge) is a matter
of association of sentences to one another and to certain
stimuli through conditioning, a process which results in a cer-

tain network of interconnected sentences or, perhaps, a certain system of dispositions to respond. Language-learning is a matter of "learning of sentences." It is impossible to make significant general statements about language or common sense theories, and the child has no concept of language or of "common sense" available to him prior to his training. In this respect, the study of language is different from, let us say, physics. The physicist works within the framework of a tentative theory. The linguist cannot, nor can the psychologist studying a "conceptual system" of the "common sense" variety, just as the child can have no "tentative theory" that guides him in acquiring and learning from experience. Apart from difficulties of interpretation noted above, this is a relatively clear formulation of a classical empiricist doctrine. It involves assumptions which may or may not be true, but for which Quine does not seem to regard evidence as necessary.

Let us briefly consider these empirical assumptions. It is, first of all, not at all obvious that the potential concepts of ordinary language are concepts characterizable in terms of simple physical dimensions of the kind Quine appears to presuppose, or conversely. It is a question of fact whether the concept "house" is characterized, for a speaker of a natural language, as a "region" in a space of physical dimensions, or, as Aristotle suggested, in terms of its function within a matrix of certain human needs and actions. The same is true of many other concepts, even the most primitive. Is a knife, to a child with normal experience, an object of such and such physical properties or an object that is used for such and such purposes; or is it defined by an amalgam of such factors, say as an object meeting certain loose physical conditions that is used for a certain sort of cutting? How would we in fact identify an object looking exactly like a knife but used for some totally different purpose in some other culture?[9] This is as much an empirical question as the question whether concepts characterized in terms of a region in a space of simple physical dimensions can be acquired in the way a child acquires his concepts. There is much to be said in this connection,[10] but it is enough to note in the present context that Quine's empirical assumptions may well be (I believe, certainly are) far too strong— more correctly, too strong in the wrong direction—and that they embody certain quite gratuitous factual assumptions.

Furthermore, consider the idea that "similarity" in a sense appropriate for psychology, the kind of "similarity" needed for an empirical theory of generalization, is definable in terms of distance in a certain space of physical dimensions. There is nothing obvious about this assumption. Two two-dimensional projections of a three-dimensional object may be "similar," in the relevant sense, for an organism that has an appropriate concept of the three-dimensional object and its properties and an intuitive grasp of the principles of projection, although there is no dimension of the presupposed sort along which such stimulations match. We could easily design an automaton which would generalize from one such presentation to another, but not from one of these to a projection of some other three-dimensional object that matched the first in some simple physical dimension. We could, of course, describe the behavior of this automaton in terms of a more abstract quality space, just as we could describe an automaton that learned English from a single sentence in these terms—see pp. 293–294 [this book], above. But this is only to say that it is an empirical problem, quite open for the time being, to determine what are the innate properties of mind that determine the nature of experience and the content of what comes to be known on the basis of (or independently of) this experience.

As far as "learning of sentences" is concerned, the entire notion seems almost unintelligible. Suppose that I describe a scene as rather like the view from my study window, except for the lake in the distance. Am I capable of this because I have learned the sentence: "This scene is rather like the view from my study window, except for the lake in the distance"? To say this would be as absurd as to suppose that I form this and other sentences of ordinary life by "analogical substitution," in any useful sense of this term. It seems hardly necessary to belabor the point, but surely it is clear that when we learn a language we are not "learning sentences" or acquiring a "behavioral repertoire" through training. Rather, we somehow develop certain principles (unconscious, of course) that determine the form and meaning of indefinitely many sentences. A description of knowledge of language (or "common sense knowledge") as an associative net constructed by conditioned response is in sharp conflict with whatever evidence we have about these matters. Similarly, the use of the term "language" to refer to the "complex of present dispositions to verbal behavior, in which speakers of the same language have perforce come to resemble one another" seems rather perverse. Assuming even that the problems noted earlier (pp. 297–298, this book) have been overcome, what point can there be to a definition of "language" that makes language vary with mood, personality, brain lesions, eye injuries, gullibility, nutritional level, knowledge, and belief, in the way in which "dispositions to respond" will vary under these and numerous other irrelevant conditions.[11] What is involved here is a confusion to be found in much behaviorist discussion. To mention just one further example, consider Quine's remarks on synonymy in his "Meaning in Linguistics."[12] Here he proposed that synonymy "roughly consists in approximate likeness in the situations which evoke two forms and approximate likeness in the effect on the hearer." If we take the terms "situation" and "effect" to refer to something that can be specified in terms of objective physical properties, as Quine would surely intend (say as involving observable stimulus condition and observable behavior or emotional state, respectively), then the qualifications in the characterization of synonymy just quoted seem misplaced, for there is not even approximate likeness in the conditions that are likely to elicit (or to serve as occasion for) synonymous utterances or in the effects of such utterances. Suppose that I see someone about to fall down the stairs. What would be the probability of my saying: "Watch out, you'll fall down the series of steps, arranged one behind and above the other in such a way as to permit ascent or descent from one level to another"; and what would the effect on the hearer be in this case? Or consider the likely circumstances and effects of "I'll see you the day after tomorrow," "I'll see you four days after the day before yesterday." This is not a matter of exotic examples; it is simply that the meaning of a linguistic expression (hence synonymy) cannot be characterized in terms of conditions of use or effects on hearers, in general. It is crucial to distinguish *langue* from *parole, competence* from *performance*.[13] What a person does or is likely to do and what he knows may be related in some way that cannot, for the moment, be made precise; the relation is, however, surely in part a factual and not a strictly conceptual one. Performance can provide evidence about competence, as use can provide evidence about meaning. Only confusion can result from failure to distinguish these separate concepts.

Finally, what about the assumption that although in physics we may work within the framework of a tentative theory, in studying language (or in learning language or in translating or interpreting what we hear), this is not possible since it is impermissible to make general statements about language or, more generally, about our "common sense theories" and since innate properties of the mind can impose no conditions on language and theories?[14] This is simply classical empiricist doctrine—perhaps "dogma" would, by now, be a more accurate term. It is difficult to see why this dogma should be taken more seriously than any other. It receives no support from what is known about language-learning or from human or comparative psychology. If it held true of humans, they would be unique in the animal world; and there is no evidence for this particular type of uniqueness. In general, it seems to me correct to say that insofar as empiricist doctrine has clear psychological content, it is in conflict with the not inconsiderable information that is now available. In any event, returning to the present theme, the particular assumptions that Quine makes about the mental processes and structures that provide the basis for human language-learning are quite unwarranted and have no special status among the many assumptions that can be imagined. They can be justified only by empirical evidence and argument. Philosophical conclusions based on these assumptions are no more persuasive than the evidence on which the assumptions rest; that is to say, for the present these conclusions are without force.

Interpreted in a psychological context, then, Quine's thesis of indeterminacy of radical translation amounts to an implausible and quite unsubstantiated empirical claim about what the mind brings to the problem of acquisition of language (or of knowledge in general) as an innate property. This claim seems to me of only historical interest. Interpreted in an epistemological context, as a claim about the possibility of developing linguistic theory, Quine's thesis is simply a version of familiar skeptical arguments which can be applied as well to physics, to the problem of veridical perception, or, for that matter, to his "genuine hypotheses." It is quite certain that serious hypotheses concerning a native speaker's knowledge of English, or the essential properties of human language—the innate schematism that determines what counts as linguistic data and what intellectual structures are developed on the basis of these data—will "go beyond the evidence." If they did not, they would be without interest. Since they go beyond mere summary of data, it will be the case that there are competing assumptions consistent with the data. But why should all of this occasion any surprise or concern?

There are other examples of empiricist speculation of a rather similar sort in modern philosophy of language. Wittgenstein's statements about language-learning in the *Blue and Brown Books* are a fairly clear example, if taken literally.[15]

He speaks of his "language games" as "the forms of language with which a child begins to make use of words," as "primitive forms of language or primitive languages," and he goes on to assert that "we can build up the complicated forms from the primitive ones by gradually adding new forms" (p. 17). He claims that "children are taught their native language by means of such games" (p. 81). Elsewhere, he speaks of children as learning language by "training" in the sense of "animal training," i.e., "by means of example, reward, punishment, and such like" (p. 77). Although the cited example is a primitive and restricted one, it is also one that Wittgenstein takes quite seriously, as we can see from later references, specifically, §17, §50, §55. Furthermore, the notion of "training" persists without qualification; cf., e.g., §7, §18. Later, "training" is distinguished from "general training" (cf. §41, §51), but the latter notion is left virtually unexplained. Although Wittgenstein does refer to the fact that training presupposes a mind that understands (p. 97), he makes no attempt to analyze or explore the significance of this fact or to determine its specific role in determining how knowledge is acquired. (And if I may interpolate a value judgment, it is just when these questions are raised that the problems become challenging and of general intellectual significance.) At the very outset of his discussion (p. 1), he divides explanations of meaning *("very roughly")* into verbal and ostensive; elsewhere, he maintains that words have meanings only when "we give them meanings by explanations" (pp. 27–28). Since the verbal definition "in a sense gets us no further," it is ostensive definitions that are crucial for language-learning. Ostensive definitions can be of two sorts (p. 12): The teaching may be "a drill," or it may supply us with a rule which is explicitly and, presumably, consciously used as "part of the calculation." Since the latter case is almost nonexistent, ostensive definition, in practice, reduces to drill. Putting these remarks together, Wittgenstein appears (on a literal reading) to be claiming that language is taught almost wholly by drill and that knowledge of language grows by training in new "language games" of the peculiar sort that he describes, the process of training being essentially that by which animals can be given an extended "behavioral repertoire."[16] These are, surely, empirical claims. One who takes them seriously should be willing to show, at least in a rough or suggestive way, how ordinary knowledge of language, the kind of knowledge that enables one to understand some simple new sentence, can be described in terms of the mechanisms exhibited in the curious examples of "language games" that are presented as paradigmatic, as constituting the core of language to which bits and pieces are added by further "training" and "drill." It seems hardly likely that one who faces the actual facts of language use will be inclined to undertake this task. Surely Wittgenstein does not.

Do these quite unsupported factual assumptions play a role in establishing any of Wittgenstein's conclusions of a philosophical nature? This is hard to say, given the narrow limitations that Wittgenstein places on philosophy. Insofar as Wittgenstein is merely stating the limitations within which he chooses to work (collecting many examples, indicating their various similarities and differences, etc.), there are, as he points out, no conclusions, hence no reference to a framework of assumptions. It is only when some assertions are made about the relevance or importance of this activity, or about certain empirical or conceptual problems, that the question of rational evaluation arises. It seems (subject to the qualifications of footnote 15) that there are such examples, and that his empirical assumptions do play some role. One of Wittgenstein's rare categorical assertions has to do with the presumed absurdity of "investigating, analyzing, the meaning of a word" (pp. 27–28). He asserts that "a word hasn't got a meaning given to it, as it were, by a power independent of us, so that there could be a kind of scientific investigation into what the word really means. A word has the meaning someone has given to it." As noted above, his view is that "we give them [words] meanings by explanations." The reference is to conscious, explicit explanations of meanings that have been given either in language-teaching or that the speaker will give when asked. If we are not ready to give any explanation, then the word does not "have a strict meaning." This point of view is central to his extremely narrow conception of language acquisition, and much of what he purports to show, or at least what others have taken him to show, is dependent on these assumptions about the meaning of words and how these meanings arise.[17]

It is important to disentangle the factual element in this. Surely there is no difficulty in principle in imagining an organism that approaches the task of language-learning with a rich system of constraints on the possible grammatical rules, possible concepts and their interrelations and relations to sensory evidence, the characteristics of physical objects and the ways in which they interact, the structure of space and time, the organization of human action and the relation of empirical concepts to certain types of human action, a theory of human needs, emotions, feelings, motives, and so on. For such an organism, we would surely want to say that the meanings of words are given to it in part by a power independent of any conscious choice; and a scientific investigation of the conditions that determine how an elaborate semantic and syntactic system was constructed on the basis of evidence would certainly be quite in order. We could imagine an organism so richly endowed that on scanty evidence it would acquire full knowledge of a human language in all its scope and subtlety, quite unconsciously, and with no element of voluntary choice and no ability to give a conscious account (explanations) of the structure of its system of concepts or its system of beliefs, the interrelations among these systems, the strict rules by which it uses language, and so on. The richer the initial endowment, the more limited can be the evidence on the basis of which these mental structures are established. We know, in fact, that some evidence is necessary—there is more than one possible human language. Beyond this, it is an empirical question what variety is possible, what is the nature of the mental structure that develops, and to what extent (if any) its development is more subject to voluntary control than the fact that under certain physical conditions a human embryo will grow two legs. A rejection of these possibilities, as seems to be entailed by a strict reading of the comments of Wittgenstein quoted above, would therefore be purely dogmatic. In fact, from what little we do know about language, it is hard to see how one can seriously doubt that the meaning of words is given largely by a power independent of conscious choice and that language is both used and learned,[18] in accordance with strict principles of mental organization, largely inaccessible to introspection, but in principle, at least, open to investigation in more indirect ways.

It seems quite clear that Wittgenstein intends that there be no empirical assumptions entering into his reasoning and analysis, that "there must not be anything hypothetical in our considerations" (*Investigations I*, p. 109). Nevertheless, as the example just given indicates, I think one can make a case that certain fairly central conclusions do, in fact, rest on empirical hypotheses which are, furthermore, of a very questionable sort. It would be interesting, but beyond the scope of this paper, to explore the matter further in detail. Possible further directions are suggested by some of the concrete examples that Wittgenstein discusses. Wittgenstein declares repeatedly that he is concerned to rid us of the temptation to search for particular mental acts accompanying thinking, meaning, wishing, expecting, and so on, a temptation which, he suggests, will disappear if we cease to imagine the whole system of language (and belief) as a kind of permanent background to what we say, a system that is "present to the mind" all at once and that participates in determining the meaning of each individual utterance that is produced or understood (*Blue and Brown Books,* p. 42). And he focuses attention rather on what actually happens in particular circumstances, for example, when one expects B to come to tea. As he correctly observes, many things may happen, with endless variations—these he refers to, curiously, as "the different processes of expecting someone to tea" (p. 20). Having collected and described various cases of "expecting," our investigation, as philosophers, is not necessarily at an end (we can go on to collect other more complicated cases); but, Wittgenstein holds, we must emancipate ourselves from the "craving for generality" which makes us dissatisfied with a collection of examples and leads us on a vain and misguided search for the "common element" in all the applications of a general term. However, there is much that is amiss in this description of "expecting." For one thing, it makes no sense at all to refer to "processes of expecting" (or to exclamations as being "acts of expecting," as in *Investigations I,* p. 586); and it is unclear what significance there is to the fact that many different things (or, nothing of relevance) may be happening during the period that one expects B to come to tea. I may be going about my business quite as usual without expecting B to come to tea any less, and alongside of expecting B to come to tea, I may also be expecting innumerable other things (e.g., that B will be less than twelve feet tall, that he will greet me warmly, that if admitted to Harvard, he will accept, etc.). Most of these expectations I will not be aware of at all; I may find out about them if, for example, something happens that is contrary to my expectations,[19] or I may never find out about them. In short, expecting, like believing, seems to involve, among other things, a finite generative mental structure that characterizes an unbounded set of possibilities. Limiting ourselves to observations of what, if anything, a person does "while expecting something," we will not even be able to raise the issues posed by an analysis of the concept "expect" and its position in the "full calculus of language." Insofar as this is correct, it is not at all absurd to speak of an "image of the world" that is available to the mind (though not in consciousness, for the most part), and to think of the content of an assertion as determined partly by this system of belief and partly by the full calculus of language that determines the intrinsic meaning of each linguistic expression. The "processes" and "acts" that Wittgenstein describes may provide the evidence that leads us to say that A expects B to come to tea—they justify us in making this assertion. But they do not constitute the meaning or content of this assertion.

Perhaps this is all irrelevant to what Wittgenstein is trying to do, however. Thus at several points he makes a distinction between "conscious mental phenomena" and states of the mind that are postulated as hypothetical constructs, to explain the conscious mental phenomena and much else. The latter are the subject matter for psychology—they are involved in determining "causes"—but are not the business of the philosopher, who is interested only in what "lies open to view," specifically with the description of a family of uses of a word. Thus he is concerned with a certain network of related events but not with the hypothetical mechanisms of mind that might explain them. Wittgenstein does not argue that there are no explanatory mechanisms of this sort. Rather, he holds that these "internal workings of the mind" do not provide the criterion for the correct use of an expression, and furthermore, that there may be no "conscious mental accompaniments" to acts and no statable reasons for performing them. In general, the philosopher's "method is *purely descriptive;* the descriptions we give are not hints of explanations" (p. 125; cf. also *Investigations I*, §§ 109, 126; also the discussion in § 156 of postulated mechanisms that "are only hypotheses, models designed to explain," as opposed to pure descriptions—the word "only" is curious here).

Thus consider the act of reading. The philosopher is concerned to dispel the temptation "to regard the conscious mental act as the only real criterion distinguishing reading from not reading" (p. 121), and his "explanation of the use of this word ... essentially consists in describing a selection of examples exhibiting characteristic features" (p. 125). This selection of examples will, presumably, provide (or suggest to a human intelligence) the criterion for distinguishing reading from not reading. When Wittgenstein refers to the "criterion for distinguishing reading from not reading," he no doubt has in mind criteria which relate to the meaning of the word "read," empirical conditions which are conceptually related in some manner to correct (i.e., true) assertion that so and so is reading, etc. But the criteria that Wittgenstein actually discusses, both here and elsewhere, are not in fact "criteria for correct assertion" in this sense, but rather "criteria for justified assertion," that is, conditions under which a rational person would be justified in stating, possibly erroneously, that so and so is reading, and so on.[20] These are criteria in the sense in which having a certain visual image might serve as a criterion that justifies my asserting that there is an oasis over there while walking through the desert, although my perfectly justified assertion might still be incorrect. It is, however, surely criteria for correct assertion that relate to problems of meaning. An account of the meaning of "oasis" will involve reference to the presence of trees, water, and so forth, not merely to the evidence, however persuasive, that justifies a rational man in saying that he sees an oasis. And just the same is true of the case of "reading." In short, it appears that Wittgenstein's rather obscure use of the notion "criterion" may indicate a belief rather akin to a belief in the possibility of phenomenalist reduction, a belief that meanings of words (and criteria for correct assertion) are some sort of "logical construction" (in a loose way, with various reservations, etc.) from criteria that justify assertion, that is, from evidence. At least, it seems difficult to make sense of his examples on any assumption other than this.

To return to the case of reading, we may ask whether anyone is subject to the temptation to regard a conscious mental event as the criterion for justified assertion, in the manner that Wittgenstein describes; is there, in fact, a temptation to be dispelled? Rather, it seems that there is a temptation to regard the unconscious mental state attributed to A as the criterion for correct (not justified) assertion of the statement that A is reading. And Wittgenstein suggests no argument to indicate that this temptation is in any way misguided. Perhaps, in fact, I have a (no doubt in part unconscious) theory involving the postulated mental states of humans performing certain acts such as reading, etc., which is related to my (also unconscious) system of linguistic rules in such a way that I assert that A is reading when I believe him to be in such a mental state, and my assertion is correct if my belief is correct. In any event, there seems to be little point in arguing at length that observed behavior provides the evidence that leads us to state that A is reading and that justifies us in making the (possibly incorrect) statement that A is reading. This is simply to prove the obvious. Nor is it necessary to elaborate on the fact that such observed behavior falls into vaguely related families; it is of the nature of bits of evidence to be fragmentary, confusing, partial, loosely related, lacking sharp boundaries, etc., that is, to exhibit only "family resemblances." This observation sheds no light on the question whether I am attributing a "criterial mental state" to a person whom I describe as reading, perhaps applying a tacit theory of human action that guides my assessments and judgments. Much as in the case of "expecting," it is questions of the latter sort that might possibly lead to an understanding of the concept "reading" and its position in the "calculus of language."

There is a curious frustration in the attempt to explore and understand Wittgenstein's thought. His examples and remarks, often brilliant and perceptive, lead right to the border of the deepest problems, at which point he stops short and insists that the philosopher can go no further. Ostensive definitions do not carry us very far toward understanding how concepts are learned, and simple "language games" barely illustrate the most superficial, largely instrumental uses of language. In general, evidence of use is merely a prerequisite for the study of meaning, as evidence of performance is merely a prerequisite for the study of competence. To make interesting and intelligent use of evidence, one has to turn to the study of what it means "to understand a language," of the nature of the "forms of life" that determine the "natural history of man," and of the nature of the mind that understands, of "that mechanism . . . born with B, which enabled him to respond to the training in the way he did" (p. 97). Why, then, does Wittgenstein's discussion break off where it does, and why does he impose such deadening limitations on the course that the philosopher may pursue?

Returning to the main theme, if we interpret Wittgenstein as intending literally what he formulates as factual assertions (about language-learning, for example), then what he says seems to fall within the framework of a narrow and dogmatic empiricism. If we interpret him as merely circumscribing the task of the philosopher, limiting it to a "purely descriptive method," to descriptions which "are not hints of explanations," then what he is proposing falls together with other, quite independent tendencies in recent study of language, specifically, with certain tendencies in descriptive linguistics which are also concerned to limit investigation to arrangement of data and "pure description" that avoids any attempt at explanation (the latter being occasionally stigmatized as a kind of infantile obsession). Both approaches make the curious, and I believe stultifying, decision to concentrate on evidence, regarded now as the subject matter of a new discipline (descriptive philosophy, descriptive linguistics), putting aside the question of what the evidence is evidence for. The traditional answer to this question was that the observed phenomena constitute evidence for an underlying mental reality; it would not have surprised any traditional theorist of language or mind that evidence falls into unilluminating networks of family resemblances. It remains to establish the fact that there is some point in restricting one's activities to arrangement of data which are no longer regarded as evidence for the construction of a theory of language or a theory of mind.

There are, of course, very significant differences between Quine and Wittgenstein in their approach to language, mind, and behavior. There also appear to be certain similarities in tacit empirical assumptions and also, apparently, similarities of a more programmatic nature. Quine consciously and purposefully follows modern behaviorism in restricting his concept of "what is learned" to a certain system of dispositions to behave, a habit system, a network of associations. Since this is an entirely inadequate concept of what is learned, his account, like that of modern behaviorism, is largely irrelevant to the problem of acquisition of language (or knowledge, or belief), whatever merits it may have in its own terms. In a parallel way, Wittgenstein (similarly, much of modern descriptive linguistics) explicitly restricts himself to descriptions that do not offer even the hint of an explanation. By thus restricting himself to data in and for itself, as the subject matter of the philosopher's exclusive attention, he necessarily turns away from many interesting and significant questions about the mental reality (language, systems of belief, the basis for perception, etc.) that might be illuminated by use of this descriptive material not merely as data but as evidence. In both cases, we find a restriction of attention to behavior, a studied refusal to examine and elaborate the mental structures[21] that underlie observed performance.[22] There can be no objection in general to restriction of attention to a limited subject matter, but one must ask always whether the domain that is delimited is viable and significant. In this case, serious doubts are in order. In linguistics, I think that the restriction to description that does not give a hint of explanations has been damaging, and an argument can be given that the same is true more generally in psychology. It is doubtful that any serious insight into the nature and organization of behavior can be achieved within these limitations; and furthermore, it is far from clear why an understanding of the organization (or control) of behavior should be regarded as comparable in importance or intellectual interest to an understanding of the underlying mental reality that can be illuminated by the use of behavior as evidence rather than as the object of study. In the specific case of Quine and Wittgenstein, it seems to me that the restrictions that they impose simply exclude from serious study the many fascinating questions that they themselves raise. Classical empiricism can, I think, be reasonably interpreted as an interesting and substantive theory of mind, which is, however, wrong in its specific assumptions and misguided in principle. But its modern variants, in philosophy or in "behavioral science," sometimes reveal a distressing tendency to exclude in principle the kinds of endeavor that might some day significantly enrich our understanding of man's essential qualities and their remarkable manifestations.

Notes

[1] I am indebted to Donald Brown, Jerrold Katz, and Charles Chihara for comments on an earlier version of this paper. This work was supported in part by The National Science Foundation under Grant GS–1430.

[2] Formal parallels between kinds of explanations offered in learning theory and evolutionary theory have frequently been pointed out. See, for example, B. F. Skinner, "The phylogeny and ontogeny of behavior," *Science,* Vol. 153, No. 3741, 9 Sept., 1966, 1205–1213, for recent discussion. Some earlier ideas are discussed by W. H. Thorpe, *Learning and Instinct in Animals,* Methuen, London, 2d edition, 1963, p. 164f. A parallel that is too infrequently noted is the difficulty, in both cases, of constructing a non-vacuous thesis of any generality.

[3] W. V. O. Quine, *Word and Object,* John Wiley and Sons, New York, and Technology Press, Cambridge, 1960. [Quine's essay "Meaning and Translation," which is selection 3 in the present collection, is an independently intelligible version of Chapter 2 of *Word and Object.* It is mainly the questions dealt with in Chapter 2 which Chomsky discusses here. Ed.]

[4] Accepting, that is, the interpretation of his remarks that is discussed above.

[5] Elsewhere, Quine states that "the learning of these wholes (sentences) proceeds largely by an abstracting and assembling of parts" and that "as the child progresses, he tends increasingly to build his new sentences from parts" (p. 13). For consistency of interpretation, we must suppose that this refers to "analogical synthesis," since the three methods enumerated are intended to be exhaustive. If something else is intended, then the scheme again reduces to vacuity, until the innate basis for the "abstracting" and "assembling" is specified.

[6] It is interesting that Russell, in his *Inquiry into Meaning and Truth,* Allen and Unwin, London, 1940, with his concept of real logical form and of logical words as expressing a mental reality, does appear to presuppose a structure that would avoid at least these very obvious problems. But a discussion of Russell's quite intricate and interesting approach to these

questions, though a useful undertaking, is impossible within the scope of this paper.

7 The reasons for this choice would take us too far afield, into a much more general consideration of Quine's thesis, developed later in the book, about the scheme of discourse that one must use in "limning the true and ultimate structure of reality" (p. 221), and in describing "all traits of reality worthy of the name" (p. 228).

8 Recall, again, that Quine is using the concept of "interlinguistic synonymy" as a device for describing not only translation but also learning of language in the first place and interpretation of what is said to him by one who knows a language.

9 Cf. Philippa Foot, "Goodness and choice," *Proceedings of the Aristotelian Society*, Supplementary Volume 35; 45–60. She comments, correctly I am sure, that we would describe such objects as looking exactly like knives, but *being* something else. See also the remarks by J. Katz on such words as "anesthetic" in his "Semantic theory and the meaning of 'good,'" *Journal of Philosophy*, Vol. 61, No. 23, Dec. 10, 1964, pp. 739–66.

10 Consider, for example, the experimental evidence that has been produced purportedly showing differences between apes and humans in ability to carry out cross-modal transfer. The difference is sometimes attributed to the "linguistic tags" available to the human. (Cf. A. Moffet, and G. Ettlinger: "Opposite responding in two sense modalities," *Science*, No. 3732, 8 July, 1966, 205–206, and G. Ettlinger, in *Brain Mechanisms Underlying Speech and Language*, F. L. Darley, ed., in press). Another possibility that suggests itself is simply that the "concepts" used in the experimental situation, being defined in terms of conjunction or disjunction of elementary physical properties (as is the general procedure in concept-formation experiments), are entirely artificial and mismatched to the "concept space" of the tested animal. The human subject, however, imposes his own system of concepts (since he understands what the experiment is about, etc.). Under the conditions of the experiment, the distinction between the artificial concepts of the experimenter and the natural concepts of the subject might well be undetectable. Hence it might be that no difference between apes and humans in cross-modal transfer (and nothing about linguistic tags) has yet been shown by such experiments, and that what is shown is merely that an animal (or human) cannot make reasonable use of concepts that are mismatched to the innate structure of his system of concepts.

11 Of the cited conditions, the one that might be regarded as relevant is "knowledge and belief." Thus it makes sense to argue that under certain conditions, a change in belief may entail a modification of language. But surely it is senseless to hold that wherever difference of belief leads to a difference of disposition to verbal behavior, there is necessarily a difference of language involved.

12 In *From a Logical Point of View*, Harvard University Press, Cambridge, 1953.

13 The issue is not simply one of observation versus abstraction but rather one of significant versus pointless idealization. A set of dispositions to repond is a construction postulated on the basis of evidence, just as is a generative grammar that attempts to characterize "knowledge of a language." In Quine's terms, the first is based on "genuine" and the second on "analytical" hypotheses, but only in a sense of "genuine" that is divorced from its ordinary meaning (or else on the basis of a value judgment that seems to me quite unsupportable). It would be more accurate to say that setting up a "complex of dispositions to respond" is merely a pointless step, since such a structure has no interesting properties, so far as is known.

14 Except, as noted earlier, for the constraints imposed by the structure of the quality space, the system of truth-functional logic, certain primitive forms of induction, and the capacity to form arbitrary associations.

15 One difficulty in interpreting Wittgenstein, however, is that it is unclear when what he says is to be taken literally. Some remarks are so outrageous that one can only suppose that something else was intended (e.g., when he asserts that thinking may be the "activity performed by the hand,

when we think by writing"). A second difficulty is the indefinite and non-committal style. Still, remarks such as those cited seem to indicate a fairly specific point of view.

Still another difficulty, in the specific case of the *Blue and Brown Books* is, of course, the question whether in detail they do or do not reflect Wittgenstein's views. In the *Philosophical Investigations,* the positions that I want to discuss are less prominent than in the *Blue and Brown Books,* though I find little there that might challenge these positions. In any event, what I will be discussing is the text of the *Blue and Brown Books,* which may or may not express what Wittgenstein really believed about these matters.

[16] This kind of terminology may suggest, erroneously, that animal training is simply a matter of adding arbitrarily selected bits of behavior to a collection of "habits." Actually, such terms are appropriate to a description of animal training only at the most superficial level. For some interesting comments on this matter, see K. Breland and M. Breland, "The misbehavior of organisms," *American Psychologist,* 16, 1961, 681–84; also Thorpe, *op. cit.,* p. 461–2 and references cited there.

[17] Similar ideas appear elsewhere. For example, D. F. Pears argues that naming is ultimately inexplicable, "that any comprehensive explanation of naming is necessarily circular" ("Universals," in A. Flew, ed., *Logic and Language,* second series, Basil Blackwell, Oxford, 1953). Ostensive definitions clearly do not in themselves explain the basis for naming, and verbal explanations do not give us an exit from the "maze of words." "Naming cannot be explained by anything which really goes beyond a reasoned choice of usage," since concepts are "completely identifiable only by their use." All that we can say about a "well-constructed series of things" (i.e., a set of things named by a word in a single sense) is just that it is well constructed. No comprehensive answers can be given to the question of what is common to such sets or how such "nameable" sets are distinguished, on general grounds, from other sets. Experimental psychology can only give "the varying tests of the good construction of a series, and not its essence." It cannot, then, characterize the essential properties of "generalization" or "concept formation," for a given organism, presumably. The desire to explain naming, beyond recording details of usage or giving tests, is "the result of the Protean metaphysical urge to transcend language."

Whether a concept is identifiable in terms of its "use" or in terms of "a reasoned choice of usage" is impossible to discuss, given the vagueness of these notions, but it certainly seems clear that the problem of determining what is a "well-constructed series of things" for a particular organism is one that can be studied in a serious way. The varying tests provided by experimental psychology can provide evidence, as can observation of usage and introspection. And on the basis of such evidence, one can try to formulate a theory regarding the "attainable concepts" and the "attained concepts," in particular, the system of concepts embedded in a person's internalized grammar. Evidently, the theory that we construct about a person's grammar (or about attainable grammars) will be underdetermined by evidence, since the task is not a triviality—the concepts that we attribute to him will not be "completely identifiable," in any interesting sense, by observed usage, without the intrusion of certain assumptions of a theoretical nature. Having arrived at a tentative theory concerning a person's grammar, we can consider the data on the basis of which he constructed this internalized grammar, which incorporates, in particular, a system of concepts. Finally, we can construct a hypothesis as to the *a priori* system of principles, conditions, and assumptions that led the person to construct this system from the given data (where the process is, no doubt, not only unconscious but also, quite likely, inaccessible to consciousness, and, quite likely, entirely deterministic insofar as the vast central areas of language are concerned). Such a hypothesis will specify, correctly or incorrectly, what can be "well-constructed sets" for a human, and will offer an explanation as to why a particular term has a specific referential scope. The problem of "explaining naming," so formulated, may be largely intractable, but it does not reflect a "Protean metaphysical urge" any more than the attempt to study various other, for the moment relatively intractable problems, for example, problems involving determinants of maturation and growth or origin of species, etc.

[18] Though certainly language is not taught in accordance with strict rule. In fact, there is no reason to suppose that language need be taught at all.

[19] But the matter is not simple. Thus one must distinguish *expecting someone* from *expecting of someone that he will do something,* or simply *expecting that something will happen or will be the case.* And one must distinguish *not expecting something to happen* from *expecting it not to happen;* and, as in the case of belief and knowledge, one must identify and analyze separately the various factors that may permit the consequences of what is expected, even those that follow by known and accepted principles, to be themselves unexpected. A better analysis of what is involved in "expecting" might build on some of the remarks in the *Philosophical Investigations I,* ¶¶ 575, 577. Although such an analysis must consider those consequences of a rule that one may draw "as a *matter of course*" (*ibid.,* ¶ 238), it will surely be inadequate if it limits itself to these, avoiding the implications of the possibility of Socratic "teaching."

[20] Whatever he may have meant by the term "criterion," his general practice is to give criteria for justified but not necessarily correct assertions. There are many examples: *Investigations I,* ¶ 344: "Our criterion for someone's saying something to himself is what he tells us and the rest of his behavior." *Investigations I,* ¶ 269: "Let us remember that there are certain criteria in a man's behavior for the fact that he does not understand a word, that it means nothing to him, that he can do nothing with it. And criteria for his 'thinking he understands,' attaching some meaning to the word, but not the right one. And lastly, criteria for his understanding the word right," *Investigations I,* §§ 154–155: "If there has to be anything 'behind the utterance of the formula' it is particular *circumstances,* which justify me in saying I can go on—when the formula occurs to me . . . for us it is *the circumstances* under which he had such an experience that justify him in saying in such a case that he understands, that he knows how to go on." Evidently, it is what a person tells us and what he does that justifies us in believing that he is saying something to himself; evidently, there is no necessary connection between satisfaction of these "criteria" and the fact of his saying something to himself. Similarly, in the other cases. Hence it is hard to imagine how one could claim that such "criteria" could somehow exhibit the meaning of such expressions as "he is saying something to himself."

For an illuminating discussion of this whole matter, see Rogers Albritton, "On Wittgenstein's use of the term 'criterion'," *J. of Philosophy,* vol. 61, 1959, pp. 845–857, reprinted, with an additional note, in G. Pitcher, ed., *Wittgenstein: The Philosophical Investigations,* Anchor Books, Garden City, N.Y., 1966.

If there were anyone who held the view that a conscious mental act (of the reader) is the real criterion for distinguishing reading from not reading, he would not be much impressed by a selection of examples exhibiting characteristic features, etc., of cases where a person is said to be reading (possibly erroneously). Rather, he would hold that these examples do, in fact, constitute a "veil of inessential features," and that evidence of usage could no more refute his conviction that reading involves a conscious mental act than citation of characteristic usages of "There is an oasis" could refute his convictions regarding the conditions under which this assertion is true and regarding the meaning of "oasis." The "transitional cases" that Wittgenstein imagines would be regarded as unclear by such a person, on the grounds that we do not have convincing evidence as to the presence of the criterial mental state. We might say that in "normal cases" criteria for justified usage do serve as criteria for correct assertion as well, but this is empty unless "normal cases" are something other than cases in which justified assertions are, furthermore, correct. The long discussion of the same matter in the *Investigations* seems to me to shed no further light on the issues.

[21] Or, potentially, their physical realizations, though it must be emphasized that this is a subject that is not, for the moment, accessible to direct study.

[22] The currency of the appellation "behavioral science" for the study of man and society is another manifestation of the same intellectual tendency in that it in effect defines this study in terms of its data rather than its natural subject matter. It is almost as though physics were renamed "science of meter-reading." What, in fact, would we expect the natural sciences to amount to in a culture that felt satisfied with a characterization of them in such terms as these?

Annotated Bibliography

The following literature is recommended for those who need to supplement their background in empiricism.

For an excellent comprehensive anthology of the great works of modern empiricism, see A. J. Ayer and Raymond Winch, eds., *British Empirical Philosophers* (London: Routledge and Kegan Paul, 1952). In addition to the basic epistemological writings of Hume and his immediate and most distinguished empiricist predecessors, John Locke and George Berkeley, this anthology includes John Stuart Mill's classic formulation of phenomenalism.

Since until very recently empiricism has been the orthodoxy of twentieth century philosophy and theory of science, I shall list only a few representative works of major figures who have accepted most or all of the orthodoxy. *Logic and Knowledge,* ed. Robert C. Marsh (New York: Macmillan Co., 1956), which is a collection of Bertrand Russell's most influential philosophical essays, contains the essential documents of Russell's philosophy of logical atomism, a logicized version of Hume's doctrine of simple and complex ideas. Another major logicization of Hume's empiricism is the philosophy of logical empiricism, of which A. J. Ayer's *Language, Truth and Logic* (London: Gollancz, 1936) is an exceedingly clear expression. Gilbert Ryle's *The Concept of Mind* (New York: Barnes and Noble, 1949) is a classic example of the use of the techniques of ordinary language philosophy in support of contemporary empiricist doctrines such as behaviorism and instrumentalism. As for empiricist works by practicing scientists, the following three books are paradigms. P. W. Bridgman, *The Logic of Modern Physics* (New York: Macmillan Co., 1927) is a pioneering account of operationalism as applied to the concepts of physics; it uses Einstein's account of simultaneity as a model of operational definition. Leonard Bloomfield, *Language* (New York: Holt, 1933) set the empiricist style of descriptive linguistics, which became orthodoxy for scientific linguistics until the advent of Chomsky. B. F. Skinner, *Verbal Behavior* (New York: Appleton-Century-Crofts, 1957), is the incursion of the world's leading behaviorist psychologist into human verbal behavior.

Another virtue of Ayer and Winch's *British Empirical Philosophers* is that it contains key criticisms of Hume and his predecessors made by Hume's contemporary, Thomas Reid. Along with Reid's works, Kant's *Critique of Pure Reason* (1781) contains the most important pre-twentieth century challenge to the principles of empiricism. The best introduction to this side of Kant's difficult book is P. F. Strawson's *The Bounds of Sense* (London: Methuen, 1966). In his 1948 paper, "The Problem of Empiricism," Roderick Chisholm first uncovers the principal reason that makes it impossible to translate or paraphrase statements about physical things into statements about sense data. This essay and other classic twentieth century criticisms of the empiricist doctrine of sense data are contained in Robert J. Swartz, ed., *Perceiving, Sensing, and Knowing* (Garden City, N.Y.: Doubleday & Co., 1965). As indicated in the Introduction to this book, Wittgenstein's argument against the possibility of a private language is a major argument against the doctrine of sense data. Although the core of Wittgenstein's remarks on private language are mostly contained in a few pages (pp. 88–104) of his posthumously published *Philosophical Investigations* (Oxford: Blackwell, 1953), it is difficult to interpret and assess these remarks. H. Morick, ed., *Wittgenstein and the Problem of Other Minds* (New York: McGraw-Hill Book Co., 1967) contains interpretations and assessments of these remarks by Wittgenstein's keenest critics as well as by his leading admirers. Also relevant to Wittgenstein's critique of sense data are his "Notes for Lectures on 'Private Experience' and 'Sense Data'" (*The Philosophical Review*, 77: 1968, pp. 275–320). Further impressive criticisms of the doctrine of sense data are to be found in J. L. Austin's *Sense and Sensibilia* (Oxford: Oxford University Press, 1962). Kant, Wittgenstein, Strawson, and Chisholm have exposed the major deficiencies and incoherencies of Humean accounts of self and self-knowledge. For Strawson and a guide to Kant see "Hume and Kant on the Self" and the rest of the section on "Soul" in Strawson, op. cit.; see also Robert Paul Wolff, *Kant's Theory of Mental Activity* (Cambridge, Mass.: Harvard University Press, 1963). For Wittgenstein, see Morick, op. cit. For Chisholm, see his "On the Observability of the Self" (*Philosophy and Phenomenological Research*, 30: 1969, pp. 7–21).

The following literature is recommended for those who wish to learn more about the major contemporary challenges to empiricism:

Ayer, A. J. *The Origins of Pragmatism.* San Francisco: Freeman, Cooper & Co., 1968. A philosopher thought of as a leading empiricist abandons the standard empiricist approach to ontology. This is an excellent introduction to the founding ideas of pragmatism. From this movement has come a formidable challenge to many of the assumptions of empiricism.

Bernstein, Richard J. "Sellars' Vision of Man in the Universe." *Review of Metaphysics,* 20 (1966), pp. 113–43; 290–316. An introduction to Sellar's philosophy.

Bohnen, Alfred. "On the Critique of Modern Empiricism." *Ratio,* 11 (1969), pp. 38–57. Bohnen argues that empiricist principles imply assumptions about the nature of perceptual processes which are incompatible with results of the scientific study of perception by psychologists such as Wolfgang Kohler and Jerome Bruner.

Carnap, Rudolph. "Testability and Meaning." *Philosophy of Science,* 1936 and 1937. Reprinted in *Readings in the Philosophy of Science,* edited by Herbert Feigl and May Brodbeck. New York: Appleton-Century-Crofts, Inc., 1953. Carnap abandons the empiricist doctrine that all concepts, including those of the sciences, are reducible to ostensive concepts. This statement marks the beginning of "liberalized" or mitigated logical empiricism.

Carnap, Rudolph. "The Methodological Character of Theoretical Concepts." In *Minnesota Studies in the Philosophy of Science,* vol. 2, edited by Herbert Feigl, Michael Scriven, and Grover Maxwell. Minneapolis: University of Minnesota Press, 1958. Further steps in the liberalization of empiricism.

Chihara, C. S., and Fodor, J. A. "Operationalism and Ordinary Language: a Critique of Wittgenstein." *American Philosophical Quarterly,* 2(1965), pp. 281–95. Reprinted in *Wittgenstein and the Problem of Other Minds,* edited by Harold Morick. New York: McGraw-Hill Book Co., 1967. Argues that Wittgenstein holds an operationalist account of our knowledge of the psychological states of others and that this facet of contemporary empiricism is untenable.

Chomsky, Noam. *Aspects of the Theory of Syntax.* Cambridge, Mass.: M.I.T. Press, 1965.

Chomsky, Noam. *Cartesian Linguistics.* New York: Harper & Row, 1966.

Chomsky, Noam. *Language and Mind.* New York: Harcourt Brace Jovanovich, 1968. *The* introduction to Chomsky; in a nontechnical way Chomsky explains fundamentals of transformational grammar and shows how it challenges empiricist assumptions.

Duhem, Pierre. *The Aim and Structure of Physical Theory.* New York: Atheneum, 1962. (French edition, 1914.) A classic forerunner of Quine's views.

Einstein, Albert. "Remarks on Bertrand Russell's Theory of Knowledge." In *The Philosophy of Bertrand Russell,* edited by Paul Arthur Schilpp. Evanston, Ill.: Northwestern University, 1944. Einstein claims that from Hume's principles "a fateful 'fear of metaphysics' arose which has come to be a malady of contemporary empiricist philosophizing" and that, contrary to Hume's principles, "the concepts which arise in our thought and in our linguistic expressions are all—when viewed logically—the free creations of thought which can not inductively be gained from sense-experiences."

Feyerabend, Paul K. "Explanation, Reduction and Empiricism." In *Minnesota Studies in the Philosophy of Science,* vol. 3, edited by Herbert Feigl and Grover Maxwell. Minneapolis: University of Minnesota Press, 1962.

Feyerabend, Paul K. "Problems of Microphysics." In *Frontiers of Science and Philosophy,* edited by R. G. Colodny. Pittsburgh: University of Pittsburgh Press, 1962.

Feyerabend, Paul K. "Materialism and the Mind-Body Problem." *Review of Metaphysics,* 17 (1963), pp. 49–66.

Feyerabend, Paul K. "Problems of Empiricism." In *Beyond the Edge of Certainty,* edited by R. G. Colodny. Englewood Cliffs, N.J.: Prentice-Hall, 1965. Selection 8 of the present collection is "a concise summary of results which I have explained in a more detailed fashion" in the first, second, and fourth of the above Feyerabend entries. In the third entry, "Materialism and the Mind-Body Problem," Feyerabend argues against the empiricist doctrine that a person's conception of what he directly experiences cannot be shaken by scientific advances.

For further development of Feyerabend's challenge to empiricism see:

Feyerabend, Paul K. "Realism and Instrumentalism." In *The Critical Approach to Science and Philosophy: Essays in Honor of Karl Popper,* edited by M. Bunge. Glencoe, Ill.: Free Press, 1964.

Feyerabend, Paul K. "Against Method." In *Minnesota Studies in the Philosophy of Science,* vol. 4. Minneapolis: University of Minnesota Press, 1970.

Feyerabend, Paul K. "Problems of Empiricism, Part 2." In *The Nature and Function of Scientific Theory,* edited by R. G. Colodny. Pittsburgh: University of Pittsburgh Press, 1970.

Fodor, Jerry A. *Psychological Explanation.* New York: Random House, 1968. An extended critique of behaviorist psychology, from which selection 14 of the present volume has been excerpted.

Fodor, Jerry A., and Chihara, C. S. See Chihara and Fodor.

Fodor, Jerry A., and Katz, Jerrold J., eds. *The Structure of Language.* Englewood Cliffs, N.J.: Prentice-Hall, 1964. The most accessible comprehensive introduction to the new linguistics approach to traditional philosophical problems. Especially noteworthy is Chomsky's "A Review of B. F. Skinner's *Verbal Behavior."*

Goodman, Nelson. *Fact, Fiction, and Forecast.* 3rd ed. Indianapolis: Hackett Pub. Co., 1973. In which Goodman poses what he calls the New Riddle of Induction, a newly discovered and so far intractable problem for empiricist epistemology.

Hanson, N. R. *Patterns of Discovery.* Cambridge: Cambridge University Press, 1958. Applies gestalt psychology to the history of science in order to challenge the distinction between observations and theories.

Harman, Gilbert. "Quine on Meaning and Existence." *Review of Metaphysics,* 21 (1967), pp. 124–51; pp. 343–67. An introduction to Quine's philosophy.

Harman, Gilbert. "An Introduction to 'Translation and Meaning,' Chapter Two of *Word and Object." Synthese,* 1968. Reprinted in *Words and Objections: Essays on the Work of W. V. Quine,* edited by Donald Davidson and Jaakko Hintikka. Dordrecht: D. Reidel Publishing Co., 1969. This collection contains a complete list of Quine's publications through 1969.

Harman, Gilbert. "Psychological Aspects of the Theory of Syntax." *Journal of Philosophy,* 64 (1967), pp. 75–87. A critical review of Chomsky's *Aspects of the Theory of Syntax,* which focuses on Chomsky's critique of empiricism.

Hempel, C. G. *Aspects of Scientific Explanation.* New York: Free Press, 1965. Twelve papers, mostly from the 1950s, in which it can be seen to what extent logical empiricism has liberalized its early strict empiricist principles. See especially "Empiricist Criteria of Cognitive Significance: Problems and Changes."

Hook, Sidney, ed. *Language and Philosophy.* New York: New York University Press, 1969. The second and by far the longest section of this collection contains symposium papers and comments dealing with Chomsky's neorationalist challenge to empiricism. Some of the contributors are Chomsky, Goodman, Quine (selection 12 of the present collection), Sidney Hook, and Gilbert Harman.

Katz, Jerrold J. *The Philosophy of Language.* New York: Harper & Row, 1966. A Chomskian view.

Katz, Jerrold J. "Mentalism in Linguistics." *Language,* 1964.

Katz, Jerrold J., and Fodor, Jerry A. See Fodor and Katz.

Kuhn, Thomas S. "Second Thoughts on Paradigms." In *The Structure of Scientific Theories,* edited by Frederick Suppe. Urbana, Ill.: University of Illinois Press, forthcoming. A reconsideration of one of the central notions, or family of notions, in *The Structure of Scientific Revolutions.*

Kuhn, Thomas S. *The Structure of Scientific Revolutions.* 2d ed., enlarged. Chicago: University of Chicago Press, 1970. Kuhn's already classic discussion of how science changes through revolutions rather than linear adjustments. The second, enlarged edition contains a thirty-five-page 1969 postscript.

Lakatos, Imre, and Musgrave, Alan, eds. *Criticism and the Growth of Knowledge.* Cambridge: Cambridge University Press, 1970. Discussion of Kuhn's *The Structure of Scientific Revolutions* by Watkins, Williams, Toulmin, Popper, Masterman, Lakatos, and Feyerabend; replies by Kuhn.

Lyons, John. *Noam Chomsky.* New York: Viking Press, 1970. Introductory overview of Chomsky's thought.

Musgrave, Alan, and Lakatos, Imre. See Lakatos and Musgrave.

Neurath, Otto. "Protocol Sentences." In *Logical Positivism,* edited by A. J. Ayer. Glencoe, Ill.: Free Press, 1959. Originally published in German in 1932, this seminal essay attacks not only phenomenalism and the empiricist notion of a necessarily private language but also contains a sketch of a positive alternative to the empiricist foundations picture of knowledge. Presages, for example, Quine's and Sellars' nonfoundations accounts of knowledge.

Polanyi, Michael. *Personal Knowledge.* Chicago: University of Chicago Press, 1960.

Polanyi, Michael. *The Tacit Dimension.* Garden City, N.Y.: Doubleday & Co., 1966.

Popper, Karl R. *The Logic of Scientific Discovery.* London: Hutchinson, 1959. A translation of Popper's *Logik der Forshung* (1935), the classic statement of Popper's views.

Popper, Karl R. *Conjectures and Refutations.* 3d ed. London: Routledge and Kegan Paul, 1969. Twenty papers ranging over topics such as the nature of science, the history of science, the history of philosophy, philosophy and language, the mind-body problem, and political life.

Putnam, Hilary. "Dreaming and 'Depth Grammar.' " In *Analytical Philosophy,* edited by R. J. Butler. Oxford: Basil Blackwell, 1962. Further light on the issues dealt with in selection 5 of this volume.

Quine, W. V. *From a Logical Point of View.* Rev. ed. Cambridge, Mass.: Harvard University Press, 1961. See especially "On What There Is" and "The Problem of Meaning in Linguistics."

Quine, W. V. *Word and Object.* Cambridge, Mass.: M.I.T. Press, 1960. See especially chapters 1 and 2.

Quine, W. V. *The Ways of Paradox and Other Essays.* New York: Random House, 1966. See especially "On Carnap's Views on Ontology" and "Posits and Reality."

Quine, W. V. *Ontological Relativity and Other Essays.* New York: Columbia University Press, 1969.

Quine, W. V. "On the Reasons for Indeterminacy of Translation." *Journal of Philosophy,* 67 (1970), pp. 178–83.

Quine, W. V., and Ullian, J. S. *The Web of Belief.* New York: Random House, 1970. Quine's most elementary exposition of his own views.

Schilpp, Paul Arthur, ed. *The Philosophy of Rudolph Carnap.* La Salle, Ill.: Open Court Publishing Co., 1963. A Carnap compendium containing Carnap's intellectual autobiography (in which he discusses his "liberalization" of empiricism), descriptive and critical essays on Carnap's philosophy by leading philosophers, and Carnap's replies and a full Carnap bibliography.

Schilpp, Paul Arthur, ed. *The Philosophy of Sir Karl Popper.* La Salle, Ill.: Open Court Publishing Co., forthcoming. A Popper compendium in the manner of Schilpp's Carnap book.

Scheffler, Israel. *Science and Subjectivity.* New York: Bobbs-Merrill Co., 1967. Defends empiricist views of the nature of scientific knowledge from attacks by Polanyi, Hanson, Feyerabend, and Kuhn.

Sellars, Wilfrid. *Science, Perception and Reality.* London: Routledge and Kegan Paul, 1963. Contains, among other papers relevant to empiricism, "Grammar and Existence: A Preface to Ontology" and the entirety of "Empiricism and the Philosophy of Mind."

Shapere, Dudley. "Meaning and Scientific Change." In *Mind and Cosmos: Essays in Contemporary Science and Philosophy,* edited by R. G. Colodny. Pittsburgh: University of Pittsburgh Press, 1966. Criticizes Kuhn and Feyerabend's views on meaning-variance.

Sumner, L. W., and Woods, John, eds. *Necessary Truth.* New York: Random House, 1969. Fourteen essays and the fullest bibliography on a key assumption of empiricism, the analytic-synthetic dichotomy.

Ullian, J. S., and Quine, W. V. See Quine and Ullian.

Unger, Peter. "On Experience and the Development of the Understanding." *American Philosophical Quarterly,* 3 (1966), pp. 48–56. Tries to show that experience is logically unnecessary for the acquisition of empirical concepts.

Warnock, G. J. "Metaphysics in Logic." In *Essays in Conceptual Analysis,* edited by Antony Flew. London: Macmillan & Co., 1963. Rejects Quine's contention that the logician can clarify problems of ontology.

Watkins, J. W. N. "Hume, Carnap and Popper." In *The Problem of Inductive Logic,* edited by Imre Lakatos. Amsterdam: North Holland Publishing Co., 1968. An excellent short discussion of similarities and differences between these three philosophers with respect to the justification of inductive inference.

Woods, John, and Sumner, L. W. See Sumner and Woods.

Notes on Contributors

Rudolph Carnap (1891–1970), late professor of philosophy at the University of California, was a member of the Vienna Circle and the leading exponent of logical empiricism. He studied in Jena and taught in Vienna and Prague before coming to the United States in 1936. He taught at the University of Chicago until 1954 and from then until his retirement at the University of California at Los Angeles. His *Logical Structure of the World* (1928) was the first attempt to carry out a full-fledged phenomenalistic account of the world, but his "Testability and Meaning" (1936, 1937) pointed the way to logical empiricism's abandonment and liberalization of key Humean doctrines. His voluminous work in the foundations of logic, mathematics, and science has been widely influential. *The Logical Syntax of Language* (1936) and *Meaning and Necessity* (1947) are two of his major works.

Willard Van Orman Quine (b. 1908) is Edgar Pierce Professor of Philosophy at Harvard University. After studying at Oberlin, Harvard, and Oxford, he became an instructor at Harvard University in 1936, where he has taught ever since, interrupted only by military service in World War II and lectures at the universities of Sao Paulo, Adelaide, Tokyo, London, and elsewhere here and abroad. Quine is an internationally recognized logician, ontologist, and philosopher of language. His work includes *Mathematical Logic* (1940), *Methods of Logic* (1950), *Word and Object* (1960), *Set Theory and Its Logic* (1963), and (with J. S. Ullian) *The Web of Belief* (1970). Some of his papers have been collected in *From a Logical Point of View* (1953), *Ways of Paradox* (1966), *Selected Logic Papers* (1966), and *Ontological Relativity* (1969).

Wilfrid Stalker Sellars (b. 1912) is professor of philosophy at the University of Pittsburgh and editor of *Philosophical Studies.* He studied at the universities of Michigan, Buffalo, and Oxford, has taught at the State University of Iowa, the University of Minnesota, and Yale University, and has been a John Locke Lecturer at Oxford University. He has written on a wide variety of subjects including metaphysics, science, and ethics. Some of his papers have been collected in *Science, Perception and Reality* (1963) and in *Philosophical Perspectives* (1967). He is the author of *Science and Metaphysics* (1968).

Hilary Putnam (b. 1926) is professor of philosophy at Harvard University. He has also taught at Northwestern and Princeton Universities and at the Massachusetts Institute of Technology. Educated at the University of Pennsylvania and the University of California at Los Angeles, he has written papers on the philosophy of science and mathematics, the philosophy of mind, and the philosophy of language. With Paul Benacerraf, he edited *Philosophy of Mathematics* (1964).

Karl Raimund Popper (b. 1902) was born and educated in Vienna. Although he has never subscribed to the early phenomenalist tendencies of logical empiricism or to the instrumentalist interpretation of scientific theories proffered by some of its adherents, the general orientation of his thought is similar to that associated with this philosophical movement. His major contributions have been to the logic of science. Popper was senior lecturer in philosophy at the University of New Zealand from 1937 to 1945, and since then has been professor of logic and scientific method at the London School of Economics. His first book, *Die Logik der Forschung* (1935), was translated as *The Logic of Scientific Discovery* (1958). Other important works of his include *The Open Society and Its Enemies* (1944, 1950) and *Conjectures and Refutations: The Growth of Scientific Knowledge* (1963, 1965, 1969).

Paul Karl Feyerabend (b. 1924) was born in Vienna and received the doctor of philosophy degree in 1951 from the University of Vienna. He is now professor of philosophy at the University of California at Berkeley and at the London School of Economics. He has written a number of important essays on the philosophy of science and the theory of knowledge and has coedited, with Grover Maxwell, *Mind, Matter and Method* (1966).

Thomas Samuel Kuhn (b. 1922), professor of the history of science at Princeton University, taught at Harvard University and the University of California at Berkeley before going to Princeton University in 1964. He received his graduate and undergraduate degrees from Harvard University. He is the author of *The Copernican Revolution: Planetary Astronomy in the Development of Western Thought* (1957) and *The Structure of Scientific Revolutions* (1962, 1970).

Mary Hesse is reader in philosophy of science at Cambridge University. She has been lecturer in mathematics at the University of Leeds and lecturer in history and philosophy of science at University College, University of London. She has been editor of *The British Journal for the Philosophy of Science* and is currently President of the British Society for the Philosophy of Science. Among her writings are *Forces and Fields* (1961) and *Models and Analogies in Science* (1963). Her work on the nature and role of models in science has been especially influential.

Avrum Noam Chomsky (b. 1928) received his graduate and undergraduate degrees from the University of Pennsylvania and is now Ferrari P. Ward Professor of Linguistics and Modern Language at Massachusetts Institute of Technology, where he has taught since 1957. He has been a visiting teacher and lecturer at Columbia University, the University of California at Berkeley, and Oxford University. He is perhaps the most influential of contemporary writers on linguistic theory. Among his publications are *Syntactic Structures* (1957), *Current Issues in Linguistic Theory* (1964), *Aspects of the Theory of Syntax* (1965), *Cartesian Linguistics* (1966), and *Language and Mind* (1968).

Henry Nelson Goodman (b. 1906), currently professor of philosophy at Harvard University, was Harry Austryn Wolfson Professor of Philosophy at Brandeis University from 1964 to 1967 and professor of philosophy at the University of Pennsylvania from 1951 to 1964. Before that he taught briefly at Tufts University. He has been visiting professor and lecturer at leading universities, including Harvard, London, and Oxford. Goodman received his graduate and undergraduate degrees at Harvard University. He has written *The Structure of Appearance* (1951), *Fact, Fiction and Forecast* (1955), *Languages of Art* (1968), and *Ways of Worldmaking* (1978), as well as important articles in philosophy of science, logic, and epistemology.

Roy Edgley is senior lecturer in philosophy at the University of Bristol. In addition to noteworthy essays he has written *Reason in Theory and Practice* (1969).

Jerry Alan Fodor (b. 1935) is associate professor of philosophy and psychology at the Massachusetts Institute of Technology, where he has been teaching since 1960. He studied at Columbia and Princeton universities. He is the author of important articles dealing with issues in psycholinguistics, the psychologies of cognition and perception, philosophy of psychology, and philosophy of language. He is coeditor (with Jerrold J. Katz) of *The Structure of Language* (1964) and is the author of *Psychological Explanation* (1968). Fodor has held Woodrow Wilson and Fulbright fellowships and was a fellow of the Center for Advanced Studies in the Behavioral Sciences.